Lecture Notes of the Institute for Computer Sciences, Social Informatics and Telecommunications Engineering   133

For further volumes:
http://www.springer.com/series/8197

Victor C.M. Leung · Min Chen (Eds.)

Cloud Computing

4th International Conference, CloudComp 2013
Wuhan, China, October 17–19, 2013
Revised Selected Papers

Springer

Editors
Victor C.M. Leung
Electrical and Computer Engineering
The University of British Columbia
Vancouver, BC
Canada

Min Chen
School of Computer Science and
  Technology
Huazhong University of Science and
  Technology
Wuhan
China

ISSN 1867-8211   ISSN 1867-822X   (electronic)
ISBN 978-3-319-05505-3 ISBN 978-3-319-05506-0   (eBook)
DOI 10.1007/978-3-319-05506-0
Springer Cham Heidelberg New York Dordrecht London

Library of Congress Control Number: 2014937396

Printed on acid-free paper

Springer is part of Springer Science+Business Media (www.springer.com)

Preface

It is a great pleasure to welcome you to the proceedings of the 4th International Conference on Cloud Computing (CloudComp 2013). This year's conference continued its tradition of being the premier forum for presentation of results on cutting-edge research in cloud computing. The mission of the conference is to share novel basic research ideas as well as experimental applications in the cloud computing area in addition to identifying new directions for future research and development.

In CloudComp 2013, we have received 84 paper submissions, and finally selected 30 regular papers.

CloudComp 2013 gave researchers a unique opportunity to share their perspectives with others interested in the various aspects of cloud computing. The conference consisted of six symposia that covered a broad range of research aspects. We hope that the conference proceedings will serve as a valuable reference to researchers and developers in the area.

We also hope that you find the papers in this volume interesting and thought-provoking. It will surely advance our understanding of cloud computing and doubtless open up new directions for research and development.

January 2014

Victor C.M. Leung
Min Chen

Organization

CloudComp 2013, the 4th International Conference on Cloud Computing, was organized by the Department of Computer Science, Huazhong University of Science and Technology (HUST) in Wuhan, People's Republic of China.

Conference Steering Committee

Steering Committee Chair

Athanasios V. Vasilakos   University of Western Macedonia, Greece

Program Committee

Narcis Cardona	Universitat Politecnica de Valencia, Spain
Woon Hau Chin	Toshiba Research Europe, UK
Melike Erol-Kantarci	University of Ottawa, Canada
Joan Serrat-Fernandez	Technical University of Catalonia, Spain
Jorge Granjal	University of Coimbra, Portugal
Harold Liu	IBM Research, PR China
Xiaofei Wang	University of British Columbia, Canada
Enzo Mingozzi	University of Pisa, Italy
Jiehan Zhou	University of Oulu, Finland
Maziar Nekovee	BT Research and Technology, UK
Han-Chieh Chao	NIU, TUN, PR China
Yan Zhang	Simula Research Lab, Norway
Shiwen Mao	Auburn University, USA
Haiyang Wang	Simon Fraser University, Canada
Gabriel-Miro Muntean	Dublin City University, Ireland
Yin Zhang	Huazhong University of Science and Technology, PR China
Honggang Wang	University of Massachusetts Dartmouth, USA
Tarik Taleb	NEC Europe Ltd., Heidelberg, Germany
Yujun Ma	Huazhong University of Science and Technology, PR China
Jaime Lloret Mauri	Polytechnic University of Valencia, Spain
Liang Zhou	NJUPT, PR China
Chin-Feng Lai	National Ilan University, Taiwan, PR China
Ning Pan	Huazhong University of Science and Technology, PR China
Choong-Ho Cho	Korea University, Republic of Korea
Daihee Park	Korea University, Republic of Korea
Hyeonjoong Cho	Korea University, Republic of Korea

Organizing Committee

General Chair

Victor C.M. Leung   University of British Columbia, Canada

TPC Chair

Min Chen   Huazhong University of Science and Technology,
                                   PR China

Program Track Chairs

Tarik Taleb   NEC Europe Ltd., Germany
Jiafu Wan   South China University of Technology, PR China
TShiwen Mao   Aubrun University, USA
Jaime Lloret Mauri   Polytechnic University of Valencia, Spain

Workshop Chair

Honggang Wang   University of Massachusetts Dartmouth, USA

International Advisory Committee Chair

Hai Jin   Huazhong University of Science and Technology,
                                   PR China
En-Dong Wang   Inspur, PR China
Roy "Xiaorong" Lai   Confederal Network Inc., USA

Publication Chair

Foad Dabiri   Google Inc., USA
Chin-Feng Lai   National Ilan University, Taiwan, PR China
Long Hu   Huazhong University of Science and Technology,
                                   PR China

Tutorial Chair

Jiehan Zhou   University of Oulu, Finland

Local Chair

Yin Zhang   Huazhong University of Science and Technology,
                                   PR China

Publicity Chairs

Xiaofei Wang   University of British Columbia, USA
Yujun Ma   Huazhong University of Science and Technology,
                                PR China

Web Chair

Liang Zhou   NJUPT, PR China

Contents

Workshop Session 2

Mobile Cloud Computing

Environment Perception
for Cognitive Cloud Gaming

Wei Cai[1]([✉]), Conghui Zhou[2], Victor C.M. Leung[1], and Min Chen[3]

[1] The University of British Columbia, Vancouver, Canada
{weicai,vleung}@ece.ubc.ca
[2] We Software Limited, Sha Tin, Hong Kong
neio.zhou@gmail.com
[3] Huazhong University of Science and Technology, Wuhan, China
minchen2012@hust.edu.cn

Abstract. Mobile cloud games utilizes the rich resources within the cloud to enhance the functionality of mobile devices, therefore, to overcome the intrinsic constraints of mobile devices. To provide a satisfying quality of experience for players in dynamic network context, we need a cognitive gaming platform which is cognitive of resources and characteristics of the cloud, the access network, and the end-user devices, and enables dynamic utilization of these resources. In this work, we develop an environment perception solution with a novel capability to learn about the game player's environment (i.e., the combination of terminal and access network) to facilitate this cognitive gaming platform.

1   Introduction

Mobile game already has a large share of application market. However, the hardware constrains of mobile devices, such as the limited storage, insufficient computational capacity, and battery drain problems, restrict the design of mobile games. To address these design issues, mobile cloud computing [1] provides a potential solution. Well recognized as the next generation computing infrastructure, the cloud is considered to provide unlimited storage and computational resources, which supports various types of online services for cloud users. With the approach of offloading [2], the cloud-based game for mobile devices utilizes the rich resources within the cloud to enhance the functionality of mobile devices and prolong the battery lifetime through better energy efficiency, therefore, to overcome the intrinsic constraints of mobile devices.

Industry is now leading the way to commercialize the Gaming as a Service (GaaS). Companies, such as OnLive[1], Gaikai[2] and G-Cluster[3] are the most famous commercial providers of gaming services on-demand. In their remonte rendering GaaS provision model, the video games are executed in their private

---

[1] http://www.onlive.com
[2] http://www.gaikai.com
[3] http://www.g-cluster.com

V.C.M. Leung and M. Chen (Eds.): CloudComp 2013, LNICST 133, pp. 3–13, 2014.
DOI: 10.1007/978-3-319-05506-0_1, © Institute for Computer Sciences, Social Informatics and Telecommunications Engineering 2014

cloud servers and the generated game video frames are transmitted to the mobile client through Internet after the encoding process. In reverse, the players' inputs are delivered to the cloud and accepted by the game content server directly [3]. In this context, the cloud is intrinsically an interactive video generator and streaming server, while the mobile devices serve as the event controllers and video receivers. Since the games are rendered in cloud servers, a less capable computer or mobile device may be used to support sophisticated games. This approach results in longer battery life for the device and longer gaming times for the user at the expense of higher consumption of communication resources. However, the remote rendering GaaS suffers from the bottleneck of Internet bandwidth, which constrains the bit rate of gaming videos, while the jitter and delay affect the quality of experience (QoE) for the players [4]. Therefore, the QoE-oriented adaptive gaming video rendering and transmission become the most promising research topic in this area. Wang and Dey [5] proposes a set of application layer optimization techniques to ensure acceptable gaming response time and video quality in the remote server based approach. The techniques include downlink gaming video rate adaptation, uplink delay optimization, and client play-out delay adaptation.

With the recent development of hardware performance, most gaming terminals, including mobile devices, are capable to perform complicated graphical rendering for game scenes. Therefore, a local rendering GaaS model become practical. As a matter of fact, the promising HTML5 browser games fall into this category. Accordingly, a more flexible solution for the provision of GaaS is suggested by [6]. In this work, cloud-based games are modeled as inter-dependant components, which work collaboratively to provide gaming services for the players. During the gaming session, the cloud intelligently transmits selected game components to the users' terminal and performs a cognitive resource allocation between the cloud and user end terminals, on the purpose of system optimization while guaranteeing QoE for players. It can be considered as an iterative 3 phases procedure: (1) to predict the resource consumption of each game component and the communication cost between these components; (2) to perform efficient and accurate real-time measurements, evaluation, and prediction on cloud performance, access network performance and end-user device status; (3) to design joint adaptive strategy to optimize the system performance.

In summary, these two approaches both envision a flexible and feasible solution that is cognitive of resources and characteristics of the cloud, the access network, and the end user devices. As a cognitive system, they are required to be capable of (i) **environment perception** to collect players' environmental data and to monitor the real-time system status; (ii) **system analysis** to evaluate the system performance and to make decisions for the service provision; (iii) **QoE-oriented adaption** to take actions for overall system optimization. In this work, we focus on **environment perception** and develop a data collecting solution with a novel capability to learn about the game player's environment (i.e., the combination of terminal and access network). To the best of our knowledge, this is the first work on the design and implementation of environment perception solution for cognitive cloud gaming, and it is also the very first work on the application of mobile agent [7] on this topic. The remaining sections of the paper is organized as follows. We review related work in Sect. 2 and describe our design of the environment perception in Sect. 3. Afterwards, in Sect. 4, we describe our implementation details. Concluding remarks are presented in Sect. 5.

2 Related Work

2.1 QoE for Cloud Gaming

The goal of environment perception is to collect the data that are have most impact on players' QoE. To provide GaaS, the relationships between cloud gaming QoE and QoS are different for distinct implementation architectures. For remote rendering GaaS, various subjective user studies have been conducted to demonstrate the relationship between cloud gaming QoE and QoS, including game genres, video encoding factors, CPU load, memory usage, and link bandwidth utilization [8], response latency, and the game's real-time strictness [9], number of users [10], network characteristics (bit rates, packet sizes, and inter-packet times) [11], and an empirical network traffic analysis of On-Live and Gaikai [12]. However, the QoE to QoS mapping shall be redefined, given the rendering component is resided on the local terminal. Due to multiple remote invoke between components, the impact of network QoS parameters will intensively impact the QoE for players.

2.2 Interval Reporting

Interval reporting is the most conventional design for status monitoring [5]. The mobile devices set up real-time monitoring on access network performance measurements, including bandwidth, latency, jitter, etc; and user-end device status measurements, including battery capacity and power consumption, network utilization, computing capacity (including the usage percentage of CPU, GPU, memories), the player input and game screen dynamics, etc, and reports these data to the cloud server at intervals. However, to select an optimal interval is still a critical issue for *Interval reporting* approach. Frequently sending detailed monitoring data makes the cloud measurement and prediction accurate, however, it also introduces more network overhead to the gaming system. Moreover, to report all status data to the cloud server is either not a smart move. As a matter of fact, not all of the status need frequently updating. Apparently, the *Interval reporting* is not bandwidth efficiency solution.

2.3 Mobile Agent for Information Collection

Mobile agents are composition of software package that is able to migrate from cloud server to user-end devices, and continues its execution on the destination terminals. It provides a potential solution to provide this distributed monitoring, decision and learning capabilities. Mobile agent has been extensively studied in collecting data for wireless sensor networks (WSN) [13], which can address the software (re)installation issue for dynamically changing application functionalities (or their requirements). As a special kind of software, a mobile agent migrates among sensor nodes to carry out task(s) autonomously. For instance, collecting sensory data from a number of source nodes with some processing defined on demand, and adaptively handling sensory data depending on time-varying network dynamics are typical application requirements of the mobile agent dispatcher (i.e., the sink node) in WSNs. Using mobile agent has been shown to be an efficient approach to enhance such capabilities of WSNs. In this work, we apply mobile agent as a information collector to our environment perception solution for cognitive cloud gaming.

3   Design of Environment Perception Solution

A key function of the situation-awareness cognitive platform is the capability to perform real-time environment perception that measures cloud performance, access network performance and end-user device status. For the performance measurement on cloud, the cloud server is capable to monitor the real-time status, including latency inside the cloud (authentication latency, processing latency, internal network latency), and processing capacity consumption and availability, etc. In contrast, access network performance and user-end device status requires a reporting mechanism between the cloud and mobile devices.

3.1   Threshold-Based Data Reporting

An intuitive data collection solution to improve the efficiency of *Interval Reporting* is *Threshold-based Data Reporting*. It sets up a threshold and reports the requested data when the variation of monitoring data exceeds the predetermined threshold.

Figure 1 depicts an screenshot of conventional interval reporting, in which the mobile devices consequently send the CPU usage, battery percentage, memory usage, and bandwidth consumption information to the cloud server in the interval of one second. As illustrated in red dot lines, if we introduce a threshold to the existing interval reporting system, the client only update the requested data when the value changes surpass the threshold, thus, the communication frequency is significantly reduced. However, to determine the value of threshold is still a critical issue, since the requirements of environment perception are subject to various of:

– **game genres and scenes:** different game genres and scenes have different QoE criteria, e.g. a First-Person Shooter Game (FPS) may always be more sensitive to network bandwidth than round-based RPG game.
– **monitoring parameters:** distinct monitoring parameters have their own characteristics. For instance, the battery keeps decreasing until the devices are connected to the power, while the memory and CPU percentage are fluctuating along with application usages.

Mobile Device Monitor

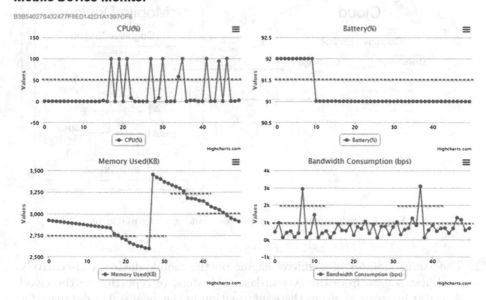

Fig. 1. Data report with threshold

- **terminals:** terminals with various hardware capacities, such as screen resolution and battery, contain unique behaviors from each other.
- **networks:** players are accessing the cloud gaming services through various network with different characteristics, especially when they are moving.

Moreover, compared to continuously reporting through Internet, environment perception procedure can be processed partially in local devices to reduce the communication cost. Therefore, a cognitive, flexible and intelligent environment perception solution is in need.

3.2 Mobile Agent Information Collection

To address these issues, we investigate the use of mobile agents [7] dispatched by the cloud to enable these real-time measurements and report the results to the cognitive platform to enable situation-aware adaptations. A task-customized mobile agent migrants from the cloud server to the user-end devices as the cognitive platform required, in order to collect in-need data and report the processed or fused information to the cognitive platform, drawing on the example of mobile agent system for wireless sensor network. The collecting mechanism, including agent design, data processing method, and agent itinerary planning, shall be both latency-sensitive and energy-efficient.

Figure 2 illustrates the environment perception procedure conducted by the cognitive control center, which is called *cognitive engine* in this context:

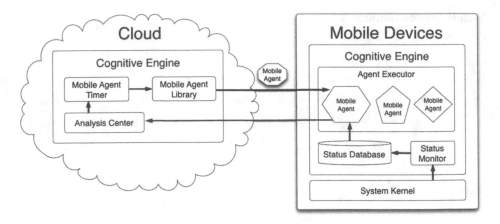

Fig. 2. Environment perception for cloud gaming platform

1. The *status monitor* of cognitive engine on the mobile devices consecutively read status data from the system kernel. Instead of reporting to the cloud server at intervals, it stores these information in the local status database for future inquiry from the cloud server.
2. In the beginning of the game session, the cognitive engine on the cloud server initiates a mobile agent with inquiry code and dispatched it to the mobile devices via network. The designated mobile agent is interpreted and executed in the *agent executor* on the mobile devices. The process of mobile agent execution, so called *local analysis*, retrieves the unread data stored in the *status database* and performs analysis to evaluate the overall performance of the access network and user-end device status.
3. Once the process of *local analysis* accomplished, the mobile agent then report the results, named *device current status*, to the *analysis center* in the cloud server through network.
4. The *analysis center* on cloud is a decision support system, which conducts the analysis of all status data, including current and historic status of access network, user-end devices status and cloud server performance. The procedure of measurement and prediction is called *cloud analysis*.
5. The *mobile agent timer*, set by the *analysis center*, triggers the *mobile agent library* to dispatch task-customized mobile agent to the mobile devices for next round status information collection.

The mobile agent information collection mechanism provides certain benefits to the cognitive engine for mobile cloud games, including:

– **Intelligent Collecting Interval:** After *cloud analysis* on *analysis center*, the cloud is able to predict the variance of the access network and user-end device status, therefore, determine an optimal collecting timing for next mobile agent.

- **Flexible Agent Design:** Also instructed by the *analysis center*, the cognitive engine in the cloud is able to create most task-specific mobile agent for dispatching, which provide flexibility to fetch the information the cloud most interested in.
- **Efficient Information Transmission:** One of most important feature of mobile agent is to execute locally to perform information retrieval, fusion and collection, which means the network transmission will be more efficient and the network overhead introduced will be reduced. This is especially important, since the cloud-based gaming system is strong network-dependant.

3.3   Design of Local Analysis

Since the *local analysis* is performed by mobile agent, the design of local analysis is intrinsically the customization of the mobile agent. As previous discussed, the mobile agent is task-oriented, and the variety of executable code in mobile agent is considered as the most significant feature. However, whatever changes, the principle of local analysis is to concern the accuracy and efficiency of the reporting data.

Here we demonstrate an example for mobile agent design. Given a set of $T = t_i, t_{i+1}, t_{i+2}, ..., t_j$ representing the duration of monitoring time and a set C representing the type of monitoring data, such as bandwidth, latency, jitter of access network and battery capacity, the usage percentage of CPU, GPU, memories of mobile devices. We denote the monitoring status value as $s(t, c)$, representing the c status value at time t. A mobile agent code focus on retrieving the raw profile of the monitoring information is designed to report the value of mean $E(c)$ and deviation $D(c)$, defined as following:

$$E(c) = \frac{\sum_{t \in T} s(t, c)}{t_j - t_i} \tag{1}$$

$$D(c) = \frac{\sum_{t \in T} (s(t, c) - E(c))^2}{t_j - t_i} \tag{2}$$

Note that, the flexibility of mobile agent is not only on the functionality of the executable code but also the interval of agent dispatching. To choose the optimal interval and appropriate mobile agent are implemented in *analysis center*, which will be discussed in next section.

3.4   Design of Cloud Analysis

The *cloud analysis* on *analysis center* is the core controller of the cognitive engine. It read all reporting information from mobile agents and perform measurement, prediction and joint-optimization for the cloud gaming platform. With the support of all status data, including cloud performance monitoring from the server script, current and historic data of access network, user-end devices status from mobile agents, the procedure of *cloud analysis* is supposed to yield two fundamental results:

– **QoE Level Factor:** The factor is an intelligent prediction from the measurement of overall system performance. It is a quantized value as the reference for the intelligent adaption of the cognitive platform.
– **System Variance Factor:** The factor predicts the variance of the overall system, which determines the time and type for next mobile agent to be dispatched.

4 Implementation of Environment Perception

4.1 Enabling Technologies

To facilitate the proposed environment perception, we have implement a experimental platform as illustrated in Fig. 3, including cloud server and mobile client.

One of the key features of this work is to make the mobile agent migrate and execute in the mobile devices. However, the code generation and compiling in various devices are long-time troubling issues for mobile agent utilization. In this work, we innovatively adopt JavaScript, an interpreted computer programming language, to construct mobile agents. JavaScript was originally implemented as part of web browsers so that client-side scripts could interact with the user, control the browser, communicate asynchronously, and alter the document content

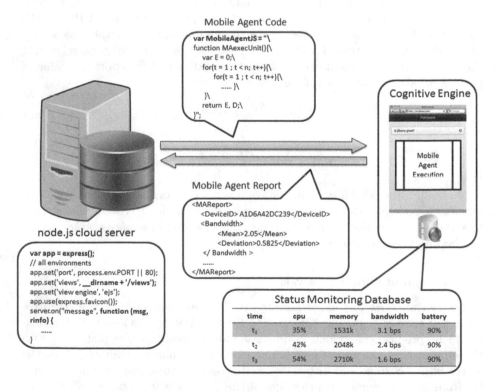

Fig. 3. Implementation of environment perception

that was displayed. More recently, however, it has become common in both game development and the creation of desktop applications.

To make the system in a constant programming style, we deploy node.js as the software system for our cloud server. Node.js is a server-side software system designed for writing scalable Internet applications, notably web servers. Programs are written on the server side in JavaScript, which enables web developers to create an entire web application in JavaScript, both server-side and client-side. This feature will facilitate our future work on mobile agents that can be running both on server and client.

For the mobile client, we embedded a WebKit-based browser to parse and execute the JavaScript mobile agent from the cloud server. In our implementation, the WebKit browser is built on Android smartphone. However, all mobile operating systems supporting browsers are able to support our cognitive platform after a small number of modification.

4.2 Stateless Connection

Mobile agent dispatching pattern in our implementation is slightly modified to the concept design. Instead of initiative mobile agent push by the cloud server, we set up the mobile agent timer on the mobile devices. When the timer expired, the mobile client post a mobile agent request to the server, and the cloud response the mobile agent code. The reason is that, if the timer is running on the cloud as designed in Sect. 3, a persistent connection between the cloud and the user-end devices shall be maintained during the whole gaming session, which is not as flexible as stateless connections. However, the mobile agent dispatching interval should always controlled by the *Analysis Center* in the cloud, therefore, the cloud need to response the mobile devices with the value of mobile agent timer, as phase 6 depicted in Fig. 4.

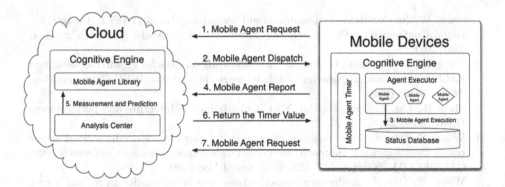

Fig. 4. Mobile agent paradigm for enviroment perception

4.3 Mobile Agent Cache

Transmitting mobile agents cost bandwidth as well. In our implementation, once a mobile agent has been fetched from the cloud server, it is cached in the *agent executor*. Whenever the client request the same agent, the cognitive engine will check with the cloud to see if the agent code is up-to-date. If no updates is in need, the *agent executor* will run the local version of mobile agent, on the purpose of saving network bandwidth.

5 Conclusion

Gaming as a Service has been introduced to the public as next generation entertaining platform. In order to provide a acceptable quality of experience for players in dynamic network context, a gaming platform is in need to provide cognitive capacity of resources and characteristics of the cloud, the access network, and the end-user devices, and enables dynamic utilization of these resources. In this work, we design a mobile agent based paradigm to implement a cognitive environment perception solution with a novel capability to learn about the game player's environment to facilitate the envisioned cognitive gaming platform. A pure JavaScript solution is adopted to overcome the compiling issues of software migration and creates an efficient information reporting for the cognitive platform.

Acknowledgement. This work is supported by a University of British Columbia Four Year Doctoral Fellowship and by funding from the Natural Sciences and Engineering Research Council.

References

1. Song, W., Su, X.: Review of mobile cloud computing. In: 2011 IEEE 3rd International Conference on Communication Software and Networks (ICCSN), pp. 1–4, May 2011
2. Yang, K., Ou, S., Chen, H.: On effective offloading services for resource-constrained mobile devices running heavier mobile internet applications. IEEE Commun. Mag. **46**(1), 56–63 (2008)
3. Shea, R., Liu, J., Ngai, E., Cui, Y.: Cloud gaming: architecture and performance. IEEE Netw. **27**(4), 16–21 (2013)
4. Wang, S., Dey, S.: Modeling and characterizing user experience in a cloud server based mobile gaming approach. In: Global Telecommunications Conference 2009, GLOBECOM 2009, pp. 1–7. IEEE, 30 Nov–4 Dec 2009
5. Wang, S., Dey, S.: Addressing response time and video quality in remote server based internet mobile gaming. In: 2010 IEEE Wireless Communications and Networking Conference (WCNC), pp. 1–6 (2010)
6. Cai, W., Zhou, C., Leung, V., Chen, M.: A cognitive platform for mobile cloud gaming. In: 2013 IEEE 5th International Conference on Cloud Computing Technology and Science (CloudCom), Dec 2013

7. Lange, D., Mitsuru, O.: Programming and Deploying Java Mobile Agents Aglets, 1st edn. Addison-Wesley Longman Publishing Co. Inc., Boston (1998)
8. Jarschel, M., Schlosser, D., Scheuring, S., Hossfeld, T.: An evaluation of QoE in cloud gaming based on subjective tests. In: 2011 Fifth International Conference on Innovative Mobile and Internet Services in Ubiquitous Computing (IMIS), pp. 330–335, 30 June–2 July 2011
9. Lee, Y., Chen, K., Su, H., Lei, C.: Are all games equally cloud-gaming-friendly? An electromyographic approach. In: Proceedings of IEEE/ACM NetGames 2012, Oct 2012
10. Choy, S., Wong, B., Simon, G., Rosenberg, C.: The brewing storm in cloud gaming: a measurement study on cloud to end-user latency. In: 2012 11th Annual Workshop on Network and Systems Support for Games (NetGames), pp. 1–6 (2012)
11. Claypool, M., Finkel, D., Grant, A., Solano, M.: Thin to win? Network performance analysis of the onlive thin client game system. In: 2012 11th Annual Workshop on Network and Systems Support for Games (NetGames), pp. 1–6 (2012)
12. Manzano, M., Hernandez, J., Uruena, M., Calle, E.: An empirical study of cloud gaming. In: 2012 11th Annual Workshop on Network and Systems Support for Games (NetGames), pp. 1–2 (2012)
13. Cai, W., Chen, M., Hara, T., Shu, L., Kwon, T.: A genetic algorithm approach to multi-agent itinerary planning in wireless sensor networks. Mob. Netw. Appl. 16(6), 782–793 (2011)

Adaptive Multimedia Cloud Computing Center Applied on H.264/SVC Streaming

Wei-Ting Cho[1] and Chin-Feng Lai[2(✉)]

[1] National Cheng Kung University, Tainan 720, Taiwan
[2] National Chung Cheng University, Chiayi 621, Taiwan
cinfon@ieee.org

Abstract. In recent years, the multimedia streaming technology becomes increasingly mature, and as network bandwidth and computing power of personal hand-held devices are developed; therefore, it leads the requirements for multimedia quality increased. In order to provide the quality multimedia content to numerous users, how to divide the loading of content servers to improve the streaming quality is an important challenge. As the concept of multimedia cloud network is formed, how to allocate multimedia streaming service to the nodes in the media cloud network is discussed in this paper. This study designs H.264/SVC streaming service at the media cloud computing center, with the video most suitable for client-side quality provided based on H.264/SVC features (temporal scalability, spatial scalability, and quality scalability) and network bandwidth. In addition, the loading balance and communication mechanisms between nodes are discussed, where the best node is selected by the evaluating node, client-side bandwidth and computing power, for determining the appropriate video streaming path that is used to provide quality multimedia streaming service. According to the experimental results, the bandwidth prediction error rate for general multimedia network streaming service can be maintained at about 6 %, while the utilization rate of various nodes of the multimedia cloud computing center is maintained in a balanced state during the period of executing multi-streaming service.

Keywords: Adaptive multimedia streaming · H.264/SVC · Cloud computing center

1 Introduction

As the internet and hand-held devices have rapidly developed, the smart phone with its multimedia related services become more and more popular. In order to provide users with the best video quality, highly compressed video formats are presented in succession. With fixed network streaming resources, almost all current streaming mechanisms use the unicast mode to transfer video of specific quality, as required by each user. However, the working efficiency of video servers is very likely to decrease as the number of users rapidly increases, thus, the needs of all users cannot be met [1–3].

V.C.M. Leung and M. Chen (Eds.): CloudComp 2013, LNICST 133, pp. 14–26, 2014.
DOI: 10.1007/978-3-319-05506-0_2, © Institute for Computer Sciences, Social Informatics and Telecommunications Engineering 2014

In general cases, in order to meet user requirements, the video server side stores massive video data, including many kinds of video, and the same video data can be subdivided according to quality, thus, the data volume is very large and consumes a lot of storage resources. In addition, the server must act as streaming server to transfer videos to appropriate users, so the computing resource is more critical [4]. As network bandwidth rapidly develops and the computing power of the PC increases, all computers are able to be a computing node in a network, resulting in the formation of a cloud computing architecture, where available nodes in the network are managed for data storage and video streaming, thus, reducing the working load of specific servers [5–7].

This study discusses a new coding technique H.264/SVC, which uses Inter Layer Prediction so the file size after coding is greatly reduced, and the play quality of video is determined by packet analysis/filtering. This study uses the cloud computing mechanism and manages the resource of computing nodes in a media cloud for specific nodes to execute storage and streaming of video data, and dynamically evaluate the network bandwidth conditions and computing power of the nodes in the media cloud, and uses an Index Node to select storage and streaming nodes, thus, providing users with the best viewing quality and using the resources in the media cloud most efficiently. The contributions of this study are, as follows:

1. Construction of an H.264/SVC analyzer and decoder.
2. Construct management and communication mechanisms for nodes in a multimedia cloud.
3. User side bandwidth prediction model.
4. Computing resource balance in a media cloud and a dynamic node selection mechanism.

2   Related Work

This section briefly provides an outline of multimedia cloud computing and relevant studies, which can help readers outside the specialty of the article to understand the paper structure.

2.1   Multimedia Cloud Computing

For the multimedia services of cloud computing, the cloud center must provide an efficient, flexible, and scalable data processing mode, in order to provide a solution for user requirements of high quality and diversified multimedia [8,9]. On the other hand, with the popularization of smart phones and wireless networks, users are no longer limited to home network services, and they can obtain multimedia information and easily enjoy ubiquitous network services by using mobile devices. However, the present mobile streaming service has a bottleneck bandwidth and different requirements for device performance, cloud computing provides multimedia content suitable for a terminal unit environment, which further considers the overall network environment and dynamically adjusts the transmission frequency of both sides and multimedia transcoding, thus, avoiding waste of overall network bandwidth and terminal equipment power [10,11]. The theses [12,13] designed a due management architecture control module for a Multimedia Content Cloud. Therefore, many studies have proposed a series of opinions on Cloud management design.

The ideal cloud computing multimedia encoding and decoding can double the efficiency of multimedia services, and there are usually three major services in a Cloud.

- Multimedia file information analysis function.
- Multimedia Codec decoding service.
- Terminal connection network quality state analysis function.

There is usually data dependence problems when decoding frames in a multimedia format; taking the decoding processes of H.264/SVC as an example, the frames can be divided into I frame, P frame, and B frame. The P frame is decoded by referring to the picture data of I-Frame of GOP (Group Of Pictures), and B frame refers to picture data other than I frame and P frame. The scalability of H.264/SVC can be divided into temporal scalability, spatial scalability, and quality scalability. Therefore, a standard H.264/SVC decoding process can be approximately divided into entropy decoding (ED), inverse quantization and inverse transform (IQ/IT), intra or inter prediction (PPC), and deblocking (DF). Therefore, many studies configure a module for each processor according to the concept of dispersal to a cloud center for computing powerparallel processing according to the decoding process [14,15], thus, as the processors share the processing load, processing is accelerated. The advantage of this mechanism is to eliminate data dependence simply and efficiently; however, its defect is that the distribution of modules is limited to the quantity of assigned tasks in cloud computing.

3 Proposed Center Architecture

This chapter introduces the proposed H.264/SVC based multimedia cloud service architecture model, which aims to provide users with real-time and high quality videos. Based on the layered coding architecture of SVC and the analytical separation of bit stream, the nodes in a media cloud are divided into Index Node, Content Node, and Streaming Node, in order to solve the excessive loading on traditional multimedia servers. In order to handle the requirements of numerous users, the traditional multimedia servers must have on-line management, data storage, and media streaming, with simultaneous functions, and if the server-side cannot dynamically assign users to nodes with better bandwidth, the overall streaming service quality will decline. Therefore, when bandwidth loading for streaming video quality is dynamically distributed to various nodes in the media cloud in order to balance the loading on the nodes, the overall streaming efficiency can be greatly increased.

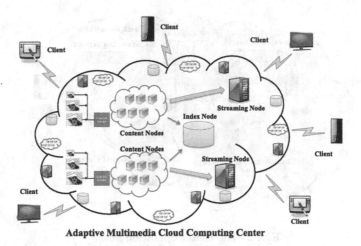

Fig. 1. The architecture of adaptive multimedia cloud computing center

3.1 Center Components

The center structure proposed in this study is shown in Fig. 1; there is one index node and multiple content nodes and streaming nodes in the media cloud, and their functions are described below. Index node, it records the dynamics of all nodes in the media cloud, including the registration and departure of nodes, records the type and IP information of nodes, and actively sends inquiry or control commands to the content and streaming nodes; Content node stores specific media segments. When a new video is added in the media cloud, it is separated into multiple segments, and dispersed for storage in multiple content nodes in the media cloud, thus, avoiding all the streaming nodes accessing the same video content node, which causes bandwidth bottlenecks; Streaming node is the node that streams video to users according to the layering characteristic of H.264/SVC; the streaming node captures specific video segments from the content node according to the user request to the index node for video, and then refers to the bandwidth of the streaming node and the lowest bit rate for playing the video segments in order to determine the level of video streaming to the user.

3.2 Center Operation Flow

This chapter introduces the practical process of center operation, and further introduces the command communications among the different nodes and the data transfer direction. As mentioned in the previous chapter, the index node records the operating state and information of all the nodes in the media cloud. Therefore, all command transfers must be actively sent and executed by the index node. Figure 2 shows the center operation flow.

First, when the client-side wants to view a video, it sends a video request to the index node, the corresponding instruction is step 1, Request Content.

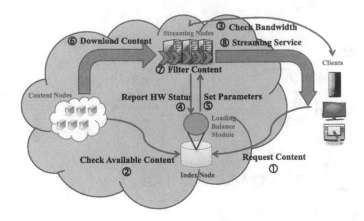

Fig. 2. The center operation flow

When the index node receives the request from the client-side, a series of Loading Balance mechanisms begin, and the index node sends information inquiring about the availability of video content to all content nodes in the media cloud, as step 2, Check Available Content. As mentioned in the previous chapter, a complete video is separated into multiple segments before it enters the media cloud, for storage in various content nodes of the media cloud. This step checks which nodes contains the video segments to be played, and then determines which content nodes have the requested video segments.

Afterwards, the index node sends a request inquiring about bandwidth to the streaming node, as step 3, Check Bandwidth, the index node sends inquires, one by one, to all the streaming nodes in the media cloud regarding bandwidth for the client-side, and then reports to the index node. Then the index node sends request inquiries about bandwidth to the screened content nodes. Finally, the values are fed back to the index node. Step 4 inquires about the hardware resource information of each streaming node in order to determine the work loading of each streaming node, and rearranges the evaluation of the equilibrium stock. After the aforesaid four steps, the results are handed to the loading balance model to evaluate the overall network and select nodes. Practical content capture, analysis, separation, and streaming are conducted after the Loading Balance Mechanism. In step 5, the index node commands the selected streaming node to set the streaming quality level, shown as Set Parameters in the figure. The index node transfers the selected content node as a parameter to the streaming node, which downloads a content based on the information, shown as step 6, Download Content, to the streaming node, and then analyzes and separates the content according to the given parameters in the Set Parameters command. Due to the layering characteristic of H.264/SVC coding, the packets can be separated according to the information stored in the NAL Header. Finally, the streaming path is fed back to the index node, which feeds the streaming address back to the client-side.

3.3   Loading Balance Model

The loading balance model which aims to render the work load of all the nodes in the media cloud consistent is discussed in this section, while providing the client-side with better streaming quality. The loading balance model contains 1: a prediction model for the bandwidth of streaming node for the client-side; and 2: the selection and balancing mechanism of the streaming and content nodes.

Prediction Model for Client-Side. The authenticity of bandwidth has a significant influence on bandwidth prediction, as it must depend on substantive historical data, and the self-designed mathematical model is used to predict future bandwidth. Therefore, the filing and authenticity of historical data significantly influence the accuracy of the overall bandwidth prediction model. In order to implement the client-side bandwidth prediction model of a streaming node, this study analyzes and predicts the bandwidth results measured at various endpoints. First, the video segment length is set as n seconds, and separated into m segments, during the play of No. 0 segment, the quality level of No. 1 video segment must be determined; therefore, this study sets every k seconds as a data group, which are analyzed and polynomial regression is used to calculate the regression polynomial curve in order to predict the data distribution pattern of data points. The polynomial regression is defined as Eq. 1, where ε is an error constant.

$$y = a_0 + a_1 x + a_2 x^2 + \cdots + a_m x^m + \varepsilon \tag{1}$$

According to the polynomial regression curve deduced from Eq. 1, extend the data into multidimensional data distribution, where the polynomial curve can be expressed, and the data distribution pattern is identical to Eq. 1. Express the distribution of polynomial curves of multidimensional data in a matrix form, as Eq. 2. Finally, the simplified results can be expressed in vector form, as Eq. 3.

$$\begin{bmatrix} y_1 \\ \vdots \\ y_n \end{bmatrix} + \begin{bmatrix} 1 \cdots x_1^m \\ \vdots \ddots \vdots \\ 1 \cdots x_n^m \end{bmatrix} \begin{bmatrix} a_0 \\ \vdots \\ a_m \end{bmatrix} + \begin{bmatrix} \varepsilon_1 \\ \vdots \\ \varepsilon_n \end{bmatrix} \tag{2}$$

$$a = (X^T X)^1 X^T y \tag{3}$$

The polynomial regression curve, as deduced from the previous data group, can be used to predict the data of the next data point in order to determine the value of A_n; use the polynomial curves obtained from $A_{n-1} \sim A_{n-5}$ in the X-coordinate of A_n to obtain a corresponding Y value, which is the predicted bandwidth, and the mathematical expression. However, as A_n is a value calculated by the mathematical model, and not a measured value, a second revision is required, as shown in Eq. 4. We can average the A_n est obtained from polynomial regression and the An rel of a real bandwidth measuring device in order to obtain the new value, A_{n_rev}. Finally, A_{n_rev} is substituted in another regression prediction curve to continuously revise the regression prediction curve for accurate prediction.

$$A_{n\_rev} = \alpha A_{n\_est} + (1 - \alpha)A_{n\_rel}$$
$$= \alpha f(A_{n-1}, \cdots, A_{n-5}) + (1 - \alpha)A_{n\_rel} \tag{4}$$

Selection and Balancing Mechanism of Streaming Nodes. The fundamental purpose of the loading balance model is to render the Work Loading of all the nodes in the media cloud consistent, while providing the client-side with better viewing quality. Therefore, the index node considers the present state of the streaming node, including the bandwidth of the streaming node of the client-side, the computing power of the streaming node and the bandwidth of the content node for the streaming node, with the operation architecture as shown in Fig. 3.

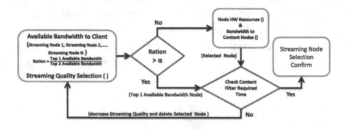

Fig. 3. Selection model of loading balance

The bandwidth of the streaming node for the client-side is the first position considered, as the fundamental purpose of the overall streaming center design is to provide users with better viewing quality, and the balance of the nodes is the second consideration. First, the index node selects the best three nodes for the client-side bandwidth from the media cloud, in descending order, and defined as Max_{BW1} and Max_{BW2}, and *Ration* defined as Eq. 5. If *Ration* is greater than bandwidth gap (defined α), meaning Max_{BW1} is far larger than Max_{BW2}, and the function of Check Computing Time is directly conducted in order to ensure the node fulfills the work within the determined time.

$$Ration = Max_{BW1}/Max_{BW2} \tag{5}$$

When the bandwidth ratio of more than two nodes in the media cloud of the client-side is less than gap, the second round of judgement must be conducted according to the work load of the streaming node. However, as the streaming nodes have different hardware specifications and computing power, using only the CPU utilization rate to determine the work load of the nodes will result in errors to some extent, thus, the hardware specifications of nodes must be calculated to judge the actual work load of the nodes. Another factor influencing the computing time is the bandwidth of the content node for the streaming node. This study uses the same streaming node selection mechanism as the loading balance model, where two better content nodes are selected for the streaming node bandwidth, and calculated at *Ration*. If *Ration* is greater than gap, the total computing time is validated. If the total computing time is longer than the predetermined time, which does not meet center requirements, this node shall be abandoned. If the $Ratio_{1-2}$ is less than gap, meaning the two content nodes have similar bandwidths, the center selects a content node at random, and validates the total computing time, and finally, the selection of the content node is confirmed.

When the streaming node and content node are selected, the data transmission path is determined, the index node transmits the result to the streaming node, and the streaming node captures the video from a specific content node, according to the path given by the index node, and analyzes and separates the video according to the user's bandwidth. Finally the video is streamed to the client-side, and the operation of the loading balance model is complete.

4 Test Results and Analysis

This study validated the bandwidth prediction model of a streaming node for the client-side, and the selection and balancing mechanism of the streaming node, as proposed in Chap. IV, the bandwidth prediction model calculates the error rate defined as Eq. 6.

$$Err = |B_{est} - B_{rel}| / B_{rel} \qquad (6)$$

In the case of varying bandwidths, and determines the precision of the bandwidth prediction model according to the Average Delay Time of the video on the client-side. The selection and balancing mechanism of the streaming node evaluates overall efficiency according to the time belt average service rate of each node, and analyzes the usability of the balancing mechanism by calculating the utilization rate and standby time of each node.

4.1 Error Rate and Video Average Delay Time of Bandwidth Prediction Model

As the bandwidth prediction model uses polynomial regression to obtain the bandwidth prediction curve, the denser the samples, the closer the prediction curve to the actual value. There is usually a rapid buffer in the transmission of massive files in a network, thus, the bandwidth transmission becomes stable after a period of time; therefore, the bandwidth measuring device requires time in order that the measured data can approximate to the bandwidth values of the network. Therefore, the sampling time and bandwidth measurement time must be balanced.

Table 1. Error rate of bandwidth estimation

Interval (s)	Limited band (Kbits)	Measured band (Kbits)	Error rate (%)
2	400	688	72
2	800	1032	29
4	400	412	3
4	800	826	3.25
8	400	405	1.25
8	800	815	1.875
10	400	405	1.25
10	800	810	1.25
20	400	402	0.5
20	800	807	0.875

Therefore, this paper analyzed the accuracy rate corresponding to the bandwidth measurement time. The analytic procedure is described below. Two bandwidth limits were set at 400 Kbits and 800 Kbits, with measurement intervals of 2, 4, 8, 10, and 20 s, the bandwidth was measured by the bandwidth measuring device under two speed limits, respectively, and their error rates were calculated. The test results are shown in Table 1.

According to the results, the error rates of the values measured by the bandwidth measuring device, at measurement intervals of two seconds, are as high as 72 % and 29 %, respectively, and the error rate is lower than 5 % when the measurement interval is larger than four seconds, thus, the bandwidth measurement interval is selected as four seconds. Meanwhile, the bandwidth prediction model proposed is used, with four seconds defined as the measurement interval, and using 20-second video segments as the examples, thus, five data can be measured, and a data group can be formed. The polynomial curve is predicted using the data of the data group, and the bandwidth for playing the next video segment can be predicted.

The delay time of each segment is calculated by Eq. 7. The client-side has a Timer, which begins counting when No. 0 segment begins to play; T_{ER} represents the real time when the video segment ends, the T_{ES} represents the scheduled time that the video segment ends, T_{SR} represents the real time when the video segment starts, and the T_{SR} represents the scheduled time when the video segment starts, not counting the delay time of other videos, thus, the delay of a single video can be independently analyzed.

$$T_{delay} = (T_{ER} - T_{ES}) - (T_{SR} - T_{SS}) \tag{7}$$

4.2   Analysis Results of Bandwidth Prediction Model

This chapter records the predicted values of an actual bandwidth prediction model measured by a bandwidth measuring device according to the real center operation results with varying bandwidths. In this test, the conditions when the bandwidth increases or decreases suddenly are tested, the initial bandwidth is

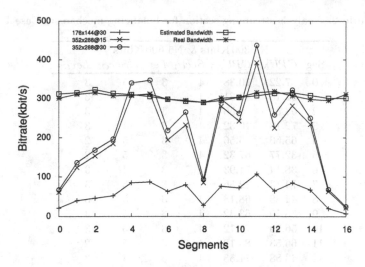

Fig. 4. Streaming bitrate of different bandwidths

limited to 300 Kbits, and the bandwidth is changed to 250 Kbits when playing the seventh video segment. The schematic diagram is shown in Fig. 4. The bandwidth prediction value, actual bandwidth value, error rate, and single video delay time, are recorded. The purple curve represents the values measured by the bandwidth measuring tool, and the cyan represents the bandwidth values predicted by the bandwidth prediction model. The data results are further discussed below.

In this experiment, No. 0 segment to No. 6 segment are limited to 300 Kbits, and this speed is adjusted to 250 Kbits from the seventh segment, as shown in Fig. 4. The error rate between the bandwidth prediction value and actual value of the seventh segment is 20 %, meaning the index node selected the wrong video level with a delay time of 2.13 s; however, the bandwidth prediction mechanism immediately corrected it. The error rates of the eighth and ninth video segments decreased to 5.8 % and 5.9 %, respectively, and the video delay was greatly reduced.

4.3   Analysis Results of Selection and Balancing Mechanism of Streaming Nodes

This chapter analyzes the node selection and node load under the streaming condition of an actual multi-node. In order to simplify the testing environment, the media cloud architecture is simplified, and includes an index node, a content node, and two streaming nodes. The actual node selections and load conditions are analyzed for two streaming nodes and two client-sides, with different bandwidths. This study analyzed the node load with two client-sides. In terms of hardware, this study used a CPU with improved computing power for Node Four, and used the worse CPU for Node Five. In terms of bandwidth, Case 1: the bandwidth of Node 4 is limited to 600 Kbits, and the bandwidth of Node 5

Table 2. Analysis streaming section for balancing mechanism Case 1

Seg	CPU_{N4}	CPU_{N5}	Sec_{C1}	Lev_{C1}	Sec_{C2}	Lev_{C2}
	N4 300 Kbits & N5 600 Kbits					
0	7.22	10.38	4	3	5	3
1	52.16	7.31	4	3	4	3
2	68.32	6.56	4	3	4	3
3	72.18	10.32	4	3	4	3
4	65.66	5.56	4	3	5	2
5	32.77	67.32	4	3	5	2
6	38.14	71.93	4	3	4	3
7	74.13	22.56	4	3	5	3
8	44.38	68.13	4	3	5	3
9	56.59	63.32	4	3	5	3
10	56.39	78.12	4	3	5	3
11	66.53	85.12	4	3	5	2
12	43.88	71.55	4	3	4	3
13	51.38	66.57	4	3	5	2
14	39.18	78.15	4	3	5	3
15	62.23	69.88	4	3	4	3
16	67.85	21.72	4	3	4	3
Avg	50.27	47.03				

is limited to 300 Kbits. Case 2: the bandwidth of Node 4 is limited to 300 Kbits, and the bandwidth of Node 5 is limited to 600 Kbits. The video play is tested, and the test results are shown in Tables 2 and 3.

According to Table 2, when two client-sides compete for bandwidth, the available bandwidth of each client-side obviously decreases; therefore, when two streaming nodes have similar bandwidths, the center adjusts the nodes according to the center load, and transfers the bandwidth demand centered in Node Four to Node Five. Finally, the measured center average load is 50.27 % and 47.03 %, respectively, which was obviously increased as compared with the single client side.

With the test results in Table 3, when bandwidth limitations are interchanged, it is obvious that the nodes are allocated to Node Four and Node Five, because although the center judges that Node Five has better bandwidth, once the node is occupied, the center load of Node Five obviously increases, thus, the center assigns the video request of the second client-side to Node Four, as it has better computing power. The test results show that the average loads of Node Four and Node Five are 45.81 % and 63.64 %, respectively.

Based on the above test, with the operation of the balancing mechanism, if a node with strong computing power is provided with better bandwidth, the center will allocate most requests for videos to the node with the stronger capability. On the contrary, if a node with weak computing power is provided with better bandwidth, the center will allocate requests for videos to the nodes in the media cloud.

Table 3. Analysis streaming section for balancing mechanism Case 2

	N4 600 Kbits & N5 300 Kbits					
Seg	CPU_{N4}	CPU_{N5}	Sec_{C1}	Lev_{C1}	Sec_{C2}	Lev_{C2}
0	2.88	7.52	5	3	4	3
1	58.34	75.41	5	3	4	3
2	61.13	69.85	5	3	4	3
3	63.99	78.15	5	3	4	3
4	63.18	76.88	5	3	4	2
5	54.18	67.32	5	3	5	2
6	52.96	72.79	5	3	4	3
7	49.86	66.13	5	3	4	3
8	51.33	71.16	5	3	4	3
9	38.41	69.32	5	3	4	2
10	44.62	62.58	5	3	4	3
11	65.39	78.55	5	3	4	1
12	66.51	79.23	5	3	5	3
13	15.32	89.16	5	3	4	2
14	48.93	68.15	5	3	4	3
15	49.52	69.47	5	3	4	3
16	38.12	61.23	5	3	4	3
Avg	48.51	63.64				

5 Conclusion

This study designs a video quality scalable streaming mechanism for the media cloud computing center, and constructs communication and management mechanisms for the media cloud, including the construction of a bandwidth measurement center and load monitoring mechanisms for nodes of specific purposes, and designs a balancing mechanism for node resources in the media cloud. During test and analysis, we discussed the error rate and client-side delay time of a bandwidth prediction model with varying bandwidths, and analyzed the actual operational effects of the multinode balancing mechanism.

Acknowledgment. The authors would like to thank the National Science Council of the Republic of China, Taiwan for supporting this research under Contract NSC 101-2628-E-194-003-MY3, 102-2219-E-194-002 and 101-2221-E-197-008-MY3.

References

1. Zhou, L., Wang, X., Tu, W., Mutean, G., Geller, B.: Distributed scheduling scheme for video streaming over multi-channel multi-radio multi-hop wireless networks. IEEE J. Sel. Areas Commun. **28**(3), 409–419 (2010)
2. Han, J., Hu, M., Sun, H.: Search engine prototype system based on cloud computing. In: Proceedings of the First International Conference on Cloud Computing, Beijing, China, pp. 332–337, 1–4 December 2009

3. Ghandeharizadeh, S., Krishnamachari, B.: C2P2: a peer-to-peer network for on-demand automobile information services. In: Proceedings of 15th International Workshop on Database and Expert Systems Applications, Zaragoza, Spain, pp. 538–542, August 30–September 3 2004
4. Wu, S.Y., He, C.E.: QoS-aware dynamic adaptation for cooperative media streaming in mobile environments. IEEE Trans. on Parallel Distrib. Syst. **22**(3), 439–450 (2011)
5. Huang, D., Zhang, X., Kang, M., Luo, J.: MobiCloud: building secure cloud framework for mobile computing and communication. In: Proceedings of the Fifth IEEE International Symposium on Service Oriented System Engineering, Nanjing, China, pp. 27–34, 4–5 June 2010
6. Ferretti, S., Ghini, V., Panzieri, F., Turrini, E.: Seamless support of multimedia distributed applications through a cloud. In: Proceedings of the 3rd IEEE International Conference on Cloud Computing, Miami, FL, USA, pp. 548–549, 5–10 July 2010
7. Diaz-Sanchez, D., Almenarez, F., Marin, A., Proserpio, D., Cabarcos, P.A.: Media cloud: an open cloud computing middleware for content management. IEEE Trans. Consum. Electron. **57**(2), 970–978 (2011)
8. Lai, C.F., Vasilakos, A.V.: Mobile multimedia services over cloud computing. IEEE COMSOC MMTC E-Letter **5**(6), 39–42 (2010)
9. Hu, G.Q., Tay, W.P., Wen, Y.G.: Cloud robotics: architecture, challenges and applications. IEEE Netw. **26**(3), 21–28 (2012)
10. Shao, L.L., Zhu, Z., Wang, Q., Sabhikhi, R.K.: Wireless network cloud: architecture and system requirements. IBM J. Res. Dev. **54**(1), 1–12 (2010)
11. Lai, C.F., Chen, M.: Playback-rate based streaming services for maximum network capacity in IP multimedia subsystem. IEEE Syst. J. **5**(4), 555–563 (2010)
12. Ali, T., Nauman, M., Hadi, F.-E., bin Muhaya, F.: On usage control of multimedia content in and through cloud computing paradigm. In: Proceedings of 5th International Conference on Future Information Technology, Busan, Korea, pp. 1–5, 21–23 May 2010
13. Chang, J.H., Lai, C.F., Huang, Y.M., Chao, H.C.: 3PRS: a personalized and popular programs recommendation system of digital TV for P2P social network. Multimedia Tools Appl. **47**(1), 31–48 (2010)
14. Huang, Y., Peng, J.L., Kuo, C.C.J., Gopi, M.: A generic scheme for progressive point cloud coding. IEEE Trans. Visual Comput. Graph. **14**(2), 440–453 (2008)
15. Chang, S.Y., Lai, C.F., Huang, Y.M.: Dynamic adjustable multimedia streaming service architecture over cloud computing. Comput. Commun. **35**(15), 1798–1808 (2012)

Vehicular Cyber-Physical Systems
with Mobile Cloud Computing Support

Hehua Yan[1], Jiafu Wan[1(✉)], Yingying Wang[1], Zhonghai Wang[2],
and Zhumei Song[3]

[1] College of Information Engineering, Guangdong Jidian Polytechnic,
Guangzhou, China
{jiafuwan_76,wyybaby}@163.com
[2] Jiangxi University of Science and Technology, Ganzhou, China
[3] Shenzhen Institute of Information Technology, Shenzhen, China

Abstract. In recent years, Vehicular Cyber-Physical Systems (VCPS) for
high-level applications have led to an increasing demand on connecting Mobile
Cloud Computing (MCC) users to VCPS and accessing the richer services. In
this paper, we first introduce the conceptual architecture for VCPS with MCC
capability. Based on the conceptual architecture, we propose a VCPS and MCC
Integration Architecture (termed VMIA), which provides mobility support for
mobile users (e.g., drivers or potential passengers) to access mobile traffic
cloud. In addition, we analyze two crucial cloud-supported components
including traffic-aware mobile geographic information system and dynamic
vehicle routing algorithms. The proposed VMIA can provide the flexibility for
enabling diverse applications.

Keywords: Vehicular cyber-physical systems · Architecture · Vehicular ad
hoc networks · Mobile cloud computing

1 Introduction

Cyber-Physical Systems (CPS) are increasingly composed of services and applications
deployed across a range of communication topologies, computing platforms, and
sensing and actuation devices [1–3]. Nowadays, vehicular networking serves as one of
the most important enabling technologies, and is producing some novel telematics
applications. Vehicular networking with the capabilities of decision-making and
autonomous control can be upgraded to Vehicular Cyber-Physical Systems (VCPS)
[4]. We believe that VCPS is an evolution of vehicular networking by the introduction
of more intelligent and interactive operations. The services and applications in VCPS
often form multiple end-to-end cyber-physical flows that operate in multi-layered
environments. In such operating conditions, each service must process events
belonging to other services or applications, while providing quality of service
assurance (e.g., timeliness, reliability, and trustworthiness).

Recently, Mobile Cloud Computing (MCC) is gradually becoming a promising
technology, which provides a flexible stack of massive computing, storage and software services in a scalable and virtualized manner at low cost [5, 6]. The integration

V.C.M. Leung and M. Chen (Eds.): CloudComp 2013, LNICST 133, pp. 27–35, 2014.
DOI: 10.1007/978-3-319-05506-0_3, © Institute for Computer Sciences, Social Informatics
and Telecommunications Engineering 2014

of VCPS and MCC is expected to facilitate the development of cost-effective, scalable and data driven VCPS platforms, which must be able to guarantee safety and improve Quality of Service (QoS) for drivers or passengers. The new mobile applications for VCPS can be rapidly provisioned and released using MCC with minimal effort. We consider MCC technology to highlight some innovative applications (e.g., historical traffic data and in-vehicle infotainment) for VCPS with richer traffic mobile video streaming, more supporting functionalities, and more reliable QoS.

For the burgeoning integration, VCPS and MCC still possess their own issues and challenges [7–9]. At the same time, this seamless integration will introduce some new problems such as system architecture. To address this challenge, we focus on the integration architecture and two crucial components in this paper. In my view, though other issues such as reliable vehicle communication are equally important for VCPS platform with MCC capability, we highlight the features and contributions as follows:

- Integrate MCC with VCPS: By incorporating the dynamic interactions between MCC and VCPS, we propose a VCPS and MCC Integration Architecture (termed VMIA) to provide more services (e.g., driving assistances).
- Analyze the Crucial Service Components in VMIA: The cloud-supported VCPS has multi-layered features, each layer provides different service contents. We analyze the crucial service components including traffic-aware mobile Geographic Information System (GIS) and dynamic vehicle routing algorithms to determine the research directions and challenges.

The remainder of the paper is organized as follows. Section 2 analyzes the multi-layered VCPS and gives the conceptual architecture for VCPS with MCC capability. In Sect. 3, we propose a cloud-supported VCPS architecture. Section 4 outlines two crucial components in VMIA, and Sect. 5 concludes this paper.

2   Developing VCPS with MCC Support

In this section, we analyze the multi-layered VCPS, and propose the conceptual architecture for VCPS with MCC capability.

2.1   Multi-layered VCPS

In VCPS, the multi-layered VCPS is shown in Fig. 1. According to the range of spatial regions, VCPS can be divided into three deferent layers (i.e., micro layer, meso layer and macro layer) described as follows:

- Micro Layer: In the vehicle range, digital platform of vehicle acquires both environment and vehicle body parameters and integrates human factors for providing high-quality man-machine interaction by means of wired/short-range wireless technologies and advanced control algorithms [10]. In this layer, the design principle is to ensure safety first and infotainment second.
- Meso Layer: The vehicular clusters usually formed by Vehicular Ad Hoc Networks (VANET) give more comfort and convenience (e.g., sharing of entertainment

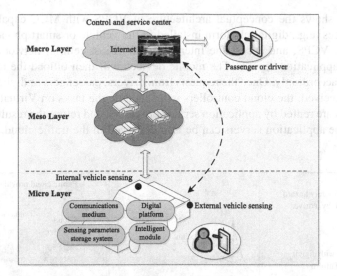

Fig. 1. Multi-layered VCPS

resources and safety information) to drivers or passengers. For the meso layer, the conspicuous challenges are computation offloading and network bandwidth limit.

- Macro Layer: The control and service center provides all kinds of services (e.g., real-time traffic information and traffic contingency plans) to improve QoS. For example, the real-time traffic information can help drivers conduct path planning and reduce congestion. With the MCC support, the macro layer can offer more services such as traffic mobile video streaming.

2.2 Conceptual Architecture for VCPS with MCC Capability

VCPS has emerged as an indispensable technology for intelligent transportation systems. In [11], the research focused on the micro layer to improve road safety and efficiency using cyber technologies such as wireless technologies and distributed real-time control theory. This research considers human factors and integrates vehicle dynamics and communication with a field theory model to predict vehicle motion in the near future for identifying safety hazards and proactive collision warning.

In this paper, the research contents extend from micro layer to multi-layers with the MCC support. The development of VCPS with MCC capability is based on two observations:

- We can develop and deploy numerous mobile applications for VCPS platforms, which can access larger and faster data storage services and processing power from the traffic cloud.
- Many mobile applications have been developed for diverse MCC environments, and these examples have provided some useful references for incorporating MCC capabilities into VCPS.

Figure 2 shows the conceptual architecture of VCPS with MCC capability. The mobile devices (e.g., digital platform installed in the vehicle or smart phone) serve as gateways for VCPS, and access the Internet via Wi-Fi or cellular networks to coordinate with application servers. The mobile devices will then offload the tasks to the traffic cloud accordingly. Once the requests from drivers, passengers or digital platform have been received, the cloud controllers will schedule the tasks on Virtual Machines (VM), which are rented by application service providers, and return the results. In some situations, the application servers can be also deployed in the traffic cloud.

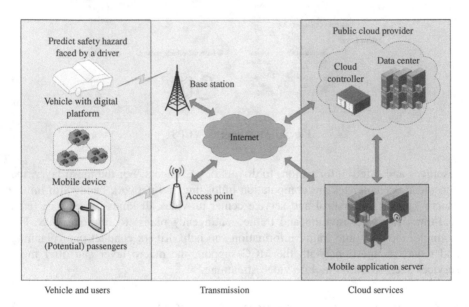

Fig. 2. Conceptual architecture for VCPS with MCC capability

3 Cloud-Supported VCPS Architecture

This paper designs cloud-supported VCPS to provide more service contents (e.g., historical traffic data) for drivers, passengers or traffic controllers. In this section, we propose a framework for an emerging vehicular networking system (i.e., VCPS) with MCC capability. Figure 3 depicts the proposed framework for VCPS platform with MCC support. This platform is comprised of three layers (micro layer, meso layer and macro layer) as follows:

- In the micro layer, the core research topic is to focus on the following two aspects: (1) design and evaluate new applications for improved traffic safety and traffic operations by integrating human factors, and (2) develop an integrated traffic-aware mobile GIS.

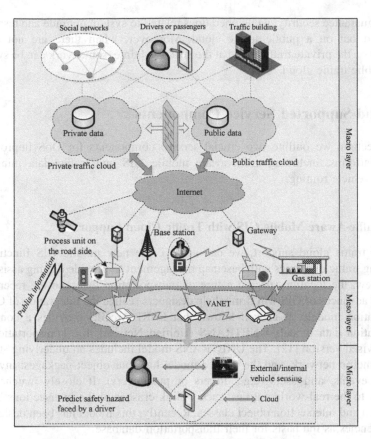

Fig. 3. VMIA: VCPS and MCC integration architecture

- In the meso layer, the vehicular clusters formed by VANET usually share entertainment resources and safety information to drivers or passengers. For example, the traffic accident information can be forwarded to the near drivers for a timely reminder when a traffic accident happens.
- The macro layer includes wired/wireless transmission, cloud services, and users. The traffic video streaming from cameras are transmitted to the adjacent routing equipment via wired or wireless transmission, and then to the traffic cloud server via Internet. The traffic cloud servers possess powerful VM resources such as CPU, memory, and network bandwidth in order to provide all kinds of cloud services such as entertainment resources. The different users such as drivers, traffic controllers, researchers, or even passengers ubiquitously acquire multiple cloud services by a variety of interfaces such as personal computers, TVs and smart phones.

For the VMIA, we further stress an important aspect: hybrid traffic cloud. In general, a hybrid cloud computing architecture can accelerate the migration from existing IT resources in transportation departments to cloud computing, make full use of resources, and reduce costs. Important traffic data and applications such as traffic contingency plans and traffic violation records can be deployed on a private traffic cloud to guarantee security, while operations related to system upgrade and testing can be carried out on a public traffic cloud. Moreover, when there are not enough resources on the private traffic cloud at the peak load time, some work can be switched to the public traffic cloud.

4   Cloud-Supported Service Components

In this section, we outline two crucial service components for QoS improvement VCPS platforms, including traffic-aware mobile GIS and traffic data mining for dynamic vehicle routing.

4.1   Traffic-Aware Mobile GIS with Traffic Cloud Support

With the traffic cloud support, we can achieve the new mobile GIS functions by integrating traffic dynamics with basemap management to provide driving assistances. In our view, the location-specific nature of transportation data and the recent technological advances of GIS will firmly help designers realize the integration of GIS and transportation models. It is well known that ESRI ArcGIS provides a conceptual transportation data models UNETRANS (Unified Network for Transportation) and later a revised version [12]. The UNETRANS model includes an underlying structure by a geometric network, and the revised model has four object packages: inventory, network, events, and users (e.g., drivers or passengers). It closely matches class behaviors to the real-world entities, such as link crashes to the intersections by handling crash and intersection object classes. Recently, this model has been designed by larger agencies as the basis for their transportation database.

Fortunately, the recently published roads and highways data model provides the best-practice templates for integrating static transportation network data and time-varying traffic flow data from a traffic cloud. However, current ArcGIS lacks necessary calculation tools for building a real-time traffic prediction model. Therefore, this is an interesting work to design a novel transportation prediction model by integrating the existing ArcGIS and an extension traffic analyst. With the support of the traffic cloud, we propose to integrate traffic monitoring and analysis with the mobile GIS functions in basemap management, traffic analysis and crash warning, and route selection.

4.2   Cloud-Supported Dynamic Vehicle Routing Algorithms

Figure 4 shows the cloud-supported traffic data mining and prediction. The Roadside Equipment (RSE) units deployed at crucial locations exchange the traffic information with On-Board Equipment (OBEs) installed on passing by vehicles. In the meso layer, both RSEs and neighboring OBEs are also interconnected and share traffic information by means of VANET. Vehicles outside the range of any RSE may still be connected to the rest of the vehicle and infrastructure network via neighboring vehicles. In this way, the vehicle and infrastructure network can generate the real-time traffic information, based on which some fundamental traffic problems such as efficiency can be well solved from a new perspective, including:

- How to accurately infer current and predict future traffic conditions at locations with or without RSE coverage.
- How to best utilize the inferred/predicted traffic information for improving traffic operations.

With the support of real-time and accurate traffic information, all the drivers will select the optimal route according to some criteria such as travel time or distance. Intuitively, these decisions will collectively result in a state of Dynamic User Equilibrium (DUE). However, for a large-scale distributed system where drivers make their own independent decisions based on the same travel time information, this may possibly lead to an extreme state similar to the result of Dynamic All-or-Nothing (DAN) assignment [13], since all the drivers from the same origin to the same destination will take the same routes. In fact, when the system is in a state of Dynamic System Optimal (DSO), the transportation network performance is optimal.

Based on the above analysis, we outline a decentralized and proactive dynamic vehicle routing algorithm to allow drivers to self-organize the traffic and shift the system state from either DAN or DUE to DSO. For example, the RSEs gather traffic information from passing-by connected vehicles. These data together with loop detector and historical traffic data from the traffic cloud are used to predict future link travel times. To avoid the DAN scenario and account for the uncertainty in travel time prediction results, we outline a stochastic route choice method based on discrete choice models by each OBE to find the optimal route. This decentralized and proactive routing process will help to move the transportation network towards a state of DSO. As shown in Fig. 3, the proposed cloud-supported dynamic vehicle routing algorithms involve two layers (the macro layer and the meso layer) of VMIA.

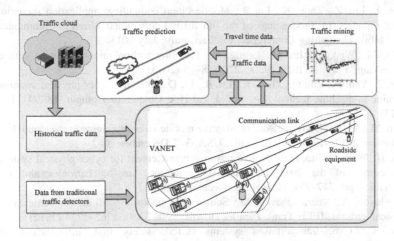

Fig. 4. Cloud-supported traffic data mining and prediction

5 Conclusions

The seamless integration of VCPS and MCC provides tremendous opportunities for future intelligent transportation systems. In this article, we provided a brief review and outlook of this promising field and discussed a cloud-supported VCPS architecture (termed VMIA). In particular, we studied the functionality and reliability of MCC services. We also suggested some crucial service components to improve performance and QoS of cloud-supported VCPS. We believe cloud-supported VCPS will attract enormous attention and research efforts in near future.

Acknowledgement. The authors would like to thank the National Natural Science Foundation of China (No. 61262013, 61363011), the Natural Science Foundation of Guangdong Province, China (No. S2011010001155), and the High-level Talent Project for Universities, Guangdong Province, China (No. 431, YueCaiJiao 2011) for their support in this research.

References

1. Zou, C., Wan, J, Chen, M., Li, D.: Simulation modeling of cyber-physical systems exemplified by unmanned vehicles with WSNs navigation. In: Proceedings of the 7th International Conference on Embedded and Multimedia Computing Technology and Service, pp. 269–275, Gwangju, Korea, September 2012.
2. Chen, M., Wan, J., Li, F.: Machine-to-machine communications: architectures, standards, and applications. KSII Trans. Internet Inf. Syst. **6**(2), 480–497 (2012)
3. Wan, J., Chen, M., Xia, F., Li, D., Zhou, K.: From machine-to-machine communications towards cyber-physical systems. Comput. Sci. Inf. Syst. **10**(3), 1105–1128 (2013)
4. Li, X., Qiao, C., Yu, X., Wagh, A., Sudhaakar, R., Addepalli, S.: Toward effective service scheduling for human drivers in vehicular cyber-physical systems. IEEE Trans. Parallel Distrib. Syst. **23**(9), 1775–1789 (2012)
5. Wan, J., Liu, Z., Zhou, K., Lu, R.: Mobile cloud computing: application scenarios and service models. In: Proceedings of the 9th IEEE International Wireless Communications and Mobile Computing Conference, Cagliari, Italy, July 2013
6. Chen, M., Wen, Y., Jin, H., Leung, V.: Enabling technologies for future data center networking: a primer. IEEE Netw. **27**(4), 8–15 (2013)
7. Wan, J., Yan, H., Liu, Q., Zhou, K., Lu, R., Li, D.: Enabling cyber-physical systems with machine-to-machine technologies. Int. J. Ad Hoc Ubiquitous Comput. **13**(3/4), 187–196 (2013)
8. Chen, M.: AMVSC: a framework of adaptive mobile video streaming in the cloud. In: IEEE Globecom 2012, Anaheim, California, USA, 3–7 December 2012
9. Yan, H., Wan, J., Suo, H.: Adaptive resource management for cyber-physical systems. In: Proceedings of the 2011 International Conference on Mechatronics and Applied Mechanics, pp. 747–751, HongKong, December 2011.
10. Miloslavov, A., Veeraraghavan, M.: Sensor data fusion algorithms for vehicular cyber-physical systems. IEEE Trans. Parallel Distrib. Syst. **23**(9), 1762–1774 (2012)
11. Qiao, C.: Cyber-transportation systems (CTS): safety first, infotainment second, Presentation Report (2010)

12. Azogu, H.: Privacy-preserving license plate image processing. In: Proceedings of the 2nd IEEE Workshop on Multimedia Communications and Services, IEEE GlobeCom 2011, Houston, TX, 5–9 December 2011
13. Sheffi, Y.: Urban Transportation Networks: Equilibrium Analysis with Mathematical Programming Methods. Prentice-Hall Inc., Englewood Cliffs (1985)

Services, Applications,
IoT on Cloud

A Simulation Study of Connected Vehicle Systems Using Named Data Networking

Tao Jiang, Xiaowei Xu, Lu Pu, Yu Hu[✉], and Zhijun Qiu

School of Optical and Electronic Information,
Huazhong University of Science and Technology, Wuhan, China
huyu.cs@gmail.com

Abstract. A Connected vehicle (CV) system is a crossing field of intelligent transportation systems (ITS) and the internet of things (IoT). The IP-based network protocol has been employed in CV systems. Recently, studies have been conducted to explore the adaptation of Named Data Networking (NDN) in certain CV applications, particularly in cloud computing-based applications and services, to enhance the QoS and lower the cost of network infrastructure. In this paper, we propose SimIVC-NDN, an federated simulation platform with the capability of performing a microscopic traffic simulation with both NDN and IP-based networking. Using SimIVC-NDN, we have conducted a quantitative simulation comparison for two CV systems powered by NDN and IP solutions, respectively, for image dissemination, a common cloud computing service. In the experiments we construct a CV system based on a calibrated traffic model of Whitemud Drive at Edmonton, Canada. The simulation results show that the NDN-based CV system lowers the packet delay by two orders of magnitude compared with the IP-based one, indicating that an NDN-based networking is a promising alternative to the conventional IP-based one for cloud computing applications of CV systems.

Keywords: Cloud computing · Named Data Networking · Connected vehicle · VISSIM · NS-3 · High level architect

1 Introduction

Connected vehicle (CV) is a crossing field of intelligent transportation systems (ITS) and internet of things (IoT), which focuses on supporting safety, mobility and environmental applications. Network protocol, affecting both communication delay and the quality of service (QoS) of traffic applications, is an essential component of the CV research. The conventional IP-based network protocol has been a mature and popular means in vehicle communication applications [8].

Recently, researchers in the CV community started to explore the adaptation of Named Data Networking (NDN) in certain CV applications, particularly in cloud computing-based applications and services, to enhance the QoS and lower the cost of network infrastructure [2, 6, 7]. NDN aims to provide secure content-oriented data transmission [1, 3]. Different from IP-based networking, NDN focuses on "what to send" (the content) instead of "where to send" (the address) [15]. In this new network

V.C.M. Leung and M. Chen (Eds.): CloudComp 2013, LNICST 133, pp. 39–48, 2014.
DOI: 10.1007/978-3-319-05506-0_4, © Institute for Computer Sciences, Social Informatics and Telecommunications Engineering 2014

architecture, a data packet will be cached in the network for future requesters, which makes NDN has great advantage in media data transmission. Studies have shown that NDN has a superior performance compared with the IP-based network in many applications [4, 5]. However, to the best of our knowledge, there is no quantitative study on the application of the NDN to CV.

In this paper, we quantitatively exploit the advantage of NDN-based CV. The major contributions of this paper are two-fold. We have proposed a high level architect SimIVC-NDN, an federated simulation platform with the capability of performing a microscopic traffic simulation with both NDN and IP-based networking. The platform is implemented based on VISSIM, a commercial traffic simulator, and NS-3, a popular academia network simulator. Using SimIVC-NDN, we have performed a quantitative comparison between NDN and IP enabled CV system for a common cloud computing-based application (image dissemination) based on a calibrated traffic model of Whitemud Drive at Edmonton, Canada. The simulation results show that the NDN-based CV system lowers the packet delay by two orders of magnitude compared with the IP-based one, indicating that an NDN-based networking is a promising alternative to the conventional IP-based one for cloud computing applications of CV systems.

The remainder of this paper includes the follows. Section 2 introduces the basic concepts of CV and NDN. Section 3 describes the architecture of the proposed federated simulation platform SimIVC-NDN, which is used in Sects. 4 and 5 for a case study comparing using NDN and IP-based networking in a CV application. The paper is concluded in Sect. 6. To the best of our knowledge, this is the first work that quantitatively studies the effectiveness of adopting NDN in the CV for cloud computing-based applications.

2 Background

2.1 Introduction to Connected Vehicle

Connected vehicle (CV) focuses on supporting mobility, safety and environmental applications [9]. Mobility applications provide a connected vehicle and infrastructure environment which is designed to facilitate better mobility. Safety applications are designed to reduce or eliminate crashes. Environmental applications both generate and capture environmentally relevant real-time transportation information and create actionable feedback to facilitate green transportation decisions.

The cloud infrastructure is an indispensable component to CV applications. The cloud infrastructure captures real-time data from equipments located either on-board vehicles or within the transportation infrastructure (e.g. the road side stations for collecting and disseminating information). The data are transmitted wirelessly and are utilized by a wide range of multi-modal applications (e.g. application that aims to make better future route planning).

2.2 Introduction to NDN

The layered architectures of IP and NDN are shown in Fig. 1.

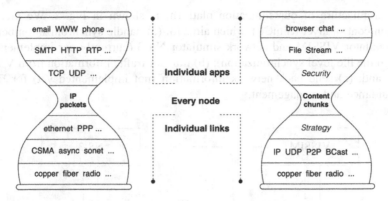

Fig. 1. IP vs. NDN layered architecture overview [1]

Unlike IP (host-to-host communication based on IP addresses), NDN is *content-centric* communication. The IP-based routers utilize IP address headers to forward packets. The NDN-based routers, however, utilize the *name prefix* (which uniquely identify a piece of data) of each packet for packet forwarding.

NDN communication is consumer-driven. Data consumer sends out request (named *Interest* under NDN terminology) with specific name prefix for desired content (named *Data*), where the name prefix of the Interest packet and that of the Data packet are identical. Due to the content-centric (instead of host-centric) nature, NDN can run over any physically connected network [1]; e.g. a network with only MAC addresses (which can uniquely identify a physical device) can also run NDN protocol directly regardless of IP addresses.

NDN-based router consists of three logical elements, *Forwarding Information Base* (FIB), *Pending Interest Table* (PIT), and *Content Store* (CS). FIB is the routing table based on name prefix instead of IP address. PIT is designed to keep the Interest packets that have not yet been responded within a certain period of time. CS is related to the *caching* mechanism of NDN; when a Data packet is sent back to the data consumer who sent out the request, the intermediate nodes along the path will cache the Data packet in their CS. With caching mechanism, when an Interest request is received by a node, the node will first check its CS; if a copy of the desired Data (within a certain range of living time) is found, the copy is sent back and the request is immediately satisfied.

The detailed description of NDN can be found in [1, 2].

3 Simulation Architecture

As to the connected vehicle simulation, depending on the needed simulation resolution of both vehicular driving behaviors and networking protocols, it is desired to develop a state-of-the-art simulator capable of performing both fine-grained microscopic traffic simulation and network simulation. We thus propose a simulation platform that integrates VISSIM and NS-3 which stems from our previous work [10].

The architecture of our simulation platform is shown in Fig. 2. We created a simulation control layer (SimCL), which aims to: (a) handle synchronization between traffic simulator VISSIM and network simulator NS-3 (currently our implementation is through the file level synchronization); (b) transfer traffic information from VISSIM to NS-3 and; (c) send back network information (not implemented yet) for further traffic guidance and management.

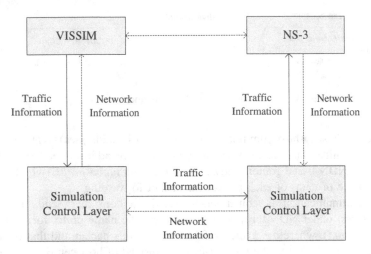

Fig. 2. SimIVC-NDN architecture overview

The new system has two main benefits [10]: (1) by using both traffic and network simulators, it provides more insights into both traffic and network simulation process; (2) because VISSIM and NS-3 are both the state-of-the-art simulation tools in either corresponding field, the coupling simulation approach (instead of implementing both the traffic and network simulator alone [13]) is more realistic and trustable. Currently, our simulation platform of coupling VISSIM and NS-3 is a unidirectional coupling, i.e. the SimCL only conveys information from VISSIM to NS-3. The implementation details are described in Sect. 4.

4   Case Study: A Comparison of NDN and IP in an Image Disseminating Application of Connected Vehicle

Based on SimIVC-NDN described in the previous section, we propose an image disseminating application scenario to conduct a comparison between NDN and conventional IP-based networking under the connected vehicle communication environment.

4.1   Application Overview

As shown in Fig. 3, the cloud server, routers, wireless stations and moving vehicles are all implemented with either IP or NDN protocol stack. Each vehicle is equipped with a Wi-Fi or cellular device for wireless communication. In our scenario, only V2I (Vehicle to Infrastructure) is involved; that is to say, vehicles can only communicate with road side stations, and cannot communicate with each other directly. To facilitate drivers' future route planning, the cloud server stores the images captured from cameras equipped at road intersections or highway entrances. The latest images stored in the server are updated with an interval of *UpdateInt*. Each vehicle periodically broadcasts request (with the request interval *VehInt*) for the latest image from certain camera.

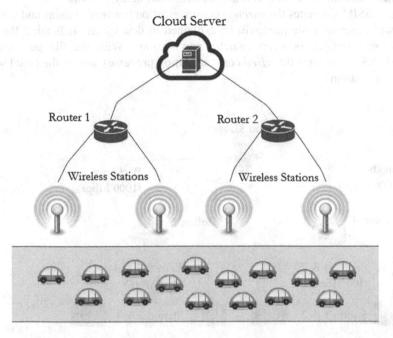

Fig. 3. Image dissemination application scenario

The *station* is equipped with both wireless and wired interfaces. On receiving a request from some vehicle, it will handle the request according to either IP or NDN rules. For cases with IP, the station will forward the request according to the routing table. For cases with NDN, the station will forward the request according to the CS, PIT and FIT which we have described in Sect. 2.2. For example, if CS has a copy of the requested image data, the request is immediately satisfied. The *router* operates in almost the same way as the station. The only difference is, the router is equipped only with wired networking interfaces. When the request reaches the top level layer (i.e. the *cloud server* in our topology), the cloud server will response the request with the desired image data if it exists.

Here we make an assumption of the name prefixes regarding cases of NDN. The name prefix has a form like *"/root/traffic/image/LuoyuRoad/GuanshanAve/20130522/1028/30"*, which means that the image is taken from the camera at the intersection of Luoyu Road and Guanshan Avenue at the time of May 22th 2013, 10:28:30.

4.2 Simulation Setup

After an overview of our proposed cloud-based image dissemination application scenario, the simulation setup details will be described in this section.

(a) Simulation Methodology
The simulation network topology corresponding to our application scenario is presented in Fig. 4. As shown in the figure, the bandwidth of either *Backbone 1* or *Backbone 2* is 1000 Mbps, while the bandwidth of either four *branches* is 100 Mbps. We assume that all wired connections' transmission delay is 1 ms.

The VISSIM simulates the *wireless* communication between stations and vehicles; and it will generate a file (that will be explained in detail later) indicating the communication frequency between vehicles and stations. With the file generated by VISSIM, NS-3 simulates the *wired* communication processes among the cloud server, routers and stations.

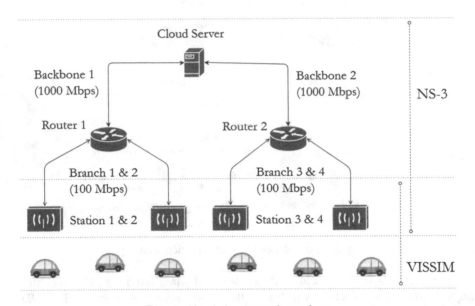

Fig. 4. Simulation network topology

(b) VISSIM Simulation
As to the traffic simulation part, we adopt a calibrated road network model of Whitemud Drive, the main east-west freeway in southern Edmonton, Canada. The road network model has been carefully calibrated with VISSIM according to the feedback of realistic traffic data [11, 12]. Within the road model, four stations are located with an interval of approximately 500 m, as shown in Fig. 5.

We utilize the Car2X functionality of VISSIM [16] to simulate the wireless communication processes between vehicles and stations, with the assumption that the communication range of each vehicle is 250 m (only within this range, a vehicle can wirelessly communicate with the nearest station).

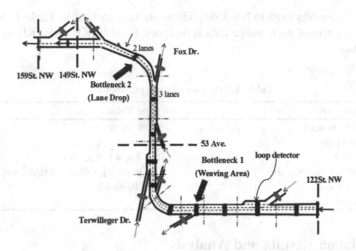

Fig. 5. Whitemud Drive road model, modeled and calibrated with VISSIM

The vehicles periodically send requests for desired image data during the simulation. The interval between each request (i.e. the *VehInt*) is designed to be 1 s, 2 s, 4 s, 8 s, and 16 s in different experiments. On receiving a request from some vehicle, the station records the current timestamp (i.e. the simulation time step) in a *request-time table* (which will then be exported to a file utilized by NS-3).

The request-time table records every request's timestamp during the simulation, thus we can obtain the communication frequency between vehicles and each station; also, the NS-3 simulation can synchronize with the VISSIM simulation by utilizing the timestamps in the table.

The runtime of the simulation is 600 s.

(c) NS-3 Simulation

As to the network simulation part, NS-3 utilizes the request-time table generated by VISSIM to keep synchronized with the vehicles' requests. We implement an application within the stations which will handle the request packets (according to either IP or NDN) sent from "virtual vehicles" according to the timestamp recorded in the request-time table. Also, on receiving the request packets, the routers and the cloud server will handle them according to either IP or NDN rules. For cases with IP, the simulation is based on the IP protocol stack implemented by NS-3 [14]. For cases with NDN, the simulation is based on the NDN protocol stack implemented by Lixia Zhang [2].

We make several assumptions here. Firstly, as the vehicles on the same section of road have a rather high possibility to request for the image captured from the same intersection or highway entrance etc., we assume that the possibility is 1. Secondly, as to the name prefix under NDN-based network, if the image updating interval *UpdateInt* is 2 s, for example, the name prefix of either Interest packet or Data packet would be like *"{…}/1028/30"*, *"{…}/1028/32"*, *"{…}/1028/34"*, and so on; and the *"{…}"* part is *"/root/traffic/image/LuoyuRoad/GuanshanAve/20130522"* (the meaning has been explained in Sect. 4.1).

All the parameters used in NS-3 simulation are summarized in Table 1. As shown in Table 1, the size of each image data is designed to be 40 KB or 80 KB in different experiments.

Table 1 NS-3 simulation parameter

Parameter	Type/Value
Protocol stack	NDN vs. IP
UpdateInt	1 s, 2 s, 4 s, 8 s, 16 s
VehInt	1 s, 2 s, 4 s, 8 s, 16 s
Request package size	[20 B, 40 B], uniform distribution
Image size	40 KB, 80 KB
Chunk data size	1 KB

5 Simulation Results and Analysis

The results of our simulation are shown below. Figure 6(a, b) shows the average delay between request packet and response packet, each for 40 KB and 80 KB image data size. Figure 6(c, d) shows the average throughputs considering the four branches and two backbones (as shown in Fig. 4), each for 40 KB and 80 KB image data size. The horizontal axis "interval" indicates the request interval (i.e. *VehInt*).

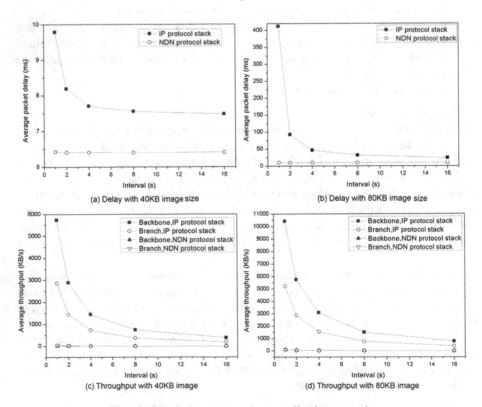

Fig. 6. Simulation results of our application scenario

As to average delay, under IP circumstance, when *VehInt* decreases, the delay increases exponentially; while under NDN, when the interval decreases, the delay almost stays the same. As to average throughput, similar phenomena can be observed. Under IP circumstance, when *VehInt* decreases, the throughput of branches and backbones increase exponentially, and the average throughput for backbones is approximately 2 times than that for branches; while under NDN, when the interval decreases, the average throughput almost stays zero.

The difference may be caused by a variety of factors. First, the caching mechanism of NDN makes immediate response of request possible. In our simulation scenario, to IP-based networking, the stations will definitely forward requests to higher level routers; to NDN-based networking, however, if a station has a copy of the desired data within its CS, the request would be immediately satisfied and with no need to travel a long distance to the cloud server, thus decreases the overall load of branches and backbones, and also reduces the delay of image dissemination packets. Second, we have only utilized the raw IP networking functionality instead of taking advantages of other more advanced application protocols such as P2P or introducing more complex IP networking infrastructure such as CDN (Content Delivery Network); out of this factor, we may not fully exploit the potential of IP; though we also only use the raw NDN networking functionality.

6 Conclusion

In this paper SimIVC-NDN, an federated simulation platform with the capability of performing a microscopic traffic simulation with both NDN and IP-based networking, is proposed. Using SimIVC-NDN, we have conducted a quantitative comparison for two CV systems powered by NDN and IP solutions, respectively, for image dissemination, a common cloud computing-based service. The simulation results show that the NDN-based CV system lowers the packet delay by two orders of magnitude compared with the IP-based one, indicating that an NDN-based networking is a promising alternative to the conventional IP-based one for cloud computing-based applications of CV systems. In our future work, a bi-directional coupling simulation platform will be proposed, and the wireless protocol components of NS-3 will be utilized to obtain a simulation result with higher precision.

Acknowledgement. This work is partially sponsored by National Science Foundation of China (61272070).

References

1. Jacobson, V., Smetters, D.K., Thornton, J.D., Plass, M.F., Briggs, N.H., Braynard, R.L.: Networking named content. In: 5th International Conference on Emerging Networking Experiments and Technologies, pp. 1–12. ACM (2009)
2. Zhang, L., Estrin, D., Burke, J., Jacobson, V., Thornton, J.D., Smetters, D.K.: Named data networking (NDN) project. NDN Technical Report NDN-0001, Xerox Palo Alto Research Center-PARC (2010)

3. Pan, J., Paul, S., Jain, R.: A survey of the research on future internet architectures. IEEE J. Commun. Mag. **49**(7), 26–36 (2011)
4. Zhu, Z., Wang, S., Yang, X., Jacobson, V., Zhang, L.: ACT: audio conference tool over named data networking. In: ACM SIGCOMM Workshop on Information-Centric Networking, pp. 68–73. ACM (2011)
5. Zhu, Z., Bian, C., Afanasyev, A., Jacobson, V., Zhang, L.: Chronos: serverless multi-user chat over NDN. NDN Technical Report NDN-0008 (2012)
6. Grassi, G., Pesavento, D., Wang, L., Pau, G., Vuyyuru, R., Wakikawa, R., Zhang, L.: Vehicular inter-networking via named data. In: ACM HotMobile Poster (2013)
7. Wang, L., Wakikawa, R., Kuntz, R., Vuyyuru, R., Zhang, L.: Data naming in vehicle-to-vehicle communications. In: IEEE Conference Computer Communications Workshops, pp. 328–333. IEEE (2012)
8. Mohammad, S.A., Rasheed, A., Qayyum, A.: VANET Architectures and protocol stacks: a survey. In: Strang, T., Festag, A., Vinel, A., Mehmood, R., Rico Garcia, C., Röckl, M. (eds.) Nets4Trains/Nets4Cars 2011. LNCS, vol. 6596, pp. 95–105. Springer, Heidelberg (2011)
9. Connected vehicle. http://www.its.dot.gov/connected_vehicle/connected_vehicle.htm
10. Xu, X., Jiang, T., Li, P., Tony Qiu, Z., Yu, H.: A high-level architecture SimIVC for simulating the traffic network. In: 2nd International Conference on Transportation Information and Safety (2013)
11. Tony Qiu, Z.: Online simulation of networked vehicle based active traffic management for freeway operation. Final Report, University of Alberta (2012)
12. Karim, M., Qiu, T.Z.: Study on calibration and validation of fundamental diagram for urban arterials. In: Transportation Research Board 91st Annual Meeting, No. 12-0637 (2012)
13. Hu, T.Y., Liao, T.Y., Chen, Y.K., Chiang, M.L.: Dynamic simulation-assignment model (DynaTAIWAN) under mixed traffic flows for ITS applications. In: Transportation Research Board 86th Annual Meeting (No. 07-1616) (2007)
14. NS-3 Internet models. http://www.nsnam.org/
15. Driving to a Content-Centric Internet, Van Jacobson speech. http://blogs.verisigninc.com/blog/entry/driving_to_a_content_centric?cmp=tw
16. Wang, Y.: Simulation-based testbed development for analyzing toll impacts on freeway travel. Transportation Northwest, No. TNW2012-16 (2012)

Interchanging Cloud Providers Instances Through Ubiquitous Devices

Tiago M.C. Simões[1], Jorge E.F. Costa[1], Joel J.P.C. Rodrigues[1(✉)], and Long Hu[2]

[1] Instituto de Telecomunicações, University of Beira Interior, Covilhã, Portugal
{tiago.simoes,jorge.costa}@it.ubi.pt, joeljr@ieee.org
[2] School of Computer Science and Technology,
Huazhong University of Science and Technology, Wuhan, China
longhu.cs@gmail.com

Abstract. Cloud computing dominates the current research landscape as a hot topic for researchers, companies, and customers where there is a growing need to transparently link services and infrastructures. Mobile devices, such as, smartphones or tablets play a key role for these purposes. The presence of dissimilar technologies among cloud providers is delivering chaos to the function of interoperability among providers. The existence of several technologies, terminologies, architectures, and business strategies are contributing to aggravate thins even further. In this paper, cloud computing providers, architecture, service, and deployment stack are discussed. Then, a cloud instance interoperability model is proposed. This model is presented to solve the interoperability issue between cloud providers. Five major components intended to ubiquitous devices are proposed in order to easily export and import computational resources, configurations, structures, virtual machines, billing information, helpdesk tickets, and further related information between cloud providers.

Keywords: Cloud computing · Ubiquitous devices · Mobile devices · Interoperability issues · Interoperability model · Cloud providers

1 Introduction

Cloud computing as become an increasingly desirable research field, countless researchers are focusing their efforts to evolve cloud computing. Although there are several definitions for cloud computing two of them stand out. The first defines cloud computing as a large-scale provision of infrastructures by cloud providers to customers through the usage of virtualization techniques [1, 2]. Secondly, cloud computing is seen as a business computing model/paradigm powered by distributed computing, parallel computing, and gird computing through the deployment of infrastructures as services [3]. Mainly, is possible to deploy infrastructures, platforms, and software through the usage of an architectural style like Simple Object Access Protocol (SOAP) or Representational State Transfer (REST).

V.C.M. Leung and M. Chen (Eds.): CloudComp 2013, LNICST 133, pp. 49–56, 2014.
DOI: 10.1007/978-3-319-05506-0_5, © Institute for Computer Sciences, Social Informatics and Telecommunications Engineering 2014

Cloud providers are an import part of cloud computing since they offer on-demand cloud infrastructure that is fully customizable by the customer [4]. They also offers a group of computing, storage, and networking services in order to meet a widely range of customer requirements. For example, Amazon offers a group of services called: Elastic Computing Cloud (EC2), Simple Storage Service (S3), and Simple Queue Service (SQS). Others like, Google provides a platform called Google App Engine to build scalable web application running on top of Google infrastructures. Microsoft also steps into play offering Microsoft Azure primarily to provide a platform as a service (PaaS) and infrastructure as a service (IaaS).

Ubiquitous devices are extra components that can be added to the cloud computing paradigm. Devices such as smartphones can offer a new opportunity to enhance people life with ubiquitous computing, at home and office computing environments, presenting a new scenario for service providing and a great opportunity to leverage computational power to perform tasks for the cloud. In this context several migration components can be created and powered by the current mobile computational power, and always-on functionality of mobile devices. On top of this, smartphone functionalities including GPS, SMS, and voice calls can enrich even more cloud components.

In the information age where there are a huge amount of devices connected to the Internet there is an increasing necessity to connect technologies and services through novel ways. In this paper, a cloud instance interoperability model used by ubiquitous devices in order to solve the issue related with the lack of convergence between different cloud providers is proposed [4]. The existence of different terminologies, functions, and architectures lead to a need of proposing this model. As core objective the model, composed by five components, is created in order to export and import cloud instances though the usage of the mobile computational power and built-in interfaces between different cloud providers.

The rest of the paper is organized as follows. Section 2 addresses the related literature with a review of cloud computing and its paradigm. Cloud computing architecture, service, and deployment stack is identified. Cloud providers presentation and categorization is also considered at Sect. 2. Section 3 gives an introduction to ubiquitous devices and their usefulness to the general population. The cloud instance interoperability model is proposed in Sect. 4, followed by a description of its operation and major components. Finally, Sect. 5 concludes the paper and pinpoints further research work.

2 Cloud Computing and Providers

Cloud computing has become an important topic for many researches, due to the capacity of providing computational resources on-the-fly as fast as possible. Cloud computing is defined as a convenient and on-demand network to provide and realize computational resources through network structures with a minimal set of interactions [5, 6]. Cloud computing is also defined as a platform with distributed systems that share its characteristics to networks as services. So, users can access cloud's resources using a low-level of expertise [7].

A cloud infrastructure is complex and composed by a diverse set of concepts. Some authors and authorities are defining the cloud infrastructure as a 4-layered architecture, a service stack, and a deployment stack. Hardware, virtualization, platform, and application layer comprise the aforementioned 4-layer architecture. The hardware layer is responsible for managing available resources of the cloud. Virtualization offers physical hardware as individual and pre-defined virtual on-demand resources. The upper layer is composed by applications designed for this environment where its software resources can be accessed through a wide range of devices [1, 8]. The service stack is the way each layered architecture is deployed to the public network [9]. In a stage of publishing the cloud to a network, a major decision should be performed concerning the deployment stack, considering it may be either public, private, or hybrid. A private cloud is only accessible via an internal network. A public cloud is the deployment appointed to mainstreaming services across a public network, namely, sharing computational resources from a cloud provider. A hybrid cloud is a combination of private and public clouds, so external cloud services are linked to a single cloud unit.

Due to growing demand for computing utility and resources deployment, several companies like Amazon, Google, and Microsoft are providing structures to enable clouds provisioning. A cloud provider can be considered at two different categories, an IaaS or a PaaS cloud provider (as illustrated in Fig. 1). The IaaS provider enables customers to consume computational resources as virtual machines, enabling the installation of applications. The PaaS provider customers are employed to build applications using internal proprietary APIs. The business model defined by each provider is different from one another. Commonly, the user pays hourly, monthly, or annually for a cloud specific structure [12].

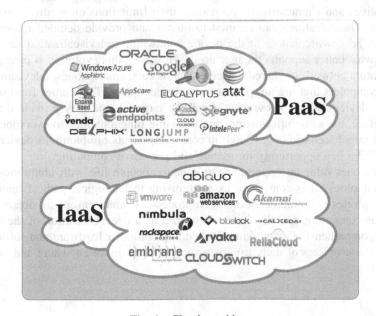

Fig. 1. Cloud providers.

Amazon Web Services (AWS) [13] are a virtual package of Web services aimed to provide a cloud computing platform. Amazon Elastic Compute Cloud (EC2) and Amazon Single Storage Service (S3) are part of this package. Amazon Elastic Compute Cloud (EC2) provides a resizable computational capacity in a cloud environment. EC2 provides a complete control of computing resources that can be provisioned through a single user interface [14]. Finally, Amazon Storage Service (S3) is an online storage facility that can be accessed by Web services.

Windows Azure [15] deploys cloud platforms and infrastructures, so it provides both platform as a service (PaaS) and infrastructure as a service (IaaS). Different programing languages, tools, and frameworks support these structures. Primarily, Windows Azure can be used to create Web applications for Microsoft datacenters [12]. Microsoft Azure also supports applications development through a public SDK and a .NET framework.

Google App Engine [16] is a platform to build scalable Web applications running on top of Google's infrastructures using a sandbox concept. A set of APIs and application model are provided in order to take full advantages of current Google services like, electronic mail (eMail), DataStore, and Memcache. The main languages used to build these services is Java, Python, and JRuby [12, 14].

3 Ubiquitous Devices

Currently, with available wireless communications and computing environments (including, at home and at office, for instance), portable devices present a new scenario for service providing. These devices, not only have access to traditional Internet services but also to location services. An evolution is bringing to portable devices new functionalities and characteristics, decreasing their limitations on hardware and software [17]. These features can be used to obtain and provide detailed information, which can be downscaled to fit the device bandwidth and visualization capacities, adopting what better supports the user needs. However, this evolution is increasingly coming into a network of shared devices, such as cars, smartphones, televisions, and desktop computers that are not personalized for each user. This comes from the fact that these devices do not know what should be targeted, and they provide the same user interface, the same information, and the same functionalities to everyone. Considering a target scenario (e.g. Cloud) in core components of ubiquitous devices, it is an identified a key opportunity for mobile and pervasive computing.

Smartphones offer an opportunity to enhance people life with ubiquitous computing technology. It is considered as a promising technological path of innovation implying wireless communications, microprocessors, and sensors as objects [18]. Ubiquitous computing can also be characterized as a decentralization of the system and their comprehensive networking. Embedding computer hardware and software in equipment and objects of daily use, they support users in an anywhere and anytime manner [19].

4 Cloud Instance Interoperability Model

Given the amount of involved technology in a cloud environment, structures and business models used by several cloud providers, the interoperability between cloud instances and cloud providers is a well-know open issue (as may seen in Table 1). The top raised question among customers is "how services furnished by a cloud provider performs in comparison to another cloud provider?". Nevertheless, this question is not related to the performance evaluation, but with the basic question "how a customer can export their data to another provider?". A customer should be able to export its custom defined structures, applications, and virtual machines (VMs) to a new cloud provider. Interoperability is discussed in the scientific community by several authors [4, 20]. Computational resources, configurations, structures, virtual machines, billing information, helpdesk tickets, and so on, are comprised in a cloud instance. Then, this paper proposes a cloud instance interoperability model used by ubiquitous devices with objective to export cloud providers instances through the usage of a smartphone. This model considers five major components that are illustrated in Fig. 2 (Cloud instance exporter/importer, interpreter, linkage, and converter component). The cloud instance exporter component is responsible for exporting a cloud image of a specific user to an internal dataset. After that, the produced cloud instance is sent to the mobile device. In a mobile device, three major components should be considered. The interpreter component will analyze the dataset and, if needed, it will retrieve missing information from the cloud instance exporter. Then, the linkage component will interconnect the request resource from the dataset to available resources from a source cloud provider (e.g. Amazon) to a target cloud provider (e.g. Microsoft). At the final stage, the linkage component uses the cloud instance importer component to export the previous created cloud instance into the target cloud provider (e.g. Microsoft).

Table 1. Cloud providers technologies.

Technologies	Amazon AWS	Windows Azure	Google App Engine
Service type	IaaS	IaaS and PaaS	PaaS
Support for (value offer)	Compute/storage	Compute	Compute
User access interface	Web APIs and command line	Azure web portal	Web APIs and command line
Virtualization	OS and Xen hypervisor	.NET container	APP Engine
Platform	Linux and Windows	Windows	Linux
Deployment model	Customizable virtual machine	Azure services	Web apps (Python, Java, and JRuby)
Deploy apps to 3rd party IaaS	No	No	No

The proposed approach offers several advantages regarding the available solutions in the related literature. The mOSAIC [21] project is providing solutions to achieve interoperability functionality between IaaS providers. APIs are used to assist the migration between clouds, however, the solution only migrates IaaS layers. Companies like RightScale are deploying solutions to multi-manage cloud providers.

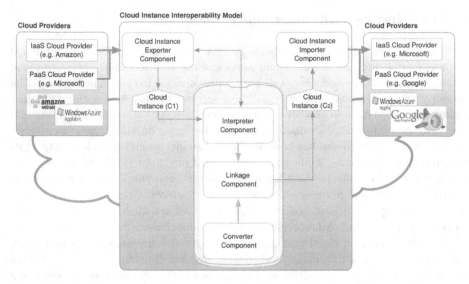

Fig. 2. Components of the proposed cloud instance interoperability model.

RightScale's MultiCloud [22] is an example of this implementation. The solution aimed to provide customers management functionalities for Amazon Web Services, CloudStack, Eucalyptus, and OpenStack. Amazon EC2 APIs, Rackspace APIs, Go-Grid's API present functionalities one-step further. They are creating APIs in order to deploy a cloud computing interface. This interface also provides interoperability among clouds. Nevertheless, the issue is in the provided technological approach. In other words, pre-constructed APIs should be deployed at root technological layers used by cloud providers. Then, the proposed solution avoids the deployment in cloud providers while uses mobile computational power to turn the representational linkage of different cloud provider architectures possible. Furthermore, this model offers the possibility to migrate not only the IaaS layer, but also the PaaS and SaaS layers. So, a complete cloud instance image is ported between cloud providers.

5   Conclusions and Future Work

Cloud computing requires an evolution of its underlying technologies, that are painting the current cloud landscape, used by both cloud providers and customers. Despite the existence of several definitions for cloud computing and its internal structure leading to a state of non-normalized approach, several authors are identifying recurring issues. A major open issue is the lack of interoperability between cloud providers where there is no convergence. The existence of different terminologies, functions, and architectures lead to this ongoing situation. Ubiquitous devices can play an important technological contribution to solve these issues. Such devices not only have access to the Internet but they also have a set of computing resources and utilities that can support cloud users and administrators.

The proposed model presents a novel approach to overlap the aforementioned open issue. This model comprises five major components (Cloud instance exporter/importer, interpreter, linkage, and converter component), each one responsible for a set of interpretation and linkage operations to be applied in cloud instances. Thus, cloud instances can be imported and exported between cloud providers offering a transparent interoperability among them. Each component will be used in a mobile computing environment with several advantages, such as mobility independence, always-on functionality, GPS location tracking, SMS usage, Voice Chat, among others.

In terms of future work the model will be deployed in a laboratory prototype and evaluated against two different testbeds. Furthermore, the interpreter, linkage, and converter component will also be deployed as hybrid components. This means that these components will be improved using different technologies, leading to a state of convergence between different terminologies, functions, and architectures present at cloud providers.

Acknowledgments. This work was partially supported by the *Instituto de Telecomunicações*, Next Generation Networks and Applications Group (NetGNA), Portugal, and by National Funding from the FCT – *Fundação para a Ciência e a Tecnologia* through the Pest-OE/EEI/ LA0008/2011 Project.

References

1. Moghe, U., Lakkadwala, P., Mishra, D.K.: Cloud computing: Survey of different utilization techniques. In: CSI 6th International Conference on Software Engineering (CONSEG 2012), Madhya Pradesh, India, pp. 1–4 (2012)
2. Kwang, M.S.: Agent-based cloud computing. IEEE Trans. Serv. Comput. 5(4), 564–577 (2012)
3. Yanxia, W.: Research on web data integration framework based on cloud computing. In: 2nd International Conference on Consumer Electronics, Communications and Networks (CECNet 2012), Yichang, China, pp. 2823–2826 (2012)
4. Prodan, R., Ostermann, S.: A survey and taxonomy of infrastructure as a service and web hosting cloud providers. In: 10th IEEE/ACM International Conference on Grid Computing, Alberta, Canada, pp. 17–25 (2009)
5. You, P., Peng, Y., Gao, H.: Providing information services for wireless sensor networks through cloud computing. In: IEEE Asia-Pacific Services Computing Conference (APSCC 2012), Guilin, China, pp. 362–364 (2012)
6. The NIST Definition of Cloud Computing. http://csrc.nist.gov/publications/nistpubs/ 800-145/SP800-145.pdf
7. Shih, W.-C., Tseng, S.-S., Yang, C.-T.: Performance study of parallel programming on cloud computing environments using MapReduce. In: International Conference on Information Science and Applications (ICISA 2010), Seoul, South Korea, pp. 1–8 (2010)
8. Liu, X.: Cloud architecture learning based on social architecture. In: 6th International Conference on Computer Sciences and Convergence Information Technology (ICCIT 2011), Seogwipo, South Korea, pp. 418–421 (2011)
9. Wei, Z., Qin, S., Jia, D., Yang Y.: Research and design of cloud architecture for smart home. In: IEEE International Conference on Software Engineering and Service Sciences (ICSESS 2010), Beijing, China, pp. 86–89 (2010)

10. Li, A., Yang, X., Kandula, S., Zhang, M.: CloudCmp: comparing public cloud providers. In: Proceedings of the 10th ACM SIGCOMM Conference on Internet Measurement (IMC 2010). New York, USA (2010)
11. Wang, L., Tao, J., Kunze, M., Castellanos, A.C., Kramer, D., Karl, W.: Scientific cloud computing: early definition and experience. In: 10th IEEE International Conference on High Performance Computing and Communications (HPCC 2008), Dalian, China, pp. 825–830 (2008)
12. Vecchiola, C., Pandey, S., Buyya, R.: High-performance cloud computing: a view of scientific applications. In: 10th International Symposium on Pervasive Systems, Algorithms, and Networks (ISPAN 2009), Kaohsiung, Taiwan, pp. 4–16 (2009)
13. Amazon AWS. http://www.aws.amazon.com
14. Lenk, A., Klems, M., Nimis, J., Tai, S., Sandholm, T.: What's inside the cloud? An architectural map of the cloud landscape. In: ICSE Workshop on Software Engineering Challenges of Cloud Computing, (CLOUD 2009), Washington, USA, pp. 23–31 (2009)
15. Windows Azure. http://www.windowsazure.com
16. Google App Engine. https://developers.google.com/appengine/
17. Bellavista, P., Corradi, A., Stefanelli, C.: The ubiquitous provisioning of internet services to portable devices. IEEE Pervasive Comput. 1(3), 81–87 (2002)
18. Nirmalya, R., Das, S.K., Basu, K., Kumar, M.: Enhancing availability of grid computational services to ubiquitous computing applications. In: 19th IEEE International Parallel and Distributed Processing Symposium, Denver, USA, pp. 92 (2005)
19. Friedewald, M., Raabe, O.: Ubiquitous computing: an overview of technology impacts. J. Telematics Inform. 28(2), 55–65 (2011)
20. Rimal, B.P., Choi, E., Lumb, I.: A taxonomy and survey of cloud computing systems. In: 5th International Joint Conference on INC, IMS and IDC (NCM 2009), Seoul, Korea, pp. 44–51 (2009)
21. Petcu, D., Macariu, G., Panica, S., Craciun, C.: Portable cloud applications from theory to practice. Future Gener. Comput. Syst. 29(6), 1417–1430 (2013)
22. Rightscale Multicloud platform. http://www.rightscale.com/products/multicloud-platform.php

Mobile Cloud Computing in Service Platform for Vehicular Networking

Yingying Wang$^{(\boxtimes)}$ and Hehua Yan

School of Information Engineering, Guangdong Jidian Polytechinc,
Guangzhou, China
wyybaby@163.com

Abstract. Recently, with the development of advanced network techniques, innovative control theories, and emerging cloud computing, vehicular networking serves as one of the most important enabling technologies. Together with an explosive growth in the usage of smart phones, their applications and emerging of cloud computing concept, mobile cloud computing (MCC) has been introduced to be a potential technology for mobile services. In this article, we first introduce the survey of vehicular networking and MCC. Next we illustrate the concept, structure and development of the service platform based on mobile cloud computing for vehicular networking. Then we give a new service model called Mobile-as-a-Personal-Proxy (MaaPP) of the service platform. Finally, we outline the relevant research challenges. We hope to inspire more technological development and progress for MCC applications.

Keywords: Mobile cloud computing · Services platform · Vehicular networking · Service model

1 Introduction

In recent years, the Internet of things (IOT) has become an information industry revolution after the computer, the Internet and mobile communication. Vehicle networking is a concentrated expression of IOT used in intelligent transportation system. With the development of advanced network techniques, innovative control theories, and emerging cloud computing, vehicular networking serves as one of the most important enabling technologies, and is producing some novel telematics application scenarios [1, 2]. These applications are more than novelties and far-fetched goals of a group of researchers and companies. Vehicular networking that aims to streamline the operation of vehicles, manage vehicle traffic, assist drivers with safety and other information, along with provisioning of convenience applications for passengers is no longer confined to theories, and test facilities of companies [3]. Up to now it has become increasingly obvious that vehicular networking opens new vistas for location-based services, such as vehicle maintenance services (VMS) and the fast-growing mobile entertainment industry [4, 5]. Obviously, vehicle networking is a large and complex system, integrating cloud computing, data communication, wireless sensing, computer networks and other advanced technologies, with the need for large amounts

V.C.M. Leung and M. Chen (Eds.): CloudComp 2013, LNICST 133, pp. 57–64, 2014.
DOI: 10.1007/978-3-319-05506-0_6, © Institute for Computer Sciences, Social Informatics and Telecommunications Engineering 2014

of data storage, processing, analysis, and provides a variety of convenient and efficient services between vehicles - road - people.

Mobile cloud computing (MCC) is the combination of mobile computing, cloud computing and mobile networks to bring benefits for mobile users, network operators, as well as cloud providers [6]. And MCC can involve other mobile devices and/or servers accessed via the Internet. Applications are run on a remote server and then sent to the user [3]. It shows that MCC has faster update, richer applications, stronger extension, individuation and sociality. Therefore, mobile cloud computing and vehicle networking combination can achieve complementary advantages and has very important practical value [7–10].

At present, the integration of vehicle networking and MCC still have their own problems, such as the structure of service platform, the service mode etc.. Consequently, we propose the concept, structure and development of service platform based on MCC for vehicular networking in Sect. 2. Section 3 analyzes a new service model called Mobile-as-a-Personal-Proxy (MaaPP). Section 4 describes the challenges of vehicle network and MCC. Finally Sect. 5 concludes this paper.

2 Concept of Service Platform for Vehicular Networking

The propose to build the service platform based on MCC for vehicular networking is to cover the owner, car manufacturers, service provider, 4S service centers, after-loading equipment manufacturers, vehicle rescue, auto insurance and car community etc., expanding the new car life industry chain model.

The platform concept is based on SoLoMo (socialization, localization, mobility) of automotive information services. So the platform give full play to the easy handling, portability, mobility and online of smart phones and the smart phones become the drivers' service access point. Through mobile data networks, smoothly upload the vehicle dynamic and static information; take the initiative to push service information from the platform. Thus the drivers, vehicle, travel, services and other information smoothly communicate between the cloud and the client to make car life safer, more convenient and more comfortable.

The platform is based on MCC technology framework to develop SaaS (Software as a Service) environment with large data center networking and to establish compute and storage resources paid on demand. By means of a variety of application markets, the platform publishes all kinds of application software which can run on Android, Ios, WindowsPhone, Blackberry and other mobile devices, and provide services for car manufacturers, service provider, 4S service centers, after-loading equipment manufacturers and other customers at the same time.

The basic structure of the platform is shown in Fig. 1. So, the development of the platform includes the following aspects:

• Universal authentication and data transmission protocol

To establish a set of common protocol for vehicle terminal authentication and data transfer, so it is safe and convenient for smart phones to connect with the vehicle

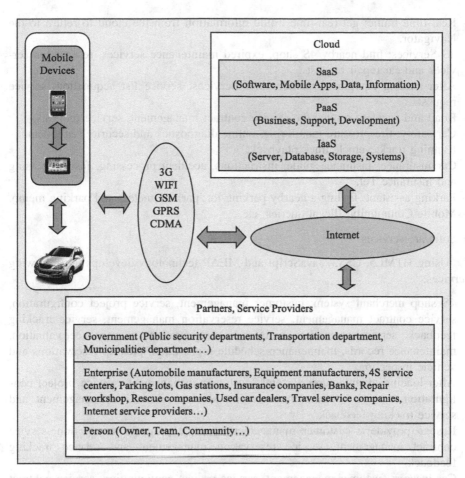

Fig. 1. A basic structure of service platform for vehicular networking

terminal, recognize identity and upload/download data through Bluetooth and other digital networks.

• Intelligent navigation based on real-time traffic weight

By getting real-time traffic information and forecast data service provided by Baidu, Google and other companies, and combining with the user's navigation need, the optimal route is calculated and sent to the user's mobile phone, and then be sent to the car intelligent terminal by the Mobile phone Bluetooth.

• Cross-platform mobile applications

Based on the open source PhoneGap mobile development framework, developing contents include:

– Bluetooth communication: mutual authentication and data transmission with vehicle intelligent terminal.

- Real-time traffic: get real-time traffic information from the cloud to return to the Navigator.
- 4S Services: find nearby 4S shop, expired maintenance services, reservation services and car repair requests.
- After-loading equipment manufacturer Services: service list acquisition, service requests.
- Road and accident rescue: the service contract management, service requests.
- Car safety: tire pressure monitoring, online diagnostics and security reminders.
- Running track: vehicle track playback.
- Car insurance: insurance guide, instructions, accident processing, fast processing and insurance Tel.
- Parking assistant: finding a nearby parking lot, parking meters and parking memo.
- Mobile Community, Illegal queries, etc.

- Software services

  Using HTML5, CSS3, JavaScript and MEAP technology develops the following services:

- 4S shop merchant system: customer management, service project configuration, service contract management, service reservation management, service tracking feedback, service promotion, maintenance registration, maintenance valuation, maintenance records, maintenance schedule registration, pick-up reservations and vehicle inspection.
- After-loading manufacturer systems: customer management, service project configuration, service contract management, service reservation management and service tracking feedback.
- Rescue providers: customer management, service project configuration, service contract management, service reservation management and service tracking feedback.
- Car insurer: customer management, service project configuration, service contract management, service reservation management and service tracking feedback.
- Owners application: vehicle condition analysis of historical data, vehicle track playback, purchase service and appointment service.
- Data applications: data analysis, data statistics, data forecasts, data charts, dashboards analysis and real-time analysis.
- Other systems.

3 Mobile Cloud Service Models of Service Platform for Vehicular Networking

Current MCC has three-type service models: Mobile-as-a-Service-Consumer (MaaSC), Mobile-as-a-Service-Provider (MaaSP), and Mobile-as-a-Service-Broker (MaaSB) [11]. In MaaSC, mobile devices are pure consumers to achieve service provided by cloud, and most existing MCC services fall into this category. MaaSP is different from MssSC in the role of a mobile device is the service provider, and the services provided by mobile devices are diverse and abundant. MaaSB can be considered as an extension of MaaSP in that it providers networking and data forwarding services for other mobile device or sensing nodes.

In the service platform based on MCC for vehicular networking, we propose a new service model called Mobile-as-a-Personal-Proxy (MaaPP) [12]. The architecture of MaaPP can be found in Fig. 2.

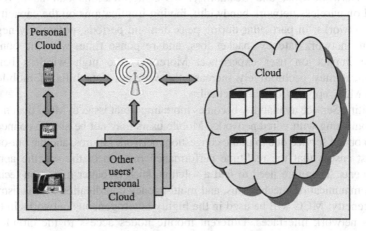

Fig. 2. Mobile as a Personal Proxy (MaaPP)

The concept of Personal Cloud (PC) is defined as the set of all mobile devices owned by a user. Each PC has a main component called Personal Cloud Hub (PCH), which is the point where the devices are registered and also provides data synchronization, communication among other PCs and secure access to the PC from Internet. Multiple PCHs, one for each user, may also be linked together creating relationships among users as it happens in social networks. Each device placed inside a PC has one component called Personal Proxy (PP).

One of the demos presented is travel application. It enables user to manage his point-of-interests while a user is traveling. Relevant data are automatically synced between the user's devices. Syncing mechanism of the app is based on the personal cloud middleware. The application enables the interaction with the in-car navigation system. When the car is parked, the smart phone can pick up the guidance.

In MaaPP, each user can be represented by PCH. Users' behaviors and attributes can be collected from real world (e.g., people, social networks, and environment or mobile devices) in real time and sent to the cloud to perform the related analysis and processing. Besides helping mobile devices execute tasks more efficiently, cloud is able to accomplish some tasks that are not possible to be achieved in traditional client-server architecture. Both physical systems and virtual systems are seamlessly connected as a whole in MaaPP. So the mobile devices and clouds are interactive and the service flow is bidirectional.

4 Challenges

The main goal of MCC is to provide users a convenient and quick way to access the data from the cloud by using their mobile devices. While enhancing the user's convenience, a lot of problems still remain in the realization of MCC [13–15]. In this section, we explain in brief the technical challenges:

- Mobile Network Cost and Scalability: MCC applications can have very high demand on wireless network bandwidth, having implications on the capacity of the mobile networks, in particular during peak demand periods, potentially negatively impacting network latency, packet loss, and response time, with the consequent negative impact on user experience. Moreover, the high wireless bandwidth requirement may prohibitively increase the wireless data bills of mobile users, making MCC applications impractical.
- Availability: Service availability becomes more important issue in MCC than that in the cloud computing with wired networks. Mobile users may not be able to connect to the cloud to obtain service due to traffic congestion, network failures, and the out-of-signal. We must ensure that the real-time performance must meet the specific application requirements. Therefore need to find a solution, such as better migration technology, better communication mechanisms, and multi-agency coordination mechanism.
- Heterogeneity: MCC will be used in the highly heterogeneous networks in terms of wireless network interfaces. Different mobile nodes access to the cloud through different radio access technologies such as CDMA, GPRS and WLAN. As a result, an issue of how to handle the wireless connectivity while satisfying MCC's requirements arises (e.g., always-on connectivity, on-demand scalability of wireless connectivity, and the energy efficiency of mobile devices).
- Information sharing: Currently, the business model of vehicular networking is not uniform, and different models have different applications. So that the information can not be shared with each other. Through MCC, solve the sharing problem, but also need to consider the transmission speed, information security etc..
- Security and privacy: Mobile devices such as cellular phone, PDA, and smart phone are exposed to numerous security threats like malicious codes and their vulnerability. In addition, with mobile phones integrated global positioning system (GPS) device, they can cause privacy issues for subscribers.
- Standards development: Vehicular networking depends on many technologies across multiple industries. But the enterprises and departments of vehicular networking industry chain alone develop with the lack of industry standards. Thus, the required scope of standardization is significantly greater than that of any traditional standards development.

5 Conclusions

In recent years, with the development of advanced network techniques, innovative control theories, and emerging cloud computing, vehicular networking serves as one of the most important enabling technologies. In this article, we first introduce the survey of vehicular networking and MCC. Next we illustrate the concept, structure and development of the service platform based on mobile cloud computing for vehicular networking. Then we give the MaaPP service models of the service platform. Finally, we outline the relevant research challenges. We hope to inspire more technological development and progress for MCC applications.

Acknowledgement. The authors would like to thank the National Natural Science Foundation of China (No. 61262013), the Natural Science Foundation of Guangdong Province, China (No. S2011010001155), and the High-level Talent Project for Universities, Guangdong Province, China (No. 431, YueCai Jiao 2011) for their support in this research.

References

1. Ge, X., Huang, K., Wang, C.-X., Hong, X., Yang, X.: Capacity analysis of a multi-cell multi-antenna cooperative cellular network with co-channel interference. IEEE Trans. Wirel. Commun. **10**, 3298–3309 (2011)
2. Humar, I., Ge, X., Xiang, L., Jo, M., Chen, M.: Rethinking energy-efficiency models of cellular networks with embodied energy. IEEE Netw. Mag. **25**, 40–49 (2011)
3. Karagiannis, G., Altintas, O., Ekici, E., Heijenk, G., Jarupan, B., Lin, K., Weil, T.: Vehicular networking: a survey and tutorial on requirements, architectures, challenges, standards and solutions. IEEE Commun. Surv. Tutorials **13**, 584–616 (2011)
4. Olariu, S., Weigle, M.C.: Vehicular Networks: From Theory to Practice. Chapman & Hall/CRC, Boca Raton (2009)
5. Xia, F., Ma, J.: Building smart communities with cyber-physical systems. In: Proceedings of ACM UBICOMP Symposium on Social and Community Intelligence, Beijing, China, pp. 1–5 (2011)
6. Chen, M.: AMVSC: a framework of adaptive mobile video streaming in the cloud. In: IEEE Globecom 2012, Anaheim (2012)
7. Fernando, N., Loke, S.W., Rahayu, W.: Mobile cloud computing: a survey. Future Gener. Comput. Syst. **29**, 84–106 (2013)
8. Verbelen, T., Pieter, S., De Filip, T., Bart, D.: Cloudlets: bringing the cloud to the mobile user. In: Proceedings of the Third ACM Workshop on Mobile Cloud Computing and Services, pp. 29–36 (2012)
9. Loke, S.: Supporting ubiquitous sensor-cloudlets and context-cloudlets: programming compositions of context-aware systems for mobile users. Future Gener. Comput. Syst. **28**(4), 619–632 (2012)
10. Chen, M., Wen, Y., Jin, H., Leung, V.: Enabling technologies for future data center networking: a primer. IEEE Netw. **27**(4), 8–15 (2013)
11. Wan, J., Liu, Z., Zhou, K., Lu, R.: Mobile cloud computing: application scenarios and service models. In: Proceedings. of the 9th IEEE International Wireless Communications and Mobile Computing Conference, Cagliari, Italy (2013)
12. Wang, Y., Yan, H., Wan, J., Zhou, K.: Mobile agents for CPS in intelligent transportation systems. In: Proceedings of the 8th International Conference on Embedded and Multimedia Computing, Taipei, Taiwan (2013)
13. Wan, J., Ullah, S., Lai, C., Zhou, M., Wang, X., Zou, C.: Cloud-enabled wireless body area networks for pervasive healthcare. IEEE Netw. **27**(5), 56–61 (2013)

14. Lai, C., Lai, Y., Chao, H., Wan, J.: Cloud-assisted real-time transrating for HTTP live streaming. IEEE Wirel. Commun. **20**(3), 62–70 (2013)
15. Zou, C., Wan, J., Chen, M., Li, D.: Simulation modeling of cyber-physical systems exemplified by unmanned vehicles with WSNs navigation. In: Park, J.J., Jeong, Y.-S., Park, S.O., Chen, H.-C. (eds.) EMC Technology and Service. LNEE, vol. 181, pp. 269–275. Springer, Heidelberg (2012)

Performance Analysis of Cloud DVR for Energy Efficiency Clustering Strategy

Zhen Zhao[✉]

Comcast Interative Media, Comcast, 1701 JFK Blvd, Comcast Center,
Philadelphia, PA 19103, USA
Zhen_Zhao@Comcast.com

Abstract. Cloud digital video recorder (cDVR) is a new service that Comcast provides to its subscribers. The primary current legal interpretation approving cloud DVR relies on a single copy in the Cablevision decision. This makes the cDVR data center running cost very high. An asynchronous service system with categorizing users by cDVR usage is employed to reduce the energy consumption. In this system, cDVRs with similar usage schedule are constructed in one cluster. The cloud recording service on this cluster goes to sleep if there has been a period with no cDVR requests. When there are one or more cDVR request arrivals, those requests are buffered in queues while the cDVR service wakes up. In this paper, a 2-class Markov Geo/G/1/K vacation model is presented to analyze the performance of this system. Different scheduling policies are compared in the simulations and experiments.

Keywords: Cloud tv · Cloud dvr · Markov process

1 Introduction

Nowadays, cloud computing is becoming popular. Comcast is providing cloud TV service to its subscribers, which gives the customers two major flexibilities: (1) watching TV on any device anytime anywhere; (2) recording the TV/Movie programs in cloud digital video record (cDVR) so they could access to cDVR to play the videos from any device later. It is straightforward to store the videos in content delivery network, hence the cDVR only need store the urls of recorded videos. However, due to the requirement of US laws, each cDVR has to provide a physical copy for any program that users record. This makes the cDVR service have much heavier load. Besides the cost of hardware, the daily energy consumption also increases a lot. To reduce the energy consumption, we deploy an asynchronous system of cDVR recording service. Clustered by the usage histogram. In this system, users with similar cDVR usage habits are categorized within one group. CDVRs of this group are put in one server cluster. If there have been a while without any requests, the cDVR recording service of the cluster goes to sleep. If some new requests arrive, the cDVR recording service is

V.C.M. Leung and M. Chen (Eds.): CloudComp 2013, LNICST 133, pp. 65–75, 2014.
DOI: 10.1007/978-3-319-05506-0_7, © Institute for Computer Sciences, Social Informatics
and Telecommunications Engineering 2014

waked up. During the wake-up period, the recording requests are buffered in the two queues. Those of recording QAM videos are put into the QAM queue and those of recording IP Streams are put into IP queue.

Our investigation employs vacation modeling results from queueing theory, to obtain blocking probabilities, and queue lengths incurred by sleeping policies for the cDVR recording service responding to the QAM and IP streaming recording requests with a finite buffer. To the best of my knowledge, this is the first work on a 2-class M/G/1/K vacation model, where two classes of requests, each with its own buffer, are processed by a server following a sleeping policy. The sleeping policy is usually characterized by three aspects: (*i*) *How does the sleeping process start?* The exhaustive policy is widely used, in which the cDVR service won't go to sleep until the buffer is empty. (*ii*) *How does the sleeping process end?* Two approaches are the most popular: termination policy and threshold policy. In the former policy, the server checks its buffer occupancy only at the time instant of sleep termination. If the buffer is empty, it goes back to sleep again. Otherwise, it starts processing requests. The latter policy requires the server to check its buffer state whenever the buffer occupancy changes. If the occupancy exceeds the threshold, the server starts processing requests. (*iii*) *What is the distribution of the sleeping process?* Usually, the sleeping process is assumed as a general distribution with an independent and identically distributed (i.i.d.) random variable (r.v.). Our work focuses on the exhaustive, termination policy, and a process with i.i.d. r.v.

The paper is organized as follows. In Sect. 2, a 2-class vacation model is described. In Sect. 3 the marginal occupancy distributions at an arbitrary time instant are derived. Section 4 presents numerical, simulation and experimental results. Conclusions are discussed in Sect. 5.

2   2-Class Vacation Model

In this section, we present a model of a server receiving and processing 2-class heterogeneous requests (see Fig. 1). Our analytical approach is to embed a Markov chain at the time slot immediately after processing completion slots. Next, we build equilibrium equations for the embedded Markov chain to obtain the marginal occupancy distributions at processing completion slots.

We consider a server with two classes of requests (class 1, 2, e.g., QAM and IP streaming), each with its own finite buffer. The request arrival of each class is a i.i.d. geometric process. The requests of a certain class are queued into the corresponding buffer if the buffer is not full and blocked otherwise. With a general scheduling function, requests from the two buffers are selected to be processed. The service order for requests of each class is scheduled by the selection function $\alpha(i,j)$, the probability that a class 1 request is chosen to be processed, while i and j requests are in class 1 and 2's buffer/queue, respectively. The processing process has a general distribution. The recording service keeps processing requests until both buffers are empty at a process completion time instant, in which case

Table 1. 2-class model notations

p_m	the probability of a request arrives in a slot of class m, where $m = 1, 2$.
μ	requests processing rate; $1/\mu$ is the mean of the general processing time distribution.
θ	service wakeup rate; $1/\theta$ is the mean of the general sleeping time distribution.
K_m	buffer size of class m, where $m = 1, 2$.
$\alpha(i, j)$	probability that a class 1 request is selected to be processed while i and j requests are in class 1 and 2 queues, respectively.
$\pi_{i,j}$	probability that i class 1 and j class 2 requests are in buffers just after processing completion slots.
$\varpi_{i,j}$	probability that i class 1 and j class 2 requests are in buffers just after sleeping termination slots.
$\pi_{i,j}^\star$	probability that i class 1 and j class 2 requests are in buffers at an arbitrary time slot.
X	the processing time random variable measured in slots.
$a(k)$	the probability distribution of X, $a(k) = \mathbb{P}(X = k)$.
Y	the sleeping time random variable measured in slots.
$v(k)$	the probability distribution of Y, $v(k) = \mathbb{P}(Y = k)$.
$\hat{B}$	remaining processing time slots for the request in service.
$\tilde{B}$	elapsed processing time slots for the request in service.
$\hat{V}$	remaining sleeping time for the node in sleep.
$\tilde{V}$	elapsed sleeping time for the node in sleep.
$G(z)$	probability generating function (PGF) of $G(k)$; $G(z) \triangleq \sum_{k=0}^{\infty} G(k)z^k$, where $0 < z \le 1$
$E(G)$	expectation of G.

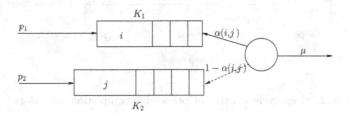

Fig. 1. Queueing model of a recording service processing 2-class requests

the recording service goes to sleep and will continue to sleep if at the sleeping termination time instant there are no requests buffered waiting for processing (Table 1).

As mentioned before, our analytical approach is to embed a Markov chain at the time instant just after processing completion slots, as is typically done for the ordinary Geo/G/1/K system. We define a couple of random variables $(N_1(k^+), N_2(k^+))$ to be the number of requests of each class in their respective buffers immediately following processing completions. Since the arrival process is Markovian, it is evident that the random process $\{N_1(k^+), N_2(k^+), k^+ = 0^+, 1^+, \ldots\}$ is a discrete Markov renewal process [18]. The vector of stationary probability masses for the embedded Markov chain is denoted by $\pi_{i,j}$, and its (i,j)th element is given by

$$\pi_{i,j} = \lim_{k\to\infty} \mathbb{P}\{N_1(k^+) = i, N_2(k^+) = j\}.$$

We denote the probability that i requests of class m $(m = 1, 2)$ arrive during a processing time $X = k$ and during a sleeping time $Y = k$ by $a_m(i)$ and $v_m(i)$, respectively,

$$a_m(i) = \sum_{k=i}^{\infty} \binom{k}{i} p_m^k (1 - p_m)^{k-i} b(k),$$

$$v_m(i) = \sum_{k=i}^{\infty} \binom{k}{i} p_m^k (1 - p_m)^{k-i} v(k).$$

and the probabilities that no less than i requests of class m $(m = 1, 2)$ arrive during a processing time X and during a sleeping time Y by $\overline{a_m(i)}$ and $\overline{v_m(i)}$,

$$\overline{a_m(i)} = \sum_{j=i}^{\infty} a_m(j), \qquad \overline{v_m(i)} = \sum_{j=i}^{\infty} v_m(j).$$

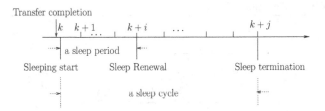

Fig. 2. Sleep cycle starting at processing completion time slots

When a sleep period completes, the server checks the buffer occupancies of the two classes. If they are empty, another sleep period with independent Y will be started. This process repeats unless there are requests waiting in at least one of the two buffers at a sleep completion time instant. We define a sleep cycle as the time interval from the time instant the server or cluster goes to sleep to the time instant it starts to processing requests. Thus, a sleep cycle is composed of one or more sleep periods (see Fig. 2). We denote the probability that i ($i < K_m$) and K_m requests of class m arrive during a sleep cycle by $\varphi_m(i)$ and $\varphi_m(K_m)$. It is easy to see that they are geometric distributions.

$$\varphi_m(i) = \sum_{j=0}^{\infty} v_m(0)^j v_m(i) = \frac{v_m(i)}{1 - v_m(0)}, \tag{1}$$

$$\varphi_m(i = K_1) = \sum_{j=0}^{\infty} v_m(0)^j \overline{v_m(K_m)} = \frac{\overline{v_m(K_m)}}{1 - v_m(0)}. \tag{2}$$

A generic term to denote the probability transition from (i, j) to (k, l) is $P_{(i,j)(k,l)}$. To find $P_{(i,j)(k,l)}$, we consider four cases: (i) $0 < k < K_1, 0 < l < K_2$; (ii) $0 < k < K_1, l = K_2$; (iii) $k = K_1, 0 < l < K_2$; and (iv) $k = K_1, l = K_2$.

Case (i) $0 < k < K_1, 0 < l < K_2$. All requests are queued in their respective buffers, excluding the processed request. The exact number of class 1 and 2 requests is $k - i$ and $l - j$, respectively.

If $i > 0, j = 0$, there is no sleep period. Only the head of line request of class 1 is processed. The case $i = 0, j > 0$ is similar. Hence, we obtain

$$P_{(i,0)(k,l)} = a_1(k - i + 1)a_2(l),$$
$$P_{(0,j)(k,l)} = a_1(k)a_2(l - j + 1).$$

If $i > 0, j > 0$, the request being proccessed is selected from class 1 with probability $\alpha(i, j)$ and from class 2 with probability $1 - \alpha(i, j)$. Thus, we have the transition probabilities $\alpha(i, j)a_1(k - i + 1)a_2(l)$ and $[1 - \alpha(i, j)]a_1(k)a_2(l - j + 1)$.

If $i = 0, j = 0$, there is a sleep cycle between the successive processing completions. When only a single class of requests is arrive during the sleep cycle, the transition probability $P_{(0,0)(k,l)}\{\text{Single}\}$ is given as

$$P_{(0,0)(k,l)}\{\text{Single}\} = \varphi_1(0)a_1(k)\Big(\sum_{j=1}^{l+1} \varphi_2(j)a_2(l - j + 1)\Big)$$

$$+ \varphi_2(0)a_2(l)\Big(\sum_{i=1}^{k+1} \varphi_1(i)a_1(k - i + 1)\Big).$$

When both classes of requests arrive during the sleep cycle, the selection function chooses a request randomly (following the general distribution $\alpha(i, j)$) from the two buffers. So the transition probability $P_{(0,0)(k,l)}\{\text{Two}\}$ is expressed as

$$P_{(0,0)(k,l)}\{\text{Two}\}$$

$$= \sum_{i=1}^{k+1} \sum_{j=1}^{l} \alpha(i, j)\varphi_1(i)a_1(k - i + 1)\varphi_2(j)a_2(l - j)$$

$$+ \sum_{i=1}^{k} \sum_{j=1}^{l+1} (1 - \alpha(i, j))\varphi_1(i)a_1(k - i)\varphi_2(j)a_2(l - j + 1).$$

Thus, the transition probability is

$$P_{(0,0)(k,l)} = P_{(0,0)(k,l)}\{\text{Single}\} + P_{(0,0)(k,l)}\{\text{Two}\}.$$

Hence, we have the equilibrium equation for Case i as

$$
\pi_{k,l} = \pi_{0,0}P_{(0,0)(k,l)} + \sum_{i=1}^{k+1} \pi_{i,0}P_{(i,0)(k,l)} + \sum_{j=1}^{l+1} \pi_{0,j}P_{(0,j)(k,l)}
$$

$$
+ \sum_{i=1}^{k+1}\sum_{j=1}^{l} \alpha(i,j)\pi_{i,j}a_1(k-i+1)a_2(l-j)
$$

$$
+ \sum_{i=1}^{k}\sum_{j=1}^{l+1} (1-\alpha(i,j))\pi_{i,j}a_1(k-i)a_2(l-j+1). \tag{3}
$$

Case (ii) $0 < k < K_1, l = K_2$. The analysis is the same as Case (i) for class 1. However, it is different for class 2 when $l = K_2$. It is possible that more than l requests arrive but are blocked due to the finite buffer size K_2. Thus, the probability of $K_2 - j$ or more requests of class 2 arrive is $\overline{a_2(K_2 - j + 1)}$ or $\overline{a_2(K_2 - j)}$. So the transition probability from $(0,0)$ to (k, K_2) is

$$
P_{(0,0)(k,K_2)} = \varphi_1(0)a_1(k)\Big(\sum_{j=1}^{K_2} \varphi_2(j)\overline{a_2(K_2 - j + 1)}\Big)
$$

$$
+ \varphi_2(0)\overline{a_2(K_2)}\Big(\sum_{i=1}^{k+1} \varphi_1(i)a_1(k-i+1)\Big)
$$

$$
+ \sum_{i=1}^{k+1}\sum_{j=1}^{K_2} \alpha(i,j)\varphi_1(i)a_1(k-i+1)\varphi_2(j)\overline{a_2(K_2 - j)}
$$

$$
+ \sum_{i=1}^{k}\sum_{j=1}^{K_2} (1-\alpha(i,j))\varphi_i^1 a_1(k-i)\varphi_2(j)\overline{a_2(K_2 - j + 1)}.
$$

And the equilibrium equation is given by

$$
\pi_{k,K_2} = \pi_{0,0}P_{(0,0)(k,K_2)} + \sum_{i=1}^{k+1} \pi_{i,0}a_1(k-i+1)\overline{a_2(K_2)}
$$

$$
+ \sum_{j=1}^{K_2} \pi_{0,j}a_1(k)\overline{a_2(K_2 - j + 1)}
$$

$$
+ \sum_{i=1}^{k+1}\sum_{j=1}^{K_2} \alpha(i,j)\pi_{i,j}a_1(k-i+1)\overline{a_2(K_2 - j)}
$$

$$
+ \sum_{i=1}^{k}\sum_{j=1}^{K_2} (1-\alpha(i,j))\pi_{i,j}a_1(k-i)\overline{a_2(K_2 - j + 1)}. \tag{4}
$$

Case (iii) $k = K_1, 0 < l < K_2$. It is readily seen that this scenario is almost the same as Case i. The equilibrium equations are obtained by exchanging $a_1(\cdot)$ and $a_2(\cdot)$ in (3), where $\cdot$ is a wild card. For brevity, we do not repeat it here.

Case (iv) $k = K_1, l = K_2$. Again, if we replace $a_m(\cdot)$ with $\overline{a_m(\cdot)}$ $(m = 1, 2)$ in (3), we get the equilibrium for π_{K_1, K_2}.

With all the above equilibrium equations and the bound condition $\sum_{i=0}^{K_1} \sum_{j=0}^{K_2} \pi_{i,j} = 1$, all the stationary probabilities can now be numerically computed.

3   Marginal Occupancy Distributions

So far, we have derived a computational procedure for obtaining the equilibrium probabilities for a Markov process embedded at the time slots of processing completion. Similarly to the analysis of a single class Geo/G/1/K, we now turn to the marginal occupancy distributions $\pi_{i,*}^\star, \pi_{*,j}^\star$ as seen at an arbitrary time slot. To focus on the quantity of interest: *buffer occupancies L_1, L_2* of both classes, we present the results directly.

The occupancies of classes 1 and 2 are given by:

$$L_1 = \sum_{i=0}^{K_1} i\pi_{i,*}^\star = \sum_{i=0}^{K_1} i(\eta_i^\star(1) + \omega_i^\star(1)), \tag{5}$$

$$L_2 = \sum_{i=0}^{K_2} j\pi_{*,j}^\star = \sum_{j=0}^{K_2} j(\chi_j^\star(1) + \omega_j^\star(1)). \tag{6}$$

In (5) and (6), $\eta_n^\star(Z), \chi_n^\star(Z), \omega_n^\star(Z)$ are the PGF functions. In the interest of space, we only show parts of class 1's results here. Class 2 is similar. Derivation details are skipped here due to the space limitation.

When $0 \leq n < K_1$, $\eta_n^\star(Z), \omega_n^\star(Z)$ satisfy:

$$\eta_n^\star(Z) = \rho' \cdot \left[\sum_{j=0}^{K_2} \sum_{i=1}^{n+1} \alpha(i,j)(\pi_{i,j} + \varpi_{i,j}) A_{n-i+1}^\star(Z) \right.$$

$$\left. + \sum_{j=1}^{K_2} \sum_{i=0}^{n} (1 - \alpha(i,j))(\pi_{i,j} + \varpi_{i,j}) A_{n-i}^\star(Z) \right],$$

$$\omega_n^\star(Z) = (1 - \rho') I_n^\star(Z),$$

where $A_n^\star(Z), I_n^\star(Z)$ are obtained by

$$A_n^\star(Z) = \frac{1}{\mu} \frac{\lambda_1^n}{(\lambda_1 + \ln Z)^{n+1}} \left[B^\star(Z) - \sum_{i=0}^{n} a_1(i) \left(\frac{\lambda_1 + \ln Z}{\lambda_1} \right)^i \right],$$

$$I_n^\star(Z) = \frac{1}{\mu} \frac{\lambda_1^n}{(\lambda_1 + \ln Z)^{n+1}} \left[V^\star(Z) - \sum_{i=0}^{n} v_1(i) \left(\frac{\lambda_1 + \ln Z}{\lambda_1} \right)^i \right].$$

The above expressions allow us to compute the buffer occupancy for each of the two classes of requests arrive at the server under a sleeping policy. Next, we present numerical, simulation and experimental results for this metric under three situations: (i) different wakeup rates; (ii) different buffer sizes; (iii) different sharing percentage of a common buffer with fixed size.

4 Numerical, Simulation and Experimental Results

In this section, we verify our modeling analysis comparing numerical with simulation and experimental results. Moreover, by varying the wakeup rate and buffer sizes of the two classes, we have an insight on the sleeping costs of servers processing heterogeneous requests. First, we describe the configurations of our simulations and experiments. Results and discussions on buffer occupancies are given later.

In our modeling, the processing process and sleeping process have general distributions. To show that, we select three distributions for processing and sleeping process: exponential, uniform, and deterministic. Unless mentioned, the simulations and experiments have the same setup. For the selection function $\alpha(i,j)$, we chose four scheduling policies: (i) LJF: longest job first. If $j \geq i$, we select class 2. The job processing length here is related to if there is in-home check, parental control tv rating check, etc. (ii) SJF: shortest job first. If $j \leq i$, we select class 2. (iii) HOL: class 2 has priority over class 1; i.e., we always processing class 2's requests first unless its buffer is empty. (iv) BER: Bernoulli model. Here, we set the probability to select either class request as 0.5.

Figure 3 shows that the average occupancy of classes 1 and 2 decreases with the increase of the wakeup rate θ and tends to be constants after θ is greater than 1. For both classes, the occupancy of LJF is greater than the one of SJF. This

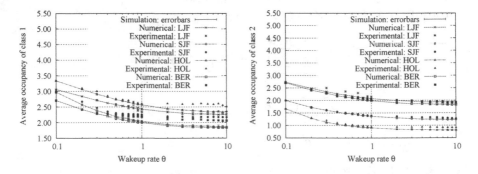

Fig. 3. Average occupancy of classes 1 and 2 varying the wakeup rate θ from 0.1 to 10. The time interval between successive wakeup time epochs is exponential. Both classes have the same Poisson arrival rate $\lambda_1 = \lambda_2 = 0.5$. The processing rate is $\mu = 1$. Each class has a finite buffer with size of 5. The same four selection policies are considered: (a) LJF; (b) SJF; (c) HOL; and (d) BER with probability 0.5 of selecting class 1.

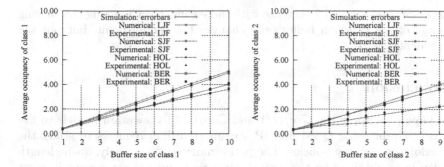

Fig. 4. Average occupancy of classes 1 (top) and 2 (bottom) with buffer size as a parameter varying from 1 to 10. Both classes have the same Poisson arrival rate $\lambda_1 = \lambda_2 = 0.5$. The processing distribution mean is $\mu = 1$. The time interval between successive wakeup time epochs is exponential with mean $1/\mu = 1$. The same four selection policies are considered: (a) LJF; (b) SJF; (c) HOL; and (d) BER with probability 0.5 of selecting class 1.

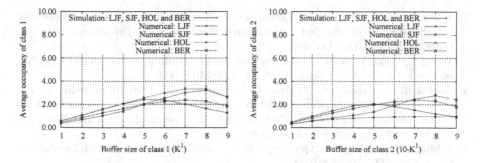

Fig. 5. Average occupancy of classes 1 (top) and 2 (bottom) with a fixed total buffer size of 10. The buffer size K_1 of class 1 is a parameter varying from 1 to 9, while $K_2 = 10 - K_1$. Both classes have the same Poisson arrival rate $\lambda_1 = \lambda_2 = 0.5$. The processing distribution mean is $\mu = 1$. The time interval between successive wakeup time epochs is exponential with mean $1/\mu = 1$. The average occupancy of each of the two classes is shown for the same four selection policies: (a) LJF; (b) SJF; (c) HOL; and (d) BER with probability 0.5 of selecting class 1.

behavior is a result of sacrificing some cost in terms of delaying requests processing. For HOL, since class 2 has priority over class 1, the average occupancy of class 2 is lower than the one of class 1 due to the increased delay of class 1.

In Fig. 4, it is evident that LJF has greater average occupancy than SJF for both classes no matter what their buffer sizes are. Similar conclusions can be drawn for HOL. Again, due to the same selection probability, BER has similar performance for both classes.

From Fig. 5, we see that while the buffer size K_1 of class 1 is less than 5 (i.e., half of the fixed total buffer size), the occupancy of classes 1 and 2 under LJF increase as class 1's buffer size increases. After that, the reverse occurs:

occupancy of classes 1 and 2 decrease with increasing K_1. Changing the sharing percentage of the common buffer only changes the saddle point, but not the curve tendency.

5   Conclusion

In this paper, we apply the $Geo/G/1$ and Geo/G/1/K vacation models to the cDRV server processing QAM and IP stream recording requests to study the cost of adopting sleeping policies. The performance costs, namely, queue length and delay were obtained by theoretical derivation and are convergent in most cases. We found that the processing time distribution does not affect the cost. We also found cases where the requests arrival process and scheduling function do affect the costs.

References

1. Wang, L., Xiao, Y.: Energy saving mechanisms in recording service networks. In: Proceedings of the 2nd International Conference on Broadband Networks (BROADNETS), October 2005
2. Wang, L., Xiao, Y.: A survey of energy-efficient scheduling mechanisms in recording service networks. Mob. Netw. Appl. **11**, 723–740 (2006)
3. Jurdak, R., Ruzzelli, A.G., O'Hare, G.: Adaptive radio modes in recording service networks: How deep to sleep? In: 5th Annual IEEE Communications Society Conference on Recording Service, Mesh and Ad Hoc Communications and Networks, SECON 2008, pp. 386–394, June 2008
4. White, H., Christie, L.S.: Queuing with preemptive priorities or with breakdown. Oper. Res. **6**(1), 79–95 (1958)
5. Avi-Itzhak, B., Naor, M.: Some queueing problems with the service station subject to server breakdown. Oper. Res. **10**, 303–320 (1963)
6. Yadin, M., Naor, P.: Queueing systems with a removable server. Oper. Res. **14**, 393–405 (1963)
7. Levy, Y., Yechiali, U.: Utilization of idle time in an M/G/1 queueing system. Manage. Sci. **22**, 202–221 (1975)
8. Fuhrmann, S., Cooper, R.: Stochastic decompositions in the M/G/1 queue with generalized vacations. Oper. Res. **33**, 1117–1129 (1985)
9. Teghem, J.: Control of the service process in queueing system. Eur. J. Oper. Res. **23**, 141–158 (1986)
10. Doshi, B.: Queueing systems with vacations - a survery. Queueing Syst. **1**, 22–66 (1986)
11. Kella, O.: Optimal control of the vacation scheme in an M/G/1 queue. Oper. Res. **38**, 724–728 (1990)
12. Li, Q., Tian, N., Cao, J.: Conditional stochastic decomposition in the M/M/c queue with server vacation. Stoch. Models **14**, 367–377 (1999)
13. Lee, T.: M/G/1/N queue with vacation time and exhaustive service discipline. Oper. Res. **32**, 774–784 (1984)
14. Frey, A., Takahashi, Y.: A note on an M/GI/1/N queue with vacation time and exhaustive service discipline. Oper. Res. Lett. **21**, 95–100 (1997)

15. Alfa, A.S.: A discrete MAP/PH/1 queue with vacations and exhaustive service. Oper. Res. Lett. **18**, 31–40 (1995)
16. Alfa, A.S.: A discrete MAP/PH/1 vacation queue with gate time-limited service. Queueing Syst. **29**, 35–54 (1998)
17. Alfa, A.S.: Vacation models in discrete time. Queueing Syst. **44**(1), 5–30 (2003)
18. Çinlar, E.: Introduction to Stochastic Processes. Prentice-Hall, Englewood Cliffs (1975)
19. Cooper, R.: Introduction to Queueing Theory, 2nd edn. North-Holland, New York (1981)

Architecture and Big Data

Boosting MapReduce
with Network-Aware Task Assignment

Fei Xu, Fangming Liu$^{(\boxtimes)}$, Dekang Zhu, and Hai Jin

Services Computing Technology and System Lab, Cluster and Grid Computing Lab,
School of Computer Science and Technology,
Huazhong University of Science and Technology, Wuhan 430074, China
fmliu@hust.edu.cn

Abstract. Running MapReduce in a shared cluster has become a recent trend to process large-scale data analytical applications while improving the cluster utilization. However, the network sharing among various applications can make the network bandwidth for MapReduce applications constrained and heterogeneous. This further increases the severity of network hotspots in racks, and makes existing task assignment policies which focus on the data locality no longer effective. To deal with this issue, this paper develops a model to analyze the relationship between job completion time and the assignment of both map and reduce tasks across racks. We further design a network-aware task assignment strategy to shorten the completion time of MapReduce jobs in shared clusters. It integrates two simple yet effective greedy heuristics that minimize the completion time of map phase and reduce phase, respectively. With large-scale simulations driven by Facebook job traces, we demonstrate that the network-aware strategy can shorten the average completion time of MapReduce jobs, as compared to the state-of-the-art task assignment strategies, yet with an acceptable computational overhead.

Keywords: MapReduce · Task assignment · Network hotspots

1 Introduction

MapReduce [1] has been widely adopted as the core technique of powering business services in big IT companies like Google, Facebook and Yahoo, through processing vast amounts of data in large-scale clusters. To improve the cluster utilization, a recent trend is to move MapReduce applications from dedicated clusters to shared clusters, such as Amazon EC2 [2] and Mesos [3].

An important challenge is that the performance of MapReduce applications can be significantly impacted by the network sharing in a shared cluster. As the network resource is shared among virtual machines hosting various applications [4] or among different computing frameworks [3], the bandwidth available for MapReduce applications becomes constrained and heterogeneous across

The research was supported in part by a grant from National Natural Science Foundation of China (NSFC) under grant No.61133006.

V.C.M. Leung and M. Chen (Eds.): CloudComp 2013, LNICST 133, pp. 79–89, 2014.
DOI: 10.1007/978-3-319-05506-0_8, © Institute for Computer Sciences, Social Informatics and Telecommunications Engineering 2014

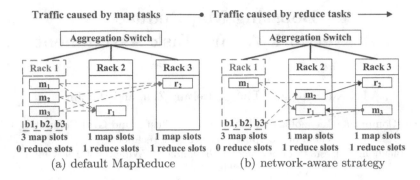

Fig. 1. Assigning 3 map (m_1, m_2, m_3) and 2 reduce tasks (r_1, r_2) of a reduce-heavy job to 3 racks. b_1, b_2, b_3 are the three input data blocks for map tasks. Congested links and racks with constrained network bandwidth are labeled with dashed lines.

racks [5]. Moreover, the network bandwidth is crucial to the MapReduce performance, as reduce tasks need to retrieve data from all map tasks across racks via the network during the shuffle phase. Hence, the issue of network hotspots in shared clusters becomes more severe than that in dedicated clusters, which would affect the completion time of MapReduce jobs [6] eventually.

To alleviate network hotspots and shorten the completion time for MapReduce applications, existing works focus on achieving the data locality of map tasks [1,7] or assigning each reduce task to the racks hosting the maximum amount of its input data [8]. However, these solutions are designed for MapReduce running in a dedicated cluster with *plenty and homogeneous* network bandwidth in racks, and *separately* optimize the assignment of map tasks and reduce tasks. There is a lack of attention devoted to the assignment of *both* map and reduce tasks in a shared cluster, with *constrained and heterogeneous* network bandwidth of racks available for MapReduce applications.

As a result, though the assignment of map tasks achieves 100 % data locality and causes zero cross-rack traffic, it is possible that large amounts of intermediate data generated by map tasks congest the racks with constrained bandwidth resource in the shuffle phase. As an example, Fig. 1 shows that greedily achieving the data locality of map tasks is not a guarantee of good performance of MapReduce applications in a shared cluster. This is because the bandwidth available for MapReduce in the rack hosting map tasks (Rack 1) is constrained, which leads to a long transfer time to shuffle large amounts of intermediate data to reduce tasks. In contrast, a network-aware strategy can alleviate the network hotspot in Rack 1 by assigning two map tasks (m_2, m_3) to Rack 2 and 3, respectively.

In this paper, we propose a network-aware task assignment strategy in shared clusters. By analyzing the relationship between the assignment of both map and reduce tasks across racks and the completion time of MapReduce jobs, we obtain insights into the time *bonus* and *penalty* incurred by assigning a task to the racks with heterogeneous bandwidth. To shorten the job completion time, we develop our strategy that integrates two simple yet effective greedy heuristics through the decomposition of the task assignment problem. To evaluate the effectiveness and overhead of our strategy, we conduct extensive simulations by replaying two MapReduce job traces from Facebook Inc. [9]. We demonstrate that our network-aware strategy can achieve a speedup of 46.1 –128.6 % on average for MapReduce jobs, in comparison to three recently proposed task assignment strategies.

The rest of this paper is organized as follows. Section 2 presents a model of the completion time of MapReduce jobs. Section 3 designs the network-aware task assignment strategy. Section 4 evaluates the effectiveness and overhead of our strategy. Section 5 discusses the related work. Finally, we conclude this paper in Sect. 6.

2 Modeling Relationship Between Job Completion Time and Task Assignment

In this section, we first model the relationship between the job completion time and the task assignment in racks. We then formulate an assignment problem of both map and reduce tasks to minimize the job completion time.

2.1 Modeling Completion Time of MapReduce Jobs

We consider a shared cluster with a set of r racks denoted by $\mathcal{R}$. In each rack $i \in \mathcal{R}$ (i.e., R_i), the numbers of available map slots and reduce slots are s_i^m and s_i^r, respectively, and the network bandwidth available for MapReduce applications is B_i. A newly-submitted MapReduce job has sets of p map tasks and q reduce tasks to be assigned, which are denoted by $\mathcal{K}_m$ and $\mathcal{K}_r$, respectively.

We then define a binary variable x_{ij} (x_{ij}^m, x_{ij}^r) to denote whether a (map, reduce) task j is assigned to R_i. We then use h_{ij} (h_{ij}^m, h_{ij}^r) to denote the amount of input data of a (map, reduce) task j stored in R_i. In particular, the sum of h_{ij} over all tasks ($\sum_{j \in \mathcal{K}} h_{ij}$) represents the network-out traffic in R_i. The sum of h_{ij} over all racks ($\sum_{i \in \mathcal{R}} h_{ij}$) represents the total input data to be read by a task j. Table 1 summarizes the important notations used in our model.

In each R_i, the transfer time of input data of a map or a reduce task can be calculated as the ratio of the amount of task input data to the capacity of network bandwidth available for MapReduce. Hence, we have $c_{ij}^m = \frac{h_{ij}^m}{B_i}$, $c_{ij}^r = \frac{h_{ij}^r}{B_i}$.

Theorem 1. *Given the amount of input data of map or reduce tasks stored in racks h_{ij}, $\forall i \in \mathcal{R}$, $j \in \mathcal{K}$ ($\mathcal{K}_m$ or $\mathcal{K}_r$), the transfer time c_i of cross-rack traffic, incurred by assigning a map or a reduce task j to R_i, can be formulated as*

$$c_i = \sum_{j \in \mathcal{K}} c_{ij} + \sum_{j \in \mathcal{K}} u_{ij} x_{ij}, \qquad (1)$$

where u_{ij} can be considered as a weight given by

$$u_{ij} = \sum_{l \in \mathcal{R}} h_{lj}/B_i - 2c_{ij}. \qquad (2)$$

Table 1. Key notations in our model

Notation	Definition
$\mathcal{K}, \mathcal{K}_m, \mathcal{K}_r, \mathcal{R}$	Sets of map/reduce tasks and racks
p, q, r	Numbers of map tasks, reduce tasks and racks
s_i^m, s_i^r	Number of available map/reduce slots in R_i
B_i	Network bandwidth available for MapReduce in R_i
$\mathcal{X}, \mathcal{X}_m, \mathcal{X}_r$	Assignment set of map/reduce tasks across racks
$x_{ij}, x_{ij}^m, x_{ij}^r$	Whether a map/reduce task j is assigned to R_i
$h_{ij}, h_{ij}^m, h_{ij}^r$	Amount of input data of a map/reduce task j stored in R_i
$c_{ij}, c_{ij}^m, c_{ij}^r$	Transfer time of input data of a map/reduce task j stored in R_i
c_i, c_i^m, c_i^r	Transfer time of cross-rack traffic in the map/reduce phase in R_i
w_i^m, w_i^m	Number of waves in the map/reduce phase in R_i
τ_m, τ_r	Average computation time of a map/reduce task

The first item of Eq. (1) is the transfer time of the total task input data stored in R_i, which is a constant as h_{ij} is given. The second item of Eq. (1) can be considered as a sum of transfer time bonus (i.e., $u_{ij} \leq 0$) or penalty (i.e., $u_{ij} > 0$) incurred by assigning map or reduce tasks to R_i.

Proof. For each R_i, c_i is the sum of transfer time of network in- and out-traffic, denoted by c_i^{in} and c_i^{ou}, respectively. Assigning a map or a reduce task j to R_i ($x_{ij} = 1$) implies that: (1) The input data of the task j on the other racks $l \neq i$ is required to be transferred to R_i, which brings an amount of network-in traffic (i.e., $\sum_{l \in \mathcal{R}} h_{lj} - h_{ij}$) to R_i. Accordingly, summing up the network-in traffic in R_i over all tasks $j \in \mathcal{K}$, and then dividing the resulting sum by B_i yields

$$c_i^{in} = \sum_{j \in \mathcal{K}} \left(\sum_{l \in \mathcal{R}} h_{lj} - h_{ij} \right) x_{ij} / B_i = \sum_{j \in \mathcal{K}} \left(\sum_{l \in \mathcal{R}} h_{lj} / B_i - c_{ij} \right) x_{ij}.$$

(2) If the task j is assigned to R_i ($x_{ij} = 1$), R_i can save an amount of network-out traffic h_{ij}. Correspondingly, subtracting the saved amount of network-out traffic (i.e., $\sum_{j \in \mathcal{K}} c_{ij} x_{ij}$) from the total network-out traffic (i.e., $\sum_{j \in \mathcal{K}} h_{ij}$) in R_i, and then dividing the resulting difference value by B_i gets

$$c_i^{ou} = \left(\sum_{j \in \mathcal{K}} h_{ij} - \sum_{j \in \mathcal{K}} h_{ij} x_{ij} \right) / B_i = \sum_{j \in \mathcal{K}} c_{ij} - \sum_{j \in \mathcal{K}} c_{ij} x_{ij}.$$

Therefore, combing c_i^{in} and c_i^{ou} together yields Eq. (1).

In general, each rack executes multiple waves to complete the assigned map and reduce tasks [1]. The execution time of all tasks T_i in each rack i is comprised of the task computation time and traffic transfer time c_i. As racks concurrently executes tasks, the *makespans* (completion time) of map phase and reduce phase can be calculated as the maximums of task execution time T_i in all racks in the two phases, respectively. As there is a time overlap between map phase and reduce phase, we *estimate* the job completion time according to [10] as below,

$$T \approx \max_i T_i^m(\mathcal{X}_m) + \max_i T_i^r(\mathcal{X}_m, \mathcal{X}_r)$$
$$= \max_i(w_i^m \tau_m + c_i^m) + \max_i(w_i^r \tau_r + c_i^r), \tag{3}$$

where τ_m, τ_r denote the average computation time of a map, reduce task, respectively. w_i^m, w_i^r denote the number of waves in the map, reduce phase of a job, respectively, and $w_i^m = \lceil \sum_{j \in \mathcal{K}_m} x_{ij}^m / s_i^m \rceil$, $w_i^r = \lceil \sum_{j \in \mathcal{K}_r} x_{ij}^r / s_i^r \rceil$.

2.2 Formulating Task Assignment Problem of MapReduce

The objective of the task assignment problem is to minimize the job completion time by optimizing the assignment of both map and reduce tasks across racks.

$$\min_{\mathcal{X}_m, \mathcal{X}_r} \quad T = \max_i(w_i^m \tau_m + c_i^m) + \max_i(w_i^r \tau_r + c_i^r) \tag{4}$$

$$\text{s.t.} \quad \sum_{i \in \mathcal{R}} x_{ij}^m = 1, \quad \sum_{i \in \mathcal{R}} x_{ij}^r = 1, \quad \forall j$$

$$x_{ij}^m \in \{0,1\}, \quad x_{ij}^r \in \{0,1\}, \quad \forall i,j$$

The formulation above is a 0-1 integer min-max optimization problem, which appears to be in the form of an *Imbalanced Time Minimizing Assignment Problem* and has been proved as NP-hard [11]. Although such a problem can be solved by a dynamic programming approach, the major drawback would be the inefficiency in iterating over all $r^{(p+q)}$ possible solutions. Since our objective is to shorten the job completion time without bringing much computational overhead to MapReduce, we seek to design a heuristic task assignment strategy that could be implemented in a real-world cluster.

3   A Network-Aware Task Assignment Strategy

In this section, we decompose the task assignment problem in Eq. (4) into two subproblems: first minimizing the makespan of a single (map or reduce) phase, and then jointly minimizing the makespans of map phase and reduce phase.

First, we focus on solving the single phase problem: Given the (map- or reduce-) input data stored in racks h_{ij}, how can we assign map or reduce tasks to racks, to shorten the makespan of map or reduce phase?

By Theorem 1 and Eq. (3), the overall task execution time[1] T_i in each R_i can be initially set as a constant time value $\sum_{j \in \mathcal{K}} c_{ij}$. Thus, we define $\max_i \sum_{j \in \mathcal{K}} c_{ij}$ as the *initial makespan* of map or reduce phase. Also, assigning a map or a reduce task j to R_i brings a time *bonus* or *penalty* u_{ij} to T_i in R_i. Accordingly, we design Algorithm 1 that greedily minimizes the maximum of T_i, by assigning the task with the minimum u_{ij} to racks one by one, until all tasks are assigned.

---

[1] Note that we fill up the available slots in racks before starting the next wave. Hence, the task computation time $(w_i^m \tau_m, w_i^r \tau_r)$ in Eq. (4) is fixed as $\lceil p/\sum_{i \in \mathcal{R}} s_i^m \rceil \tau_m$, $\lceil q/\sum_{i \in \mathcal{R}} s_i^r \rceil \tau_r$. It is omitted when calculating the phase makespan for simplicity.

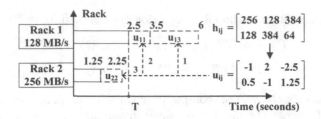

Fig. 2. An example of Algorithm 1: minimize the makespan T of map or reduce phase, when assigning 3 map or reduce tasks to 2 racks. The dashed rectangle means a time *bonus*.

Example 1. We consider the example shown in Fig. 2. Algorithm 1 first assigns each rack with an initial time, i.e., $T_1 = \sum_{j \in \mathcal{K}} \frac{h_{1j}}{128} = 6$, $T_2 = \sum_{j \in \mathcal{K}} \frac{h_{2j}}{256} = 2.25$, and u_{ij} is generated by Eq. (2). As u_{ij} has three elements that are less than zero, we first select R_1 with the maximum execution time T_i, and assign task 3 with the minimum u_{ij} to the selected R_1. As a result, T_1 becomes $6 - 2.5 = 3.5$. Then, we proceed to assign task 1 to R_1, and task 2 to R_2 sequentially. The resulting makespan of map or reduce phase is 2.5 eventually.

Algorithm 1. Minimize makespan of map or reduce phase

1: **Initialize** $T_i \leftarrow \sum_{j \in \mathcal{K}} c_{ij}, \forall i \in \mathcal{R}$; Set of racks with available slots $\hat{\mathcal{R}} \subseteq \mathcal{R}$
2: **while** exists unassigned tasks **do**
3:    **if** set of racks $\hat{\mathcal{R}}' \subseteq \hat{\mathcal{R}}$ that meet $u_{ij} \leq 0$ is empty **then**
4:       Find a rack $i' \in \hat{\mathcal{R}}$ with the minimum T_i
5:    **else**
6:       Find a rack $i' \in \hat{\mathcal{R}}'$ with the maximum T_i
7:    **end if**
8:    Assign the task $j' \in \mathcal{K}$ with the minimum $u_{i'j}$ to the rack i', $x_{i'j'} \leftarrow 1$
9:    Update $T_{i'} \leftarrow T_{i'} + u_{i'j'}$
10: **end while**
11: **return** the task assignment set $\mathcal{X}$

Remark 1. The procedure of Algorithm 1 fits well with the mechanism of task scheduling in MapReduce, where the master node of MapReduce assigns tasks one by one via heartbeats from each slave nodes (racks) [1]. In addition, the complexity of Algorithm 1 is $\mathcal{O}(|\mathcal{K}| \cdot r)$.

Next, we solve the two phases problem, which can be considered as a multi-objective optimization problem: Given the map-input data h_{ij}^m and reduce-input data generated by map tasks L_j, how can we assign map tasks to racks, to jointly shorten the makespan of map phase and initial makespan of reduce phase?

To obtain a Pareto optimal solution [11] for such an optimization problem, we adopt the weight sum method that minimizes $sum_{i=1}^2 \alpha_i T_i(\mathcal{X})$, i.e., minimizes the sum of makespan of map phase and initial makespan of reduce phase when the weights α_i are set as 1. Accordingly, we design Algorithm 2 that greedily minimizes the sum of increased makespans of map phase and reduce phase, by assigning the map task with the maximum reduce-input data L_j to racks one by one [11], until all map tasks are assigned. In particular, ΔT^m and ΔT^r are the increased makespans of map phase and reduce phase, respectively.

Example 2. We consider the example shown in Fig. 3. The input data blocks of three map tasks (i.e., m_1, m_2, m_3) are stored in R_1, R_2 and R_1, respectively. As the amounts of reduce-input data L_j generated by each map task j are 384, 128, 512 MB, respectively, Algorithm 2 first chooses to assign m_3 with the maximum reduce-input data to racks. If m_3 is assigned to R_1, $\Delta T^m = 0$ because the map-input data of m_3 is stored in R_1, and $\Delta T^r = \frac{512}{128} = 4$. If m_3 is assigned to R_2, $\Delta T^m = \frac{128}{256} = 0.5$ because the map-input data of m_3 is transferred to R_2, and $\Delta T^r = \frac{512}{256} = 2$. Accordingly, assigning m_3 to R_2 achieves the minimum sum of ΔT^m and ΔT^r. Similar to the assignment procedure of m_3, we sequentially assign m_1 to R_1, m_2 to R_2, to minimize the sum of T^m and T^r.

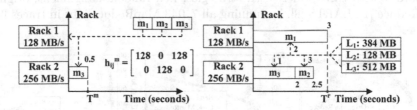

Fig. 3. An example of Algorithm 2: jointly minimize the makespan of map phase T^m and initial makespan of reduce phase T^r, when assigning 3 map tasks to 2 racks.

Algorithm 2. Jointly minimize the makespan of map phase and initial makespan of reduce phase

---

1: **Initialize** T_i^m, $T_i^r \leftarrow 0$, $\forall i \in \mathcal{R}$; Set of racks with available slots $\hat{\mathcal{R}} \subseteq \mathcal{R}$
2: **while** exists unassigned map tasks **do**
3:     Find a map task $j' \in \mathcal{K}_m$ with the maximum L_j
4:     Find a rack $i' \in \hat{\mathcal{R}}$ to host task j' such that $\Delta T^m + \Delta T^r$ is minimized
5:     Assign the task j' to the rack i', $x_{i'j'}^m \leftarrow 1$
6:     Update $T_{i'}^m \leftarrow T_{i'}^m + h_{i'j'}/B_{i'}$, $T_{i'}^r \leftarrow T_{i'}^r + L_{j'}/B_{i'}$
7: **end while**
8: **return** the map task assignment set $\mathcal{X}_m$

Remark 2. Algorithm 2 cooperates with Algorithm 1 to minimize the completion time of MapReduce jobs. After Algorithm 2 outputs a map task assignment set $\mathcal{X}_m$ that jointly minimizes the makespan of map phase and initial makespan of reduce phase, Algorithm 1 proceeds to find an assignment of reduce tasks $\mathcal{X}_r$ that further shortens the makespan of reduce phase. In addition, the complexity of Algorithm 2 is $\mathcal{O}(p \cdot r)$.

4   Experimental Evaluation

In this section, we evaluate the effectiveness and computational overhead of our strategy. Specifically, we build a simulator with $1,100$ lines of C code, driven by two one-day MapReduce job traces from Facebook Inc. [9]. We set up a 600-server shared cluster. To make the simulation practical, the parameters are chosen according to Microsoft's Cosmos cluster [6]. We set the number of servers in a rack as 30, the number of racks r as 20, the number of map, reduce slots s^m, s^r in a rack as 60, the size of a data block as 128 MB, and the capacity of network bandwidth of a rack as 10 Gbps. In addition, we generate the background traffic in each rack randomly, and set the average computation time of a map task τ_m and a reduce task τ_r as $5\,\mathrm{s}$ and $\frac{3 \cdot \tau_m \cdot p}{q}\,\mathrm{s}$ [12], respectively.

4.1   Effectiveness of Network-Aware Task Assignment

To illustrate the effectiveness of our network-aware task assignment strategy, we compare it with three widely-used strategies, i.e., random assignment, original MapReduce [1], LARTS [8], by running all $7,043$ MapReduce jobs in traces [9].

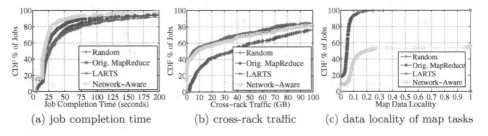

(a) job completion time   (b) cross-rack traffic   (c) data locality of map tasks

Fig. 4. Performance comparison of MapReduce jobs with four task assignment strategies.

- Random: Map and reduce tasks are randomly assigned to available racks.
- Original MapReduce [1]: Each map task greedily achieves the data locality. Reduce tasks are randomly assigned to available racks.
- LARTS [8]: Each map task greedily achieves the data locality. Each reduce task is assigned to the rack hosting the maximum amount of its input data.

Figure 4 shows that our strategy can save a significant amount of time to complete MapReduce jobs, while incurring little amount of cross-rack traffic and sacrificing the data locality of map tasks for around 50 % of jobs, compared to the three other task assignment strategies. Specifically, the network-aware strategy outperforms the other strategies in shortening the job completion time, as shown in Fig. 4(a). The reason is that our strategy takes the network bandwidth of racks into account and jointly optimizes the assignment of map and reduce tasks to racks. Although LARTS achieves the least cross-rack traffic than other strategies, as shown in Fig. 4(b), it is not a guarantee of good MapReduce performance. This is because its selected rack hosting the maximum input data of a reduce task would be a network hotspot, which inevitably prolongs the network transfer of cross-rack traffic. Moreover, the cross-rack traffic with our strategy is slightly more than that with LARTS and original MapReduce. Figure 4(c) shows that our strategy breaks 100 % map data locality, compared to the original MapReduce and LARTS. The rationale is that, our strategy jointly considers the makepan of map phase and initial makespan of reduce phase of a job during the assignment of map tasks. Table 2 quantitatively shows the mean values of simulation results.

Table 2. Mean values of simulations results with four task assignment strategies.

	Random	Orig. MR	LARTS	Net-aware
Job completion time	85.5 s	69.4 s	108.6 s	47.5 s
Cross-rack traffic	182.5 GB	147.9 GB	143.9 GB	151.7 GB
Data locality of map tasks	5.1 %	100 %	100 %	51 %

Furthermore, we compare the completion time of 4, 712 map-only jobs and 2, 198 map- and reduce-heavy jobs in traces [9], respectively, in order to examine the effectiveness of our strategy on minimizing the makespans of map phase and reduce phase. Figure 5(a) shows that our network-aware strategy outperforms the other strategies for around 50 % of map-only jobs. This is because LARTS and the original MapReduce greedily achieve the data locality in the map phase. Such policies are oblivious to the constraint on available map slots in racks, which would produce more waves to run jobs than our strategy. Figure 5(b) shows that our network-aware strategy can save more 30 s for 40 % of map- and reduce-heavy jobs, compared to the other strategies. The rationale is that, our strategy jointly minimizes the makespan of map phase and initial makespan of reduce phase by optimizing the assignment of map tasks. After that, the assignment of reduce tasks is further optimized to shorten the makespan of reduce phase.

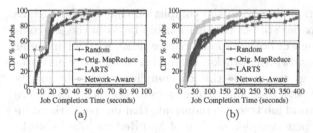

(a)   (b)

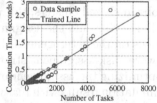

Fig. 5. Performance comparison of (a) map-only jobs and (b) map- and reduce-heavy jobs.

Fig. 6. Training computation time of network-aware strategy by the least squares method.

4.2 Computational Overhead of Network-Aware Task Assignment

To analyze the computational overhead of our strategy, we use the least squares method to train the data samples of strategy computation time collected in simulations. As shown in Fig. 6, we observe that (1) the computation time of our strategy is approximately linear to the number of tasks as the number of racks is fixed. This is consistent with the complexity analysis of our strategy in Sect. 3. (2) Our strategy is able to optimize the assignment of 8,000 tasks (i.e., 1 TB input data) within 3 s, when running on a commodity server (one quad-core Intel Xeon E5620 2.40 GHz processor). Such an overhead is acceptable and can be amortized over the execution of MapReduce jobs, as the average reduction of job completion time is more than 20 s shown in Table 2.

5   Related Work

There have been a number of works on reducing the cross-rack traffic by optimizing the assignment of map or reduce tasks separately, to shorten the completion time of MapReduce jobs. Reference [6] computed the optimal assignment of reduce tasks across racks by minimizing the transfer time of cross-rack traffic over all possible task assignment permutations. Yet, this approach would incur a high computational overhead when the number of reduce tasks or racks is large. Reference [8] designed a heuristic algorithm that assigns each reduce task to the rack hosting the maximum amount of its input data, without consideration of the bandwidth available for MapReduce in racks. A recent work [13] studied the relationship between the data locality of map tasks and the numbers of tasks and servers. Reference [4] placed input data blocks near to map and reduce tasks to improve the processing efficiency of MapReduce. Reference [12] analyzed the impact of the execution order of tasks and jobs on the job completion time. Orthogonal to these works, our work analyzes the assignment problem of both map and reduce tasks across racks to shorten the job completion time by taking the network bandwidth of racks into account.

6   Conclusion and Future Work

To mitigate network hotspots and shorten the completion time of MapReduce jobs in shared clusters, this paper studies the relationship between the job completion time and the assignment of both map and reduce tasks, with a particular focus on the heterogeneous bandwidth of racks. We further develop the network-aware task assignment strategy to shorten the job completion time, by jointly optimizing the assignment of both map and reduce tasks across racks. Extensive simulation results with real-world job traces demonstrate that our network-aware strategy can shorten the average completion time of MapReduce jobs by 46.1–128.6 %, compared to the recently proposed task assignment strategies.

As our future work, we plan to implement our network-aware task assignment strategy in Hadoop and evaluate its effectiveness in a shared cluster. We also plan to incorporate the disk I/O into our model and extend our task assignment strategy, as it is another key factor that impacts the MapReduce performance.

References

1. Dean, J., Ghemawat, S.: MapReduce: simplified data processing on large clusters. In: Proceedings of OSDI, December 2004
2. Zaharia, M., Konwinski, A., Joseph, A.D., Katz, R.H., Stoica, I.: Improving MapReduce performance in heterogeneous environments. In: Proceedings of OSDI, December 2008
3. Hindman, B., Konwinski, A., Zaharia, M., Ghodsi, A., Joseph, A.D., Katz, R.H., Shenker, S., Stoica, I.: Mesos: a platform for fine-grained resource sharing in the data center. In: Proceedings of NSDI, March 2011
4. Palanisamy, B., Singh, A., Liu, L., Jain, B.: Purlieus: locality-aware resource allocation for MapReduce in a cloud. In: Proceedings of SC, November 2011
5. Ballani, H., Jang, K., Karagiannis, T., Kim, C., Gunawardena, D., O'Shea, G.: Chatty tenants and the cloud network sharing problem. In: Proceedings of NSDI, April 2013
6. Ananthanarayanan, G., Kandula, S., Greenberg, A., Stoica, I., Lu, Y., Saha, B., Harris, E.: Reining in the outliers in Map-Reduce clusters using mantri. In: Proceedings of OSDI, October 2010
7. Zaharia, M., Borthakur, D., Sarma, J.S., Elmeleegy, K., Shenker, S., Stoica, I.: Delay scheduling: a simple technique for achieving locality and fairness in cluster scheduling. In: Proceedings of Eurosys, April 2010
8. Hammoud, M., Sakr, M.F.: Locality-aware reduce task scheduling for MapReduce. In: Proceedings of CloudCom, November 2011
9. Chen, Y., Ganapathi, A., Griffith, R., Katz, R.: The case for evaluating MapReduce performance using workload suites. In: Proceedings of MASCOTS, July 2011
10. Jalaparti, V., Ballani, H., Costa, P., Karagiannis, T., Rowstron, A.: Bridging the tenant-provider gap in cloud services. In: Proceedings of SOCC, October 2012
11. Aora, S., Puri, M.C.: A variant of time minimizing assignment problem. Eur. J. Oper. Res. 110(2), 314–325 (1998)
12. Chen, F., Kodialam, M., Lakshman, T.V.: Joint scheduling of processing and shuffle phases in MapReduce Systems. In: Proceedings of Infocom, March 2012
13. Guo, Z., Fox, G., Zhou, M.: Investigation of data locality in MapReduce. In: Proceedings of CCGrid, May 2012

Towards a Trusted Launch Mechanism for Virtual Machines in Cloud Computing

Juan Wang[1,2]([✉]), Xuhui Xie[1], Qingfei Wang[1], Fei Yan[1,2], Hongxin Hu[3], Sijun Zhou[1], and Tao Wang[1]

[1] School of Computer, Wuhan University, Wuhan 430072, Hubei, China
[2] Key Laboratory of Aerospace Information Security and Trust Computing, Ministry of Education, Wuhan 430072, Hubei, China
jwang@whu.edu.cn
[3] Delaware State University, Dover, DE 19901, USA
hhu@desu.edu

Abstract. Although cloud computing enables us to dynamically provide servers with the ability to address a wide range of needs, this paradigm also brings forth many new security challenges. The security of virtual machines (VM) is one of such critical challenges for cloud computing. However, existing techniques for VM security, such as Terra, tboot and TXT, mainly focus on the security of VM running environment. There is a lack of protection mechanism for VMs themselves in clouds. In this paper, we propose a trusted launch solution for virtual machines (TLVM), including four systematic mechanisms, image encryption, measurement, attestation and security-enhanced authentication, for protecting VMs in clouds. We also discuss a proof-of-concept implementation of our approach. Our experimental results demonstrate the feasibility of our solution to protect the whole launch process of a VM.

Keywords: Cloud security · VM · Measurement · Attestation

1 Introduction

The emerging cloud-computing paradigm is rapidly gaining momentum as an alternative to traditional information technology due to the reason that it provides an extensible and powerful environment for growing amounts of services and data. However, the security of current cloud infrastructures is a key challenge, probably hindering the development of cloud computing.

For infrastructure as a service (IaaS) in cloud computing, virtual machines are leased to users. Some sensitive user data is stored in the virtual machines. Once the data is leaked outside of the virtual machines, it will damage the interests of users. Thus, how to protect the security of virtual machines is crucial in IaaS. However, the existing techniques for VM security like Terra [1], TXT [2] and tboot [3] mainly focus on the security of VM running environment, such as the

V.C.M. Leung and M. Chen (Eds.): CloudComp 2013, LNICST 133, pp. 90–101, 2014.
DOI: 10.1007/978-3-319-05506-0_9, © Institute for Computer Sciences, Social Informatics and Telecommunications Engineering 2014

security of host and virtual machine monitor (VMM) [4,5]. There is a lack of protection mechanism for VMs themselves in clouds.

To address such a critical problem, we propose a trusted launch solution for virtual machines (TLVM). In TLVM, four systematic mechanisms including image encryption, measurement, attestation and trusted-enhanced authentication are used to protect virtual machines. The image encryption mechanism can prevent illegal users to start a VM. The measurement and attestation mechanisms can protect the integrity of a VM. The trusted-enhanced authentication mechanism can achieve two-way authentication between a user and a VM. Consequently, the overall solution can protect the whole launch process of a VM in cloud computing.

The remainder of this paper is organized as follows. In Sect. 2, we describe our goals and the framework of TLVM. In Sect. 3, we present the detailed design of our systematic mechanism for protecting VM security. Section 4 presents the implementation of TLVM. Section 5 discusses the experimental evaluation of our solution. Finally, Sect. 6 concludes this paper.

2 Trusted Launch of Virtual Machines

2.1 Trust and Attack Model

In our trust and attack model, an administrator is able to copy VM images to outsides of a trusted domain. The trusted domain comprises trusted nodes. The trusted nodes including hosts and VMM can be achieved by tboot, TXT and dynamic measurement technology, such as SICE [8] and TEE [5]. Furthermore, the attackers including the administrators of IaaS can tamper with VM images. In addition, since a user can not trust the identity of the VM, the user suffers from the VM phishing attack.

A VM instance is considered trusted in the current attack model if and only if it fulfills the following criteria:

(1) The VM image used for the instance is not tampered with.
(2) The VM instance is launched on a trusted domain.
(3) The identity of the VM is trusted.

In above criteria, the second one can be insured by tboot, TXT and dynamic measurement [9,10] technology, such as SICE and TEE. These methods are not our major focus in the paper. Instead, we investigate the trust issue for VM launch.

2.2 Overview

Trusted Computing [6] is a technology developed and promoted by the Trusted Computing Group. With Trusted Computing, a computer will consistently behave in expected ways, and those behaviors will be enforced by computer hardware and software. Enforcing those behaviors is achieved by building a trusted chain based on trusted base. Five main key technologies: endorsement key, secure input and output, memory protected execution, sealed storage, and remote attestation, can be used to ensure the trust of a protected platform.

Based on the trusted computing technology, TLVM provides a security protection mechanism for virtual machines in a cloud computing platform which can guarantee the confidentiality, integrity and authentication of a user's VM. In TLVM, we add the modules of image encryption, measurement and attestation in VMM. Furthermore, the authentication module based on Usbkey and trusted platform module (TPM) is added in VMs. These mechanisms provide a systematic solution of secure launching a VM.

2.3   Trusted Launch Process of a VM

The framework of TLVM and secure launch process of a VM are depicted as Fig. 1. The system is composed of a cloud management center including a user management module, a VM management module, a key management and attestation server, a host where virtual machines are running, an Usbkey administrator and users. The launch process of a VM is shown as following.

(1) A user requests to register in the cloud management center.

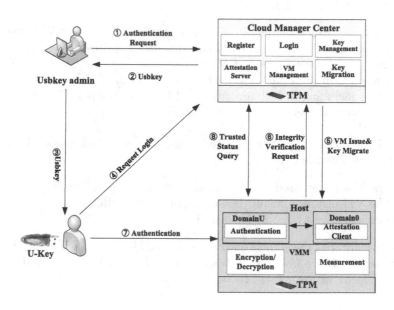

Fig. 1. Trusted launch process of a VM

(2) An Usbkey administrator requests a certificate, a private key and a symmetric key to the cloud management center server. The cloud management center generates a certificate, a private key and a symmetric key and then writes them to an Usbkey. Meanwhile, the symmetric key which is encrypted with the storage

root key (SRK) of the TPM on the cloud management server will be saved to the cloud key management center.

(3) The Usbkey administrator issues the Usbkey to the user.

(4) The user logins to the cloud management center and applies for a virtual machine. The cloud manager center creates a virtual machine for the user.

(5) The encrypted virtual machine image is launched on a host to run. Meanwhile, the symmetric key will be migrated to the host by TPM key migration command and then be protected by the local TPM.The VMM image encryption and decryption module will decrypt the image with the migrated symmetric key. Then the virtual machine image will be measured by measurement module.

(6) The measurement result including measurement value and report signed by TPM in the host will be sent to remote attestation server to verify the integrity of the image.

(7) The user will login to the VM using the Usbkey. The VM will communicate to the host and get the migrated key. The VM and the user will mutually authenticate by the symmetric key in the Usbkey and the migrated key.

(8) When the user logins the VM. The trust query module in VM will communicate with the attestation server and get the VM's measured result. Then the trusted status will be shown on the VM's desktop.

2.4 Detailed Design

In TLVM, the encryption/decryption mechanism of image, measurement, attestation and security-enhanced mechanism based on TPM are added. The detailed design of them is described as following.

2.4.1 Encryption Mechanism of VM Image

In clouds, a virtual machine's images are possible to be started by unauthorized users. For example, administrators possibly copy a virtual machine image to outside of trusted domains and then start the virtual machine. In order to protect the user's VM from unauthorized starting, the strongest method is full virtual machine disk image encryption [11], which makes it difficult to recover the image for unauthorized users. However, it is obviously a time-consuming process. To achieve a tradeoff between security and performance, we only encrypt the main disk information of a virtual machine image. For a common disk file, we could encrypt the master boot record (MBR), Boot, and some logic partitions. But in a cloud environment, some virtual machines may have the same MBR or boot. It is easy to copy a VM to attack other VMs. Thus, we have designed an image file encryption which is based on the file system and user's configuration. We first get the user's symmetric key which is protected by TPM, and get the partition and file system type information from the MBR, then read the user's encryption configuration. Finally, we encrypt the file contained in the configuration, and then encrypt key information of a file system, such as index structure.

The encryption process of a VM image is summarized as follows:

(1) Decrypt the symmetric key which is migrated to the host where VM is running when the VM launches and is protested by the TPM's SRK in the host.

(2) Get the partition and operating system's file system. For every image, partition table is in the end of MBR. We can get the partition information such as initial location, size, file system etc.

(3) Load the user's crypto configuration. Every VM has a crypto configuration which has been protected by the VM's symmetric key. Every operating system has a default configuration.

(4) Check whether the image file has been encrypted. In order to avoid repeating encryption, we have set a flag to identify the image file's crypto status. If the status shows that the image file has been encrypted, the crypto process will be broken.

(5) Encrypt the file included in a configure file. In order to balance the encryption performance and security, we have provided elastic encryption. The configuration includes some kernel file which may be common for the same operating system. For windows 7, it must include the boot, registry, bootmbr, ntldr, boot.ini, winlog.exe and some important files. These files are invisible for users, and users can also add other important files to encrypt.

(6) Encrypt import partition for certain file systems. Different file systems have different organizations of the files. For a Linux system, we search every partition, and get the basic information about the partition from super block and traverse all block groups. Then, we encrypt group descriptors table,block bitmap, inode bitmap, inode table of every block group. Because the image files are in general large, we only rewrite the encrypt section to the image file.

2.4.2 Measurement Mechanism of VM

The measurement mechanism of VM provides integrity measurement of a VM before it starts. The integrity of a system is a semantic concept that indicates whether the system has been modified in an unauthorized manner. To measure an entire system is very expensive in practice. One efficient way is to associate the integrity semantics with some important files. In our mechanism, we measure the most important files of different systems and some files defined by users. For Linux systems, we have measured the boot, grub, kernel, kernel modules, binaries shared libraries and dynamic libraries. For Linux users, we should measure the data and applications. If the VM is a web server, we should measure httpd, mod_access.so, and libjvm.so.

The measurement process of a VM image is described as follows:

(1) Get the configuration file of measurement by VM's UUID. If the configuration file does not exist, a default one will be used.

(2) Get the partition and operating system's information.

(3) Mount every partition and measure the files defined in the configuration file. Use sha1 algorithm to compute the hash value of each file. All hash values will be saved in a measurement log file.

(4) Iterate the hash values in the measurement log as the final measurement values.

(5) Call the attestation client module to send and verify the measurement values.

2.4.3   Attestation Mechanism

Remote attestation [7] does the integrity verification of a system. It can prove whether system data is tampered with. It also provides a credible platform status report to a verifier. For remote attestation, TPM is the trusted root of the report. It helps ensure the report deriving from the current integrity measure values.

There are some differences between the remote attestation of VM and the general remote attestation protocol. The general process of remote attestation is shown in Fig. 2.

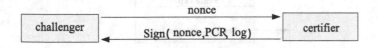

Fig. 2. Remote attestation protocol

A platform (Challenger) sends a challenging message and a nonce to another platform (Certifier), asking for one or more PCR values in order to verify the status of the platform. Certifier uses attestation identity key (AIK) to sign PCR values specified by the challenger, attached to the corresponding measure log entries and AIK certificate, sending to the challenger. Then challenger verifies the value. The validation process includes three steps, (1) re-compute the hash value according to the measure log; (2) verify the AIK certificate; and (3) match the signature value with the expected value.

For VM attestation, the measurement values cannot store in TPM's PCR, because the number of current TPM PCR is only 24, but there are a lot of VMs on a host and the number of VMs is not fixed. Moreover, the measurement values need to be sent to attestation server when a VM starts. The process of remote attestation in our mechanism is shown in Fig. 3. After measuring of VM, the measurement module invokes the attestation client, transfer the measurement value and log to the attestation client. Attestation client receives them, and then triggers the attestation server to send a nonce to the attestation client. After the attestation client gets the nonce, it uses SHA1 algorithm to calculate a hash value of the measurement value, then loads a private signing key from TPM to sign the hash value, forming an integrity report. The report includes nonce, measurement value, hash value, signature value and some other information about the VM. Finally, the attestation client sends the integrity report and measurement log to the attestation server. The attestation server checks nonce, verifies hash and signature, and then judges the platform's credibility by comparing the signature and the expected value.

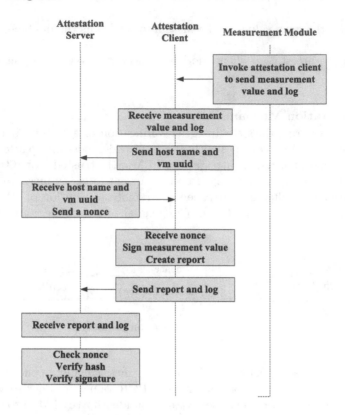

Fig. 3. Process of remote attestation

2.4.4 Trusted Authentication Mechanism of VMs

When the integrity of a VM is achieved by measurement and remote attestation, the VM will be started. However, currently VMs can authenticate users in clouds, but users can not authenticate VMs. Hence, a user easily suffers from a VM phishing attack. To address the issue, we propose a mutual authentication mechanism between VMs and a user based on migrated symmetric key from the TPM of cloud management center and Usbkey. When a user sends request to a VM to login, a VM agent will generate a random N1 and encrypt with the symmetric key K2 migrated from the TPM of cloud management center. The VM agent sends the encrypted N1 to the user. The user decrypts the N1 with the symmetric key K1 issued by the cloud administer. The Usbkey of user side also generates a random N2 and encrypts the sequence (N1, N2) with K1 sent to the VM agent. The VM agent receives the sequence and gets the random N1. If the random N1 is same with the original random N1, the VM can ensure the user is legal. Furthermore, the VM agent uses K2 to encrypt random N2 and sends this random to the user. The user compares the N2 with the initial random N2. If they are same, the user can believe that the VM is legal. If one of them fails, the manual authentication will terminate.

When the mutual authentication succeeds, the user logins to the VM. The VM pops up a web page which accesses the attestation server and gets the integrity verification result of VM image, displaying the trusted status of the VM. According to this measurement verification result, a user can judge that if the VM has been tampered with.

3   Implementation

We have implemented our proposed mechanisms based on Xen and Eucalyptus. The detailed implementation environment of our system is shown in Table 1.

Table 1. Implementation environment of the system

Name	Configuration
Cloud platform	Eucalyptus 3.1
VMM	XEN 4.1.2
Host	HUAWEI RH2288
Domain0 OS	SUSE Linux Enterprise 11SP2
Virtual-Machine OS	Windows 7, ubuntu 10.10
TPM	STM 1.2.7.0
TSS	Trousers 0.3.10
Database	PostgreSQL9.0

For implementing the crypto of a virtual machineimage file, the VM's image should be decrypted before the VM starts and encrypted when the VM shuts down. We also consider some exceptional situation, for example the host where the VM is running suddenly powers off when a VM image is being encrypted. In that situation, we should be able to recover the VM image file when the host powers on. We have modified the source code of Xen to support our approach. The number of modified code is about 1000 lines. We adopted 256-bits Advanced Encryption Standard (AES) as our crypto algorithm.

The principle of encrypting a VM image file system is as following. For Linux system, the file system is ext2, ext3 or ext4 and the basic storage cell of ext is block. One partition has a server block group. Every group block has a number of blocks. The group descriptors table, block bitmap, Inode bitmap and Inode table are stored in front of each block group's description information. The block group 0 has a super block. The super block includes a number of information about this partition such as block size, block number, block group number, and file system flag, node number. The super block has several backups in some block groups. We encrypted the above image file descriptor. For Windows systems, the file system is NTFS. In NTFS, the most important structure is Master File Table (MFT). It includes some system files and file area. Every file has a record in MFT. For every partition it has a backup for MFT. We can encrypt the files to prevent an attacker from opening the VM image file.

For measuring the VM image, such as Linux and Windows 7 virtual machine images, we modified the source code of Xen mainly in XendXm and Python. The amount of modification is about 2000 lines of code. Xen supports two types of virtualization technologies: full-virtualization and para-virtualization. Different types have different implementation mechanisms and image files. We measure the VM image based on the full-virtualization. We should first obtain the OS type, and load the measurement nodes based on the OS type. All measurement nodes are stored serially in a XML configuration file. The XML file can be modified by the manager, if the manager wants to measure more files. Then, we should read the partition information from MBR and measurement each partition. In addition, we firstly mount the boot files and measure them. Furthermore, other partitions are mounted and measured. We store all measurement log and hash values in a XML file. The hash value is iterated as the final hash value.Finally, the measurement module will call attestation module to sign and send the final value and measurement the log file to attest the measurement values.

The attestation module will additionally send the measurement values to the attestation server to verify its integrity. The remote attestation implementation includes two main modules: client signature module and server verification module. First, the client computes hash of the measurement value outside of TPM. Then, the client invokes an interface to implement the signature in TPM. We sign the hash value by using "$Tspi\_Hash\_Sign$". The sign key is loaded by the VM UUID. Then, the signature value is returned to form an integrity report.

The attestation server receives the integrity report "report.xml" from the attestation client through the web service. Then the attestation server desterilizes report.xml into a java content tree. We use JAXB provided by java to implement unmarshalling process. Marshaller class marshals the given object to a given javax.xml.transform.result. Result is a tagging interface that basically represents an XML output abstraction. The Unmarshaller class reads from the given javax.xml.transform.source, and returns the object read. As with Result, source is a tagging interface that has three concrete implementations. After parsing the report, the server checks the nonce, verifies the hash, uses public signing key to verify the signature. The public signing key is stored in cloud management center. When the server wants to verify the signature, it will ask the cloud management center for the public signing key. The attestation module contains about 4700 lines of code.

Finally, the user and the VM will mutually authenticate when the VM is started. For implementing the mutual authentication based on Usbkey and TPM, we customized a new Credential Provider (CP) for VM images. In the new CP, we added functions, like data encryption, data decryption, key transmission, etc. For the user side, we also added authentication client program to implement data encryption and decryption. Usbkey provider provides Usbkey functions interfaces. In order to ensure the security of the new function, we encapsulated our program to the system library file. We used Openssl to protect their data transmission to guarantee the security of the communication between VM agents and users. The total code of mutual authentication based on TPM and Usbkey including the Usbkey driver and API is about 6400 lines.

4   Evaluation

We have measured the runtime performance of our TLVM solution at the implementation environment shown in Table 1. We have launched the VM of Windows 7 img with 10 G 100 times. The total average time of TLVM is 20.076 s. The average time of each stage is show in the Table 2.

Table 2. Performance of TLVM for a VM

	Decryption	Measurement	Attestation	Authentication
T(s)	4.714	1.382	6.277	7.663

The total time of decrypting VM img is about 4.717 s, including decrypting key with TPM SRK taking about 3.852 s, saving temp file taking 0.223 s, decrypting the img disk file system taking 0.267 s, decrypting file specified in configuration file taking 0.368 s.

The total time of measurement is 1.382 s, including mounting the image file taking 0.186 s, measuring the kernel taking 0.241 s, measuring dynamic link libraries taking about 0.432 s, measuring boot files taking 0.164 s and measuring drivers taking 0.459 s.

The attestation time is about 6.277 s. Generating measurement report based measurement files takes 0.569 s. Signing the measurement hash value will cost 3.872 s. Verifying the signature and comparing the value with baseline values takes 0.684 s. The remaining is the time of communication with the attestation server.

The authentication time with a Usbkey is about 7.663 s including the gentgeneration time of nonces, communication time and encryption/decryption time.

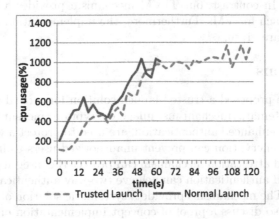

Fig. 4. The performance of multiple VM launched

Because the input PIN speed of different people vary greatly, we have ignored the time of inputing PIN.

In order to show the trusted launch performance impact on the host, we have launched 22 virtual machines with windows 7 image simultaneously. The tested host is HUAWEI RH2288 with 24 core CPUs. Generally, a VM runs in a CPU core. As shown in Fig. 4, normally starting 22 virtual machines takes 63 s, and the CPU usage increase quickly. Trusted launch time is about 120 s. The CPU usage increases slowly. Taken as a whole, the performance overhead is acceptable.

5   Related Work

Santos et al. [12] presented the design of a trusted cloud compute platform, which ensures VMs are running on a trusted cloud node. In the paper, a trusted coordinator and a trusted virtual machine monitor are leveraged to ensure VMs are running on a trusted cluster. The limitation of such a solution is that a trusted coordinator (TC) which is inside an external trusted entity beyond the cloud platform like VeriSign is needed, which makes it hard to be adopted in practice. In addition, they only gave a framework and protocols, but did not implement them. Mudassar Aslam et al. [14] proposed a secure VM launch protocol using Trusted Computing. However, they still focused on the integrity of VM running environment, not the security of the VMs themselves. The difference between our approach and their work is that their work mainly focus on building a trusted execution environment for VMs, such as the trust of host and VMM. But our approach considers the trust of VMs themselves.

Schiffman et al. [13] proposed a centralized verification service called cloud verifier (CV). A user can request to CV to verify the trust of a VM and a host. Nicolae Paladi et al. [15] provided a protocol to ensure the launch of a VM instance. But their method lacks the measurement and remote attestation mechanism for VMs. Moreover , they can not provide a proof-of-concept implementation. In contrast, our TLVM mechanism provides a comprehensive protection approach for VMs. Furthermore, the implementation and evaluation of our approach are given.

6   Conclusions

In this paper, we proposed a trusted launch solution for virtual machine which includes four systematic mechanisms, image encryption, measurement, attestation and security-enhanced authentication, are used to protect a virtual machine in clouds. Image encryption can prevent unauthorized users to initialize a VM. Measurement and attestation mechanism can protect the integrity of a VM. The security-enhanced authentication can achieve two-way authentication between a user and a VM. The mechanisms provide a systematic solution of secure launching a VM. We also discuss a proof-of-concept implementation of our approach. Our experimental results demonstrate the feasibility of our solution to protect the whole launch process of a VM.

Acknowledgment. This work is sponsored by National Natural Science Foundation of China (61173138 and 61103628) and the Huawei Technologies Co., Ltd. collaborative research project.

References

1. Garfinkel, T., Pfaff, B., Chow, J., Rosenblum, M., Boneh, D.: Terra: a virtual machine-based platform for trusted computing. ACM SIGOPS Operating Syst. Rev. **37**(5), 193–206 (2003)
2. Intel Corp. Intel Trusted Execution Technology. http://www.intel.com/technology/security/
3. Intel Corp. Trusted Boot (tboot). http://sourceforge.net/projects/tboot (2007)
4. Azab, A.M., Ning, P., Wang, Z., Jiang, X., Zhang, X., Skalsky, N.C.: HyperSentry: enabling stealthy in-context measurement of hypervisor integrity. In: Proceedings of the 17th ACM Conference on Computer and Communications Security, pp. 38–49. ACM (2010)
5. Dai, W., Jin, H., Zou, D., Xu, S., Zheng, W., Shi, L.: TEE: a virtual DRTM based execution environment for secure cloud-end computing. In: Proceedings of the 17th ACM Conference on Computer and Communications Security (CCS 2010), New York (2010)
6. Challener, D., Yoder, K., Catherman, R.: A Practical Guide to Trusted Computing. Pearson Education, Indianapolis (2008)
7. Brickell, E., Camenisch, J., Chen, L.: Direct anonymous attestation. In: Proceedings of 11th ACM Conference on Computer and Communications Security, ACM Press (2004)
8. Azab, A.M., Ning, P., Zhang, X.: DSICE: a hardware-level strongly isolated computing environment for x86 multi-core platforms. In: Proceedings of the 18th ACM Conference on Computer and Communications Security (CCS '11), pp. 375–388. ACM, New York (2011)
9. Suh, G.E., Clarke, D., Gassend, B., et al.: Hardware mechanisms for memory integrity checking[R]. MIT LCS TR-872 (2003)
10. Maheshwari, U., Vingralek, R., Shapiro, W.: How to build a trusted database system on untrusted storage. In: Proceedings of the 4th USENIX Symposium on Operating System Design and Implementation (2000)
11. Tomonori, F., Masanori, O.: Protecting the integrity of an entire file system. In: First IEEE International Workshop on Information Assurance (2003)
12. Santos, N., Gummadi, K.P., Rodrigues, R.: Towards trusted cloud computing. In: Proceedings of the 2009 Conference on Hot Topics in Cloud Computing, HotCloud2009. USENIX Association, Berkeley (2009)
13. Schiffman, J., Moyer, T., Vijayakumar, H., Jaeger, T., McDaniel, P.: Seeding clouds with trust anchors. In: Proceedings of the 2010 ACM Workshop on CloudComputing Security, CCSW 2010, pp. 43–46. ACM, New York (2010)
14. Aslam, M., Gehrmann, C., Rasmusson, L., Bjorkman, M.: Securely launching virtual machines on trustworthy platforms in a public cloud - an enterprise's perspective. In: Leymann, F., Ivanov, I., van Sinderen, M., Shan, T. (eds.) CLOSER, pp. 511–521. SciTePress, Copenhagen (2012)
15. Paladi, N., Gehrmann, C., Aslam, M., Morenius, F.: Trusted launch of virtual machine instances in public iaas environments. In: Kwon, T., Lee, M.-K., Kwon, D. (eds.) ICISC 2012. LNCS, vol. 7839, pp. 309–323. Springer, Heidelberg (2013)

Dynamic Resource Provisioning in Cloud Computing: A Heuristic Markovian Approach

Hamid Reza Qavami[1(✉)], Shahram Jamali[1], Mohammad K. Akbari[2], and Bahman Javadi[3]

[1] University of Mohaghegh Ardabil, Ardabil, Iran
qavami@gmail.com, jamali@iust.ac.ir
[2] Amirkabir University of Technology, Tehran, Iran
akbarif@aut.ac.ir
[3] University of Western Sydney, Richmond, Australia
b.javadi@uws.edu.au

Abstract. Cloud computing provides more reliable and flexible access to IT resources, which differentiates it from other distributed computer paradigms. Managing the applications efficiently in cloud computing motivates the challenge of provisioning and allocating resource on demand in response to dynamic workloads. Most of investigations have been focused on managing this demand in physical layer and very few in application layer. This paper focuses on resource allocation method in application level that allocates appropriate number of virtual machines to an application which demonstrates a dynamic behavior in terms of resource requirements. By the knowledge of authors this is the first fully estimation based investigation in this field. Experimental results demonstrate that the proposed technique offers more cost effective resource provisioning approach considering cloud user demands.

Keywords: Cloud computing · Dynamic resource provisioning · Adaptive resource provisioning · Estimation · Markov chain

1 Introduction

With recent progressions in Information Technology the need for computations when ever and where ever on the one hand and also the need of individuals and organizations for cost effective heavy duty computation powers on the other hand, have increased the desire for computation as a utility paradigm. Cloud computing is the latest answer to these tendencies where IT resources are offered as services. Cloud computing also offers the user an infinite resource pool (e.g. processing capacity, Memory, Storage etc.); an intrinsic feature of cloud computing that severs it from traditional hosting services.

The fact that the average data center consumption was estimated to be something as many as 25,000 households [1] plus the huge amount of those data centers in the world, clearly shows the necessity of an optimizing resource provisioning policy. In addition an efficient resource provisioning is able to utilize the resources for reducing user payments.

V.C.M. Leung and M. Chen (Eds.): CloudComp 2013, LNICST 133, pp. 102–111, 2014.
DOI: 10.1007/978-3-319-05506-0_10, © Institute for Computer Sciences, Social Informatics and Telecommunications Engineering 2014

Generally the term Resource Provisioning in Cloud Computing is used for the taking in, deploying and managing an application on Cloud infrastructure. One of the main ideas in resource provisioning is to provision resources to applications in a way that reduces power and cost by optimizing and utilizing available resource. Hence some power management techniques are considered in this field in some of investigations. As a whole there are two generic way of resource provisioning:

One is Static Resource Provisioning which usually provides the peak time needed resource all the time for the application. In this kind of provisioning most of the time the resources are wasted because the workload is not peaked in reality. The other is Dynamic Resource Provisioning which its basic fundamental idea is to provision the resources based on the application needs (Fig. 1). This type of provisioning enables cloud provisioner to use pay-as-you-go billing system which is one of the end users' favorite advantages of cloud computing. We have developed a learning based dynamic resource provisioning approach in the present investigation.

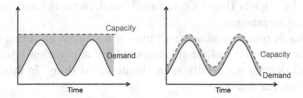

Fig. 1. Static resource provisioning vs. dynamic resource provisioning

The rest of this paper is organized as follows. Section 2 presents a review of related works. Section 3 describes the proposed methodology from approach to implementation. Section 4 discusses experimental results. Section 5 concludes the paper.

2   Related Works

One of the headmost investigations about power management was carried out by Pinheiro et al. [2] the idea was about addressing power conservation for clusters of workstations or PCs. Elnozahy et al. in [3] combined Dynamic Voltage Frequency Scaling with dynamically turning on/off method called VOVO (vary-on/vary off) to reduce power consumption. Kusic et al. [4] used Limited Lookahead Control (LLC). The goal was to maximize the resource provider's profit by minimizing both power consumption and SLA violation. Kalman filter was used to predict the number of next coming requests to predict the future state of the system and perform necessary reallocations. Verma et al. [5] solved the problem of power-aware dynamic placement of applications using Bin Packing problem. Van et al. [6] developed an optimization method and by modeling both provisioning and allocating problem they used Constraint Satisfaction Problem (CSP). Lin et al. [7] purposed a new Round Robin algorithm called Dynamic Round Robin (DRR) to allocation and migration of Virtual Machines between hosts. Lin et al. [8] introduced a dynamic Virtual Machine-Varying

Based resource allocation using a threshold. Using this threshold their algorithm decides that the current counts of virtual machines which are assigned to an application are sufficient or not, it is the same for over provisioning. The basic differences and advantages of our study as compared to the latter are that first, our work does not need any human admin interferences and is able to approximate next workload instead of a reactive action. Calheiros [9] et al. addressed workload prediction and resource adaption using a queuing model and analytical performance, like previous work, there is a human control parameter in this.

Iqbal et al. [10] aimed a bottle neck detection system for multi tier web application using a heuristic approach, this mechanism is able to detect bottle necks in every tier of system. Jeyarani et al. in [11] developed a dispatcher using a new PSO (Particle Swarm Optimization) method Called SAPSO (Self-Adaptive PSO) to dispatch virtual machine instances among physical servers efficiently. Zaman et al. [12] showed a new bid based (capital market model) approach for responding to the users' requests. Islam et al. [13] advanced a new machine learning technique by developing a Neural Network system called ECNN (Error Correction Neural Network) and using it side by side with a Linear Regression.

Most of methods relied on allocating physical resources to virtual resources and load balancing methods. Few of them considered the application layer. And among these rare studies there is not a fully approximate based study. In this paper authors tried to cover these leakages.

3   Proposed Methodology

We explored a number of existing investigations on resource provisioning techniques, some of them like [8] and [10] seemed to be good but not feasible in a real cloud environment, because they are reactive approaches and take action when the workload has already arrived, while creating a virtual machine is not instantaneous. The other problem is dependencies on parameters like [9], which is not favorable for an autonomous system. Also, more complexity imposes more overhead in a system. It will make an approach difficult to be accepted. Considering all above, we have chosen a simple learning system which is fully autonomous. The system can predict future needs of a cloud application using estimations. A quasi-DTMC[1] [14] heuristic approach which is suitable for dynamic workloads has been chosen to overcome the variety of the environment. The proposed method is not too complex so it can be implemented for each user in Cloud manager or in broker, even in the client side of the cloud system.

3.1   Approach

A basic discrete time Markov Chain (DTMC) is a memory less system with finite or countable number of states and transitions between them. The term memory less

---

[1] Discrete-time Markov chain.

means that the following action (state) depends only on current state and not preceding events. Each state have the probability P_i which indicates the happening chance of state i. In each state there are transitions to the other states with probability $\pi_{i,j}$ which means transition probability from state (i) to state (j). When we are in state (i) and $\pi_{i,j}$ exist, the chance of going to state (j) is $P_i \times \pi_{i,j}$ While $\Sigma_j \, \pi_{i,j} = 1$ and $\Sigma_k \, P_k = 1$.

In presented model, there is a state output diagram just like DTMC and there are transition probabilities $\pi_{i,j}$ too, although with some differences. Here we have $\Sigma_m \Sigma_n \pi_{m,n} = 1$.

There is not any probability for each state individually here but just alike the former one new state depends on the previous one. Probabilities $\pi_{i,j}$ are not fixed anymore and they vary during the time depending on the environment changes. New state is chosen based on previous state and the $\pi_{i,j}$ between them which owns the greatest chance to choose.

Beside the state machine a learning part works as well. The learning algorithm is a punishment/reward based one and uses the average virtual machines utilization as a feedback to understand which action among is the proper action. Also in each state, when the corresponding action must be taken, the learning algorithm would control the aggression amount of the action looking to virtual machines utilization.

For a state diagram system with (N) transitions there are these relations for initialization and carrying on the work:

In the beginning the chance of all transitions is equal and would be initiated using these equations:

$$\Pi_{m,n} = \frac{1}{N} \tag{1}$$

The learning algorithm rewards the transition chance to the proper state from current state and punishes the other transitions by decreasing their chance. Considering the punishment value as a Decrement Step, the reward (Increment Step) would be gained as below:

$$\text{IncrementStep} = (N - 1)\,\text{Decrement Step} \tag{2}$$

Using mentioned principles for this investigation, a three state machine with seven ($N = 7$) transitions, was developed to control the number of allocated VMs to a specific workload dynamically (Fig. 2):

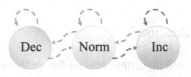

Fig. 2. Proposed state machine

Decrement state (briefly Dec) means that the workload was over provisioned, Normal state (briefly Norm) means that the workload was provisioned just enough and Increment state (briefly Inc) means that the workload was under provisioned.

Global transition updates provide a short memory for the system and this is one of the key differences to the DTMC.

3.2   Problem Formulation

The purpose of this study is to minimize the amount of rented virtual machines from the provider by the user, considering application demands. For a particular arriving workload (W) we want to minimize the number of virtual machine instances while providing appropriate amount of resources for the application. So the total processing power in MIPS[2] must be greater than total workload in MI[3] (Fig. 3):

$$\text{Object for: } \min \left(\sum_{n=1}^{MaxVM} VMlist_n^W \right) \tag{3}$$

$$\text{Subject to: } \sum_{1}^{MaxOnlineVMs} MIPS_{VirtualMachines} > \sum_{1}^{CurrentCloudLetNumber} MI_{CloudLets} \tag{4}$$

Also the average utilization of virtual machines under workload (W) with allocated virtual machine number (OnlineVMs) is needed to be calculated which has been formulated as below:

$$VMs\ Avg.\ Utilization^W = \frac{\sum_{i=1}^{OnlineVMs} VM_i^W\ Utilization}{OnlineVMs} \tag{5}$$

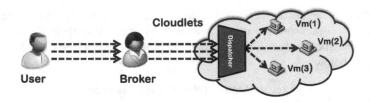

Fig. 3. Implemented architecture in Cloudsim. System contains two basic components. First is a broker allocated out of the cloud body which observes application workloads (from the cloud user's side) and communicates with cloud (provider) to adapt resources. The other is a dispatcher in cloud body which allocates VMs to workload appropriately.

4   Performance Evaluation

The proposed Learning Based algorithm (called Smart Virtual Machine Provisioner - SVMP) is implemented using Cloudsim which is suitable for resource provisioning simulating [15]. However this tool typically is not able to simulate Dynamic Virtual

---

[2] Million Instructions Per Second.

[3] Million Instructions.

Machine provisioning beside the disability to resource provisioning in application layer, which the authors purpose to simulate, so new components and attributes have been added to the simulator to enable it to handle Dynamic VM provisioning in application layer.

Apart from SVMP, a workload dispatcher was developed to dispatch user workloads (called cloudlets in the Cloudsim) among available VM instances. This dispatcher fulfills each VM with incoming cloudlets until VM utilization is under 80 %, the remaining 20 % is reserved for eventual heavy loads. With this method VMs would be utilized in a reasonable manner, moreover over provisioned VMs remain empty of load and can be easily shutdown. For some cases like web servers this threshold is considered 85 % [10, 16], but SVMP is designed for more general applications besides it is a learning based system and take some time to learn, so our threshold was set to 80 %.

Based on decision table (Table 1), if the algorithm was in the proper state it would do the right action, else it would update the probabilities into the proper state and do the action of the current state (although it is not the proper one) until it reaches (so Learns) the right action. The aggression of actions differs and learning system decides how many virtual machine(s) must be added or to be removed based on the average utilization amount.

Table 1. Decision table of the algorithm.

	Average utilization > 80	80 ≥ Average utilization≥70	Average utilization < 70
Probably condition	Under provisioned	Normal	Over provisioned
Proper state to be select	Inc	Norm	Dec
Action of the state	Add VM(s)	Do nothing	Remove VM(s)

To evaluate our proposed system, we performed three experiments using three different approaches. 1st and 2nd experiments demonstrate the cloud behavior using two specific static provisioning approaches. Experiment 3 shows the cloud behavior using the proposed dynamic VM provisioner.

The system has been tested under Normal Distribution Workload (Fig. 4). The workload starts from small amount of MI, then goes to a peak and then starts falling; this pattern happens a lot in real word with different peaks and slopes.

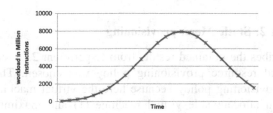

Fig. 4. Workload generation profile for all experiments.

As mentioned before, we have simulated our study using Cloudsim with three different experiments. First of all for demonstrating the studies we have defined a scenario as below (Table 2):

Table 2. SLA parameters for running the scenario

SLA parameters				
Workload type	Max VMs	VMs CPU core(s)	Core processing power	VMs RAM
CPU intensive	30	1	250 MIPS	512 MB

Cloud user deploys an application in the cloud on several virtual machines (Web server e.g.).

4.1 Experiment 1: Static Max Provisioning (Over Provisioning)

Experiment 1 describes behavior of the system under a static provision policy using the maximal virtual resource provisioning. Number of virtual machines is 30 instances. We have obtained this number considering the maximum virtual machine number provisioned by our dynamic approach. So the processing power is would be 12000 MIPS (Fig. 7), constantly. Figure 5 demonstrates average VMs utilization during this Experiment.

There is not any saturation area in this plot which means there is not any under provisioning. This is completely expectable because this is an over provisioning policy. However the highest average utilization of virtual machines that was obtained is 66.25 % (Fig. 5). This means high amount of waste in resources. This usual type of traditional resource provisioning for applications inflicts unnecessary cost to the application extender as a cloud user.

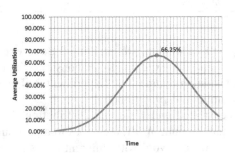

Fig. 5. Average utilization of provisioned virtual machines during Experiment 1.

4.2 Experiment 2: Static Mean provisioning

This section describes the obtained results from Experiment 2. A static provisioning using mean virtual resource provisioning policy was chosen. The term mean is referred to this provisioning policy because here the virtual machine number is the mean of minimum allocate able virtual machine (1) and maximum allocate able virtual machine (used in previous experiment). So the processing power is 6000 MIPS (Fig. 7), constantly. Obviously this is a conservative strategy which is cheaper than latter strategy. However this approach is not able to detect saturation in virtual machines so user suffers from under provisioning in time that workload is above average. The average utilization generally seems better (Fig. 6) comparing to Experiment 1, but both under and over utilization problems are still remained.

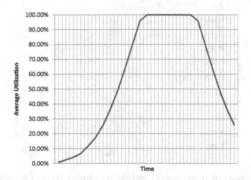

Fig. 6. Average utilization of provisioned virtual machines during Experiment 2.

4.3   Experiment 3: Dynamic Provisioning Using Proposed System

This section describes the results of Experiment 3 using our proposed algorithm, the SVMP (Smart Virtual Machine Provisioner). Unless two previous approaches this is an adaptive approach. The processing power is adapting to the workload and is not constant any more (Fig. 7). First system starts from normal state and tries to evaluate the environment and guesses the next state of the workload. The SVMP curve flat areas in Fig. 7 are the times that system is in normal or learning state.

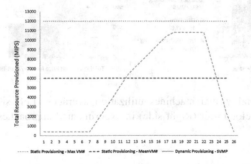

Fig. 7. Comparing total MIPS estimated and provisioned by different approaches.

SVMP tries to meet application needs in one hand and reducing cloud user cost in the other. By utilizing allocated virtual machines to user's workload, number of provisioned virtual resources to user is reduced. So here total utilization of virtual machines is the feedback parameter so becomes very important. As Fig. 8 demonstrates the SVMP tries to keep this utilization up and where ever this amount drops, it will bring it back up (Fig. 8. The Point **B**) by removing unnecessary allocated virtual machines. Besides that, SVMP detects under provisions– when utilization grows and goes to 100 % – and pulls it down by adding extra virtual machines up (Fig. 8. The Point **A**), so keeps Qos parameters.

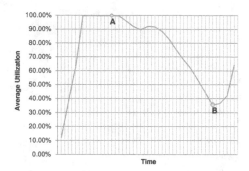

Fig. 8. Average utilization of provisioned virtual machines during Experiment 3. The SVMP detects application demands by monitoring utilization of virtual machines and scales up or down when resources are under or over provisioned, respectively.

From experimental result it can be extracted that SVMP owns not only the best average utilization and price (Fig. 9) even the least saturation time among the all (Figs. 6, 8). Both results show advantages of proposed dynamic provisioning approach (SVMP) comparing to the static provisioning method.

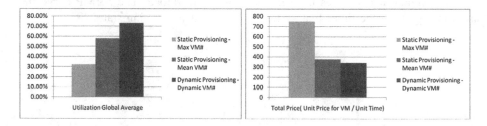

Fig. 9. Comparing total virtual machines utilization averages (Left side) and total virtual machines cost for the cloud user (Right side) in experimented approaches.

5   Conclusion

Dynamic resource provisioning enables cloud users to execute their tasks considering QoS elements in more cost effective way. A true application layer dynamic resource provisioner must predict the users' workload and provide the resources before workload arrival; this is important because providing resources in this layer (virtual machines) is not instantaneous and for a virtual machine instance it takes some time to start and become functional. The experiment presented in this paper addressed dynamic resource provisioning with a learning based system called SVMP to reduce the cost while keeping requirements of cloud user application. We are currently extending our system to employ other learning algorithm to improve performance of resource provisioning scheme.

References

1. Kaplan, J., Forrest, W., Kindler, N.: Revolutionizing Data Center Energy Efficiency. McKinsey & Company (2008)
2. Pinheiro, E., et al.: Load balancing and unbalancing for power and performance in cluster-based systems. In: Proceedings of the Workshop on Compilers and Operating *Systems* for Low Power (2001)
3. Elnozahy, E.N.M., Kistler, J.J., Rajamony, R.: Energy-efficient server clusters. In: Falsafi, B., VijayKumar, T.N. (eds.) PACS 2002. LNCS, vol. 2325, pp. 179–196. Springer, Heidelberg (2003)
4. Kusic, D., et al.: Power and performance management of virtualized computing environments via lookahead control. In: Proceedings of the 2008 International Conference on Autonomic Computing, pp. 3–12. IEEE Computer Society (2008)
5. Verma, A., Ahuja, P., Neogi, A.: pMapper: power and migration cost aware application placement in virtualized systems. In: Issarny, V., Schantz, R. (eds.) Middleware 2008. LNCS, vol. 5346, pp. 243–264. Springer, Heidelberg (2008)
6. Van, H.N., Tran, F.D., Menaud, J.M.: Performance and power management for cloud infrastructures. In: 2010 IEEE 3rd International Conference on Cloud Computing (CLOUD) (2010)
7. Lin, C.-C., Liu, P., Wu, J.-J.: Energy-aware virtual machine dynamic provision and scheduling for cloud computing. In: 2011 IEEE International Conference on Cloud Computing (CLOUD) (2011)
8. Lin, W., et al.: A threshold-based dynamic resource allocation scheme for cloud computing. Procedia Eng. **23**, 695–703 (2011)
9. Calheiros, R.N., Ranjan, R., Buyya, R.: Virtual machine provisioning based on analytical performance and QoS in cloud computing environments. In: 2011 International Conference on Parallel Processing (ICPP) (2011)
10. Iqbal, W., et al.: Adaptive resource provisioning for read intensive multi-tier applications in the cloud. Future Gener. Comput. Syst. **27**(6), 871–879 (2011)
11. Jeyarani, R., Nagaveni, N., Vasanth Ram, R.: Design and implementation of adaptive power-aware virtual machine provisioner (APA-VMP) using swarm intelligence. Future Gener. Comput. Syst. **28**(5), 811–821 (2012)
12. Zaman, S., Grosu, D.: An online mechanism for dynamic VM provisioning and allocation in clouds. In: 2012 IEEE 5th International Conference on Cloud Computing (CLOUD) (2012)
13. Islam, S., et al.: Empirical prediction models for adaptive resource provisioning in the cloud. Future Gener. Comput. Syst. **28**(1), 155–162 (2012)
14. Papoulis, A., Pillai, S.U.: Probability, Random Variables and Stochastic Processes, vol. 1, 4th edn., 852 p. McGraw-Hill, Boston (2002)
15. Buyya, R., Ranjan, R., Calheiros, R.N.: Modeling and simulation of scalable Cloud computing environments and the CloudSim toolkit: Challenges and opportunities. In: International Conference on High Performance Computing & Simulation 2009 (HPCS '09), (2009)
16. Allspaw, J.: The Art of Capacity Planning: Scaling Web Resources. O'Reilly Media, Sebastopol (2008)

Cloud-Assisted Pervasive Computing and Services

Research on Sports Teaching Resource Platform Based on Cloud Computing

Zhang Jian[1] and Song Wanjuan[2(✉)]

[1] College of Sport Engineering and Information Technology,
Wuhan Institute of Physical Education, Wuhan, China
[2] College of Computer, Hubei University of Education, Wuhan, China
zjgo1979@163.com

Abstract. To improve sports teaching, the sports teaching resource platform based on cloud computing is designed. This paper introduces the structure of Cloud Computing and its functions firstly. And then we describe this platform's framework and its module. According to the advantages of Cloud Computing we discuss how this platform is arranged in the Cloud Computing. So this platform can store multimedia material efficiently. And Teachers can share the sports multimedia material and design a dynamic courseware in this platform. The students can view this dynamic courseware through the platform's GUI. So it will be convenient for students to learn themselves.

Keywords: Cloud Computing · Sports teaching · Multimedia database · Dynamic courseware

1 Introduction

Now, many of universities have their own teaching resource management systems [1]. But there are some same problems in these systems such as the restrictions of storing multimedia data, or insufficient sharing. And other problems caused by these such as the flexibility of system is not enough and utilization rate is not high [2]. All of these restrict the popularization of information technology in education and are unfavourable for the teacher's teaching and student's learning.

And in the traditional sports teaching teachers always show the sports action themselves. Even in the sports theory teaching they seldom use courseware. This is related to the way of sports teaching. And at the same time this is also related to the computer technology which the teachers know. This teaching module has obvious disadvantage. If students want to review the content of courses, they will only depend on their memory. And if a teacher can not grasp a new sports technology completely, he can not teach his students.

This work was supported by the Huber Provincial Department of Education (No. B2013304 and No. B2013016).

V.C.M. Leung and M. Chen (Eds.): CloudComp 2013, LNICST 133, pp. 115–121, 2014.
DOI: 10.1007/978-3-319-05506-0_11, © Institute for Computer Sciences, Social Informatics and Telecommunications Engineering 2014

The sports teaching resource platform based on cloud computing is designed to solve above problems [3, 4]. This platform has the advantages of cloud computing such as super computing power, storage capacity and performance [5]. And teachers can share the sports multimedia material and design a dynamic courseware in this platform. Teachers can upload the multimedia material such as text, picture, voice and video to the platform which is in the cloud computing service. Platform will manage them. It can share the resource completely. Teachers can design teaching program in this platform and add different types of multimedia material to the program. After this, a dynamic courseware will be complete. The students can view this dynamic courseware through the platform's GUI. So it will be convenient for students to learn themselves. And platform can provide a succinct program editing function. The advantages are simple operation and easy to use. Even the teachers who operate computer unskilled also can design a good teaching program and multimedia courseware.

2 The Overview of Cloud Computing

There is not a general concept module about Cloud Computing. It is a development of Parallel Computing, Distributed Computing and Grid Computing. It includes concepts of Virtualization, Utility Computing, Iaas (Infrastructure as a Service), Paas (Platform as a Service) SaaS (Software as a Service) [3, 4]. Generally speaking, Cloud Computing can concentrate the resource in the network and provide many services (Computing, storage and software) for network users. According to the actual demand, users can get service resource any time and any place. Cloud Computing is a new concept. It breaks the resource constraints in the traditional module. As long as the users connect the network, they will get super computing ability, storage ability and software resource.

Cloud Computing can manage and schedule a lot of computer resource in the network such hard disk, platform and service. This forms a resource pool to provide services for users. Its architecture is given in Fig. 1.

The architecture of Cloud Computing includes fore layers: physical resource, resource pool, management middleware and SOA (Service-Oriented Architecture). The physical resource includes computer, storage, network equipment, database and software. Resource pool assembles the resource as their types. The main works of resource pool are assembling and management. Management middleware manages the resource of Cloud Computing. And it also schedules the application tasks and makes the resource provide efficient and security service. SOA packages the performance of Cloud Computing as a standard web services and manages it. Resource pool and management middleware are the primary keys of architecture. The functions of SOA most depend on external features.

The works of management middleware are resource management, task management, user management and security management. Resource management balances every point of cloud resource and detects the point's failure and recovers or shields it. At the same time it will monitor and gather the data of resource. Task management

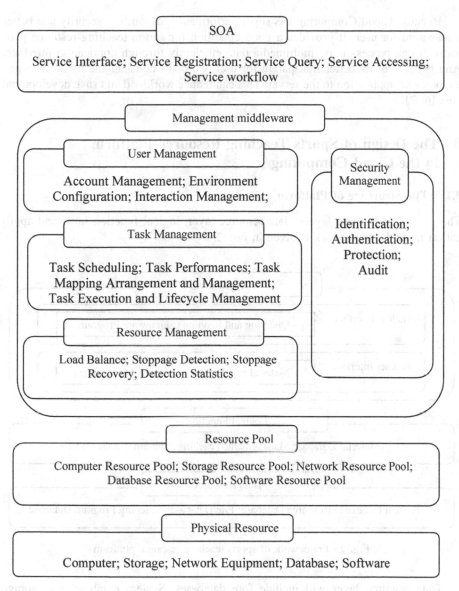

Fig. 1. Architecture of cloud computing

will perform the mission which is submitted by user or application. It includes the arrangement and management of user task mapping, task scheduling, task execution and the task lifecycle management. User management is important for accomplishing the business module of Cloud Computing. It includes providing user interface, managing and identifying the user, creating the environment for user's program and counting the cost. Security management can ensure the device safety. It includes identification, authentication, protection and audit.

Because Cloud Computing has super performance, capability, security and better transparent for user, it provides a good condition for sports teaching resource platform. It can process mass multimedia data efficiently through application interface. And because of its better transparent for user, we don't consider the hardware when we place an application to the server. This can reduce workload and save development cost [6, 7].

3   The Design of Sports Teaching Resource Platform in the Cloud Computing

3.1   The Structure of Platform

The platform has three layers: data resource layer, logical function layer and application layer. Its framework is given in Fig. 2.

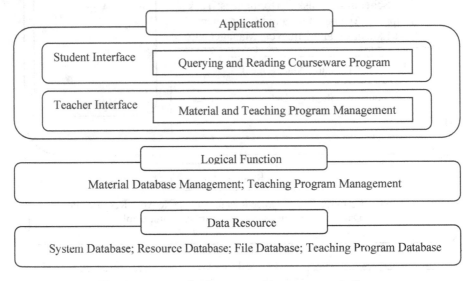

Fig. 2. Framework of sports teaching resource platform

Data resource layer will include fore databases. System database will storage system information such as user information. Resource database will store the ordinary teaching material such as text and image. File database will store special multimedia material such as voice and video. Teaching program database will store the final teaching program. This structure can depart the data as its logic and facilitate to arrange database.

Logical function layer will realize the logic between resource data and teaching program. It will process data as its type. At the same time it will accept the user's service request and return the result to the user. There are two modules in this layer:

(a) The module of material database. This module will manage the multimedia material database including adding and deleting material, and creating, altering and dropping the type of material, and querying material.
(b) The module of teaching program. Through this module user can design a teaching program, select appropriate material from database and add it to the teaching program. So a dynamic courseware is shown to us. The operation will include adding, altering and delete the material for program, and saving and sharing the program.

Application layer will provide different service interface for different user. The students can query and read the courseware program through the student interface. Through the teacher interface teachers can manager their own course and its material database. The teachers who teach same course can share this course's material database and edit their own teaching program.

3.2   The Development of Sports Teaching Resource Database

3.2.1   The Development of Multimedia Material Resource

This development is the kernel of system. The multimedia information has different type and includes large data. It is hard to store in the normal database. Especially in the sports students are interested in animation and video. Only text courseware is not appropriate for teaching. And Cloud Computing has powerful processing capability. It can manage and store multimedia information efficiently. At the same time it also provides the functions of querying, uploading and downloading.

The material resource is managed by teacher. Every course has a director. This director will check the multimedia material. Other teachers who have same course can upload the multimedia material and share it each other.

3.2.2   The Development of Teaching Program Resource

The teaching program resource is an characteristic of system. The ordinary CAI software always adds all the multimedia material in the courseware. This is inconvenient for updating, storing and conveying. In this part, we propose a method about teaching program based on Cloud Computing. Teachers can not edit a courseware by pages. This courseware will be replaced by class program. Its materials will come from the multimedia material database in the Cloud Computing. When the teachers design a class program, they only need find an appropriate resource from the database and link it to the program. Then a dynamic courseware is finished. And it will be stored into database. The students who learn this course can query these teaching programs through the interface. When students want to learn a section in the class program, the material linked to this section will be shown. If the teachers find a better material, they will only edit the link about this program and will not adjustment the whole program.

3.3   The Design of Platform

This platform placed on the Cloud Computing. It can improve the degree of resource sharing and constructing. And it can also implement the storage functions of large capacity and high speed about multimedia information. For the clients, they can view the teaching resource from the browser and can not install any other software. The server program can upload to a Cloud Computing Platform. It can save the money using to buy hardware and can provide the high quality information services (Fig. 3).

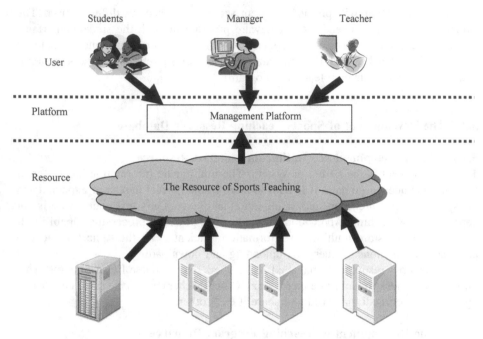

Fig. 3. The design of sports teaching resource platform

This design can utilize advantages of the Cloud Computing in the resource sharing and service. Users can get information they need from the complex and different construction data source. And at the same time the resource service will be intelligence. The resource sharing will be ultimate extent.

4   Conclusions

This paper designs a sports teaching resources platform based on cloud computing and discuss the structure of this platform and the arrangement in the Cloud Computing. Cloud Computing service can concentrate and integrate the sports teaching resources. It can provide open service about resource sharing for the network users. Placing the teaching resource to the Cloud Computing is an effective solution for ultimate sharing of teaching resource.

References

1. Jiling, Z.: Network education mode of information technology research and practice that based on constructivism learning theory. Exam. Week **54** (2010)
2. Hu, L.: The malpractice and strategy of over dependence on the multimedia in college teachiing. In: The Memoir of the Second Nationwide Agriculture and Forestry Colleges Educational Science Postgraduate Academic Forum (2010)
3. Foster, I., Zhao, Y., Raicu, I., Lu, S.: Cloud computing and grid computing 360-degree compared. In: Grid Computing Environments Workshop, pp. 1–10 (2008)
4. Kaplan, J., Forrest, W., Kindler, N.: Revolutionizing data center energy efficiency. Technical report, McKinsey & Company (2008)
5. Gruman, G., Knorr, E.: What cloud computing really means. Technical report, Info World Inc. (2008)
6. Environmental Protection Agency: EPA report to congress on server and data center energy efficiency. Technical report, US Congress (2007)
7. Brill, K.: The invisible crisis in the data center: The economic meltdown of Moore's law. Technical report, Uptime Institute (2007)

Delay-Optimized Offloading for Mobile Cloud Computing Services in Heterogenous Networks

Kan Zheng[1]([✉]), Hanlin Meng[1], Hua Zhu[1], Kai Lin[2], Wei Cai[3], and Hang Long[1]

[1] Wireless Signal Processing & Network Lab, Key laboratory of Universal Wireless Communication, Ministry of Education, Beijing University of Posts & Telecommunications, Beijing 100088, China
zkan@bupt.edu.cn
[2] School of Computer Science and Engineering, Dalian University of Technology, Dalian, Liaoning, China
[3] Electrical and Computer University of British Columbia, Vancouver V6T 1Z4, Canada

Abstract. Offloading is an efficient method for extending the lifetime and speeding up the execution rate of mobile devices by executing remotely in mobile cloud computing (MCC) networks. Meanwhile, heterogeneous network (HetNet), which has multiple types of radio access nodes in the network, is widely accepted as a promising way to satisfy the increased traffic demand. In this paper, we first propose two delay-optimized offloading control schemes in LTE-Advanced heterogeneous networks. One of them is to control the number of offloading users by setting a threshold. Another is to determine whether the users are suited to offload by estimating the execution delay. Both of them take the traffic load of serving cell and neighbouring cells into account. For comparison purpose, the delay performance of different schemes are evaluated by simulations in not only heterogeneous network but also macro-only network.

Keywords: Mobile cloud computing (MCC) · Heterogeneous Network (HetNet) · Offloading

1 Introduction

In recent years, mobile cloud computing (MCC) is introduced as an integration of cloud computing into the mobile environment to overcome the limitations of mobile devices (MDs). However, it has to face many technical challenges because of the integration of two different fields [1]. One of the challenges is computing offloading technique. It is proposed to migrate the large computations and complex processing from resource-limited MDs to remote servers with the objective of extending the battery life and speeding up the operating rate, which avoids requiring changes in the structure or hardware equipment [2]. Experiments in [3] show that offloading is not always the effective way to improve performance.

V.C.M. Leung and M. Chen (Eds.): CloudComp 2013, LNICST 133, pp. 122–131, 2014.
DOI: 10.1007/978-3-319-05506-0_12, © Institute for Computer Sciences, Social Informatics and Telecommunications Engineering 2014

So how to offload the application to the remote servers becomes very important at present.

There are generally two kinds of offloading techniques, called full offloading and partial offloading. Full offloading is to move all computation tasks of mobile applications from the MD to the remote cloud. However, different computation tasks of an application may have different characteristics that make them more or less suitable for offloading. Application can offload only the sub-parts that benefit from the remote execution for more energy saving. So partial offloading has gained more attention, where the application is divides into unoffloadble tasks and offloadble parts. In [4], a simple but basis model is proposed to analyze whether the energy can be saved by computation offloading. It is shown that moving image processing to the remote server reduces 41 % for energy consumption [5]. System is modeled within a Markovian dynamic control framework [6], in which the associated energy versus delay trade-off is studied. The power consumption is minimized in [7] by solving two constrained optimization problems, which are setting the optimal clock frequency of local processor and data transmission rate of each time slot for cloud execution within time delay. Then the offloading decision is made with smaller energy consumption. A dynamic offloading algorithm based on Lyapunov optimization is proposed in [8] to make the offloading decision for all the computation tasks while satisfying given application execution time requirement.

Although existing works have improved the basic model from various aspects, there are still some open problems, especially when the offloading data is transmitted via heterogeneous network (Hetnet), in which the base stations with lower transmit power (e.g., pico, femto, really eNodeB) are deployed besides the macro eNodeB with high transmit power [9]. The offloading decision of an application is made based on the estimation of execution time or energy consumption. However, almost no literature considers traffic load of MD's serving cell and neighboring cells which may affects the offloading decision so far. Traffic load at MD's serving cell impacts on wireless channel gains at the scheduling instants of MDs. Meanwhile, the increased traffic load in the neighboring cells may results in heavy interference situation. Both of them may affect power consumption and execution delay. Therefore, we propose the delay-optimized offloading control schemes in Hetnet environment with the consideration of traffic load, which reduces the average delay of all the mobile users. Simulation results demonstrate the effectiveness of the proposed scheme in terms of average delay.

This paper is organized as follows. Section 2 gives a brief overview of the system and problem formulation. The delay-optimized offloading control schemes are proposed in Sect. 3. Then, Sect. 4 gives the simulation results. Finally, Sect. 5 concludes this paper.

2   System Model

The LTE-Advanced heterogenous network with macrocell and picocell is considered in this paper. An picocell eNodeB is deployed in each sector of macrocell [10]. There are M sectors in a single macrocell.

2.1   Flow Model

A dynamic flow model with elastic traffic for mobile applications is assumed, where a new flow arrives at the network with a finite-length file request, and leaves the system after the file is transmitted. The flow of user n arriving at cell m in the network follows a Poisson distribution with an average arrival rate of $\lambda_n^{(m)}$. There are N_m active users served by the eNodeB in cell $m, 0 \leq m \leq M$. Note that cell 0 represents the macrocell while others indicate picocells.

The main purposes of computation offloading are to save the power consumption of MDs and speed up the application processing. However, the above two goals may not always be achieved depending on the particulars of the computation task, the server load, and the connectivity to the network. For example, a task with high computation and low communication requirements is more likely to benefit from offloading than a task with low computation and high communication requirements. Therefore, a judicious decision has to be made on whether to offload a computation task or not. For simplicity, a mobile application is assumed to be executed either locally in the mobile device or remotely in the remote cloud servers by full offloading. Let the binary vector $\mathbf{B}^{(m)} = \{b_n^{(m)}|b_n^{(m)} \in \{0,1\}\}_{1 \times N_m}$ describe the offloading decision, where $b_n^{(m)} = 1$ denotes that the application of user n in cell m is executed locally, otherwise $b_n^{(m)} = 0$.

2.2   Network Model

For offloading cases, the total execution time for an application consists of the time spent sending the task and data to the cloud servers, idly waiting for the cloud to complete the task, and receiving the result of the task. However, due to the large computation ability of cloud servers, the delay caused by the wireless transmission between the MD and cloud servers especially in the uplink may dominate the total execution time. In this case, the data transmission rate between the mobile device and cloud servers has significant impact on offloading decisions.

The basic radio resource unit for OFDM transmission can be described as a two-dimensional (2-D) time-frequency grid that corresponds to a set of OFDM symbols and subcarriers in the time and frequency domains. In LTE-Advanced networks, the basic unit for data transmission is a pair of resource blocks (RBs) that correspond to a 180-kHz bandwidth during a 1 ms subframe. In this paper, all the radio resources, i.e., K RBs, are assumed to be fully reused between picocells and macrocell. Let the binary matrix $\mathbf{A}^{(m)} = \{a_{k,n}^{(m)}|a_{k,n}^{(m)} \in \{0,1\}\}_{K \times N_m}$ describe the resource allocation among the users, where $a_{k,n}^{(m)} = 1$ denotes that RB k in cell m is assigned to user n, otherwise $a_{k,n}^{(m)} = 0$. Then, the achievable rate of user n on RB k in cell m is given by

$$\eta_{k,n}^{(m)} = W \log_2 \left(1 + \frac{\beta_n^{(m)} h_{k,n}^{(m)} P_{k,n}^{(m)}}{\zeta_{k,n}^{(m)} + \sigma_N^2} \right), \tag{1}$$

$$1 \leq k \leq K \,, 1 \leq n \leq N_m \,, 0 \leq m \leq M \,,$$

where W is the bandwidth per RB, $\beta_n^{(m)}$ is the pathloss (PL) from the eNodeB in cell m to user n, $P_{k,n}^{(m)}$ is the transmit power of user n at RB k in cell m, $h_{k,n}^{(m)}$ is the independent, identically distributed (i.i.d.) Rayleigh fading channel gain between the eNodeB in cell m to user n at RB k, i.e., $h_{k,n}^{(m)} \sim \mathcal{CN}(0, \sigma^2)$[1], with $\sigma^2 = \mathbb{E}[|h_{k,n}^{(m)}|^2]$, σ_N^2 is the noise power of the additive white Gaussian noise (AWGN), and $\zeta_{k,n}^{(m)}$ is the interference between cells, i.e.

$$\zeta_{k,n}^{(m)} = \sum_{j=0, j \neq m}^{M} \sum_{i=1}^{N_j} a_{k,i}^{(j)} b_i^{(j)} \beta_i^{(j)} h_{k,i}^{(j)} P_{k,i}^{(j)} . \tag{2}$$

3   Delay-Optimized Offloading Control Schemes

3.1   Delay Analysis

If an application of user n in cell m is decided to be offloading to cloud servers for processing, the total execution time can be calculated by

$$\tau_n^{(m)} = \tau_{U,n}^{(m)} + \tau_{C,n}^{(m)} + \tau_{D,n}^{(m)} , \tag{3}$$

where $\tau_{U,n}^{(m)}$ and $\tau_{D,n}^{(m)}$ denotes the transmission delay in the uplink and downlink, respectively, and $\tau_{C,n}^{(m)}$ is the idle time waiting for cloud to complete the task. Compared to the transmission delay, the processing time in cloud servers is quite smaller and can be omitted. On the other hand, some kind of typical cloud computing services has much more amount of task data in the uplink than of the completed result in the downlink. Moreover, the uplink transmission ability is usually the bottleneck of the wireless networks instead of the downlink. Therefore, the total execution time may approximately equal to the delay due to uplink transmission, i.e.

$$\tau_n^{(m)} \approx \tau_{U,n}^{(m)} . \tag{4}$$

Otherwise, this application is executed in the mobile device with the local execution time $\tau_{L,n}^{(m)}$. Then, the average delay of all the users in the heterogenous network can be expressed by

$$\overline{\tau} = \frac{1}{\sum_{m=0}^{M} N_m} \sum_{m=0}^{M} \sum_{n=1}^{N_m} \{ b_n^{(m)} \tau_{U,n}^{(m)} + (1 - b_n^{(m)}) \tau_{L,n}^{(m)} \} . \tag{5}$$

As we know, the delay due to uplink transmission is highly determined by the achievable data rate $\mu_n^{(m)}$ and the byte number of the transmitted data $D_n^{(m)}$, i.e.

$$\tau_{U,n}^{(m)} = \frac{D_n^{(m)}}{\mu_n^{(m)}} . \tag{6}$$

---

[1] A circularly symmetric complex Gaussian RV x with mean m and covariance R is denoted by $x \sim \mathcal{CN}(m, R)$.

It is noted that the different offloading control scheme and scheduling algorithm may result in the different achievable data rate, i.e.

$$\mu_n^{(m)} = \sum_{k=1}^{K} a_{k,n}^{(m)} b_n^{(m)} \eta_{k,n}^{(m)} . \tag{7}$$

Meanwhile, the local execution time $\tau_{L,n}^{(m)}$ can be given by

$$\tau_{L,n}^{(m)} = \frac{C_n^{(m)}}{X_n^{(m)}} , \tag{8}$$

where $C_n^{(m)}$ is the computation complexity for application in term of instruction number, and $X_n^{(m)}$ is the speed of the local execution at user n.

3.2   Delay-Optimal Offloading Control Scheme

The offloading decision problem is to find $\mathbf{A}$ and $\mathbf{B}$ such that an objective function is optimized. In this paper, the optimization problem with the objective of minimizing the average system delay is needed to be solved for offloading decision, i.e.

$$\arg\min_{\mathbf{A},\mathbf{B}} \overline{\tau} ,$$

$$s.t. \quad a_{k,n}^{(m)} \in \{0,1\} ,$$

$$b_n^{(m)} \in \{0,1\} ,$$

$$1 \le k \le K , 1 \le n \le N_m , 0 \le m \le M . \tag{9}$$

By integrating (6), (7) and (8) into (9), we can easily find that the optimization problem is non-concave. To find its optimal solution, exhaustive search over all the possible solution set is needed, which has prohibitively high computational complexity. Therefore, considering the implementation feasibility, it is necessary to deal with the offloading decision problem in the heterogenous network by other methods.

For simplicity, not only the computation complexity of application but also the speed of the local execution for all users are assumed to be same, i.e., $C_n^{(m)} = C$ and $X_n^{(m)} = X$. Then, the local execution time $\tau_{L,n}^{(m)}$ becomes the constant, i.e., $\tau_{L,n}^{(m)} = \tau_L = C/X$. Moreover, the amount of data bytes that needed to be transmitted on the link for all users is assumed to be fixed, i.e., $D_n^{(m)} = D$. Now, the average delay of all the users in the heterogenous network can be simplified as

$$\overline{\tau} = \frac{1}{\sum_{m=0}^{M} N_m} \sum_{m=0}^{M} \sum_{n=1}^{N_m} \{b_n^{(m)} \tau_{U,n}^{(m)} + (1 - b_n^{(m)})\tau_L\} . \tag{10}$$

It can be further rewritten as

$$\overline{\tau} = \rho \overline{\tau}_O + (1 - \rho)\tau_L , \tag{11}$$

where ρ is the ratio of the applications in the network that needs to be offloading, i.e.

$$\rho = \frac{\sum_{m=0}^{M} \sum_{n=1}^{N_m} b_n^{(m)}}{\sum_{m=0}^{M} N_m} . \tag{12}$$

The average execution time for all the applications to be offloading is expressed by

$$\bar{\tau}_O = \frac{\sum_{m=0}^{M} \sum_{n=1}^{N_m} b_n^{(m)} \tau_{U,n}^{(m)}}{\sum_{m=0}^{M} \sum_{n=1}^{N_m} b_n^{(m)}} . \tag{13}$$

It can be seen that $\bar{\tau}_O$ is not only dependent on the ratio of offloading applications but also on the scheduling algorithm and wireless channel characters of offloading users, i.e.

$$\bar{\tau}_O = f(\rho, \mathcal{S}, \gamma) , \tag{14}$$

where $\mathcal{S}$ represents the scheduling algorithm such Round Rubin, max C/I and so on, γ represents the wireless channel characters of offloading users. We propose two methods to perform the offloading decision in order to decrease the average delay as much as possible.

Threshold-Based Method. Given that $\mathcal{S}$ in (14) is fixed, then the τ_O only depends on the ratio ρ and the channel condition γ. Furthermore, in order to find the solution with low complexity, γ is ignored. So, the τ_O can be expressed by $f(\rho)$. When the following conditions can be satisfied for $f(\rho)$, the optimal solution of $f(\rho)$ exists in the network, i.e., (i) $f(\rho)$ increases monotonically in ρ, (ii) $f(\rho)$ is strictly convex. Finally, the offloading ratio ρ can be obtained. When an application becomes active in the MD, the random variable with the uniform distribution in $[0, 1]$ is first generated by the offloading controller. Then, the value of this random variable is compared with a certain threshold (i.e., offloading ratio ρ). If it is no more than the threshold, the offloading controller decides that this application is to be offloading. Otherwise, it will be executed locally.

Rate-Prediction Method. Unlike the above method, we take account of the channel characters for more energy saving at the cost of larger complexity. When an application arrives at the cell m in the time t, the MD n sends the offloading request to its donor eNodeB. Then, the eNodeB estimates the average transmission rate per RB of MD n according to its channel characters in the time t, i.e.

$$\tilde{\eta}_{RB,n}^{(m)}(t) = \frac{\sum_{k=0}^{K} \eta_{k,n}^{(m)}(t)}{K} , 0 \le m \le M , 0 \le k \le K . \tag{15}$$

Next, the average achievable data rate of user n is predicted by

$$\tilde{\mu}_n^{(m)}(t) = \frac{K \times \tilde{\eta}_{RB,n}^{(m)}(t)}{N_m^{(t)}} , 0 \le m \le M . \tag{16}$$

The delay due to uplink transmission is approximately estimated by

$$\tilde{\tau}_{U,n}^{(m)}(t) = \frac{D}{\tilde{\mu}_n^{(m)}}(t) .$$ (17)

If this estimated delay is no more than the local execution time, i.e., $\tilde{\tau}_{U,n}^{(m)}(t) \leq \tau_L$, this application is decided to be offloading. Otherwise, it has to be processed locally. This offloading decision is sent to the MD from the eNodeB. By this method, the system not only has a good control of the offloading ratio, but also choose the mobile users with better channel state as the offloading users, which can reduce the average delay effectively.

4   Simulation Results

In this section, simulation results are presented to evaluate the delay performances of the proposed offloading control schemes in LTE-Advanced heterogenous networks (HetNet). Here only one macrocell with three picocell is considered. For comparison purpose, the performances of the network with macro-cell only are also given.

Detailed simulation parameters including channel model and system assumptions are summarized in Table 1 [10].

In order to determine the threshold value for offloading decision, the performance of the networks, in which the applications may be offloading according to the given probability, i.e., threshold, are firstly given. The offloading ratio ρ can be varied from 0 to 100 %. In these simulations, different scheduling algorithms are adopted under different scenarios. Figure 1(a) shows that the average

Table 1. Parameters assumption in LTE-Advanced wireless networks.

Parameters	Values
Carrier (GHz)	2
Bandwidth (MHz)	10
Time slot duration (ms)	0.5
Resource block separation (kHz)	180
Number of resource blocks	50
Channel model	VA, Speed=3 km/h
Arrival rate	2 applications/sub-frame
Offloading file size (Kbytes)	10
Target SNR (dB)	10
Transmit power in eNodeB (dBm)	46 in Macro/30 in Pico
UE power class (P_{max}) (dBm)	23
Antenna configuration	Tx × Rx= 1 × 1
Pathloss model in Macro	128.1+37.6log10(R), R in km
Pathloss model in Pico	140.7+36.7log10(R), R in km
Scheduling algorithm	RR, Max C/I
Power control	Open loop with full pathloss compensation

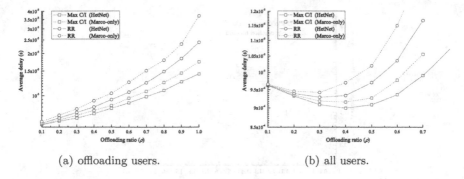

(a) offloading users.   (b) all users.

Fig. 1. Delay performances of (a) and (b) with different offloading ratio.

delay of users whose applications are decided to be offloading. It can be seen that the delay is increased with the larger offloading ratio. When the number of application that needed to be offloading becomes large, the radio resource that can be allocated to each user is decreased. Correspondingly, the achievable data rate of users become less so that the transmission delay is increased. Due to the scheduling gain, the performances of the networks with Max C/I algorithm are better than those with Round Rubin (RR) algorithm. Moreover, the delay in Hetnet is much less than that in macro-only network. It is because that the radio resources are reused between the macro-cell and pico-cell, which leads to more number of RBs to users for transmitting the offloading data. It can be observed that the average delay is increased with offloading ratio ρ and is the convex function of ρ under all simulated scenarios. According to the analysis in Sect. 3, there exists a optimal offloading ratio ρ, which can be used as the threshold for offloading decision.

Then, the average delay performances of all users whose application are offloading are shown in Fig. 1(b), where the local execution time is set to be fixed, i.e., $\tau_L = 1$ ms. As expected, the average delay of all the users becomes smaller first and then larger with the increase of the offloading ratio ρ. It is noted that the optimal offloading ratio is highly dependent on the scheduling algorithm and network environment. For example, in HetNet scenarios, the optimal offloading ratio of 40 % can be taken as the threshold in case of Max C/I scheduling algorithm while 30 % is in case of RR scheduling algorithm. So, we have to find the different threshold values for the threshold-based offloading control scheme by simulations.

In Fig. 2, we present the average delay performances of the network with our two proposed offloading control schemes while different local execution time is assumed. With the larger value of the local execution time, more applications are likely to be offloading so that the radio resource competition in the network becomes more intense. Then, the delay becomes larger due to the less achievable data rate for each user. Although the threshold-based scheme is simple, it can not always make the best decision. Compared to the threshold-based scheme,

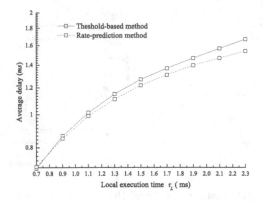

Fig. 2. Performance comparison with different offloading control methods in HetNet.

the delay performance of the network with the rate-prediction scheme is better no matter which scheduling algorithm is applied. It is because that not only the channel state information but also the number of all users are taken into account in the rate-prediction method.

5   Conclusion

Energy saving and execution speed gains have attracted increasingly attention due to the limitations of the mobile devices. In this article, we propose two offloading control schemes to meet the delay requirements of mobile cloud applications. The performances of the proposed methods with typical scheduling algorithms are studied under various scenarios. Execution delay can be reduced effectively by threshold-based scheme, which is simple but less flexible. Since not only the network environment but also the channel characters are taken into account, the rate-prediction scheme can achieve better delay performances and can be easily extended to various cases.

Acknowledgment. This work was supported by the National Natural Science Foundation of China (No. 61271183), Program for New Century Excellent Talents in University (NCET-11-0600), the National Key Technology R&D Program of China under Grant (2012ZX02001-2), and Chinese Universities Scientific Fund under Grant 2013RC0116.

References

1. Dinh, H. T., Lee, C., Niyato, D., Wang, P.: A survey of mobile cloud computing: architecture, applications, and approaches. Wireless Communications and Mobile Computing (2011)
2. Mayo, R.N., Ranganathan, P.: Energy consumption in mobile devices: why future systems need requirements-aware energy scale-down. In: Falsafi, B., VijayKumar, T.N. (eds.) PACS 2003. LNCS, vol. 3164, pp. 26–40. Springer, Heidelberg (2005)

3. Rudenko, A., Reiher, P., Popek, G.J., Kuenning, G.H.: Saving portable computer battery power through remote process execution. J. ACM SIGMOBILE Mob. Comput. Commun. Rev. **2**, 19–26 (1998)

4. Kumar, K., Lu, Y.-H.: Cloud computing for mobile users: can offloading computation save energy? Computer **43**, 51–56 (2010)

5. Kremer, U., Hicks, J., Rehg, J.: A compilation framework for power and energy management on mobile computers. In: Dietz, H.G. (ed.) LCPC 2001. LNCS, vol. 2624, pp. 115–131. Springer, Heidelberg (2003)

6. Gitzenis, S., Barnbos, N.: Joint task migration and power management in wireless computing. IEEE Trans. Mob. Comput. **8**, 1189–1204 (2009)

7. Wen, Y., Zhang, W., luo, H.: Energy-optimal mobile application execution: taming resource-poor mobile devices with cloud clones. In: 2012 Proceedings of the IEEE INFOCOM, Orlando, pp. 2716–2720. IEEE (2012)

8. Huang, D., Wang, P., Niyato, D.: A dynamic offloading algorithm for mobile computing. IEEE Trans. Wirel. Commun. **11**, 1991–1995 (2012)

9. Lei, L., Zhong, Z., Zheng, K., et al.: Challenges on wireless heterogeneous networks for mobile cloud computing. IEEE Wirel. Commun. **20**, 1 (2013)

10. 3GPP TR 36.814, v2.0.0.: Further Advancements for E-UTRA, Physical Layer Aspects (2010)

Exploring Critical Risks Associated with Enterprise Cloud Computing

Guo Chao Alex Peng[1(✉)], Arnab Dutta[1], and Alok Choudhary[2]

[1] Information School, University of Sheffield, Regent Court,
Sheffield S1 4DP, UK
{g.c.peng, ADutta2}@sheffield.ac.uk
[2] Management School, University of Sheffield, IWP Building,
Sheffield S10 2TN, UK
a.choudhary@sheffield.ac.uk

Abstract. While cloud computing has become an increasingly hot topic in the industry, risks associated with the adoption of cloud services have also received growing attention from researchers and practitioners. This paper reports the results of a study that aimed to identify and explore potential risks that organisations may encounter when adopting cloud computing, as well as to assess and prioritise the identified risks. The study adopted a deductive research method based on a cross-sectional questionnaire survey. The questionnaire was distributed to a group of 295 carefully selected and highly experienced IT professionals, of which 39 (13.2 %) responses were collected and analysed. The research findings identified a set of 39 cloud computing risks, which concentrated around diverse operational, organisational, technical, and legal areas. It was identified that the most critical risks were caused by current legal and technical complexity and deficiencies associated with cloud computing, as well as by a lack of preparation and planning of user companies.

Keywords: Cloud computing · Risks · Legal · Organisational · Operational · Technical

1 Introduction and Background of Study

In order to sustain business competitiveness in the digital age, modern organisations have implemented and used an increasing number of information technology (IT) applications and possessed an ever complicated IT infrastructure. These IT resources (such as, data, software, PCs, CPUs, memory cards, and servers) are traditionally hosted and maintained by user organisations internally. However, the increasing number of internal IT facilities and resources has now become very costly and time-consuming for user companies to maintain. Consequently, organisations nowadays are facing the dilemma to remain high usage of advanced IT applications to sustain competitiveness on the one hand, and to substantially reduce their IT operation and maintenance costs on the other hand. With the development of new IT and web technologies, cloud computing emerges in late 2000s as a solution to this IT dilemma.

V.C.M. Leung and M. Chen (Eds.): CloudComp 2013, LNICST 133, pp. 132–141, 2014.
DOI: 10.1007/978-3-319-05506-0_13, © Institute for Computer Sciences, Social Informatics and Telecommunications Engineering 2014

Cloud computing is an advanced IT model to host and share both software and hardware resources over the Internet. It allows organisations to use a pool of IT resources and applications as services virtually through the web, without physically holding these computing resources internally [1]. Nowadays organizations are increasingly looking for adopting the various cloud services for supply-chain integration and access to real-time data. Cloud computing provides the facility to access shared resources and common infrastructure, offering services on demand over the network to meet changing business needs [1]. It also promises to deliver high-quality and advanced IT services to organisations with substantially reduced costs [2], such as reduced hardware investments, less maintenance fees, and lower electricity consumption associated with IT usage. In this context, cloud computing can also be perceived as one of the green technologies that enables environmentally sustainable use of IT in modern organisations in the long term.

However, despite these very attractive facts, migrating the hitherto internal IT resources and sensitive business data to a third-party cloud vendor is never an easy decision to be made by CEOs, CIOs and IT managers. In fact, the adoption of cloud computing is associated with a wide range of potential risks and challenges. For instance, the inherent features of cloud computing determine that IT operation within a third-party cloud provider will be by no means transparent to user companies, who also have limited control on the subscribed cloud services [3]. Such lack of transparency and control may raise potential risks related to the security and privacy of business and customer data stored in the cloud [1]. Moreover, user companies need to make a range of internal changes (e.g. designing new business processes, refining IT roles, and downsizing IT department) to prepare themselves to the new cloud environment [4]. This however may potentially lead to job dissatisfaction of in-house IT and business staff. Consequently, fully exploring and understanding these cloud risks and challenges is fundamental for organisations to decide strategically whether or not cloud computing is the right tool for them, as well as to better prepare them to deal with the potential cloud problems and thus avoid severe technical failure and business disasters.

This paper reports a study that aimed to identify, explore and assess a comprehensive list of risks associated with cloud computing. A systematic literature review was carried out at the early stage of the research. As a result of this extensive review, the researchers established a theoretical risk ontology that contains 39 potential risks that organisations may encounter during cloud computing adoption and usage. A questionnaire was constructed based on this theoretical risk ontology and it was used to seek IT professionals' perceptions of the established cloud risks. This paper is organized in the following manner. The next section of the paper presents the research methodology including a discussion of the theoretical risk ontology and the research questionnaire design. Section 3 presents the analysis and results derived from the questionnaire survey. Finally, Sect. 4 concluded this study with a note of its research and practical implications.

2 Research Methodology

2.1 The Theoretical Risk Ontology

In order to establish an explicit IT lens to frame the study and generate data collection tools, a desktop study, based on the process of a critical literature review, was carried out at the early stage of the research. As discussed above, an initial literature review of the study identified that current research on cloud computing risks has been very limited and focused mainly on security and privacy aspects. Faced with this scarcity of studies on the topic, a more extensive literature review was conducted. This critical review followed the systematic approach proposed by Peng and Nunes [5, 6]. Specifically, apart from reviewing studies that directly address cloud computing risks, this systematic review also covers general IT and computing journal papers, conference proceedings, books, industrial white papers, and technical reports. The purpose here was "to identify broadly any possible factors and issues that might lead to potential" cloud computing failure [5]. This endeavour resulted in the identification of a large amount of valuable literature, which addressed various IT, cloud computing, legal, and business issues. Subsequently, these retrieved articles and materials were "systematically and critically analysed, compared and synthesised, and then used as raw materials to construct arguments and standpoints for risk identification" [5]. Consequently, through this extensive and critical literature review, the researchers established and proposed a set of 39 potential cloud computing risks. A risk ontology is then developed to organise and present these identified cloud risks (Fig. 1 below).

As shown in Fig. 1, the established cloud risks were organised into 4 main categories and 12 sub-categories in the risk ontology. The 4 main risk categories include:

- *Organisational risks (OGR).* Cloud adoption can lead to significant impacts on diverse organisational aspects, such as IT governance, compliance to industrial regulations, in-house IT experts, and IT planning. Risks related to these organisational and managerial aspects are categorised as organisational risks.
- *Operational risks (OPR).* The adoption of cloud computing significantly changes the hitherto internal IT and business operations in user companies. Risks affecting daily business and IT operations are thus categorised as operational risks.
- *Technical risks (TR).* The complicated cloud infrastructure and inherent IT deficiencies existed in the company can raise a set of technical risks during cloud computing adoption.
- *Legal risks (LR).* The nature and inherent features of cloud computing can lead to a range of legal risks related to data privacy, intellectual property, and contracts.

In order to examine and explore the suitability of this theoretical risk ontology in current cloud computing practices, a deductive research design based on a cross-sectional questionnaire survey was selected and used as the suitable data collection tool of this study, as further discussed below.

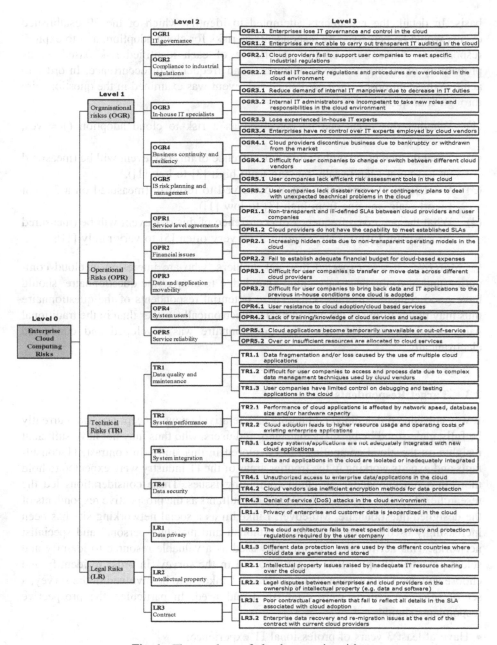

Fig. 1. The ontology of cloud computing risks

2.2 The Questionnaire Design

The questionnaire began by asking general questions related to respondents' previous experience of IT, cloud computing, and risk assessment. Subsequently, the main part of the questionnaire was designed by using the cloud risk ontology as the theoretical basis. In detail, the researchers attempted to identify which of the 39 established events would be perceived by respondents as risks for cloud adoption, and to explore respondents' perceptions on the importance of each identified risk based on its probability of occurrence, level of impact, and frequency of occurrence. In order to achieve these purposes, each predefined risk event was examined in the questionnaire through four questions:

(1) Whether this event can be perceived as a risk to cloud adoption (1 = yes, 2 = no).
(2) What the perceived probability of occurrence of this risk event will be (measured on a 3-point Likert scale, ranging from high [3] to low [1]).
(3) What level of impact this risk is perceived to result in (measured on a 3-point Likert scale, ranging from high [3] to low [1]).
(4) What the perceived frequency of occurrence of this risk event will be (measured on a 5-point Likert scale, ranging from very often [5] to very rarely [1]).

Moreover, it was expected that stakeholders, who are interested in cloud computing and have the necessary cloud knowledge to answer the questionnaire, should have good computer literate skills. These potential respondents of the questionnaire thus may prefer filling in the questionnaire electronically, rather than in the traditional paper-based format. Therefore, this questionnaire was developed and conducted electronically.

2.3 Target Respondents

It was considered that cloud computing as a relatively new concept may not currently be fully understood by business managers and users, who thus may not have sufficient insights on the cloud computing risks explored in this study. In contrast, IT consultants and experts working in the frontier areas of the IT industry were expected to hold more in-depth knowledge on cloud computing issues. These considerations led the researchers to select IT professionals and consultants as the prospective respondents of the designed questionnaire. Moreover, Linkedin as a social networking site has been increasingly used by professionals to establish and maintain personal and specialist networks. This networking site was thus used as a valuable resource to identify and select potential IT specialists to get involved in the survey. In order to identify and choose suitable IT professionals registered on Linkedin to be involved in the survey, a set of selection criteria were established and used. In particular, the prospective respondents should:

- Have at least 3 years of professional IT experience;
- Have experience and/or knowledge of cloud computing;
- Have experience in IT risk assessment and management.

By using these criteria, a sample of 295 highly-qualified IT professionals registered on Linkedin was identified and selected to participate in this questionnaire survey. An invitation email, which contained (1) a covering letter to explain the purpose of the study, and (2) the URL to the online questionnaire, was sent to these 295 IT professionals. Three weeks after the original email, a reminder was sent out. With these efforts, a total of 39 valid and usable responses were received, representing a response rate of 13.2 %.

3 Data Analysis and Findings

3.1 Overall Risk Findings

The questionnaire findings show that all of the 39 events contained in the risk ontology were perceived by the majority (86 %) of the respondents as risk events to cloud computing adoption. Nonetheless, these risks were perceived to have different levels of importance. In particular, the questionnaire asked respondents to assess the importance of each risk item from three dimensions, namely perceived probability of occurrence, level of impact, and frequency of occurrence. The need for all this information lies in the fact that from a risk management perspective, a risk event that has a high probability of occurrence may not have a high impact, and vice versa. Moreover, while probability refers to 'how likely' a risk event may occur, frequency refers to 'how often' this event may happen. Therefore, when evaluating the importance of a risk event, it is necessary and vital to take into account all these three risk aspects [7]. Consequently, and in order to facilitate risk assessment, the following formula was developed:

$$Risk\ score\ of\ each\ cloud\ computing\ risk = \Sigma[W * (Probability + Impact + Frequency)]$$

This formula was initially established and proposed by Peng and Nunes [7] and then further improved by Pan et al. [8], which aimed to identified and assessed ERP post-implementation risks. Because the structure of this formula is consistent with and clearly reflects the questionnaire design of this research, it is adopted as a suitable method to assess cloud computing risks in this study. Based on this formula, the calculation of the risk score for each identified risk event should go through the following 3 steps:

Step 1 *(Probability + Impact + Frequency)*: sum up the values given by each respondent for the three independent dimensions of a risk event, namely perceived probability of occurrence (i.e. high = "2", medium = "1", low = "0.5"), perceived level of impact (i.e. high = "2", medium = "1", low = "0.5"), and perceived frequency of occurrence (i.e. 5 values from very often to very rarely = "2", "1.5", "1", "0.75" and "0.5").

Step 2 *W*(Probability + Impact + Frequency)*: 'W' refers to whether or not the respondent perceived this risk event as a cloud computing risk, with '1' stands for 'yes' and '0' means 'no'. In case that the respondent did not perceive the given risk event as a cloud computing risk, the formula will turn the value generated from Step 1 into 0.

Step 1 and 2 thus generate the individual score that each respondent gave for a specific risk event.

Step 3 Σ [W*(Probability + Impact + Frequency)]: sum up the individual score that each of the 39 respondents of the survey gave for a particular risk event, and thus generate the total risk score that this risk event received.

By using this formula, the researchers calculated the risk scores for all of the 39 cloud computing risks identified, and then prioritised these risks based on their risk scores. The top 10 cloud risks ranked by their risk scores are shown in Table 1. These top 10 risks were identified as the most critical to current cloud computing practice.

Table 1. Top 10 cloud computing risks as perceived by IT experts

Rank	Risk ID	Top 10 critical risk events for cloud computing	Risk score (n = 39)
1	LR1.1	Privacy of enterprise or customer data is jeopardised in the cloud	153.50
2	LR1.3	Inconsistent data protection laws adopted by different countries where cloud data are generated and stored	151.75
3	OGR4.2	Difficult for user companies to change cloud vendors even in the case of service dissatisfaction (also known as vendor lock-in)	148.50
4	OGR5.2	User companies lack disaster recovery and contingency plans to deal with unexpected technical issues in cloud environment	147.75
5	LR3.2	Enterprise data re-migration difficulties at the end of the cloud contract	140.25
6	OPR4.2	Inadequate user training/knowledge on cloud services and usage	139.75
7	OPR5.1	Cloud applications become temporarily unavailable or out-of-service	137.25
8	OPR2.1	Increasing hidden costs due to non-transparent operating models in the cloud	136.00
9	TR4.3	Denial-of-Service (DoS) attacks in the cloud environment	135.50
10	TR4.1	Unauthorised access to enterprise data/applications	135.00

As discussed above, when sensitive business and customer data is processed by third-party service providers outside the organisation, business managers of user companies are less immediately aware of the occurrence of any risks in the cloud, and also have no direct ability to control and manage these risks [9]. These inherent features in the cloud raise immediate concerns and risks related to data privacy and security, which have been the main focus of the majority of current academic studies [e.g. 10–12] and industrial reports [e.g. 9] on cloud computing. The findings of this study confirmed that data privacy and security risks represent some of the significant challenges in the cloud. However, the findings also identified that the most critical cloud computing risks do not just cluster around privacy and security aspects. That is, critical cloud risks as shown in Table 1 were also found across diverse legal, operational and business areas. Therefore, it seems that potential failure of cloud computing adoption may not just be simply attributed to privacy and security risks, but may also be triggered by various operational, organisational, and managerial problems related to both cloud vendors and user companies. In order to validate this conclusion, a further bivariate analysis was carried out to explore potential casual relationships between the cloud computing risks identified, as presented below.

3.2   Correlations Between the Identified Cloud Computing Risks

A bivariate analysis is a statistical technique that aims at identifying the correlation between two variables. In this study, the researchers used bivariate analysis to explore potential relationships between the identified cloud computing risks. Specifically, we aimed to explore that when the probability of occurrence of Risk A (e.g. inconsistent data protection laws adopted by different countries where cloud data are stored) was perceived to be high/low in practice, whether the probability of occurrence of Risk B (e.g. data privacy is jeopardised) would be correspondingly perceived as high/low. If so, then we interpret that Risk A is likely to have influence on Risk B. As illustrated earlier, Likert scales were used in the survey to examine the perceived probability of occurrence of each identified risk, data variables generated were therefore ordinal data sets. According to Field [13] and Bryman and Cramer [14], Spearman's rho (rs) is the most common and appropriate approach to use to measure bivariate correlations between ordinal variables. As a consequence, Spearman's rho was adopted for this study. Moreover, one-tailed test was used to test further the statistical significance (P value) of each correlation identified. By following this approach, the researchers identified 18 statistically significant correlations between all the 39 identified risks. Figure 2 presents a conceptual map to summarise and represent these correlations.

By scanning this conceptual map, it becomes immediately apparent that in the perceptions of IT professionals, the identified cloud computing risks, especially the top 10 critical risks (as highlighted with grey colour in the map), are interwoven and

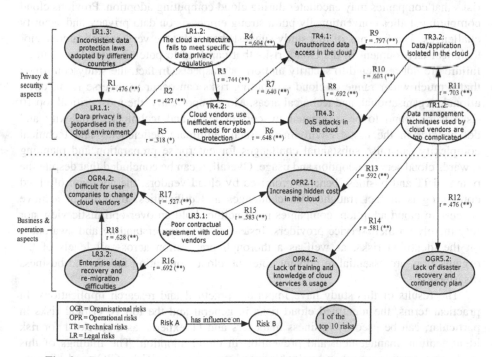

Fig. 2. Conceptual map of correlations between identified cloud computing risks

closely related with each other. Therefore, the occurrence of these critical risks proves to be very difficult for user companies to manage, mitigate and contain. Moreover, by further investigating the conceptual map, it emerges that about half of the identified correlations was related with privacy and security risks (e.g. LR1.1, TR4.1 and TR4.3). These findings thus confirm the importance of privacy and security issues in cloud computing adoption. More importantly, the findings also identified that these critical privacy and security risks can be originated by current legal and technical complexity and difficulties in the cloud (e.g. LR1.2, LR1.3 and TR1.2). On the other hand, the second half of the correlations shown in the conceptual map was found between various organisational and operational risks (e.g. OGR5.2, OPR4.2, OGR4.2 and LR3.2). These business-related risks were also triggered by legitimate deficiencies (e.g. LR3.1) and IT infrastructure complexity (e.g. TR1.2) in the cloud.

Overall, the results of this bivariate analysis supported the early conclusion by confirming that within the sophisticated virtualized cloud environment, critical risks, which are interrelated and can cause potential failure of cloud computing, can occur in not just privacy and security aspects but also across different IT operation and business areas.

4 Conclusions

The study reported in this paper employed a questionnaire survey to explore potential risks that companies may encounter during cloud computing adoption. Previous cloud computing studies conventionally put a strong emphasis on data privacy and security challenges. The findings of this study suggest that under the very complicated socio-technical environment in the cloud, risks that can lead to potential cloud computing failure are not restricted to security and privacy aspects. In fact, the study confirmed that a much wider range of cloud computing risks can occur in diverse legal, operational, organisational, and technical areas. More importantly, the most critical top 10 risks were found to be originated by current legal and technical complexity and deficiencies in the cloud environment. Such legitimate deficiencies and technical complexity can raise substantial challenges for enterprise preparation and planning towards cloud service adoption and usage. Overall, it can be concluded that despite the potential IT and business benefits promised by cloud vendors, the adoption of cloud computing is in fact fraught with challenges and difficulties. In order to achieve success in cloud adoption, companies must neither hold an over-optimistic view nor rely merely on their service providers. Instead, a clear understanding and awareness on the identified risks, as well as a thorough preparation across all levels of the organisation, are essential to prevent potential cloud computing failure and business disasters.

The results of this study have important practical and research implications. In practical terms, the identified cloud risks in general and the top 10 critical risks in particular, can be used by business managers and IT experts, as a checklist for risk identification, management and prevention in cloud adoption. The findings of this study also provide useful and valuable insights to support CEOs, CIOs and IT managers in the process of strategic planning and decision making towards successful cloud adoption. In research terms, the comprehensive risk ontology established in this study does not just fill the current knowledge gap in cloud computing risk, but can also serve as a starting point and theoretical foundation for IS researchers to carry out further investigation in this increasingly important research area.

References

1. Voorsluys, W., Brober, J., Buyya, R.: Introduction to cloud computing. In: Buyya, R., Broberg, J., Goscinski, A. (eds.) Cloud Computing Principles and Paradigms, pp. 1–41. Wiley, New Jersey (2011)
2. Marston, S., Li, Z., Bandyopadhyay, S., Zhang, J., Ghalsasi, A.: Cloud computing - the business perspective. Decis. Support Syst. **51**(1), 176–189 (2011)
3. Chow, R., Golle, P., Jakobsson, M., Shi, E., Staddon, J., Masuoka, R., Molina, J.: Controlling data in the cloud: outsourcing computation without outsourcing control. In: Proceedings of the 2009 ACM Workshop on Cloud Computing Security, pp. 85–90, Chicago, USA (2009)
4. Ali, K.H.: Cloud migration: a case study of migrating an enterprise IT system to IaaS. In: Proceedings of the 3rd IEEE International Conference on Cloud Computing, pp. 450–457, Miami, Florida (2010)
5. Peng, G.C., Nunes, J.M.B.: Surfacing ERP exploitation risks through a risk ontology. Ind. Manage. Data Syst. **109**(7), 926–942 (2009)
6. Peng, G.C., Nunes, J.M.B.: Establishing and verifying a risk ontology for surfacing ERP post-implementation. In: Ahmad, M., Colomb, R.M., Abdullah, M.S. (eds.) Ontology-Based Applications for Enterprise Systems and Knowledge Management, pp. 43–67. IGI Global, Hershey (2012)
7. Peng, G.C., Nunes, J.M.B.: Identification and assessment of risks associated with ERP post-implementation in China. J. Enterp. Inf. Manage. **22**(5), 587–614 (2009)
8. Pan, K., Nunes, J.M.B., Peng, G.C.: Risks affecting ERP post-implementation: insights from a large Chinese manufacturing group. J. Manuf. Technol. Manage. **22**(1), 107–130 (2011)
9. Heiser, J., Nicolett, M.: Assessing the security risks of cloud computing. http://www.globalcloudbusiness.com/SharedFiles/Download.aspx?pageid=138&mid=220&fileid=12 (2008). Accessed Mar 2012
10. Mather, T., Kumaraswamy, S., Latif, S.: Cloud Security and Privacy: An Enterprise Perspective on Risks and Compliance. O'Reilly, Sebastopol (2009)
11. Onwubiko, C.: Security issues to cloud computing. In: Antonopoulos, N., Gillam, L. (eds.) Cloud Computing Principles, Systems and Applications, pp. 271–288. Springer, London (2010)
12. Bisong, A., Rahman, S.S.M.: An overview of the security concerns in enterprise cloud computing. Int. J. Network Secur. Appl. **3**(1), 30–45 (2011)
13. Field, A.: Discovering Statistics Using SPSS: And Sex, Drugs and Rock 'n' Roll, 2nd edn. SAGE Publication, London (2005)
14. Bryman, A., Cramer, D.: Quantitative Data Analysis with SPSS 12 and 13: a Guide for Social Scientists. Routledge, East Sussex (2005)

Management and Virtualization
for Cloud

A Capability-Based Matchmaking Mechanism Supporting Resource Aggregation within Large-Scale Distributed Computing Infrastructures

Feng Liang[1][✉], Hai Liu[1], Yunzhen Liu[1], Shilong Ma[1],
Siyao Zheng[2], and Pan Deng[3]

[1] State Key Lab of Software Development Environment,
Beihang University, Beijing 100191, China
{liangfeng,liuhai,liuyunzhen,slma}@nlsde.buaa.edu.cn
[2] The Laboratory of Embedded Systems, Beihang University, Beijing 100191, China
zhengsiyao@les.buaa.edu.cn
[3] Lab of Parallel Software and Computational Science, Institute of Software,
Chinese Academy of Sciences, Beijing 100190, China
dengpan@iscas.ac.cn

Abstract. Facing the large-scale, heterogeneous dynamic resource and the complex constraints of computation-intensive parallel scientific applications, collaborating large-scale computation resource for these applications within Large-Scale Distributed Computing Infrastructures like grids and clouds are challenging. This paper addresses this issue by proposing a Resource Capability Model and implementing a corresponding language GSO and an information service Application Information Service to ensure not only the resource description, aggregation, matchmaking but also life cycle management of the reservations and tasks. Experiment result shows that our mechanism is scalable in both Grid and Cloud environment.

Keywords: Grid Service Object · Large-scale Distributed Computing Infrastructures · Resource Capability model · Application Information Service

1 Introduction

As Lage-scale Distributed Computing Infrastructures (LDCI) like grids and clouds become robust, more and more computation-intensive parallel scientific applications want to utilize them. But because of the following reasons, it is not easy to matchmake the suitable resource for these applications. (1) The large-scale clusters increases the time to search for the suitable resource. (2) The diverse heterogeneity of the nodes makes it hard to compare the resource capability. (3) The dynamic feature of the nodes requires more concern on the availability of the nodes. (4) The computation-intensive scientific applications

V.C.M. Leung and M. Chen (Eds.): CloudComp 2013, LNICST 133, pp. 145–154, 2014.
DOI: 10.1007/978-3-319-05506-0_14, © Institute for Computer Sciences, Social Informatics
and Telecommunications Engineering 2014

demands large-scale computation resource. (5) The resource collaboration constraints lead to the life cycle management of the reservations and tasks.

With large-scale, diverse heterogeneity and dynamic resource and complex resource requirement of the applications, it is required to establish a resource matchmaking mechanism for fine-grained resource description, proper resource aggregation, and optimized resource matchmaking. To address these issues, this paper proposes a Resource Capability Model and its XML implementation Grid Service Object language to support the resource description, aggregation and matchmaking and life cycle management.

The contributions of this paper include two aspects: firstly, we propose the Resource Capability model to measure the capability of a single resource and aggregated resources. Secondly, we propose a Grid Service Object language based on the Resource Capability model and implement it in an Application Information Service, so as to support the matchmaking for aggregated resources. Experiments show that our methods are acceptable for production-level LDCI.

This paper is structured as follows: we begin with a discussion of related work in Sect. 2. The Resource Capability Model is given in Sect. 3. Section 4 presents the GSO and AIS in details. Section 6 presents experimental results that evaluate the scaling and effectiveness of our mechanism. In Sect. 7 we summarize the contributions of this paper and present some areas of future work.

2   Related Work

To proper describe the resource and the request, a proper and complete resource and request description model is required for resource discovery and matchmaking. Up to now the existing models can be categorized into three classes: the request description models, the resource description models and the symmetrical models.

2.1   Job Description Models

The request description models are used mainly for task requirement description. The typical models are RSL (Resource Specification Language) [4] and JSDL (Job Submssion Description Language) [2]. RSL is used mainly in Globus Toolkit, it uses the {*attribute, value*} key-value pair for requirement description and utilizes operations &, | and + for single task description, the logical relationships between tasks and the resource set respectively, but its format is not friendly for collaborate with other LDCI. Proposed by the Open Grid Forum and implemented in XML format, JSDL is used widely in Grid, but it can support only task descriptions. JSDL can be considered as an extended RSL, as it allows the user and the grid machines to add new keys for extra attributes.

2.2   Requirement Description Models

The resource description models are for the resource description. The most widely accepted models are GLUE (Grid Laboratory for a Uniform Environment) [1]

and DRMAA (Distributed Resource Management Application API) [10]. GLUE
is the proposed by the Open Grid Forum using the accumulated experience from
piratical Grid Projects. It encapsulate the computation resource into a Computing Element and uses the $\{attribute, value\}$ for description. The Monitoring and
Discovery Service from Globus Toolkit implements GLUE in XML and manages the Computing Elements in hierarchy. But this model does not support the
resource aggregation. DRMAA is a Open Grid Forum proposed generalized API
for distributed resource management systems in order to facilitate the development of portable application programs and high-level libraries. DRMAA includes
detailed definitions about resource descriptions in aspects such as os version, cpu
architecture, etc.

2.3   Symmetrical Models

The symmetrical models include ClassAds (Condor classified Advertisement) [9]
and GODsL (Grid Object Description Language) [6]. ClassAds is used in Condor, every ClassAds is an entity to describe both the resource attributes, the job
attributes and the preference attributes. ClassAds uses the $\{attribute, value\}$
for description and allow the users to define constraints in job type, access
control, time, resource requirement. But it does not support resource aggregation. GODsL is an object-oriented extensible description model, it defines Grid
Object (GO) to define the job and its resources. Each GO includes 5 containers,
namely the Resource Container, the Server Container, the Machine Container
and the Backup Container, each container can contain one or more profiles about
resource, used machine, file path, backup location. GODsL is mainly used for job
migration and recovery and is written in C, which is not proper for collaboration.
      From all the listed resource and request description models, we can see
although the current existing models do support detailed description of single resource and request, but there is no model supporting resource aggregation and collaboration, which is essential for accurate matchmaking for those
computation-intensive scientific parallel computing applications.

3   Resource Capability Model

As the crucial factor of LDCI systems, the computation node evaluates its capability in different metric such as task execution time, success rate and its availability, etc. These metric can be measured using the attributes of nodes such
as the CPU speed, memory volume, network bandwidth, etc. According to the
effects of the nodes in different aspects, the node capability can be split into 5
aspects: Computation Capability, Communication Capability, Memory Capability, Availability Capability and the Software Support Capability.

3.1   Capability-Based Matchmaking for a Single Node

The capability of a single resource $node_i$ is described as in $C_i = \{Ssup_i, Comp_i, Comm_i, Memo_i, Avai_i\}$. The 5 aspects and its meanings are as follow. $Ssup_i$, the

Software Support Capability of $node_i$, means the Software Environment of the node for computation, including the Operating System, the runtime software, the third party library, etc. $Comp_i$, the Computation Capability of $node_i$, measures the processing ability of the processor by the CPU speed. A multi-core processor is considered as several equal CPU processors. $Comm_i$, the Communication Capability of $node_i$, measures the data transfer of the the the node's network by both the latency and the bandwidth. $Memo_i$, the Memory Capability of $node_i$, measures the memory of the nodes by the memory volume. $Avai_i$, the Availability Capability of $node_i$ measure the availability of the node by the online time percentage of the node.

During the matchmaking process for a single computation node, the capability requirement should be satisfied by the node candidate. Assuming the capability of the request and the node are described as $C_r = \{Ssup_r, Comp_r, Comm_r, Memo_r, Avai_r\}$ and $C_a = \{Ssup_a, Comp_a, Comm_a, Memo_a, Avai_a\}$ respectively, then its matchmaking for 5 aspects are defined below.

$Ssup$ is a qualitative attribute, usually the requirement and the node should be equal in this attribute to ensure an execution. $Comp_a, Comm_a, Memo_a, Avai_a$ are quantitative attributes. As this paper aims mainly for the execution of computation-intensive parallel applications, so the node should has bigger capability than the requirement for $Comp_a, Comm_a, Memo_a, Avai_a$ respectively.

3.2   Matchmaking for Aggregated Resource

As the parallel computation program normally need multiple nodes, so it is essential to aggregate their capability and match with the requirement. Assume the capability requirement of a parallel application is defined in $CReq = \{C_R, N\}$ and $C_R = \{Ssup_R, Comp_R, Comm_R, Memo_R, Avai_R\}$. Within it, C_R means the requirement of each node, N means the required node number. Assuming there exists N nodes $\{C_i | 1 \leq i \leq N\}$, These nodes need to be aggregated first to match with the requirement. Assume the aggregated capability of these nodes is $CAgg$, as shown in $CAgg = \{C_A, N\}$ and $C_A = \{Ssup_A, Comp_A, Comm_A, Memo_A, Avai_A\}$. When $CAgg$ satisfies $CReq$, there should be $Ssup_A = Ssup_R, Comp_A \geq Comp_R, Comm_A \geq Comm_R, Avai_A \geq Avai_R, Memo_A \geq Avai_R$. As the N nodes might be heterogeneous, so the aggregation process for the $Ssup$ and $comp$ capabilities are listed as $Ssup_A = Ssup_i, 1 \leq i \leq N$ and $Comp_A = min_{i=1 \cdots N}(Comp_i)$. The others are similar.

As a qualitative attribute, the required capability of $Ssup_A$ should be equal to each of the N nodes. As a quantitative attribute, the required capabilities $Comp_A, Comm_A, Memo_A, Avai_A$ should be equal to the lowest value among the nodes as the execution time of a parallel application mostly depends on the lowest node.

3.3   Matchmaking for Co-reservation

For a single reservation, it can be described as q, and then the request for co-reservation is $Q = \{q_1, q_2, \cdots, q_l\}$ $(l \in N)$, i.e. each co-reservation request Q has multiple sub-request q. The resource set is $R = \{r_1, r_2 \cdots, r_k\}$ $(k \in N)$, a R includes multiple r. $R(q)$ means all the r that satisfies q. t means the start time, d means the duration, then the quadruple $A = \langle q, r, t, d \rangle$ means to allocate a resource r from time t with the duration of d to satisfy the requirement q. Then the total allocation result would be in $TA(Q, R) = \{\langle q, r, t, d \rangle\} = \{A \mid \bigcup q_A = Q, \forall A \neq B, r_A \neq r_B\}$, it means an executable solution for resource allocation.

For a $TA(Q, R)$, it has to satisfy the temporal and spatial constraints. Suppose a single constraints is $sc(A)$. Then the $TA(Q, R)$ has to satisfy all single constraints, as is shown in $SC = \bigcup_{q_l \in Q, r_k \in R(q_l)} sc(q_l, r_k, t, d) = \bigcup_{A \in TA(Q,R)} sc(A)$. Assume two arbitrary node allocations A, B and their network allocation C, then the temporal constraint among these three is $tc(A, B, C)$, and the spatial constraint is shown in $pc(A, B, C) = pc_{net}(A, B, C) \cup pc_{nnt}(A, B)$ including both the network constraint and the non-network constraint. If the constraints among multiple sub tasks is $mc(ASet)$ and $ASet$ is shown in $mc(ASet)$, $ASet = \{A_1, A_2, \cdots, A_l\}$.

So the final constraints for $TR(Q, R)$ can be described as in $(\bigcup_{A \in TA(Q,R)} sc(A))$ $\bigcup(\bigcup_{A,B,C \in TA(Q,R)} pc(A, B, C) \bigcup tc(A, B, C)) \bigcup(\bigcup_{ASet \subseteq TA(Q,R)} mc(ASet))$.

4   Grid Service Object Language

To ensure the execution of the Grid application with co-reservation, a information model is required to support the resource description, resource aggregation and the life cycle management of the task and reservations. As an earlier Grid resource information model, GODsL defined an extensible information model to describe the resource, applications, service and data within Grid. But this language did not support resource capability description, resource aggregation or the life cycle management of the task and reservations, besides, it used the C language syntax, therefore not suitable to exchange information with the modern Grid systems using XML. So Based on the Grid Object Description Language (GODsL), the Grid Service Object model (GSO) is proposed to address these issues. This model refines the GODsL according our Resource Capability Model and add the support about resource aggregation and the life cycle management of the tasks and reservations. XML Scheme is used to implement this language to ensure its compatibility with the other Grid Systems.

GSO model can be seen as in Fig. 1. Every GSO object owns a global unique id and a version number, to identify it. Besides, it also contains three sub-object, so called container, namely *RequirementContainer*, *ExecutionContainer* and *ResourceContainer*. These three containers can include 1 or more sub members. The contents of each container is listed as below:

RequirementContainer. It is used to describe the requirement of the resource capability, including the specifications about resource and the reservations. The *RequirementContainer* contains one or more *ResourceProfile*. It describes the Capability of nodes, shown in Table 1. In order be compatible with more distributed resource systems, the *RequirementContainer* adapt the DRMAA API standards for resource requirement description. Besides these *ResourceProfile*,

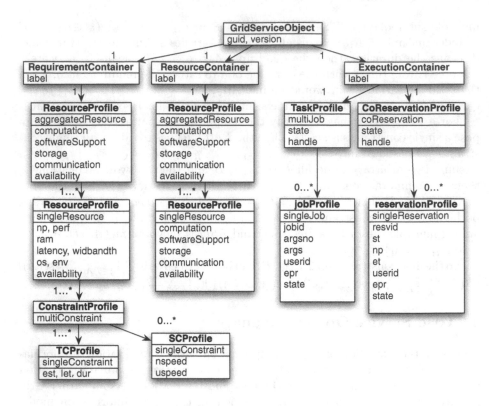

Fig. 1. GSO model

Table 1. The ResourceProfile within the RequirementContainer and the Resource-Container

Capability	Name	Meaning	Format
Computation	np	number of processors	positive integer
	perf	processor performance	positive integer (GHz)
Memory	ram	memory	positive integer (GB)
Communication	band width	the bandwidth	positive number (MB/s)
	latency		positive number (ms)
	os	OS name and version	String_version number
SoftwareSupport	env	runtime name and version	multiple String_version, split using ";"
Availability	online ratio	the online time length within the last 100 days	percentage (%)

the *RequirementContainer* also contains zero or more *ConstraintProfile* (to describe the constraints), which include *SCProfile* (for spatial constraints) and *TCProfile* (for temporal constraints).

ExecutionContainer. It is used to describe to related attributes and status of the tasks and reservations during the execution process, so mainly the life cycle management the tasks and the reservations.

ResourceContainer. It is used to describe the resource capability and status, including the computation capability, the storage capability, the communication capability, the software support capability and the availability. It is mainly for the resource management. The contents are the same as the *RequirementContainer*. Besides, it also includes the unique url of the resource.

5   Application Information Service in Migol

Migol [5,7,8] is a grid middleware, it aims at providing fault tolerance functionality to ensure the robust execution of the computation-intensive parallel applications. Composed of a set of loosely-coupled service, Migol follows the Open Grid Service Architecture (OGSA) [3]. Migol makes use of some basic components form Globus Toolkit, such as GRAM and MDS. This modularized service-oriented design allows Migol to collaborate with other Grid Middleware or to utilize the Cloud resource. As shown in Fig. 2, Migol uses GSO as the basic metadata model to store all the related information of the applications to ensure their execution.

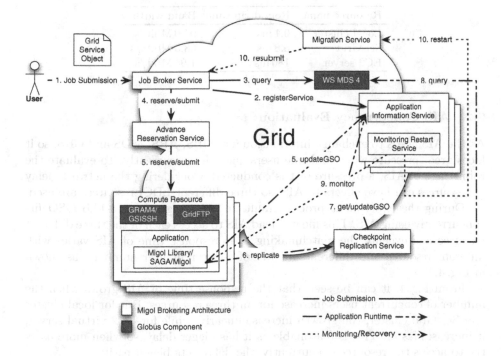

Fig. 2. Migol architecture

Application Information Service (AIS) is a registry service for LDCI applications within Migol. It stores all the GSO. Before the application execution, the user should registry the application's GSO to AIS. After the registration, the GSO contains information such as resource requirement, resource location, application task states, reservation states, etc. Meanwhile, the updated information of the used resource, tasks and reservations are collected from MDS, JBS, ARS and CRS respectively.

6   Experimental Results

6.1   Testbed Configuration

In order to evaluate the efficiency of the AIS service, an experiment is conducted to test for its currency. The experiment include 2 server nodes for services such as JBS and AIS and 3 different LDCI resources, a local cluster, a SeisGrid resource site and an Amazon EC2 virtual server. The two server nodes each has 1 GB memory, AMD Opteron 2.2 GHz processor with Globus Toolkit 4.0.5 and JRE 1.5.0_14 installed. The 3 resource are shown in Table 2 and the testbed is deployed as shown in Fig. 3.

Table 2. Site network configurations

Resource name	Roundtrip time	Band width
Local cluster	0.1 ms	95.0 Mbit/s
SeisGrid	5.8 ms	68.5 Mbits/s
EC2 server	180 ms	1.98 Mbit/s

6.2   AIS Concurrency Evaluation

As the AIS needs to exchange information with JBS, ARS, MDS and CRS, so it faces great pressure when multiple users query it concurrently. To evaluate the robustness of AIS, a pressure test is conducted. Considering the network delay of resources can have effects to AIS, so three different LDCI resources are used.

During the experiment process, multiple users registers a 3.1 kb GSO file concurrently using AIS. This file will lead AIS to access each of the three different resource and execute the matchmaking. The response time of AIS varies with different resource and different number of concurrent user numbers, as shown in Fig. 4.

From Fig. 4, it can be seen that the response time of AIS grows when the number of concurrent users increase for all three resources. But for local cluster and SeisGrid cluster, the growth increase linearly, while for EC2 virtual server, it increases faster. This is reasonable as it has bigger delay, so when more users try to access the resource concurrently, the delay gets bigger easily.

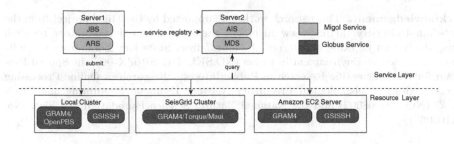

Fig. 3. Testbed deployment

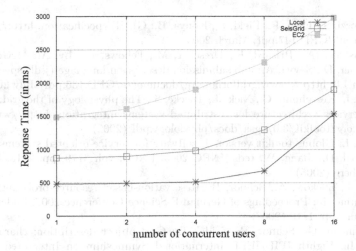

Fig. 4. The comparison of AIS response time with different resource delays and different number of concurrent user numbers

7   Conclusions

The middleware for utilizing LDCI should support optimized resource matchmaking so as to ensure the automatic resource collaboration. As the resource in LDCI are large-scale, dynamic, and heterogeneous, and the resource requirement of the computation-intensive parallel scientific applications are complex and include multiple constraints, so a mechanism is required for fine-grained resource description, proper resource aggregation, optimized resource matchmaking. Different from the current resource description models, this paper proposes a Resource Capability Model to enable resource description, aggregation and optimized matchmaking. Based on the Resource Capability model, a XML-based GSO language and the Application Information Service is developed to implement the matchmaking process. The experiment result shows that our mechanism is scalable in both Grid and Cloud environment.

Acknowledgement. This research work was supported by the Migol project from the Potsdam University (http://www.migol.de), the self-conducted exploratory research program "Green Lighting in Internet of Things" from State Key Laboratory for Software Development Environment in China (NO.SKLSDE-2010ZX-06), the Special Program for Seism-Scientific Research in Public Interest "Research in Online Processing Technologies for Seismological Precursory Network Dynamic Monitoring and Products" (NO. 201008002) and the National Natural Science Foundation of China (No. 61100066)

References

1. Andreozzi, S., Ehm, F., Field, L., Kónya, B.: GLUE specification. http://ogf.org/documents/GFD.147.pdf. March 2009
2. Anjomshoaa, A., Brisard, F., Drescher, M., Fellows, D., Ly, A., McGough, S., Pulsipher, D., Savva, A.: Job submission description language (jsdl) specification, version 1.0. http://www.gridforum.org/documents/GFD.136.pdf. July 2008
3. Foster, I., Kesselman, C., Nick, J., Tuecke, S.: The physiology of the grid: an open grid services architecture for distributed systems integration. http://www-unix.globus.org/toolkit/3.0/ogsa/docs/physiology.pdf (2002)
4. Foster, I.: Globus toolkit version 4: software for service-oriented systems. In: Jin, H., Reed, D., Jiang, W. (eds.) NPC 2005. LNCS, vol. 3779, pp. 2–13. Springer, Heidelberg (2005)
5. Jeske, J., Luckow, A., Schnor, B.: Reservation-based resource-brokering for grid computing. In: Proceedings of German E-Science Conference 2007, Baden-Baden, Germany, pp. 1–10 (2007)
6. Lanfermann, G., Schnor, B., Seidel, E.: Grid object description: characterizing grids. In: Eighth IFIP/IEEE International Symposium on Integrated Network Management, Colorado Springs, Colorado, USA, March 2003
7. Luckow, A., Schnor, B.: Migol: a fault-tolerant service framework for mpi applications in the grid. Future Gener. Comput. Syst. - Int. J. Grid Comput. **24**(2), 142–152 (2008)
8. Migol Research Group: Migol, Migration in the Grid OGSA Lite. http://migol.de/. (2010)
9. Thain, D., Tannenbaum, T., Livny, M.: Distributed computing in practice: the condor experience. Concurrency - Pract. Experience **17**(2–4), 323–356 (2005)
10. Troger, P., Brobst, R., Gruber, D., Mamonski, M., Templeton, D.: Distributed resource management application API version 2 (DRMAA). http://www.ogf.org/documents/GFD.194.pdf. January 2012

The Framework of SCADA System
Based on Cloud Computing

Miao Liu[⊠], Changbing Guo, and Mancang Yuan

China Petroleum Longhui Automation Engineering Co., Ltd.,
China Petroleum Pipeline Bureau, Langfang, China
{lhbj_liumiaol,guochangbin,yuanmancang}@cnpc.com.cn

Abstract. SCADA (Supervisory Control and Data Acquisition) system is
computer control system based on supervisory. SCADA system is very
important to oil and gas pipeline engineering. Cloud computing is fundamen-
tally altering the expectations for how and when computing, storage and networking resources should be allocated, managed and consumed. In order to
increase resource utilization, reliability and availability of oil and gas pipeline
SCADA system, the SCADA system based on cloud computing is proposed in
the paper. This paper introduces the system framework of SCADA system
based on cloud computing and the realization details about the private cloud
platform of SCADA system.

Keywords: SCADA system · Cloud computing · Private cloud platform

1 Introduction

SCADA (Supervisory Control and Data Acquisition) system is computer control
system based on supervisory. The SCADA system of oil and gas pipeline can manage
sequential control transmission of petroleum pipeline, equipment monitoring, data
synchronization transmission record and monitoring operation conditions of every
station control system. In addition, the SCADA system has more features, such as
leaking detection, system simulation, water hammer protection in advance, and so on.
SCADA system can continuously monitor equipments which are scattered over the
wide regions and it can operate remote devices from the control center so that
the operating efficiency is improved, the energy is saved and the cost is reduced. And,
the SCADA system can guarantee the integrity of pipeline by continuous monitoring
the key parameters of system, such as pressure, flow, oil tank liquid level and so on
[1]. So, SCADA system is very important to oil and gas pipeline engineering.

Cloud computing, as a current commercial offering, started to become apparent in
late 2007 [2]. It was intended to enable computing across widespread and diverse
resources, rather than on local machines or at remote server farms. Although there is no
standard definition of Cloud Computing, most authors seem to agree that it consists of
clusters of distributed computers (Clouds) providing on-demand resources or services
over a network with the scale and reliability of a data centre [3]; notions familiar from
resource virtualization and Grid computing. Where these clusters supply instances of
on-demand Cloud computing; provision may be comprised of software (e.g. Software

V.C.M. Leung and M. Chen (Eds.): CloudComp 2013, LNICST 133, pp. 155–163, 2014.
DOI: 10.1007/978-3-319-05506-0_15, © Institute for Computer Sciences, Social Informatics
and Telecommunications Engineering 2014

as a Service, SaaS) or of the physical resources (e.g. Platform as a Service, PaaS). The Amazon Elastic Compute Cloud (Amazon EC2) [4] is an example of such an approach, where a computing platform is provided. In common with many commercial approaches *provision* is the primary objective; management and governance handled via redundancy or replication, scaling capacity up or down as required. In contrast the authors proposed a Cloud Coordination framework in 2005 with the notion of a Cloud being a system of loose boundaries, which interacts and merges with other systems [5]. This definition of a Cloud is refined to a federation of interacting services and resources, which share and pool resources for greater efficiency. Thus governance, in general, and scalability are handled as part of the separated coordination framework.

In order to increase resource utilization, reliability and availability of oil and gas SCADA system, the SCADA system based on cloud computing is proposed in the paper.

The remainder of this paper is organized as follows. In Sect. 2, traditional structure of SCADA system is described. The framework of cloud computing and the key features and characteristics of cloud computing are detailed in Sect. 3. Section 4 the system architecture of SCADA system based on cloud computing is proposed. In Sect. 5, the realization details about the private cloud platform of SCADA system is described. Finally, the paper concludes in Sect. 6.

2   Traditional Structure of SCADA System

The SCADA system adopts distributed supervisory control and centralized management. The traditional structure of SCADA system is described in Fig. 1. The system is organized by the supervision center, a lot of site control systems and communication medium. The supervision center (master station) is the core of system and in charge of controlling and managing system running. It is organized by a lot of data processing servers and database servers. The outside site is the intelligent measure and control module by microprocessor or DSP. It can collect and process the data of remote sites, control local sites and communicate with remote supervision center.

The SCADA system includes: information acquisition subsystem, information transmission subsystem and information processing subsystem. The information acquisition subsystem includes all kinds of sensors and controllers. It takes charge of data collection and devices controlling of local site. The information transmission subsystem can transport collected data and system controlling signal of local site by efficient communication technologies. It is the bridge of information acquisition subsystem and information processing subsystem. It includes RTU (Remote Terminal Unit), modem and central communication controller. The information processing subsystem is located at supervision center and it can gather, process and analysis the data of remote sites. It includes master computer and all kinds of expert software.

However, the current SCADA system has problems as follow:

(1) Reliability problem

Servers of supervision center are the command center of system. They can gather the pipeline running data, state and warning information and provide the real-time database for all operating sites. Now, the SCADA system of oil and gas pipeline adopts

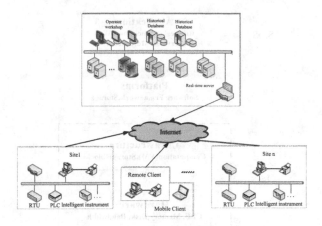

Fig. 1. The structure of SCADA system

Hot Standby as the way of redundant configuration to ensure the reliability of system. When master server is working online, the slave server monitors work state of master server and get the data from master server for keeping the data consistency between the master server and slave server. Once the master server breaks down, the slave server takes over the work from the master server immediately, and the slave server becomes the master server, the repaired master server becomes the slave server. As the controlling core of SCADA system, the central servers are responsible for data collecting and controlling of all line. It is important to ensure the data transmission between the servers and site control system for all SCADA system network normal operation. The single backup server cannot ensure the reliability of system completely.

(2) Source wasting problem

Hot Standby is used for ensuring the reliability of system. With system scaling out constantly, the number of server increases. Redundant configuration can cause wasting server source and the workload of operation administration and maintenance increasing. So, it is necessary to find more advanced resource configuration mode to increase resource utilization rate.

(3) Load balancing problem

With SCADA system of oil and gas pipeline scaling out constantly, the number of server increases. There is lots of operation and data are processed on different servers. However, CPU load is different with different site data. So, different servers have different load, some servers overload but some servers just are idle. It is necessary to study new load balancing strategy for improving the performance of system.

3 The Framework and the Key Features of Cloud Computing

Generally, the architecture of a cloud computing environment can be divided into 4 layers, as shown in Fig. 2 [6].

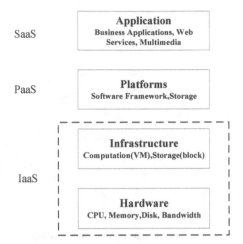

Fig. 2. The architecture of cloud computing

The hardware layer: This layer is responsible for managing the physical resources of the cloud, including physical servers, routers, switches, power and cooling systems. In practice, the hardware layer is typically implemented in data centers. A data center usually contains thousands of servers that are organized in racks and interconnected through switches, routers or other fabrics. Typical issues at hardware layer include hardware configuration, fault tolerance, traffic management, power and cooling resource management.

The infrastructure layer: Also known as the virtualization layer, the infrastructure layer creates a pool of storage and computing resources by partitioning the physical resources using virtualization technologies such as Xen [7], KVM [8] and VMware [9]. The infrastructure layer is an essential component of cloud computing, since many key features, such as dynamic resource assignment, are only made available through virtualization technologies.

The platform layer: Built on top of the infrastructure layer, the platform layer consists of operating systems and application frameworks. The purpose of the platform layer is to minimize the burden of deploying applications directly into VM containers. For example, Google App Engine operates at the platform layer to provide API support for implementing storage, database and business logic of typical web applications.

The application layer: At the highest level of the hierarchy, the application layer consists of the actual cloud applications. Different from traditional applications, cloud applications can leverage the automatic-scaling feature to achieve better performance, availability and lower operating cost. Compared to traditional service hosting environments such as dedicated server farms, the architecture of cloud computing is more modular. Each layer is loosely coupled with the layers above and below, allowing each layer to evolve separately. This is similar to the design of the OSI model for network protocols. The architectural modularity allows cloud computing to support a wide range of application requirements while reducing management and maintenance overhead.

4 The System Framework of SCADA System Based on Cloud Computing

Compare to traditional structure of SCADA system, the SCADA system based on cloud computing used cloud computing technologies to integrate server resource of supervision center, manage and assign this resource uniform, but not allocate a certain server to be in charge of a certain pipe line. In addition, the local site control systems are redeployed at the cloud server of remote private cloud platform. The structure of SCADA system based on cloud computing is shown in Fig. 3.

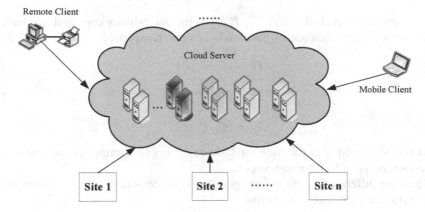

Fig. 3. The structure of SCADA system based on cloud computing

The virtualization technology enables the abstraction or decoupling of the application payload from the underlying physical resource. The physical resource can then be carved up into logical or virtual resources as needed. This is known as provisioning. With server virtualization, we can create complete logical (virtual) servers that are independent of the underlying physical infrastructure or their physical location. We can specify the computing, network and storage resources for each logical server (virtual machine) and even move workloads from one virtual machine to another in real-time (live migration). Every practitioner of server virtualization is aware of how virtualization can result in "Virtual Machine (VM) Sprawl" and the associated management burden it creates. VM Sprawl is a result of the ease with which new VMs can be created and proliferated on virtualized servers. This is however not the only factor affecting management complexity. Since VMs are cheaper to setup and run than a physical server, load balancers, routers and other applications that required physical servers are all now being run as in VMs within a physical server. Consequently, we now have to manage and route network traffic resulting from all these VMs within a server as well as the network traffic being routed across server. Adding to this confusion are the various OS vendor, each offering the other vendor's OS as a "guest" without providing the same level integration services. This makes the real life implementations, very management intensive, cumber some and error-prone to really operate in a heterogeneous environment. It is our contention that the cost of this additional management may yet offset any cost benefits that virtualization has enabled through consolidation. A traditional management system with human-dependency is just an untenable solution for cloud computing.

The SCADA system model of oil and gas pipeline is created as follow:

The real-time data processing tasks of SCADA system are expressed by $T = \{T_1, T_2, ..., T_n\}$. Each task of SCADA system is independent and the task is non-preemptive.

Each real-time task can be defined as

$$T_i = \left(d_i, T_i^1, T_i^2, T_i^3\right) \tag{1}$$

d_i is the deadline of real-time task; T_i^1, T_i^2, T_i^3 is the one primary copy and two backup copies, respectively; the code of three tasks is same completely.

$$T_i^1 = (C_i, s_i^1, \rho_i^1) \tag{2}$$

$$T_i^2 = (C_i, s_i^2, \rho_i^2) \tag{3}$$

$$T_i^3 = (C_i, s_i^3, \rho_i^3) \tag{4}$$

There, s_i^1, s_i^2 and s_i^3 is the time for tasks to be began running; ρ_i^1, ρ_i^2 and ρ_i^3 are processors assigned to three task copies.

There are different execution time for different processors so defining a computing time vector for each task T_i as follow,

$$C_i = [c(i, 1), ..., c(i, m)] \tag{5}$$

There c_{ij} represents the execution time for T_i^1, T_i^2, T_i^3 on processor P_j.

If SCADA system can tolerate 2 processors disable, the sum of primary copy execution time and backup copy execution time should be less than or equal to deadline.

$$\forall i \in [1, n], \left(c\left(i, \rho_i^1\right) + c\left(i, \rho_i^2\right)\right) \le d_i \wedge \left(c\left(i, \rho_i^1\right) + c\left(i, \rho_i^3\right)\right) \le d_i \tag{6}$$

For each processor P_i of SCADA system

$$\forall i \in [1, m], \sum_{T_i^1 \in \Delta_j} c(i, j) + \sum_{T_i^2 \in \Delta_j} c(i, j) \le d_i, \sum_{T_i^1 \in \Delta_j} c(i, j) + \sum_{T_i^3 \in \Delta_j} c(i, j) \le d_i \tag{7}$$

5 Realization Details About the Private Cloud Platform of SCADA System

The physical architecture of Private cloud includes: controller node, compute nodes, NFS server and network devices. It is shown in Fig. 4.

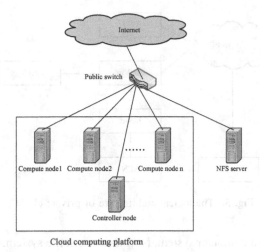

Fig. 4. The physical architecture of private cloud

The function of Controller node includes showing, monitoring, management and scheduling. The controller node provide a database and web server to support the management interface of system. The users issue control commands and operate the system by the management interface of the controller node. Information of other nodes must register to the controller node and the controller node schedule the resource constantly.

Compute nodes is the operating foundation of virtual machine. They are in charge of the specific operating work of private cloud system. Compute nodes compose the resource pool together and provide the resource with form of virtualization. The virtual machines which privat cloud system provide for outside users to use run in compute nodes. Compute nodes are dominated and managed by the controller node.

NFS server provides NFS service which supports dynamic extension function of private cloud system.

Network devices include routers and switches. They connect every devices of private cloud system and access to network. In addition, they take charge in network address assignment.

The logical architecture of Private cloud is shown in Fig. 5.

Graphic interface management is the external interface of system. The users manage and operate the system by GUI. It is the web service based on web server and database. Users can enter the management interface by accessing to the port of related server via internet without setting up client. In addition, users can access and manage all system, anytime and anywhere, by all kinds of network terminal to master running state of system and find and solve the problem in time.

ConVirt is the core of system. It provides all kinds of data to management interface and monitor all system. Also, it is the real manager of system. It converts all operations on management interface by users to computer instruction and sends the instruction to every execution parts of system. ConVirt is programmed by python and

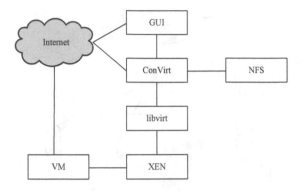

Fig. 5. The logical architecture of private cloud

it is fit for all kinds of computer system. NFS is network file system. The private cloud can copy and migrate virtual machine conveniently without redeploying by the function of shared catalog and files provided by NFS.

Libvirt provides a set of reliable and convenient interface for all kinds of virtualization tools to shield the difference of instruction of virtualization tools.

Xen is a virtualization solution. It can realize virtualization function of x86 framework. The virtual machine of private cloud system is made by Xen directly. Users operate the virtual machine on graphic management interface is passed on layers and layers by ConVirt converting to computer instructions. The running condition of virtual machine is collected and fed back to users by ConVirt.

6   Conclusion

Oil and gas pipeline project is an industrial system with highly systemic. The running data of pipelines can be obtained real-time, processed scientifically and made decision by SCADA system. For improving the reliability and resource utilization of traditional oil and gas pipeline SCADA system, the application framework of oil and gas pipeline SCADA system based cloud computing is proposed and the system model is designed in the paper. This application framework can realize real-time data multi-copy execution and history data multi-restore. So, the new application framework is with more reliability and higher resource utilization. Next, the real-time scheduling algorithm for the SCADA system based on cloud computing can be researched.

References

1. Yang, L., Cao, X.: Research on FNN-based security defense architecture model of SCADA network. In: Proceedings of IEEE CCIS, pp. 1829–1833 (2012)
2. IBM: IBM Introduces Ready to Use Cloud Computing. IBM Press Release, 15 Nov 2007
3. Grossman, R.L.: The case for cloud computing. IT Prof. **11**(2), 23–27 (2009)

4. Amazon Elastic Compute Cloud (EC2). http://www.amazon.com/gp/browse.html?node=201590011
5. Miseldine, P., Taleb-Bendiab, A.: A programmatic approach to applying sympathetic and parasympathetic autonomic systems to software design. In: Czap, H., et al. (eds.) Self-Organization and Autonomic Informatics (1), pp. 293–303. IOS Press, Amsterdam (2005)
6. Zhang, Q., Cheng, L., Boutaba, R.: Cloud computing: state-of-the-art and research challenges. J. Internet Serv. Appl. **1**, 7–18 (2010)
7. XenSource Inc., Xen. www.xensource.com
8. Kernal Based Virtual Machine. www.linux-kvm.org/page/MainPage
9. VMWare ESX Server. www.vmware.com/products/esx

Cloud Services Platform of Public Resources Trading Integration

Jianbin Xiong[1(✉)], Qinruo Wang[2], Jianqi Liu[3], Qiong Liang[1],
and Keliang Zhou[4]

[1] Guangdong University of Petrochemical Technology, Maoming, China
276158903@qq.com
[2] School of Automation, Guangdong University of Technology,
Guangzhou, China
[3] College of Information Engineering, Guangdong Jidian Polytechnic,
Guangzhou, China
[4] Jiangxi University of Science and Technology, Ganzhou, China

Abstract. Considering China's public resources trading platform does not implement in the true sense of integration, information sharing still exist in isolation, security is not strong, large resources, poor timeliness, and efficiency is low, so we put forward a public resources trading platform based on cloud services. This system not only realize the public resources trading center insider, wealth, and the unity of the business process management, meanwhile to achieve resource virtualization, services can be quantified, and one-stop service online.

Keywords: Cloud computing · SOA · One-stop service · Measurement of service

1 Introduction

With the advancement and deepening of China's institutional reform, in order to standardize public resources trading markets, and promote the public resources trading to develop healthily in the direction of fairness, justice and openness, currently, the public resources centers in area units have sprung up across the country [1]. At present, while a lot of public resources centers have been set up across the country, but most of the public resources centers are still only staying on the surface of the integration, though with various department personnel working together [2]. In the workflow, information sharing is still isolated, and strictly speaking, there is no real sense of integration. The main cause of this phenomenon is that the original business belong to the management of different government departments, the departments involved are very wide, including: the National Development and Reform Commission (NDRC), Housing Construction Bureau, Finance Bureau, Water Conservancy Bureau, Department of Transportation, Health Bureau, Land Bureau, Bidding Management Office, etc., but no one integrated platform is to provide uniform service for the public resources trading, the problems existing in SOA-based integration platform of the public resources trading have following features [3]: (1) Lead to changes in

V.C.M. Leung and M. Chen (Eds.): CloudComp 2013, LNICST 133, pp. 164–176, 2014.
DOI: 10.1007/978-3-319-05506-0_16, © Institute for Computer Sciences, Social Informatics and Telecommunications Engineering 2014

organizational structure. There is a center of excellence (COE) in the center of each SOA. COE is a new entity that controls the technology development of SOA and provides the rest of the organization with professional knowledge. SOA COE for any organization is newly added, and thus launches, when it is strong enough and the decisions made here will affect other personnel of the organization, its introduction may lead to conflict. (2) Changes in the structure of organization power. Putting the ownership and control of the service into the business field, will change the power structure of the organization. Doing so will often encounter resistance from those who have the privilege to maintain the status. (3) Business faces new challenges. IT business must be given more guidance. Business lines must enhance the ownership of the services and be responsible for it, so as to start the development and change cycle, because they will facilitate this process. This is not a typical supplement of the business lines, which can result in inappropriate changes. (4) IT will be more and more complex before it becomes easier. In order to implement SOA, we use a set of such as business process execution engine and ESB technology. Adding this technology into IT planning won't make it simple, even when its advantages far outweigh its costs. IT planning, however, more complex doesn't mean that it can't appear in a more simple form. The launch of this service let IT's complexity become a secret. Consumers of these services don't need to know how the internal services run. As a result, any rationalization operations occurred in the backend. It can be hidden in the service interface. (5) No data view. The standard service interface requires a unified data view. This unified view usually doesn't exist, and trying to develop a unified view often finds a very different view of the organization. (6) Transformations are not easy. There are lots of problems such as many unsafe factors, large resource input, poor timeliness and low efficiency, etc. It's not easy for transformation and organizations to become "service-centered". The organizations created in the traditional form of islands need to change their structure, make fully using become the advantage of the "service-centered". This transformation is complex and expensive, and never lack of the opponents of this change [4].

So it needs to establish a set of cloud services platform which can cover the public resources trading business integration, this article is not only to achieve the unified management of the internal personnel, financial, material and business process of the public resources trading center, but will also face the necessary related services of each superior administration and all kinds of enterprises.

2 Related Works

Service-oriented architecture (SOA) is defined with neutral manner. It should be independent of the hardware platforms, operating systems and programming languages that achieve services. This allows the services built on a variety of systems like that can interact in a unified and general form [5]. The feature of this neutral interface definition (not mandatory to bind to a specific implementation) is called loose coupling between services. Two advantages of loosely coupled systems are: (1) flexibility. (2) when the internal structure of each service and implementation composing the entire application program changes gradually, it can continue to exist, but on the other hand, tight coupling means that the interface between the different components of the application program and its function and structure are closely linked, so when it needs to make some form of change on the part or entire application program, they are very fragile [2, 5].

While the service-oriented architecture is not a relatively new thing, but it is the alternative model of the more traditional object-oriented model, object-oriented model is tightly coupled, and it has been around for more than twenty years [4, 6]. Although SOA-based system does not preclude the use of object-oriented design to build a single service, its overall design is service-oriented. Because it takes into account the objects within the system, so, while SOA is based on the object, but as a whole, it is not object-oriented [7]. The difference lies in the interface itself. A typical example of SOA system prototype is Common Object Request Broker Architecture (CORBA), it has been around for a long time, the concept it defined is similar to the SOA.

Now, however, the SOA is somewhat different, because it relies on some updated progress, this progress is based on the eXtensible Markup Language (XML). By using XML-based language (called Web Services Description Language, WSDL) to describe the interface, the service has been turned to more dynamic and flexible interface system.

In addition, dynamic business workflow can include not only the operation between departments, but also even the operation it carried out with the not being controlled external partners. Therefore, in order to improve the efficiency, it needs to define the strategy that how to know the relationship between services, this strategy is often in the form of service level agreements and operating strategies [8].

In view of the disadvantages existing in SOA, the emergence of the cloud changes the technical basis of the Internet, and will even affect the pattern of the whole industry. Within a few years, the foreign cloud computing has been become today's hot technology from emerging technology. From the core file published by Google in 2003, to the commercial applications of Amazon EC2 (Amazon Elastic Compute Cloud) in 2006, and to the Synaptic Hosting services launched by the U.S. telecommunications giant AT & T (American Telephone and Telegraph Company), cloud computing, from the cost-saving tool to the driver of profit, from the ISP (Internet Service Provider) to the telecom enterprise, apparently successfully evolved into public service from the built-in IT system [9].

In the domestic, following the personal computer revolution, the Internet revolution, the cloud computing, viewed as the third wave of IT, is an important part of China's strategic emerging industries. It will bring the fundamental change of life, production mode and business model, becoming the focus of the whole society's attention. China's cloud computing industry is divided into market run-up, take-off stage and mature stage. Currently, China's cloud computing industry is still in the import and preparation stage. The advantages of combining SOA technical architecture and cloud computing technology concept with public resources trading platform include the following [8]:

(1) Providing high speed channels of human interaction and coordination, improving the efficiency of trading centers.
(2) Providing tools and services, promoting the rationalization and streamlining of the process.

(3) Integrating the complex, heterogeneous data sources, providing unified service information for trade centers.
(4) Connecting the people, process and information of trading centers.
(5) Extending the value of the previous asset investment, realizing the capitalization of information resources.

3 Integrated Service Cloud Platform Architecture

In this paper, it uses SOA-based architecture to build the integrated service cloud platform that meets the trading business of the public resources trading center. The overall structure of the cloud platform is shown in Fig. 1, according to the hierarchical logical model to design, it composed of five intermediate core layers and two support systems.

SOA-architecture-based cloud platform of public resources trading integration service divides from bottom to top: infrastructure layer, data support layer, SOA architecture platform support layer, application layer and access layer.

LaaS infrastructure layer: using the LaaS concept of cloud computing technology, to build infrastructure in the lowermost environment platform, mainly including: server equipment, data storage, backup device, application software environment, network environment and other application infrastructure, and using virtualization technology to implement the LaaS platform structures [10].

Data support layer: is the core data of the integrated service cloud platform, data center is based on all kinds of trading business data as the main content, depending on the database management technology, in accordance with the unified standards, and establishes the organization, management, maintenance and updating systems of the public resources trading center's scale data-base. It specifically includes: engineering trading libraries, government procurement library, land transactions libraries, medical device procurement libraries, bidders library, agency library, experts vault, rating system libraries, code base as well as unstructured information repository and so on [11].

SOA architecture platform support layer: namely the platform layer of the SOA architecture base, in this layer, the SOA architecture providing each business subsystem provides operation support environment, specifically including: the system integrated platform Portal Framework that used to unify the organizational structure, unify the personnel and unify the management rights; the Star Flow (BPM) that used to support the workflow system. The GLR that used for service resource management; the ESB that used to provide a trading service bus functions and so on, can use the products of ChinaSoft International own.

SaaS application layer: namely the SaaS applications that the integrated service platform needs to construct, is composed of the practical application business functions of the project. They are respectively Engineering Trade cloud, government procurement clouds, land transactions cloud, Medical Device trading systems, integrated management cloud, trade-sharing clouds, etc.

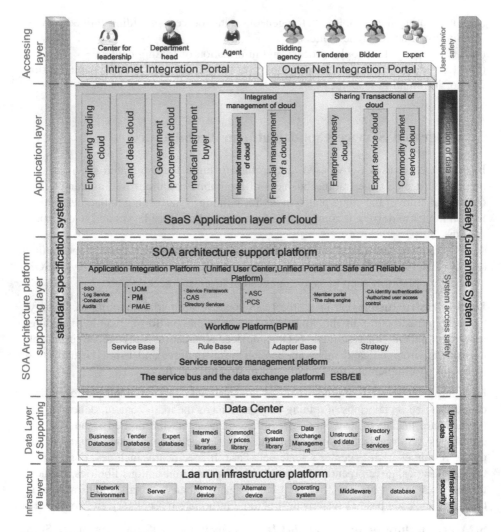

Fig. 1. Cloud platform of public resources trading integration service based on SOA architecture

Access layer: in fact involves the form of the whole application system for the end users. Around the core layer, is respectively with the security system, the standard system to constitute the system's support system.

Security system: from the physical environment security, network security, operating system security, database security, middleware security, application security, user security, access security, etc. multiple levels to protect the overall system in three-dimensional.

Standards and regulations system: is the necessary basis of the system construction of the standard trading center, including the documents compilation of the bidding policies and regulations, industry standards, data standards, exchange standards, etc.

The work that this article needing to construct can be roughly divided into three aspects are respectively the standard system construction of the integrated service cloud platform, the development of the integration service cloud platform, and the security system construction of the integration service cloud platform.

3.1 IaaS Cloud Platform Basis Design

IaaS (Infrastructure as a Service) infrastructure is namely service, IaaS is also the base layer construction of the integrated cloud service platform. Consumers can gain the service from the perfect computer infrastructure through the Internet. Services provided to the consumer is the use of all facilities, including processing, storage, networks, and other basic computing resources, Users can deploy and run their own software. Consumer does not manage or control any cloud computing infrastructure, but can control the choice, storage space, the deployment application of operating system, also possible to obtain the control of restricted network components (eg, firewalls, load balancers, etc.) [8–12]. In this paper, platform can provide consumers with the required cloud storage. Cloud storage is a system which is through the clustering application, grid technology and distributed file system, etc. To make a large variety of different types of storage devices work together through software applications, then to commonly externally provide data storage and business-access functions. When the computing and processing core of cloud computing system is the storage and management of large amounts of data, cloud computing systems need to configure a large number of storage devices, cloud storage is a cloud computing system with data storage and management as the core, as shown in Fig. 2.

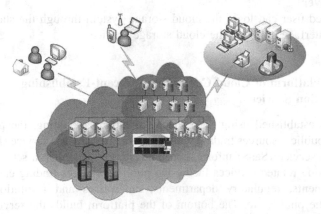

Fig. 2. Cloud storage system architecture diagram.

The structure model of cloud storage system consists of four layers:

(1) Storage layer

Storage layer is the most basic part of cloud storage. Storage devices can be FC fibre channel storage devices, can be IP storage devices such as NAS and ISCSI, etc., can also be DAS storage devices such as SCSI or SAS, etc. The number of storage devices in cloud storage is often large and distributed in different regions, and through wide area network, Internet, or FC fibre channel network to connect each other together.

Over the storage devices is a unified storage device management system, it can achieve the logic virtualization management of storage device, more link redundancy, and condition monitoring of hardware equipment and fault maintenance.

(2) Basic management layer

Basic management is the core part of the cloud storage, as well as the most difficult part to achieve of the cloud storage. Basic management is via the cluster, distributed file systems and grid computing technologies, to implement the collaborative work between multiple storage devices of cloud storage, enabling multiple storage devices to provide external with the same kind of service, and to provide bigger, stronger and better data access performance.

CDN content distribution systems, data encryption technology ensure the data in cloud storage will not be accessed by unauthorized users, meanwhile, through a variety of data backup and disaster recovery technology and policy to ensure that the data stored in the cloud storage is not lost, and to ensure its own security and cloud storage stability.

(3) Application interface layer

Application interface layer is the most flexible part of the cloud storage. It can develop different application service interface, and provide various application service according to the actual business types of the public resources trading. Such as network hard disk reference platform, remote data backup application platform, etc.

(4) Access layer

Any authorized user can login the cloud storage system through the standard utility application interface, to enjoy the cloud storage service.

3.2 Cloud Platform of Cloud Computing Concept-Establishing Integration Service

The platform established using the concept of cloud computing, the platform will combine the public resources trading with the infrastructure as a service (IaaS) and the software as a service (SaaS) information innovatively, establish a set of cloud platforms to provide related services facing the public resources trading center, government departments, regulatory departments, enterprises and institutions, industry experts and the public, etc. The bottom of the platform builds the server group and mass storage through the virtualization technology. The virtualization technology can effectively improve the use efficiency of the equipment, for the view of system pressure, multiple application service nodes can be set up in the virtual machine, to achieve the load balancing, both structured data and unstructured data are stored in the safe and efficient cloud storage devices, these will serve as the infrastructure services layer for the cloud platform. In the application, according to the actual needs of the business to build the major application systems such as engineering trading cloud, land transactions cloud, government procurement cloud, medical device procurement cloud, integrated management cloud and deal-sharing cloud, etc., so as to achieve the construction work of the integrated service's cloud platform.

3.2.1   Using the SOA Framework to Build the Entire System

The entire cloud platform of the public resources trading integration service is designed and constructed with the SOA framework, it's convenient for the data interchange and function call between various components of the system, and then implementing the loose coupling of the whole system and improving the scalability of the whole system.

SOA is a distributed software model. The three elements of SOA architecture are: service providers, service registry, service consumers. Each entity in the service-oriented architecture plays one (or more) of these three roles, the service provider, the requestor and the registry. Its relational schema is shown in Fig. 3.

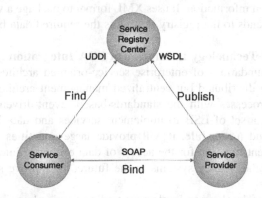

Fig. 3. The three elements of SOA architecture

(1) Service Requester: Service requester is an application, a software module or another service that needs a service. It launched a query in the registry's service, bind the service through transport, and perform the service function. The service requester performs the services according to the interface contracts.

(2) Service Provider: Service provider is an entity that can be addressed through the network. It accepts and executes the request from the requestor. It will release their own service and interface contracts to the service registry, so that the service requester can discover and access the service.

(3) Service Registry: The service registry is a supporter of the service discovery. It contains a repository of available services and allows the service requesters interested in lookup the service provider interface.

SOA software model involves the following techniques:

Web Service is also called the XML Web Service. Web Service is via the software service provided by SOAP on the Web to describe using WSDL file, and is via UDDI to register.

XML: Extensible Markup Language. Facing the short-term temporary data processing, and the World Wide Web, is the foundation of the SOAP.

SOAP: Simple Object Access Protocol. It is the communication protocol of XML Web Service. After finding the WSDL description document via the UDDI, users can call one or more operations of Web services via SOAP. SOAP is the specification of the invocation method of XML document. It can support different underlying interfaces, such as HTTP (S) or SMTP.

WSDL (Web Services Description Language) WSDL file is an XML document, used for describing a set of SOAP messages and how to exchange these messages. In most cases, it automatically generates and uses by the software.

UDDI (Universal Description, Discovery, and Integration) is a system framework of Web Service Integration. It contains the standard specification of the service description and discovery. Before the user invoking the Web Service, they must determine which methods contained within this service, and find the invoked interface definitions. UDDI use SOAP message mechanism (standard XML/HTTP) to publish, edit, browse and locate the registration information. It uses XML format to package a variety of different types of data, and sends to the registry or returns the required data by the registry.

3.2.2   Using ESB Technology to Implement SOA Integration

ESB, one of the foundations of enterprise service-oriented architecture, enables the enterprise in highly distributed but centralized management architecture to integrate applications and processes with the standards-based, event-driven service. Current project will deploy a set of ESB to implement services and data integration across multiple systems and meanwhile, it will provide large quantities of data exchange schedule management function for the access of data exchange interface and process arrangement with other legacy systems in the future, to improve service efficiency, lower overall cost.

(1) Using ESB technology to implement trading service bus

In the SOA-based system structures of the public resources trading integration service cloud platform, the design concept of the ESB will be used, in which the transaction service bus can use a lightweight ESB.

Trading service bus implements the service virtualization of various trading business logic, and provides a global, virtual view of the service, to simplify interact of various components of the system. Service users do not have to focus on what approval system the service is in, and what kind of interface data format it uses. Just need using the unified interface that released by transaction service bus, to use the service according to the unified data format [10–12].

To ensure the correct handling and forwarding messages of the transaction services bus, it needs to develop the following standards and specifications:

(1)   Unified service release specifications;
(2)   Unified standard message format.

Therefore, the transaction service bus is the combination of ESB and unified data standard specification.

To ensure the flexibility and scalability of the system, information transmission between each composition system should try to adopt the way of messaging, and implement via the transaction service bus.

(2) Using ESB technology to implement bidirectional data exchange

The cloud platform of public resources trading integration service contains city, district/county level secondary deployment, is essential to the realization of the municipal and district/county level 2 trade integrations, and data exchange. Using the unified data exchange standard of transaction service bus and fast, flexible system integration model of ESB, the trading system of secondary public resources trading center can implement the bidirectional data exchange in the form of fast and loose coupling.

On the one hand, the real-time trading data of district/county can timely centralize in the municipal trading platform, so as to realize the unification of transaction management and supervision. On the other hand, the public trading repository built on the municipal trading platform can provide district/county with the shared information resources.

Meanwhile, public resources transactions involves many government departments, including: Development and Reform Bureau, Finance Bureau, Housing Bureau, Water Bureau, Transportation Bureau, Health Bureau, Land Bureau, tender management office and so on, therefore, the cloud platform of integrated services also needs to exchange data with the information systems of the departments, Such as various types of enterprise's credit file information, all kinds of project approval information, transaction results record information, and the regulatory information of transaction process, etc., are all required to achieve horizontal data exchange via the ESB, so as to really realize data interconnection, communication, sharing.

(3) Using ESB technology to realize automatic business process

Currently, the popular ESB generally supports BPEL (Business Process Execution Language), namely the Business Process Execution Language (BPEL). BPEL is a specification language for business process automation, very suitable for the combination of business component of public resources trading integration service cloud platform. For example: fences standard series of standard components may contain more than one judgment strategy, these judgments strategies complete the function of fences standard series standard component together. Using BPEL, can flexibly assemble these judgments strategy components. At the same time, after implementing the new judgment logic can be quickly added to the task in the chain, as shown in Fig. 4.

(4) Using ESB technologies to realize unified trading shared services

Relying on the trading service bus to publish the sharing and inquiry service of unified trading information, trading sharing service system decouples the Trading sharing data and its users, to improve system's extensibility.

At the same time, it will implement the unified configuration of the sharing information, related to trading, which is scattered stored in transactions underlying database and e-government exchange platform, and provides a global, virtual trading share data "view". Inquirers only need to request to the inquiry service of trading-

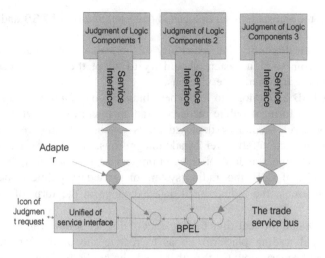

Fig. 4. Using BPEL of trading service bus to combine business components

sharing information that released by trading service bus, it is up to the shared service system to decide from where to get the actual share information according to the configuration of the Shared information . If the shared information is stored in a centralized transaction basis database, then read directly, otherwise will forward the query to the e-government data exchange platform for sharing information query, as shown in Fig. 5.

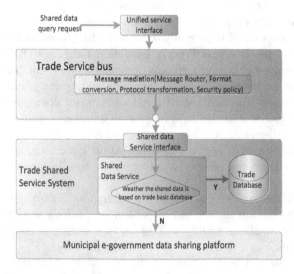

Fig. 5. Using the transaction service bus to achieve the unified trading -sharing services

(5) Using ESB technology to achieve the data exchange of internal and external network security

In the cloud platform of public resources trading integration services, online trading service hall system deployed outside the network, the remaining components of the system belong to the intranet system. Online trading service hall systems directly receive transaction data provided from the Internet, but also directly facing various possible attacks. Therefore, the online trading service hall systems and internal composition systems should ensure secure data exchange.

For the flexibility and security of data exchange, both internal and external network data exchange service use Web Service to provide services, use the transaction Service bus to accomplish through messaging. Since the ESB itself can flexibly set the security policy, so on the basis of the hardware network security equipment, using the transaction service bus, is conducive to the deployment of inside and outside network security isolation equipment, simplify the setting of security exchange policy, so as to improve the security of the system.

4 Conclusions

In order to realize the government's public resources data sharing. This paper puts forward the integration of public resources trading on cloud service platform, combining SOA architecture and cloud services. In this paper, we have implemented ESB bidirectional data exchange, automatic business process, inside and outside network security data exchange, one-stop online service.

References

1. Feng, D., Zhang, M., Zhang, Y., Xu, Z.: Study on cloud computing security. J. Softw. **22**(1), 71–83 (2011)
2. Tian, G., Meng, D., Zhan, J.: Reliable resource provision policy for cloud computing. Chin. J. Comput. **33**(10), 1859–1873 (2010)
3. Chen, K., Zheng, W.: Cloud computing: system instances and current research. J. Softw. **20**(5), 1337–1359 (2009)
4. Zhang, Y., Zhou, Y.: A new cloud operating system: design and implementation based on transparent computing. Acta Electron. Sinica **39**(5), 985–991 (2011)
5. Lai, C., Lai, Y., Chao, H., Wan, J.: Cloud-assisted real-time transrating for HTTP live streaming. IEEE Wirel. Commun. **20**(3), 62–70 (2013)
6. Wan, J., Ullah, S., Lai, C., Zhou, M., Wang, X., Zou, C.: Cloud-enabled wireless body area networks for pervasive healthcare. IEEE Network **27**(5), 56–61 (2013)
7. Chen, M., Wan, J., Gonzalez, S., Liao, X., Leung, V.: A survey of recent developments in home M2M networks. IEEE Commun. Surv. Tutor., January 2014
8. Chen, M., Wan, J., Li, F.: Machine-to-machine communications: architectures, standards, and applications. KSII Trans. Internet Inf. Syst. **6**(2), 480–497 (2012)
9. Chen, M., Wen, Y., Jin, H., Leung, V.: Enabling technologies for future data center networking: a primer. IEEE Network **27**(4), 8–15 (2013)

10. Wan, J., Liu, Z., Zhou, K., Lu, R.: Mobile cloud computing: application scenarios and service models. In: Proceedings of the 9th IEEE International Wireless Communications and Mobile Computing Conference, Cagliari, Italy, July 2013
11. Lai, C., Lai, Y., Wang, M.: An adaptive energy-efficient stream decoding system for cloud multimedia network on multi-core architectures. IEEE Syst. J. (2012)
12. Lai, C., Wang, H., Zhou, L., Chen, M.: Multi-appliance recognition system with hybrid SVMGMM classifier in ubiquitous smart home. IEEE Syst. J. (2012)

Cloud Security

Trusting Identity Based Authentication on Hybrid Cloud Computing

Hazem A. Elbaz[✉], Mohammed H. Abd-elaziz,
and Taymoor Nazmy

Faculty of Computer Science and Information System,
Ain-Shams University, Cairo, Egypt
{hazem.baz,ntaymoor19600}@gmail.com,
mhashem100@yahoo.com

Abstract. Nowadays users outsourcing their data to cloud provider, the most challenge on research works in cloud computing are access control and data security. Security problems come from the different kinds of cloud services for internet users provided by companies. Currently the majority of cloud computing systems provide digital identity for user to access their services, this will bring some inconvenience for hybrid cloud that include private clouds and, or public clouds. Recently identity based cryptography and Hierarchal identity based cryptography have been proposed to solve the internet applications threads. This paper based on using identity management on hybrid cloud, each user and server will have its own trusted unique identity, the unique key distribution and mutual authentication can be greatly simplified.

Keywords: Cloud computing · Hybrid cloud · Identity based cryptography · Hierarchal identity based cryptography · Cloud security · Authentication · Privacy

1 Introduction

Cloud Computing defined by National Institute of Standard Technology (NIST) it is: "a model for enabling convenient, on-demand network access to shared pool of configurable computer resources, that can be rapidly provisioned and released with minimal management effort or service provider interaction" [1]. Cloud Computing comes from development of Infrastructure as a services (IAAS), Platform as a Service (PAAS), and Software as a Service (SAAS). The private networks that offer cloud computing services for a restrictive set of users within the internal network called Private Cloud or internal cloud. Public cloud or external cloud called to cloud that enterprise provide cloud computing services for public users. Hybrid cloud which contains multiple private and public clouds.

With a large amount of resources given by cloud computing, user can smoothly solve their problems of computation and storage, cloud provide flexibility to for its users. The cloud computing services serve their users to store their critical data in servers and they could access to their data anywhere they can via internet [2].

V.C.M. Leung and M. Chen (Eds.): CloudComp 2013, LNICST 133, pp. 179–188, 2014.
DOI: 10.1007/978-3-319-05506-0_17, © Institute for Computer Sciences, Social Informatics and Telecommunications Engineering 2014

Cloud computing also concerned on data security, to increase demands and data confidentiality, authentication, and access control, where as data owners store their data on external servers. These concerns come from the fact that cloud server are operated by commercial providers, which are outside of trusted domain of users. Using asymmetric and symmetric cryptography is mostly used in cloud computing, but at recent identity based cryptography have attention by it characteristics which seem fit to cloud computing requirements.

It is easy to provide security in private cloud and public cloud, comparing with hybrid cloud, that's where private cloud or public cloud has only one provider in cloud, but in hybrid cloud it consisting multiple services providers that much more difficult for mutual authentication and key distribution. Accessing to service in the cloud, users need digital identity for servers in the cloud to manage the access control. Using identity based management is most recent techniques for each user to have his unique digital identity to allow him to access cloud computing servers [3].

The technology of identity-based cryptography is a public key technology, the user use public identifier as a public key. Hierarchal identity based cryptography is deployment from it to make solution of scalability problem in cloud computing.

This paper based on using identity management on cloud, that's where each user and server will have its own unique identity, with this unique, the key distribution and mutual authentication can be greatly simplified.

The reset of this paper is organized as follows: Sect. 2 gives introduction to cloud security, what the threads it face and solutions. Section 3 presents concepts of identity based cryptography and hierarchal identity based cryptography. Section 4 describe a propose of using friendly identity based management. Section 5, shows our performance analysis and results of our proposed protocol. Section 6 concludes the paper and outline for future research.

2   Cloud Computing Security

Cost reduction, resources sharing, and time saving are the most advantages of cloud computing. New challenges come to cloud computing systems, especially data security and privacy, while most software and data that users use reside over the internet. The characteristics of cloud computing is complicated to provide security in its environment, where each application may use resource from many servers, multiple location are potentially these serves and the services are provided by different infrastructures via clouds across many organizations. Users in cloud computing need to be taken various security issues, such as authentication, confidentiality, and integrity to ensure enough security in cloud environment. Cloud computing security concerns, when creating cloud environment inside a firewall, it provides users less exposure to internet threads. Inside private cloud computing, the internal connections can be responsible to access to services rather than public internet connections, that make existing security measures and standards easy to use, which make private cloud suitable for services with important data that should be protected. However, in hybrid cloud, it have more than one domains, which make the security more difficult to provision, especially mutual authentication and key management. Because of hybrid cloud include more than one kind of cloud; this make different security policies and different kinds of network conditions, so that it is much difficult to provide efficient security techniques to protection.

A strong and friendly way for users to gain access services in the cloud system are provided by cloud computing. The user needs to get a digital identity to run and application in the cloud. Simply the identity is a lot of bytes which related to user. Depends on the identity the cloud can know what is the privilege of user has and what he allowed to do in the cloud system. So these clouds computing provide their users, a unique digital identity [4].

The main problem here is that this digital identity can only used in one cloud, private one or public one. Users in a hybrid cloud may be want to access services that provided by different cloud, so it need multiple identities for each one of services on these clouds. Here is show clearly not user friendly.

This paper proposed to solve this problem by using identity management in clouds with hierarchal identity based cryptography, where this proposed scheme allow users from one cloud to access to service in other one with single digital identity, and also allow them in hybrid cloud to simplified a mutual authentication and key distribution.

3   Identity Based Cryptography

In 1984 Shamir was proposed the idea of identity based cryptography (IBC), which was the overcome the problem of binding between a public key and its owner, which was a new approach of public key cryptography [5].

The idea was using an identity of participant as a public key, rather than creating crafted integer. For example; when email sending to your partner, it is importance to know the email address to encrypt the message better than grabbing the corresponding public key from the public server.

Identity based cryptography used for two parties to exchange data and effectively verify each other's signature, as a new approach of public key cryptographic. IBC doesn't seem public key scheme which a public key is a random string, IBC use for encryption and signature verification a unique identity that user is used as a public key. Most advantages of IBC are, making ease key management complexity as public keys are not required to be distributed securely to other. IBC encryption and decryption operation can be done offline, without the key generation center [6].

Dan Boneh and Matthew K. Franklin defined completely [7] the approach of identity based cryptography, firstly the private key generator (PKG) creates a "master" public key and corresponding "master" private key. PKG makes "master" public key public for all users. A user can create his public key by using "master" public key and his identity. A user can get his private key by contact the PKG via his identity. The PKG use the user identity and his "master" private key to create user private key.

Hierarchal identity based cryptography (HIBC) come to solve the problem of one PKG in large network, which is PKG will have a Cumbersome job. HIBC creates in large network, root PKG to generate a private key for sub-domains PKGs, and the sub-domains PKGs generate private keys for users bellow. HIBC is the suitable choice for large network scale which reduce the workload of root PKG. HIBC improves the security of large network because each sub-domain responsible to do the user authentication and privacy key distribution [8] (Tables 1 and 2).

Table 1. Approach of identity based cryptography

Name	Description
Setup	PKG creates master key K_m, system parameters P, K_m is secret. P is public
Extract	User requests his private key from PKG
Encryption	User uses P, receiver's identity and MSG, to generate ciphertext
Decryption	User receiving a ciphertext, he use P, his private, to decrypt MSG

Table 2. Approach of hierarchal identity based cryptography

Name	Description
Root setup	Generate the Root PKG system parameters. It are publics for all sub-domains and users. Root secret. It is private
Sub-domain setup	Got the Root PKG system parameters to generate its own secret key with its own identity. Generate private keys for all users in its domain
Extract	User asks its key secret from its sub-domain PKG by identity. The sub-domain PKG by the identity and system parameters required private key from the root PKG, to be able to establish the user's private key

4   Trusting Identity Based Management in Cloud Computing

4.1   Trusting Identity Based Management

A user may be want to get access to external networks, or he is external network user want to access to an internal network. Friendly using identity based authentication is enhanced to deal with this security issue. It gives ability to share, between internal networks and external networks and enables the portability of identity information to access to different networks. The most advantages of friendly identity, increases the security of networks, where it needs a user to identity and authenticate himself to the system for one time, and his identity information will be used in different networks. Trusting identity also makes users from different networks to trust each other.

Trusted authority in PKGs at hybrid cloud computing are used. This paper propose to use trusted and friendly identity based management with HIBC at Hybrid cloud computing. PKGs will acts as PKGs in identity based cryptography system and also allocate hierarchal identities to users in sub-domains. Each cloud has root in overall domain, and within this cloud, each sub-domain (private or public) has also its PKG. the role of root PKG is manage whole cloud, the first level contains the private clouds or public clouds, second level it contains users and servers. Allocating and authenticating identities for all clouds (private or public) also done by root PKG. For example, root PKG creates identity *ID_Uni* to a private cloud of a University. Identities of all users and servers in a private cloud or public cloud manage and allocate by using sub-domain PKG. A hierarchal identity created for user and server, which is combine both identity of the user or server and the identity of the sub-domain. For example, the identity of email server in the private cloud of a University can be *ID_Uni.email_server*.

4.2   Cloud Computing Key Generation

Key generation and distribution is an important part at hybrid cloud computing using HIBC. As described in [8, 9], using of admissible pairing is the base for the security of HIBC.

Let G1 and G2 be two groups of some large prime order q, G1 is an additive group, G2 is a multiplicative group, we can call ê an admissible pairing if (ê : G1 × G2 → G2) have the following properties:

a. Billinear: for all P, Q ∈ G1 and a, b ∈ Z^*_q, $\hat{e}(aP, bQ) = \hat{e}(P, Q)^{ab}$.
b. Non-degenerate: there exits P, Q ∈ G1, such that $\hat{e}(P, Q) \neq 1$.
c. Computable: for all P, Q ∈ G1, there exists a efficient way to calculate $\hat{e}(P, Q)$.

An admissible pairing can be generated by using a Weil pairing or Tate pairing [9]. Hybrid cloud use two levels PKG, root PKG is $level_0$ PKG, and the PKGs in private or public clouds are $level_1$. The root setup can be done as follow:

1. Root PKG generates G1, G2 and admissible pairing $\hat{e}(aP, bQ) = \hat{e}(P, Q) \neq 1$ (G1,G2,ê,P0,Q0,H1,H2) ê : G1 × G2 → G2.
2. Root PKG chooses $P_0 \in$ G1 and $s_0 \in Z^*_q$ and set $Q_0 = s_0 P_0$.
3. Root PKG chooses hash function H1: $\{0, 1\}^* \rightarrow$ G1 and H2 : G2 → $\{0, 1\}^n$.

The system parameters are (G1,G2,ê,P0,Q0,H1,H2) and are public available, s_0 is the root PKG's secret key, and is known only by the root PKG.

For the lower level PKGs, and users and servers in the hybrid cloud computing, they use the system parameters and their identities to generate its public key. And users or servers in the cloud connect the PKGs in their cloud sub-domain to get their private keys.

For example, the private cloud of University with identity *ID_Uni*, its public key generated as $p_{ID\_Uni} =$ H1 (*ID_Uni*), and the private key generated by root PKG as $s_{ID\_Uni} = s_0 p_{ID\_Uni}$.

A user in the University can generate its identity as follow: the public key $p_{usr} =$ H1 (ID_Uni ‖ usr), and the University PKG creates the user private key as $s_{usr} = s_{ID\_Uni} + s_{ID\_Uni} \, p_{usr}$.

4.3   Identity Based Authentication and Secret Key Exchange

Communicating over insecure channel, between two users needs authentication key agreement protocol to create a shared secret key to be guaranteed that they are indeed sharing this secret key with each other [10].

Later, increasingly researched have been on identity based authenticated key agreement protocol, because of simplicity of public key management. Bilinear pairings on elliptic curves is most using on identity based two parties key agreement schemes as proposed in [10, 11].

According to Sanjit Chatterjee, Palash Sarkar [2], each of two parties in the system using identity based cryptography, has its own private key and public key of each other, to calculate the secret shared key between them. For example, Alice and Bob are two parties in the cloud with their public keys and private keys P_{Alice}, Q_{Alice}, P_{Bob}, Q_{Bob}, can calculate the secret shared key by computing: $K_s = ê(Q_{Alice}, P_{Bob}) = ê(Q_{Bob}, P_{Alice})$.

Now, Hybrid cloud that using HIBC, each user and server wants to communicate without message exchange by using a secret shared key when they calculate it. The advantage of identity based cryptography show here, which is reduce the message transmission and avoid detection of secret shared key among transmission.

HIBC use the secret shared key for encryption/decryption operations, but also use to establish the mutual authentication. Assume the we want to authenticate between, Alice as a user with identity Alice@Uni, and the server with identity Email@google in the cloud. Firstly, Ks the secret shared key should be calculated between them. Then Alice send a message to server as: Alice → server: Alice@Uni, M, f(Ks, Alice@Uni, Email@google, M). Which M is randomly selected message, f() One way hash function, to compute the correct value, a correct value need Ks, Ks is computed by Alice's private key that allocated from the PKG in the private cloud of University.

At the same way, the server authenticate itself to Alice. We notice that this mutual authentication does not need any certification from third party.

5   Performance Analysis and Results

In this section, discussing performance comparison between IBAKE [12, 13] and TIBA, then gives the results.

5.1   Communication Cost

The comparison communication cost between two different protocols is shown in Table 3. Note that only communication is considered, i.e. encrypted and signed messages, which may have the greatest consumptions of network bandwidth.

Table 3. Comparison of communication cost.

TIBA		IBAKE	
1 IBE ciphertext	1 IBS signature	3 IBE ciphertext	0 IBS signature

Reference [10] shows that communication cost of IBAKE is 3 IBE ciphertext and no signatures. However, in the TIBA, the communication cost id only one IBE ciphertext and only one 1 IBS signature.

5.2   Computation Cost

The comparison of computational cost between two different protocols is shown in Table 4. Note that only computation is considered, i.e. encryption, decryption, and authentication.

Table 4. Comparison of computational cost

	TIBA		IBAKE	
Client side	1 encryption	1 signature	2 encryption	1 decryption
Server side	1 decryption	1 verification	1 encryption	2 decryption

Kolesnikov et al. [13] showed that in IBAKE, the computation cost of client was 2 encryption and one decryption. The computation cost of server was one encryption and two decryption. However, in the TIBA, the computation cost of client is one encryption and one signature. The computation cost of server is one decryption and one verification.

5.3   Simulation and Experiment Results

5.3.1   Simulation Platform and Reference

The platform of simulation experiment is rackspace private cloud computing V2.0 [14, 15]. Special users and resources can be generated by rewriting these interfaces. This aligns well with various users and resources of cloud computing. Rackspace has developed Rackspace Private Cloud Software, a fast, free, and easy way to download and install a Rackspace Private Cloud powered by OpenStack in any data center. Rackspace Private Cloud Software is suitable for anyone who wants to install a stable, tested, and supportable OpenStack private cloud, and can be used for all scenarios from initial evaluations to production deployments. Therefore, it is feasible to simulate our proposed authentication protocol of cloud computing by Rackspace private cloud.

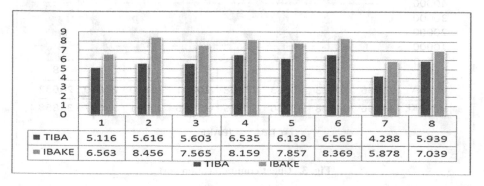

	1	2	3	4	5	6	7	8
■ TIBA	5.116	5.616	5.603	6.535	6.139	6.565	4.288	5.939
■ IBAKE	6.563	8.456	7.565	8.159	7.857	8.369	5.878	7.039

Fig. 1. Client computation cost

5.3.2   Simulation Results and Analysis

Figure 1 illustrates the client computation time of TIBA is approximate 5.72 ms while that IBAKE is about 7.49 ms. That is to say, client computation time of TIBA is 76 % of IBAKE. Figure 2 illustrates the computation time of server for TIBA is approximate 10.3275 ms, while that for IBAKE is 15.97513 ms. That is to say, computation time of server for TIBA is 65 of that for IBAKE. The simulation results confirm that both client and server of TIBA are more lightweight than those of IBAKE.

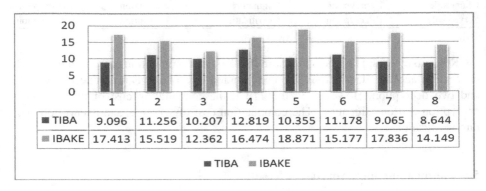

Fig. 2.   Server computation cost

Figure 3 shows the client communication cost of TIBA is approximately 20812.88 bytes while that of IBAKE is 35027.13 bytes. That is to say, client communication cost of TIBA is 60 % of that IBAKE. Figure 4 obtains the communication cost of server of TIBA is 27738 bytes while that of IBAKE is 38999.5 bytes. That is to say server communication cost of TIBA is 71 % of that IBAKE. The simulation results confirm that the communication cost of TIBA is less and the authentication time is shorter.

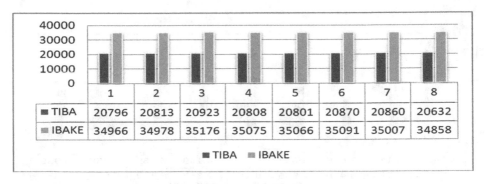

Fig. 3.   Client communication cost

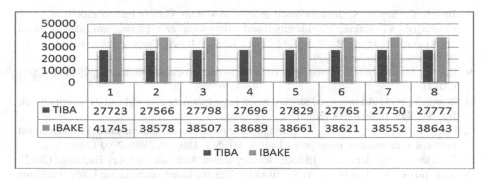

	1	2	3	4	5	6	7	8
■ TIBA	27723	27566	27798	27696	27829	27765	27750	27777
■ IBAKE	41745	38578	38507	38689	38661	38621	38552	38643

Fig. 4. Server communication cost

6 Conclusions

Security in hybrid cloud computing have some disadvantages in key management and authentication. This paper presented an introduction of cloud computing security problems, concepts of identity based cryptography and hierarchal identity based management and how it suitable to solve the problem in hybrid cloud authentication. We proposed using friendly identity based management and HIBC in cloud, explained how can the system generate and distribute the public and private keys to users and servers. Also we showed how two parties in the hybrid cloud can generate secret shared key without certificate (message exchange) and authenticate each other with simple way using identity based cryptography. We indicated that performance analysis at authentication protocol is more efficient and lightweight than IBAKE. This aligned well with idea of hybrid cloud computing to allow users with average to outsource their computational tasks to more powerful servers.

References

1. Mell, P., Grance, T.: The NIST definition of cloud computing. NIST Spec. Publ. **800**(145), 1–7 (2011)
2. Chatterjee, S., Sarkar, P.: Identity-Based Encryption. Springer, Heidelberg (2011)
3. Sanka, S., Hota, C., Rajarajan, M.: Secure data access in cloud computing. In: 2010 IEEE 4th International Conference on Internet Multimedia Services Architecture and Application (IMSAA). IEEE (2010)
4. Yan, L., Rong, C., Zhao, G.: Strengthen cloud computing security with federal identity management using hierarchical identity-based cryptography. In: Jaatun, M.G., Zhao, G., Rong, C. (eds.) Cloud Computing. LNCS, vol. 5931, pp. 167–177. Springer, Heidelberg (2009)
5. Shamir, A.: Identity-based cryptosystems and signature schemes. In: Blakely, G.R., Chaum, D. (eds.) CRYPTO 1984. LNCS, vol. 196, pp. 47–53. Springer, Heidelberg (1985)
6. Schridde, C., et al.: An identity-based security infrastructure for Cloud environments. In: 2010 IEEE International Conference on Wireless Communications, Networking and Information Security (WCNIS). IEEE (2010)

7. Boneh, D., Boyen, X.: Identity-based-encryption system. Google Patents (2009)
8. Chatterjee, S., Sarkar, P.: Identity-based encryption and hierarchical identity-based encryption. In: Joye, M., Neven, G. (eds.) Identity-Based Cryptography, vol. 2, p. 45. IOS Press, Amsterdam (2009)
9. Lin, C.: Identity-based cryptography on hidden-order groups. Procedia Eng. **29**, 2067–2071 (2012)
10. Wang, S., et al.: An improved identity-based key agreement protocol and its security proof. Inf. Sci. **179**(3), 307–318 (2009)
11. Cao, X., Kou, W., Du, X.: A pairing-free identity-based authenticated key agreement protocol with minimal message exchanges. Inf. Sci. **180**(15), 2895–2903 (2010)
12. Cakulev, V., Sundaram, G.: IBAKE: Identity-Based Authenticated Key Exchange (2012)
13. Kolesnikov, V., Sundaram, G.S.: IBAKE: identity-based authenticated key exchange protocol. IACR Cryptol. ePrint Archive **2011**, 612 (2011)
14. Rackspace private cloud software getting started guide. V2.0 (2012-11-21) Copyright 2012 rackspace all rights reserved. http://addff702607deedcafc3-81cc2db876f4430c0f6e1367cfd 71afd.r1.cf1.rackcdn.com/rackspace-private-cloud-releasenotes-alamo2.pdf
15. Rackspace private cloud software Release Notes. V2.0 (2012-12-05) Copyright 2012 rackspace all rights reserved. http://addff702607deedcafc3-81cc2db876f4430c0f6e1367cfd 71afd.r1.cf1.rackcdn.com/rackspace-private-cloud-gettingstarted-1121.pdf

A Dual Cloud Based Secure Environmental Parameter Monitoring System: A WSN Approach

B. Pooja, M.M. Manohara Pai$^{(\boxtimes)}$, and M. Pai Radhika

Department of Information and Communication Technology,
Manipal Institute of Technology, Manipal University, Manipal, India
poojab2789@gmail.com,
{mmm.pai,radhika.pai}@manipal.edu

Abstract. Advancement of technologies has made the presence of Wireless Sensor Networks (WSNs) ubiquitous. The adequacy of WSNs to gather critical information has provided solution to applications in areas such as transport, health care systems, environment monitoring etc. However, due to the limitations of WSNs in terms of memory, computation and scalability, efficient management of WSN data to provide information services to users is a hindrance. In the midst of these issues the resources of cloud computing act as a remedy. But, once the data enters the cloud the owner has no control over it. This imposes a barrier on the confidentiality and integrity of the data being stored in the cloud. In this paper we propose secure sensor-cloud architecture by integrating two different clouds. In this architecture, the sink node outsources data into the cloud after performing the respective hash and the encryption operations. Since the encrypted data and the key required to perform this operation are stored in different databases, the path for a third party to obtain the sensitive information stored in the cloud is being blocked. As the IaaS resources, SaaS and PaaS environments of Cloud Computing are provided by two different cloud service providers (CSPs), both the CSPs will not have complete information of the architecture. This provides inherent security as data storage and data processing are done on different clouds. Therefore the proposed framework provides better services to the users.

Keywords: WSNs · Cloud computing · Sensor-cloud architecture · Integration of clouds · Confidentiality · Integrity

1 Introduction

In the current technological world, Wireless Sensor Network (WSN) is one of technology used for gathering critical information in applications such as health care, environment monitoring, agriculture, telemetric, disaster monitoring and many more. The raw data obtained from these WSNs need to be processed and analyzed in order to provide better information services to the users. But due to the limitation of WSNs in terms of memory, energy, computation and scalability, management of WSNs data to provide efficient observation services to the users is an important issue to deal with.

V.C.M. Leung and M. Chen (Eds.): CloudComp 2013, LNICST 133, pp. 189–198, 2014.
DOI: 10.1007/978-3-319-05506-0_18, © Institute for Computer Sciences, Social Informatics
and Telecommunications Engineering 2014

To address this problem a scalable storage infrastructure and a powerful high-performance computing environment is essential for real-time processing, storing and analysis of WSN data. Cloud computing is one among the new generation technologies which provides these features and thus a remedy to this issue.

Cloud computing is a pioneer technology to provide a flexible stack of massive computing, storage and software services in a scalable and virtualized manner at low cost [1]. As defined by the NIST standard "cloud computing is a model for enabling convenient, on demand network access to a shared pool of configurable computing resources (e.g., networks, servers, storage, applications and services) that can be rapidly provisioned and released with minimal management effort or service provider interaction" [2]. This paradigm renders services in three elementary levels; Software as a Service (SaaS - for example, application level programs), Platform as a Service (PaaS - for example, operating platforms) and Infrastructure as a Service (IaaS - for example, storage and server). These three levels provide the users with dynamically scalable and virtualized resources through the Internet on "pay per usage" basis. [1]. Thus in order to overcome the shortfall of WSNs in terms of storage and computation it is integrated with the cloud computing environment, leading to the introduction of sensor-cloud infrastructure [1].

A Sensor-Cloud "is a unique sensor data storage, visualization and remote management platform that leverage powerful cloud computing technologies to provide excellent data scalability, rapid visualization, and user programmable analysis through a simple API" [3]. The sensor-cloud collects and process data from several sensor networks and enables the users to access, monitor, visualize, analyze, store and share the data among different users. Though the resources provided by the sensor-cloud can be used to provide better observation services, the owner becomes totally dependent on availability of these services and has no control over the data that enters the cloud. This creates a hindrance on the confidentiality and integrity factor of the data stored in the cloud. Thus in this paper we propose a secure sensor-cloud architecture.

The paper is organized as follows. Section 2 gives an overview of the related work. Section 3 introduces the proposed scheme. Section 4 provides experimental setup details and Sect. 5 concludes the paper.

2   Related Work

This section gives an overview of the work related to integration of WSNs with the cloud computing paradigm. Yuriyama and Kushida [6] has suggested an infrastructure where the WSNs can be configured as virtual sensors. Although the user can request and release the resources on demand, it is not very much user friendly, as the end user needs to do most of the processing and provisioning. M.M. Hassan et al. [7] proposed a framework for sensor-cloud integration based on the pub-sub broker model. This model is used for channelization of sensor data to the SaaS application. A. Deshwal et al. [8] has also provided an end to end solution to access data generated from remotely located WSN by using a smart device. The IaaS paradigm of cloud computing was utilized to provide virtualization of sensor. Also, R. Hummen et al. [5], introduced a sensor-cloud architecture that is suitable for different kinds of sensors.

Though the work of Hassan et al. [7], Deshwal et al. [8] and Hummen et al. [5] have proposed different architectures to integrate WSNs into cloud neither of these architecture provides security features to the outsourced WSN data.

Apart from the above work, there also exists many services that provide sensor-cloud infrastructure to store and process the sensor based information. Few of them are Nimbits [9], Pachube Platform [10], IDigi [11] and ThingSpeak [12]. Although the above sensor-cloud provides observation services, they lack secured access to the data.

The NIST has identified certain high level security objectives in order to address the threats that are specific to outsourcing of data to the cloud [4]. These objectives are confidentiality, integrity, availability, assurance and accountability. R. Hummen [5] has discussed the essentiality of these five objectives with respect to sensor-cloud scenario.

Thus considering the confidentiality and integrity factor of the outsourced data we propose secure sensor-cloud architecture.

3 The Proposed System Architecture

3.1 Design of the Proposed Architecture

This section discusses the proposed sensor-cloud architecture. The system architecture is shown in Fig. 1. The architecture is designed by taking the following assumptions into consideration. Within the boundaries of the sensor network, we assume that data is transferred securely to the gateway. Considering the gateway, we assume that its configuration is secure and access control mechanisms are implemented properly. With respect to assurance, we assume that the IaaS and PaaS provider ensure compliance to the security standards. Most importantly, the cloud service provider does not handover the data to an unauthorized third party.

As shown in the Fig. 1 the overall system comprises of WSNs henceforth represented as sensor networks, gateway, virtual sensor cloud, service cloud and the client device. Each subsystem is discussed below.

(1) Client Device
Client devices are the devices that the end user interacts with, in order to access the applications. Any device that has internet and web-browser facility can be used as a client device. These devices can either be a smart phone, tablet, laptop or a desktop. The end user can request for the different services using the client device.

(2) Sensor Networks
The sensor network consists of a group of wireless sensors that can communicate with each other using the standard communication protocols like ZigBee, Bluetooth etc. These sensors can be used to measure different parameters (like temperature, pressure, amount of different gases in the environment etc.) periodically. This raw data is forwarded to the sink node or the gateway directly or through multiple hops.

(3) Gateway
The gateway acts as an interface between the sensor network and the cloud network. The gateway or the sink node receives raw data from various sensor nodes. The received data consists of various parameters like sensor identity, observation values,

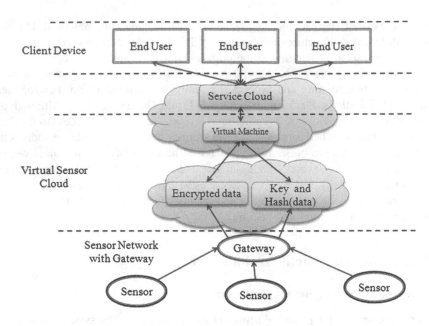

Fig. 1. An overview of sensor-cloud architecture

geo-location, manufacture information and many more. The gateway extracts the sensor observation values to perform the integrity and encryption operations and accesses the services of cloud computing to store data into the cloud.

(4) Virtual Sensor Cloud

The virtual sensor cloud refers to the interface between the storage services provided by the IaaS architecture of a CSP and data processing services provided by another CSP. This subsystem is responsible for sensor data management and sharing operations. The sensor data may be requested for different applications by the service cloud. Based on the requirements the sensor data needs to be represented accordingly. To support these operations a virtualization layer is essential. The virtualization layer consists of two different levels. These levels are:

(a) Virtual Sensors: The virtual sensor consists of databases to store the data. The infrastructure services for storage are provided by the CSP, say CSP_A. We consider that each gateway has a one to one connection with two virtual sensors. This is shown in Fig. 2. The data virtual sensor is used to store the encrypted data and key virtual sensor is used to store the computed hash value and the key that was used for performing the encryption operation. In order to identify the key used for encrypting the data, the timestamp at which the operation is performed is also stored in the corresponding databases.

(b) Virtual Machines: The virtual machine is spawned on the request of the service cloud. Based on the request of the service cloud the Virtual Machines (VMs) extract the information from the virtual sensors and process it. These processing services are provided by the second CSP say CSP_B. The connection between the

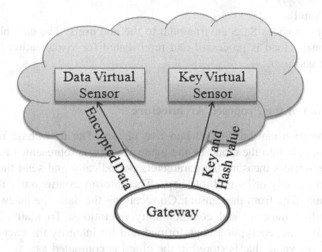

Fig. 2. Interface between the gateway and the virtual sensors (database).

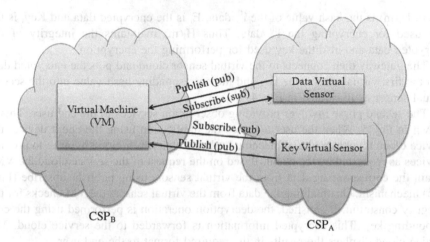

Fig. 3. Interconnection between virtual machine and virtual sensors (database) using pub/sub mechanism

VMs and the virtual sensors follow a publish/subscribe mechanism which is as shown in the Fig. 3. Once the encrypted data, key and the hash values are obtained the corresponding integrity and decryption operations are performed. The decrypted data is sent to the service cloud.

There are many advantages of using the above IaaS based architecture when compared to ad-hoc based solutions and thread based solutions as explained in [8]. Thus deployment of IaaS based architecture with virtualization makes the proposed architecture suitable to any working environments.

(5) Service Cloud

This subsystem provides SaaS environment to the end users. The data obtained from the virtual sensor cloud is processed and represented for visualization based on the request of the end user.

3.2 Operation of the Proposed Architecture

The entire operation can be divided into two phases. The first phase involves outsourcing of the data into the cloud by the gateway. This is represented as a flowchart in Fig. 4. The sensors measure the parameters periodically and send the data to the gateway either directly or by multiple hops. The gateway continuously monitors if it has received any data from the sensors. On receiving the data, the gateway performs the corresponding integrity and confidentiality operations. To maintain the confidentiality of the data, encryption is performed and for integrity the encrypted data is hashed. The hash value that is stored in the cloud is computed as:

$$H_i(m) = \text{Hash}(E_i(m) \| \text{Key}_i) \tag{1}$$

where $H_i(m)$ is the hash value of the ith data, E_i is the encrypted data and Key_i is the key used for encrypting the ith data. Thus $H_i(m)$ maintains the integrity of the encrypted data and also the key used for performing the encryption.

The gateway then connects to the virtual sensor cloud and puts the encrypted data into the first virtual sensor, the key and the corresponding hash value into the second virtual sensor as illustrated in Fig. 4.

The second phase involves providing observation services to the end user. This is shown in Fig. 5. When the user accesses the application using the client device, the service cloud invokes a virtual machine in the virtual sensor cloud in order to provide services as requested by the client. Based on the request of the service cloud the VMs obtain the corresponding data from the virtual sensors using publish/subscribe (Pub/Sub) mechanism. On obtaining the data from the virtual sensors the VM checks for the integrity constraint. If satisfied, the decryption operation is performed using the corresponding key. This decrypted information is forwarded to the service cloud. The service cloud displays the results in the required format to the end user.

In the proposed architecture we observe that the encryption and the hash operations are performed at the gateway before outsourcing the data to the cloud. As the encrypted data and the key required for performing the encryption are stored in different virtual sensors (databases), the attacker must obtain the database in which the key is stored to decrypt the data. Since the cloud architecture provides IaaS paradigm to several users, finding the exact pair of databases is a challenge.

Hence, the path for an attacker to obtain the sensitive information from the cloud is obstructed to a major extent. Therefore, the proposed architecture maintains the confidentiality and integrity of the data stored in the cloud. Thus the sensor-cloud architecture helps in providing better observation services to the end user, in-turn helping the customers to perform better analysis. Also this architecture provides dynamic provision of services to the customers; as a result the users can access relevant information from anywhere and at anytime.

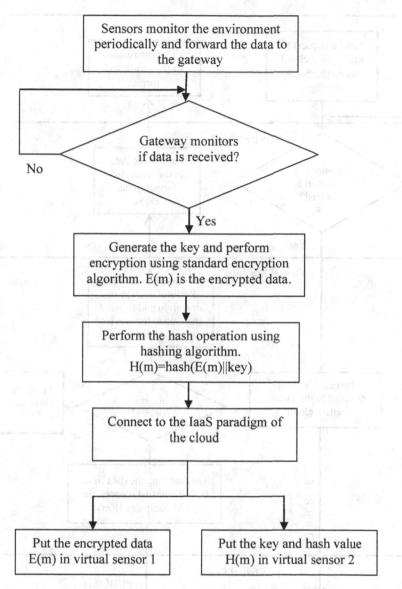

Fig. 4. Phase –I Gateway outsourcing the data into the cloud after performing encryption and hashing operations

Apart from this the storage services are provided by the CSP_A and processing services are provided by CSP_B. Thus, neither of the two service providers have complete information of the overall architecture. CSP_A either knows the contents of the database or the application for which this data needs to be processed and CSP_B does not have the stored data. As a result this architecture provides inherent security as the data storage and data processing are performed by two different clouds.

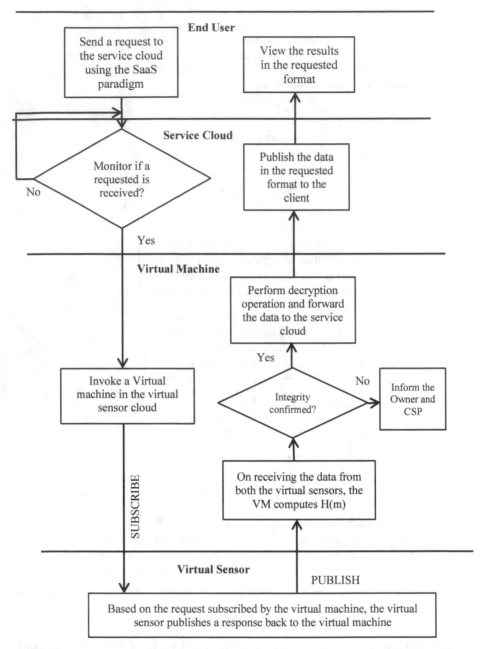

Fig. 5. Phase –II Flowchart showing the steps involved in providing observation services to the end user

4 Experimental Setup

As discussed in Sect. 3, the system architecture consists of 4 subsystems, namely client device, service cloud, virtual sensor cloud and the wireless sensor networks. For each of these subsystems the following tools are used for implementation.

We consider the client device to be a laptop or a desktop. SQL service of CSP_A is used for the implementation of Virtual sensor. Java Virtual machines provided by CSP_B is used for virtualization and service cloud. Thus the storages services are provided by CSP_A and processing services are provided by CSP_B. For demonstration purpose we have measured the levels of oxygen and carbon-dioxide in an air-conditioned room. To measure these values oxygen sensor (SK-25) [15] and carbon-dioxide (TGS-4116) [15] of Libelium Company [13] are used. These sensors are embedded on the Waspmote board [14] provided by Libelium Company.

Java platform is used for programming with the help of NetBeans-7.3 IDE [16]. Any of the standard encryption/decryption algorithm and hashing algorithm (which provides both pre-image resistance and second pre-image resistance) can be used. In this work, DES algorithm is used to perform the encryption and decryption operations and SHA-256 is used to perform hash operations. Thus if an attacker tries to access the data stored in cloud, the task of finding the pair of databases in order to decrypt the data is a challenge. Thus the path for a third party attacker to manipulate the data is obstructed, thereby making the overall system more secure.

5 Conclusion

Though the advancement of technologies has made the presence of WSNs ubiquitous, cloud computing is a solution to overcome the limitations of WSNs. The integration of WSNs with cloud computing paradigm has led to the evolution of sensor-cloud architecture. The sensor-cloud architecture has provided better provision for storing, processing and analyzing the data. But, once the data is outsourced to the cloud the owner has no control over the data. This imposes a barrier on the confidentiality and integrity factor of the data stored in the cloud. As a support to this issue, the proposed solution in this paper provides the required security features and blocks the path for an attacker to manipulate the data stored in the cloud.

As a part of future work, in order to reduce the latency we are planning for a virtualized distributed computing model.

References

1. Alamri, A., Ansari, W.S., Hassan, M.M., Hossain, M.S., Alelaiwi, A., Hossain, M.A.: A survey on sensor-cloud: architecture, applications and approaches. Int. J. Distrib. Sensor Netw. (Hindawi Publishing Corporation) 2013, 1–18 (2013)
2. Dash, S.K., Sahoo, J.P., Mohapatra, S., Pati, S.P.: Sensor-cloud: assimilation of wireless sensor network and the cloud. In: Meghanathan, N., Chaki, N., Nagamalai, D. (eds.) CCSIT 2012, Part I. LNICST, vol. 84, pp. 455–464. Springer, Heidelberg (2012)

3. Sensor-Cloud. http://sensorcloud.com/system-overview
4. Stoneburner, G.: Underlying technical models for information technology security. In: NIST Special Publication 800-33. National Institute of Standards and Technology (2001)
5. Hummen, R., Henze, M., Catrein, D., Wehrle, K.: A Cloud design for user-controlled storage and processing of sensor data. In: 4th International Conference on Cloud Computing Technology and Science. IEEE Computer Society (2012)
6. Yuriyama, M., Kushida, T.: Sensor-cloud infrastructure -physical sensor management with virtualized sensors on cloud computing. In: 13th International Conference on Network-Based Information Systems (NBiS), pp. 1–8, 14–16 Sept 2010
7. Hassan, M.M., Song, B., Huh, E.-N.: A framework of sensor-cloud integration opportunities and challenges. In: Proceedings of the 3rd International Conference on Ubiquitous Information and Data Management and Communication (ICUIMC), Suwon, South Korea, 15–16 Jan 2009
8. Deshwal, A., Kohli, S., Chethan, K.P.: Information as a service based architectural solution for WSN. In: 1st IEEE International Conference on Communications in China (ICCC), pp. 68–73, Beijing, China, 15–17 Aug 2012
9. Nimbits Data Logging Cloud Sever. http://www.nimbits.com
10. Pachube Feed Cloud Service. http://www.pachube.com
11. iDigi—Device Cloud. http://www.idigi.com
12. IoT—ThingSpeak. http://www.thingspeak.com
13. Libelium- Connecting Sensors to the Cloud. http://www.libelium.com
14. Waspmote Sensors Overview. http://www.libelium.com/products/waspmote/sensors
15. Gases 2.0 Libelium. http://www.libelium.com/uploads/2013/02/gases-sensor-board_2.0_eng.pdf
16. NetBeans IDE 7.3. http://www.netbeans.org/community/releases/73/

Data Possession Provability on Semi-trusted Cloud Storage

Wei Fu[✉], Bo Yan, and Xiaoping Wu

Department of Information Security, Navy University of Engineering,
Wuhan, People's Republic of China
lukeyoyo@tom.com

Abstract. In cloud storage applications, users cannot trust storage service provider as before. They need reliable methods to verify the possession of their data as well as replicas on such semi-trusted platform. In this paper, PPoDT scheme is carefully designed based on Data Tag to prove data possession with a Challenge-Response model. Furthermore, MPPoDT scheme is presented to validate multiple replicas possession provability. After procedure of file blocking, encrypting, Data Tag computing, challenge generating, evidence producing and validating, the client can be certain of the existence and integrity of its data/replica with very high probability. Prototype implementation and experiments show that the schemes are both effective and efficient.

1 Introduction

Cloud Computing is an emerging computing paradigm, which is regarded as the biggest evolvement of distributed computing technology after Grid computing [1]. It enables on-demand access to computing and data storage resources, which can be configured to meet unique constraints of the clients with minimal investment and management overhead. Cloud computing represents one of the newest developing trend of information technology. It is widely accepted because of the simplicity, centralization, scalability and specialization [2].

With the rapid development of information technology and the explosive growth of data capability, requirements on massive data management become more and more rigorous. Researches show that overhead of data management is as much as 2−3 times more than that of data acquisition. Therefore, a special kind of cloud platforms appeared with the emerging of cloud computing technology, which solved data-intensive issues in particular. With existing technologies such as cluster, grid and distributed file system, these platforms integrate heterogeneous storage devices to accomplish complex data management task cooperatively and provide online data storage/access functions. Generally they are called Cloud Storage Systems [3]. In fact, more and more applications adopt cloud storage technology to manage their data.

This paper is supported by NSF of China (NO. 61100042), NSF of Hubei Province (NO. 2012 FB06901) and Chinese postdoctoral Fund (NO. 2013M532170).

V.C.M. Leung and M. Chen (Eds.): CloudComp 2013, LNICST 133, pp. 199–209, 2014.
DOI: 10.1007/978-3-319-05506-0_19, © Institute for Computer Sciences, Social Informatics and Telecommunications Engineering 2014

Typical representatives of them include Amazon S3 (Simple Storage Service) and EMC Atmos.

Comparing with traditional technologies, Cloud Storage has several advantages. Firstly, the system can be quickly deployed, configured or reconfigured with Virtual Machine technology. Secondly, it can be conveniently scaled up and down according to individual requirements. Thirdly, it provides a pay-as-you-go pricing model. In this commercial model, the cloud storage providers charge to the users according to storage capacity, storage duration, network bandwidth, etc., helping them to cut down their managing and maintaining overhead heavily.

Cloud Storage tries to provide an infrastructure of data management, which can greatly save social resources and energy. However, it also brings many security problems, such as malicious tampering and data lost to server commitment. In cloud storage platform, users' data is stored in the manner of outsourcing. In this circumstance, the relationship between users and cloud storage provides is evolved from the traditional "Server/Client" to "Seller/Customer". In other words, the provider cannot be totally trusted any more. In this paper, we call them the Semi-trusted Cloud Storage.

Semi-trusted cloud storage correctly operates at most of the time, but it will break its promise sometimes. For example, if a cloud storage system is hacked or failed to perform normal operations, it will damage user's data security passively. Furthermore, if there is no sufficient monitoring or supervision mechanism, cloud storage provider would actively violate data security for tremendous economic benefit.

One of the most challenging problems is to prove that user data are still integrated and can be accessed at any time. This is because that cloud storage provider will just conceal or simply shirk responsibilities when data loss occurs due to its own consideration. Only when the storage providers could provide methods to verify the existence and accessibility of user data, and continuously improve the quality of storage service, can cloud storage is widely applied.

Furthermore, cloud storage service provider usually replicate user data in different locations to avoid unexpected data corruption. If one of the locations suffers data loss problem, the system would automatically switch to the backup node, so as to eliminate the availability reduction problem. However, multiple replicas will bring storage capacity pressure to the service provider if they follow the contract or agreement with users. Meanwhile, in order to ensure those copies available, more additional servers are required to run at the same time, which would bring economic pressure to the service provider (mainly refers the huge electricity charge). In order to alleviate these pressures, the cloud storage service providers may reduce the number of backup storage by cheating, or temporarily shut down some backup nodes to reduce electricity payout. Therefore, the users would suffer greatly loss if the existing insufficient backup nodes fail to work.

In this paper, a data possession proving scheme is presented to guarantee storage providers to loyally maintain the availability and integrity of data. Then, the scheme is evolved to solve the possession proving of multiple replicas. Finally, an experimental system is designed and implemented to validate the two schemes. The main contributions of the paper are listed as follows:

1. A novel scheme is proposed to solve data possession proving problem on semi-trusted cloud storage system;
2. The former scheme is modified to solve multiple replica possession proving problem on the same system;
3. A prototype system is carefully designed and implemented;
4. Experiments are executed to show the effectiveness and efficiency of the schemes.

2 Related Work

Many literatures focused on the problem of data possession or retrievability. They can be divided into two types: Schemes based on symmetric cryptography and schemes based on asymmetric cryptography.

Sentinel-based Proof of Retrievability (POR) [4] protocol developed by Juels of RSA Laboratories and Kaliski of EMC Corporation is a typical representative of symmetric cryptograph possession proving scheme. The basic idea of POR is: POR protocol uses symmetric cryptograph to encrypt the file data and code it with error correcting code, and then randomly embeds a set of randomly-valued check blocks called sentinels. The verifier challenges the server by specifying the positions of a collection of sentinels and asking the server to return the associated sentinel values. The authors prove that if the server could make effective response with a certain probability or greater than it, the data file is recoverability. The advantage of this scheme is its small computational overhead, but the disadvantage is that it needs consume a sentinel each time, so the times of challenge are limited. In additional, if the data file need to update, this scheme requires finding out all unused sentinels, and then re-coding the data file and re-embedding sentinels, so it's efficiency is low.

Bowers et al. proposed a theoretical framework of POR [5] based on Juels and Kaliskis' research [4]. It is an improved scheme of POR that could achieve lower storage overhead and higher error detection rate. They indicate that the file update and public verification are remaining unresolved open problems. Besides, similar work can be found in [6–8]. However, all of them focus on static data.

The HAIL [9] scheme proposed by them makes some copies or redundant among several storage provider, and then uses POR to verify whether the file data is damaged. If the file data stored in one of those storage providers is damaged, then the file data could be recovered via the other providers.

Almost at the same time with presence of POR, Ateniese et al. proposed a provable data possession model (PDP) [10, 11], which is the typical representative of asymmetric cryptograph possession proving scheme. The principle of this model is: Let N be a RSA modulus, F is a large integer represents the file, the verifier saves $k = F \bmod \phi (N)$; As in challenge, the verifier sends a random element g in Z_N, and the server return $s = g^F \bmod N$; the verifier verifies whether $g^k \bmod N = s$, so as to make sure the existence of original data file. The original PDP scheme can only process static data, and its computational overhead is high, efficiency is low.

Based on original PDP scheme, Ateniese et al. proposed SPDP scheme [12], attempted to improve PDP efficiency. Chris et al. proposed DPDP solution [13], attempting to provide the support of data dynamic update. Erway [14] proposed a new DPDP scheme based on [10] to support dynamic operations of outsourced data with rank-based authenticated skip lists [15]. Their protocol can insert new blocks by eliminating the index information in the tag. Also in this paper, a variant of the DPDP scheme using RSA trees is presented, instead of skip lists. Besides, Yan Zhu et al. combined with hybrid clouds background and proposed EPDP scheme [12], attempting to solve the high efficiency data possession proving with multi servers and multi files. In general, these possession proving schemes derived from the original PDP scheme mainly based on RSA asymmetric cryptography.

Zhu [16] present a CPDP scheme based on homomorphic verifiable response and hash index hierarchy to prove data possession in a multi-prover zero-knowledge proof system. However, it is designed for Multi-Cloud environment and lacks of efficiency. Ren [17] propose an improved fairness and dynamic provable data possession scheme that supports public verification. Comparing with all the solution above, it needs a trusted third party auditor.

According to the analysis and comparison of the schemes above, we conclude that the existing schemes have following drawbacks: (1) Most of the schemes require a lot of modular exponentiation calculation, causing high computational overheads and inefficiency, especially for big data; (2) These schemes do not consider the confidentiality of data; (3) Replica possession has not been considered sufficiently. Therefore, we consider that the problem of data possession proving on cloud storage is still necessary for further research.

3   Data Possession Proving Model

Traditionally, users verify the presence of data possession by means of data accessing. This method is widely used in on-line storage system, mass storage system, database storage system, and so on. Users download data to their local, then check data integrity manually or automatically. After that, users can confirm that their data are kept by servers and available at present. Obviously, this method needs both frequent accessing to servers and massive data transferring. In cloud storage environment with mass data, the method described above is obviously inefficient and un-suitable for cloud storage applications, so we won't discuss it any more.

Traditional proving schemes have several drawbacks. Therefore, a new possession proving model based on "Challenge-Response" is proposed here. Firstly, client selectively challenges some data blocks. Then server generates corresponding possession evidences and sends back to client according to the client's challenge requirement. Finally, the client judges the validity of the evidences. The data possession proving model is presented as Fig. 1 illustrated.

There are two roles involved in this model: the data owner and storage server. And the model mainly includes four steps of the two phases:

(1) Data storage phase: includes step① and step② in Fig. 1.

Data owner pre-processes the data file, i.e., slices and encrypts the data, extracts some sampling information from data slice, etc. The purpose of above process is to obtain the treated persistent data and metadata m that used to verify the possession of

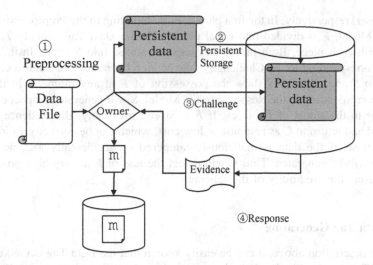

Fig. 1. The data possession proving model. Data file will be pretreated and transferred to cloud storage for persistent store. At any time, data owner can challenge cloud storage about data's existence.

data later; then data owner uploads the persistent data to server side for long-tern storage, and saves the metadata m in client in security.

(2) Data proving phase: includes step③ and step④ in Fig. 1.

In the lifetime of persistent data, data owner initiates a data possession proving challenge to server side. According to the data owner's requirement, the server side extracts some specific persistent data; After data operation processing, the server side could obtain an evidence which is used to prove the existence of data. Then the evidence is returned to data owner. Finally, data owner processes the evidence and the metadata m previously saved, and verifies whether the persistent data is stored in the server side validly according to the processing result.

Compared with traditional storage system data existence proving, this model only need to send a few challenge information (generally only a few bytes) in challenge phase; In server response phase, the model can take full advantage of the powerful cloud computing capacity to generate evidence. Generally speaking, the evidence information has only a few dozen bytes, up to a few hundred bytes. Therefore, it can significantly save network bandwidth resources, which makes it very suitable for cloud storage applications with powerful aggregating computing power and huge amount of data.

4 The Basic Data Possession Proving Scheme

4.1 Phrases of the Scheme

In this paper, a basic data possession proving scheme based on Data Tag (PPoDT for short) is presented. The PPoDT scheme presented consists of three phrases. Let F stands for the original large data file, S for cloud storage service, and C for the cloud user (owner) respectively. In the first phrase, corresponding to the Preprocessing in the Proving Model, F is divided into equal pieces. Then a Data Tag, namely T, is generated with each piece. Both pieces and tags are stored into S by C. In the second phrase, corresponding to the Challenge in the Model, C creates and sends a challenge request to S and requires S show the possession of F at any moment. In the third phrase, corresponding to the Response in the Model, S will generate compact evidence according to the status of F pieces. If F is stored invariably, the evidence will be generated and return to C as response at low cost, which can be correctly validated by C. Otherwise, if the data is maliciously tampered or accidentally lost, no correct evidence will be generated. Thus C will detect the loss of F at very high probability, which ensure the credibility of the scheme.

4.2 Data Tag Generating

From the description above, it can be easily known that the Data Tag is the key point of PPoDT scheme. Firstly, let's introduce the generating formula of Data Tag T. Suppose that the original file F can be divided into c blocks. Each block is encrypted into cryptograph text, labeled as M_i which can be converted to a big number. Then its Data Tag can be calculated as the follows:

$$T_{i,M_i} = \left(h(W_i) * g^{M_i}\right)^d \bmod n \tag{1}$$

- $W_i = v \parallel i$, where i is the index of the file block M_i, v is a security prime number that is randomly generated in file Preprocessing process. The index file is encrypted after connecting the v and i, that can ensure the variable and unpredictable of the W_i to meet the security requirement.
- g is a security prime number, which meets the equation condition that: $g \bmod n \equiv 1$.
- n is a safe prime in RSA algorithm, and d is the private key of C generated in phrase one.
- $h(.)$ is a hash algorithm.

From formula (1), it can be found that the calculation of data label is a large number modular exponentiation algorithm. In order to meet the security requirement, Data Tag uses M_i, and d as exponential, whose values directly determine the computational overhead of the PPoDT scheme.

4.3 Possession Evidence Calculation and Validation

In the phrase of challenge, C produces challenge information $chalset = (i_1, i_2, \ldots i_c)$ and sends it to S, where i_j stands for the random selected data pieces indexes. Then in the phrase of verifying, after receiving the challenge information $chalset$, S calculates the possession evidence, which consists of two parts: $evid = (T, \zeta)$.

Firstly, the index information should be permutated by a random permutation function: $i_j = \pi_K(j)$, where K stands for a secret shared by S and C. Secondly T is calculated as follows:

$$T = T_{i_1,m_{i_1}}\ldots T_{i_c,m_{i_c}} = \left(h(W_{i_1})\ldots h(W_{i_c}) * g^{m_{i_1}+\ldots+m_{i_c}}\right)^d \bmod n \qquad (2)$$

$$\zeta = h\left(g_s^{m_{i_1}+\ldots+m_{i_c}} \bmod n\right) \qquad (3)$$

where s stands for another secrete shared by S and C, and g_s is the shortening format of $g^s \bmod n$.

At the phrase of validation, C receives *chalset* from S, then it executes the validating algorithm as Fig. 2 shows:

> *input* : *evid* $= (T,\zeta), e, v, s, chalset = \{i_1, i_2, \ldots i_c\}$
>
> *output* : *TRUE   or   FALSE*
>
> *begin* :
>
> *For* $1 \le j \le c$
>
> $\{$
>
> $\quad W_{i_j} = v \| i_j\,;$
>
> $\}$
>
> $\gamma = \dfrac{T^e}{\prod\limits_{j-1}^{c} h(W_{i_j})} \bmod n;$
>
> *if* $(h(\gamma^s \bmod n) == \zeta)$
>
> $\quad$ *return   TRUE*;
>
> *else*
>
> $\quad$ *return   FALSE*;
>
> *end.*

Fig. 2. The pseudo-code description of validating algorithm, where e is the public key of C in RSA algorithm, v and s are the same meanings with those described in Sect. 4.2.

If the algorithm returns *TRUE*, then C can believe with high probability that his data file F is completely stored on the cloud storage.

4.4   Proof of the PPoDT Scheme

Suppose that F is not modified, then according to PPoDT,

$$\because T = T_{i_1,m_{i_1}}\ldots T_{i_c,m_{i_c}} = \left(h(W_{i_1})\ldots h(W_{i_c}) \cdot g^{m_{i_1}+\ldots+m_{i_c}}\right)^d \bmod n;$$

$$\therefore T^e = (h(W_{i_1})\ldots h(W_{i_c}) \cdot g^{m_{i_1}+\ldots+m_{i_c}})^{d.e} \bmod n = h(W_{i_1})\ldots h(W_{i_c}) \cdot g^{m_{i_1}+\ldots+m_{i_c}} \bmod n$$

$$\therefore \gamma == \frac{T^e}{\prod\limits_{j=1}^{c} h(W_{i_j})} \bmod n = g^{m_{i_1}+\ldots+m_{i_c}} \bmod n$$

Since $g_s = g^s \bmod n$,

$$\therefore \gamma^s \bmod n = g^{s(m_{i_1}+\ldots+m_{i_c})} \bmod n = g_s^{(m_{i_1}+\ldots+m_{i_c})} \bmod n$$

Therefore, $h(\gamma^s \bmod n) \neq \zeta$, which indicates that F is correct.

However, if $F = (m_1, \ldots m_i)$ has been modified, even a few bits, then $(m_{i_1} + \ldots m_{i_c})$ will be changed at very high probability. In other words, $(m_{i_1} + \ldots m_{i_c})$ in Formula (2) won't be equal to that in Formula (3). Since $h(\gamma^s \bmod n) \neq \zeta$, the modification will be detected by C with high probability.

5   Multiple Replica Possession Proving Scheme

5.1   Basic Idea of MPPoDT Scheme

On cloud storage platform, replica technology is often employed to obtain high availability. Multiple copies will be distributed at different physical locations to provide coinstantaneous data service. For example, Google file system will keep 3 copies of one data block at any time. However, under semi-trusted circumstance cloud storage will not or cannot keep enough replicas. Thus some technique is needed to prevent this to happen.

The PPoDT scheme described above cannot solve this new problem. Because servers can deceive users by helping each other to forge the evidence of replica existence, which is commonly called colluding attack. In this paper, an effective and efficient solution is proposed on the basis of PPoDT scheme, namely MPPoDT. At first, the original data will be divided and encrypted respectively. Then different replicas are produced by XOR operations on cryptograph text and some random-choosed mask codes. After that, Data Tags will be calculated one by one as what happens in PPoDT scheme. During the Challenge-Response phrase, user can challenges the possession of all replicas by module-power operation on Data Tag at one time.

5.2   Multiple Replicas Generating

Before persistent storage, F is divided into pieces as PPoDT scheme does. Then each pieces will be encrypted as cryptograph text, represented as: $F = \{b_1, \ldots, b_n\}$, where $b_i = E_k(M_i), 1 \leq i \leq n$, and E_k is a pseudo-random permutation, defined as:

$$E_k : \{0,1\}^k \times \{0,1\}^\beta \to \{0,1\}^\beta \tag{4}$$

where β is the length of file pieces.

If u replicas are needed, each file piece should be handled as follows:

$$F_u = \{m_{u,1}, \ldots, m_{u,n}\}, m_{u,i} = b_i + r_{u,i}, 1 \le i \le n \tag{5}$$

where $r_{u,i}$ is a safe random number, $r_{u,i} = f_k(u \parallel i)$ and $f(.)$ is a pseudo-random function.

Now Data Tag can be generated as shown in Formula (1), excepted that M_i should be replaced by b_i. Finally all replicas F_u will be transferred to S together with their Data Tags.

5.3 Multiple Data Tag Generating and Possession Validating

The validating process in MPPoDT is very similar with that in PPoDT, except for some replica-related parameters. The algorithm and its proof is almost the same as those described in Sect. 4. Limited by the length of the paper, here only the differences will be listed below:

(1) Data Tag generating:

$$T_{i,b_i} = \left(h(W_i) * g^{b_i}\right)^d \bmod n \tag{6}$$

(2) Evidence validating:

$$T = T_{i_1,b_{i_1}} \ldots T_{i_c}, b_{i_c} = \left(h(W_{i_1}) \ldots h(W_{i_c}) * g^{b_{i_1}, \ldots, b_{i_c}}\right)^d \bmod n \tag{7}$$

$$\zeta = h\left(g_s^{m_{u,i_1} + \ldots + m_{u,i_c}} \bmod n\right) \tag{8}$$

6 Experiments and Evaluation

In order to check the correctness and efficiency of both PPoDT and MPPoDT, a prototype system is implemented with Java programming, shown as Fig. 3:

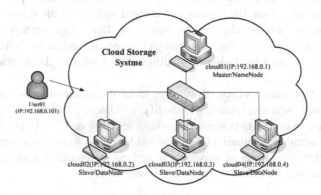

Fig. 3. The prototype system topology, built up based on the Hadoop system. Cloud storage platform consists of one Namenode and 3 DataNodes.

All nodes are installed on IBM x3650 M2 rack servers, with dual Intel Xeon CPU of 2.4 GHz, 4 GB DDR3 memory, 2*146 GB SAS disk and 1000 Mbps Ethernet adapter. Experiments show that: even one single bit is modified, validating phrase can detect it. And the more data piece indexes to be challenged is included in *chalset*, the lower probability for the system to deceive the user.

Different parameters are tested in MPPoDT, including the size of data pieces and the size of whole data file. The replica number is 3. Firstly, a 10 MB file is chosen as a sample. Table 1 shows that with different size of data pieces, the time cost of three phrases. It is easy to find that when data file is divided into 4 KB pieces, the overall time cost is the smallest. Secondly, the data piece size is fixed to 4 KB, and data file with different size are tested. The result is shown in Table 2. It reveals that the total time span will increase with the file length growth. However, the total time cost is within a reasonable level.

Table 1. The time span in different phrases when handling 10 MB data file (*unit: second*).

Size of pieces	1 KB	2 KB	4 KB	8 KB	16 KB	32 KB
Preprocessing	32.5	26.3	21.0	20.7	20.8	20.1
Challenge-Response	13.6	11.1	10.3	11.9	13.1	15.8
Evidence check	5.6	5.8	6.1	8.2	11.3	13.0
Total	51.7	43.2	37.4	40.8	45.2	48.9

Table 2. The time span in different phrases when handling different data file (*unit: second*).

Size of data file	10 KB	100 KB	1 MB	10 MB	100 MB	1 GB
Preprocessing	21.0	21.0	32.5	21.0	21.0	20.7
Challenge-Response	10.3	10.3	13.6	10.3	10.3	11.9
Evidence check	6.1	6.1	5.6	6.1	6.1	8.2
Total	37.4	37.4	51.7	37.4	37.4	40.8

7 Conclusion

In cloud storage applications, users have to confirm that their data's possession under semi-trusted context. From the view of precautions against all the rivals including the service providers, two novel schemes based on Data Tag, namely PPoDT and MPPoDT, are presented. By using an interactive proof similar to "zero knowledge proof", users can detect the losing or modification of original data/replica with high confidence.

With the evolvement of cloud storage technology, the demand of modifying existing data will increase, including "Modify", "Delete", "Insert", "Append", etc. So the feasible dynamic data possession proving schemes on Cloud Storage need to be developed. In addition, synthesizing several evidences to form a new evidence could increase the challenge times of verification, reduce computational and storage overhead. All these could be carried out in our future work.

References

1. Foster, I., Kesselman, C.: The Grid 2: Blueprint for a New Computing Infrastructure. Morgan Kaufmann Publishers Inc., San Francisco (2003)
2. Feng, D.G., Zhang, M., Zhang, Y.: Study on cloud computing security. J. Softw. **22**(1), 71–83 (2011)
3. Kamara, S., Lauter, K.: Cryptographic cloud storage. In: Sion, R., Curtmola, R., Dietrich, S., Kiayias, A., Miret, J.M., Sako, K., Sebé, F. (eds.) FC 2010 Workshops. LNCS, vol. 6054, pp. 136–149. Springer, Heidelberg (2010)
4. Juels, A., Kaliski, B.: PORs: proofs of retrievability for large files. In: 14th ACM CCS, pp. 584–597 (2007)
5. Bowers, K.D., Juels, A., Oprea, A.: Proofs of retrievability: theory and implementation. In: CCSW 09, pp. 43–54. ACM Press, New York (2009)
6. Dodis, Y., Vadhan, S., Wichs, D.: Proofs of retrievability via hardness amplification. In: Reingold, O. (ed.) TCC 2009. LNCS, vol. 5444, pp. 109–127. Springer, Heidelberg (2009)
7. Juels, A., Kaliski, B.S.: PORs: proofs of retrievability for large files. In: CCS'07: Proceedings of the 14th ACM Conference on Computer and Communications Security, pp. 584–597. ACM (2007)
8. Shacham, H., Waters, B.: Compact proofs of retrievability. Cryptology ePrint Archive, Report 2008/073. http://eprint.iacr.org/ (2008)
9. Bowers, K.D., Juels, A., Oprea, A.: HAIL: a high-availability and integrity layer for cloud storage. In: CCS 2009, pp. 187–198. ACM Press, New York (2009)
10. Ateniese, G., Burns, R., Curtmola, R.: Remote data checking using provable data possession. ACM Trans. Inf. Syst. Secur. **14**(1), 12–34 (2011)
11. Ateniese, G., Burns, R., Curtmola, R., et al.: Remote data checking using provable data possession. ACM Trans. Inf. Syst. Secur. **14**(1), 12:1–12:34 (2011)
12. Ateniese, G., Pietro, R.D., Mancini, L.V.: Scalable and efficient provable data procession. In: SecureComm, Istanbul, Turkey, pp. 1–10 (2008)
13. Chris, E., Alptekin, K., Papamanthou, C.: Dynamic provable data procession [EB/OL]. ePrint Archieve (2009)
14. Erway, C., Kupcu, A., Papamanthou, C., Tamassia, R.: Dynamic provable data possession. In: CCS '09: Proceedings of the 16th ACM Conference on Computer and Communications Security, pp. 213–222. New York (2009)
15. Pugh, W.: Skip lists: a probabilistic alternative to balanced trees. Commun. ACM **33**, 668–676 (1990)
16. Zhu, Y., Hongxin, H., et al.: Cooperative provable data possession for integrity verification in multi-cloud storage. IEEE Trans. Parallel Distrib. Syst. **23**(12), 2231–2244 (2012)
17. Ren, Z., Wang, L., Deng, R., Rongwei, Yu.: Improved fair and dynamic provable data possession supporting public verification. Wuhan Univ. J. Nat. Sci. **18**(4), 348–354 (2013)

Workshop Session 1

A BPEL-Based Web Service Flow Engine
in the Early Warning of the Volcano Effusion

Jingyuan Pang[1(⊠)], Chen Wang[2], Pan Deng[3], Yanhong Lu[1],
and Hao Liu[1]

[1] Earthquake Administration of Jilin Province, Changchun 30117, China
{vv.v8,363970142,1256164300}@qq.com
[2] Institute of Geophysics, China Earthquake Administration, Beijing, China
578043315@qq.com
[3] Laboratory of Parallel Software and Computational Science,
Institute of Software Chinese Academy of Sciences, Beijing 100190, China
33421255@qq.com

Abstract. Web service flow engine is the core of the service assembling and cooperating system in volcano early warning data-shared platform. We design and realize a lightweight web service flow based on BPEL standard. It takes charge of parsing the service flow model constructed by users, checking-up the syntax and logic of the service flow file, constructing the basic elements of the given service flow, and then executing it according to the BPEL standard. Then the engine collects all the executing information and invoking results, at the same time it also supervises the execution of web services, managing the invocation of services. Finally it returns the results back to users. Experimental results show that our engine can work correctly, the time efficiency is high and the occupancy rate of system resources is nearly zero.

Keywords: Web service · Web service flow engine · BPEL · Early warning of volcano · Data-shared platform

1 Introduction

In recent years, there is an increasing tendency in the frequency of the earthquake and the surface deformation in Changbai Mountain Tianchi [1]. It is possible to effuse volcano again. So, we research into the early-warning of the volcano effusion and create the volcano early warning data-shared platform. Organizing these services effectively and ensuring these services work together are important for the stability and efficiency of NGG [2].

Traditional web service faces many problems when applying it in the volcano early warning and other applications. In the volcano early warning, a single service

This work was supported by the special fund of earthquake 《Experimental Research on the Applications of the Early Warning of Volcano Effusion in Changbai Mountain Tianchi》 (No. 201208005), and National Natural Science Foundation of China (No. 61100066)

V.C.M. Leung and M. Chen (Eds.): CloudComp 2013, LNICST 133, pp. 213–221, 2014.
DOI: 10.1007/978-3-319-05506-0_20, © Institute for Computer Sciences, Social Informatics and Telecommunications Engineering 2014

can't finish the early-warning task. It is necessary to combine several services together to finish the early-warning, but the traditional web service mechanism doesn't support the combination of several services. Due to the huge volume of the data and the complexity of the computation in the volcano early warning data-shared platform, in order to make system stable and reliable is important to response immediately to the activity state. Due to the "no-state" of the traditional web service, it can not provide the state information needed in the service call, which poses serious problems for the usage of the platform. Furthermore, when the professionals develop a certain application, they will need a convenient and effective development tool to make the services collaborative, which can support the rapid building of the application and improve work efficiency.

So, based on the above analysis, we propose to design and realize a lightweight web service flow engine based on BPEL [3]. In our proposed web service flow engine, we firstly modeling the web service flow according to the user demand, and then provide the execution basis for each instance of the web service flow based on BPEL. Specially, the web service flow engine perform the following task: analyzing the model of the web service flow, creating instances for each service based on the execution flow, and then finally controlling and monitoring the instance of the services.

2   Related Works

Work flow has been widely used in many E-commerce and E-government fields, such as office automation (OA), customer relationship management (CRA), and so on. It has been accepted and used by more and more government departments and enterprises and institutions. There developed a Workflow Management Coalition (WFMC), the members of which include IBM, ORACLE and BEA. Now, there are many open source work flow engine projects which can divided into several categories: the engine based on Extensible Markup Language (XML) and the engine based on the Web, and so on.

Shark [4] engine is a XML-based open source work flow engine. The implementation of Shark is based on WFMC [5] standard completely, which can be extended easily. Shark uses XML Process Definition Language (XPDL) to define the process and the WFMC tool agent API used to execute the active node in the server. Each component in the Shark, such as the persistence layer, transactions managers, scripting engine and process database can be executed according to the standard and also can be extended and replaced by the specific project.

Bonita [6] engine is a web-based open source work flow engine, which conforms to WFMC standard. As a flexible collaborative work flow engine, Bonita is realized based on the web browse. It enclosures the existing work flow methods using the data binding technology of Symbolic Optimal Assembly Program (SOAP) and XML, and then release them in the web service form based on J2EE.

jBpm [7] is another extendible, open source work flow engine system developed by tom baeyens which combines the convenience of the work flow application development and the ability of Enterprise Application Integration (EAI). jBmp consists of a Web application and a scheduling program. jBmp is based on several components, and can be deployed as a J2EE application clusters.

Beside the above engines, there are many commercial web service flow engines, for example, WLI of BEA, Holosofx of IBM, NetWeaver of SAP, Workflow Designer for Exchange of MicroSoft, LOUSHANG and eBuilder of TongFang.

3   The Main Function of Web Service Flow Engine

In order to execute successfully the web service flow of the volcano early warning platform, we need to create a whole service flow model to define the execution sequence of every service of the service flow, the transmission process of the data, and provide a reliable basis for the execution of the service flow. The service flow engine is mainly responsible for the following works: analyzing the normative web service flow to extract the basic services in the flow, checking and binding these basic services, then executing these services according to the execution sequence defined in the service flow language, and finally returning the results to the users. Once we create the web service flow engine, the user only need to input the necessary data to the engine, and the engine will be responsible for the subsequent monitoring of the execution of every service and communications between the services. So the engine can simplify the user operation greatly.

Based on the above analysis, the engine should include the following functions: grammar and logic check, work flow construction and flow execution, and so on. The architecture is shown in Fig. 1.

(1) Grammar check. Grammar check is to check whether the user uploaded web service file meet the specification of BPEL. BPEL is based on XML, so we can use Crimson (a parser for XML) to parse the BPEL file. It will firstly check the element keywords and then check the structure. It will return the error report if it find errors.

(2) Logic check. The work of the logic check is to check if there are link errors or data dependency definition error. The check is based on the execution sequence between the activities and data transmission between the service calls.

(3) Basic Element Construction. It constructs the basic element of the workflow model, which include service workflow, activity, service and variable, and then create the state of these elements and the I/O buffer.

(4) Workflow execution. The work of it is to execute the workflow, start the activities, and then wakeup these activities based on the dependence relations.

(5) Activity execution. It is responsible for the executing of the activity, initializing the input buffer, collecting the entry data, and executing the entire conditional branch, and then returning the results.

(6) Service execution. This model is used to execute the service, which includes initializing the input buffer, collecting the entry data, and sending the request to service call model, and then returning the results.

(7) Service scheduling interface. It executes the requests from the models based on the services and sends the call requests.

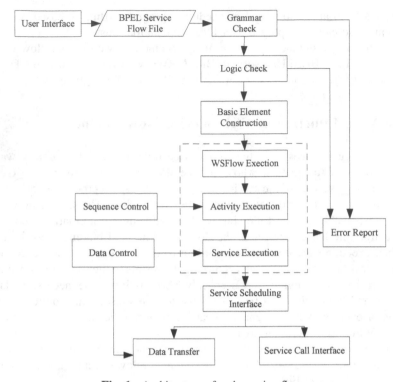

Fig. 1. Architecture of web service flow

(8) Sequence control is used to start the basic element according to the structure defined by the web service workflow model.

(9) Data control. According to the defined data relation, it is responsible for the operations of synchronization, waiting, and so on.

4 Realization of the Web Service Flow Engine

4.1 Construction of the Basic Element of Web Service Flow Engine

Once the workflow engine receives the BPEL file from the user, it will do the following works:

(1) Use Crimson to parse the file according to the structure of the XML DOM tree, and then create three empty lists: activity list, service list and variable list.

(2) Extract the XML elements from the workflow file. If the element name is *Process*, then instantiate the *WSFlow* class; if the element name is the basic activity name of BPEL, for example, *Receive*, *Reply*, *Invoke*, *Assign*, and so on, then add the element into activity list and instantiate the *Activity* class; if the element name is *Partnerlink*, then add the element into service list and instantiate the *Service* class; if the element name is *Variable*, then add the element into variable list and add a attribution named *VariableValue* for the element.

(3) When the workflow engine starts up, *WSFlow* need to activate all its *Activity* instances. Each *Activity* class will search the variable list firstly, collect the entry parameter of the activity, and then activate all its *Service* instances. Each *Service* class needs to call the appointed service and return. When the activity is over, it needs to modify the value of *VariableValue*, which is the important part of the data transfer. Finally, the results of the workflow are all recorded in the variable list.

4.2 Service Flow Execution

The entry of the service flow execution module is maybe the root node of the service flow tree of the first class, or maybe the root node of the service flow tree which is produced by certain activity. So the service flow execution module will need to make a judgment about the type of the root node firstly.

If it is the root node of the service flow tree of the first class, i.e. it is the entry of the whole BPEL service flow. It needs to receive source data (includes the entry parameter of the service flow and the WSDL address of the service, and so on) from the client, and then searches the activity list circularly. If there are activities which have not been executed, then activate this activity and extract the entry parameter from the variable list. If the extraction fails, it means that the activity can not be executed because of the data transmission. The activity then needs to wait for the modification of the data. Execute the above process circularly until all the activities are executed.

If it is the root node of the service flow tree which is produced by certain activity, we then need to create a sub-tree of the service flow and set the root node again. Add all the activities in the sub-tree into the sub-list of the activities, create a new list pointer and then search the activity list circularly. The subsequent process is same with the former case (introduced in the last paragraph.)

4.3 Activity Execution

After the *activity* class is waked up by the web service flow execution module, the execution module will do the following works: firstly search the variable list, secondly collect the entry parameter and instantiate *activity* class, start the activity, and finally judge the type of the activity according to the name of the root node of the activity:

(1) If the activity is *Receive*, then receive the source data, and judge whether the source data is null. If it is not null, then write the source data into the *VariableValue* attribution of the *Input* variable, and the activity is over. Or else the activity returns.

(2) If the activity is *Reply*, then search the variable list, extract the *VariableValue* attribution of the *Output* variable, and return attribution value to the client. The activity is over.

(3) If the activity is *Assign*, then search the variable list, extract the *VariableValue* attribution of the *From* sub element, then write the attribution value into the *VariableValue* attribution of the *To* sub element. The activity is over.

(4) If the activity is *Invoke*, then firstly prepare the entry parameter of the service and check whether the service is usable. If the service is not usable, then the activity returns directly and is over. Or else the activity calls the service and collects the returned results, search the variable list, modify the *VariableValue* attribution of *outputVariable* variable and the activity is over.

(5) If the activity is *Flow*, decompose into independent web service flow and create the corresponding thread, and then switch to the previous module, i.e. the web service flow execution module.

(6) If the activity is *Sequence*, then switch to the web service flow execution module.

4.4 Activity Execution

Only the *Invoke* activity can call web service directly, so only the *Invoke* activities can instantiate *Service* class. The service execution module will firstly decompose the attribution of the root node of the *Invoke* activity, and then judge the name of the attribution:

(1) If it is the *Partnerlink* attribution, then search the service list, and then extract the name of the service, PartnerlinkType and namespace, and finally return the address of the service.

(2) If it is the *PortType* attribution, then extract the type of the port directly.

(3) If it is the *Operation* attribution, then extract the method to call the service directly.

(4) If it is the *Variable* attribution, then search the variable list, and extract *Inputvariable* and *Outputvariable*.

When the engine receives the five parameters, i.e. service name, service address, port type, call method and input parameter, it will instantiate a Service class. Search the WSDL files according to the source data and analyze the file. Check the parameter, if the parameter is not correct, it will return wrong information and exit service call module. If the parameter is correct, it will call the corresponding activity using the Call.invoke() in Axis. If the call fails, it will return the wrong information and exit. If the call success, it will collect the result, and then write into the attribution *VariableValue* of the variable *Outputvariable*, and then exit.

5   System Testing and Performance Analysis

In the Web service flow file "JJCCBPEL1.bpel", it calls two web services, which are Cube.jws and Square.jws. The former is to compute and return the result of a cube of a given parameter, and the latter is to compute and return the result of a square of a given parameter. The specific content of the file is shown in Fig. 2.

We firstly need to submit the file "JJCCBPEL1.bpel" to the engine. For convenience, the needed two WSDL files have been stored in the folder "Axis", and what the user need to is only to submit a source data. We firstly deploy the web service under Axis, store the WSDL file into the folder "Axis", and then start the Tomcat server, finally stat the engine. The user interface is shown in Fig. 3.

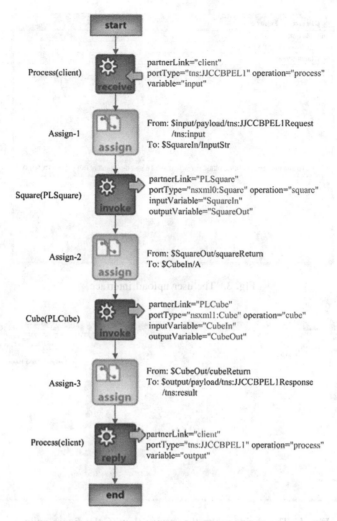

Fig. 2. The content of the service file "JJCCBPEL1.bpel"

The client provides two type of operation mode: OP1 and OP2. OP1 is to execute the web service flow in the background of the engine, and return the results after the execution is over. OP2 is to step the web service flow, so the users can watch and control the running state of the web service flow. We firstly choose OP1 mode, and the average of the computation is 2 seconds. When the engine finishes the computation, the client returns the result: 1,000,000, which is the right results (referring to the file content in Fig. 2). When we choose OP2 mode, the engine will firstly return an empty interface. When we click "Start" button on the interface, the engine will return the graph of the web service flow. The interface is as follows (Fig. 4):

The yellow buttons in the left the above interface represent the activities the flow includes and the relative sequence and relationships between the activities. When we

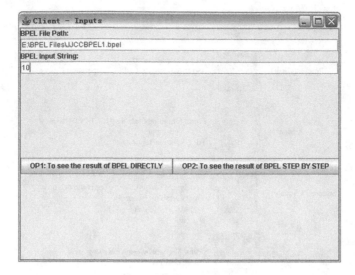

Fig. 3. The user upload interface

Fig. 4. The engine return the service flow (Color figure online)

click these buttons, the engine will execute the corresponding activity, and at the same time return the results of the single step. The waiting time of single step is smaller than one second.

From the above experiments, we can see that our proposed Web service flow engine can return the results correctly. The time efficiency of our engine is very effective and the occupancy rate of system resources is nearly zero.

6   Conclusions

In this paper, with reference to the idea of the Web service flow engine, we create a lightweight Web service flow engine based on BPEL. Our engine includes the following functions: analyzing the application service flow modeling which is inputted by the user, carrying out the grammar check and the logic check to the service flow file, constructing the basic component of the service, executing the service according to the standard, collecting all kinds of the execution information and the results, monitoring the service execution, managing the service calls and finally returning the execution result to the users. Experimental results show that the resource consumption of our proposed engine is very small, and it is easy to maintain and extend. The above advantages contribute to the wide use of our proposed engine.

References

1. Yuwen, T., Tienan, L., Mingzhi, Ma., Xuemei, L., Xin, Z.: Characteristics of volcano and earthquake activity in the Changbai Mountain Tianchi. Sci. Technol. Inf. **05**, 214–215 (2011)
2. Zhang, J., Deng, P., Wan, J., Yan, B., Rong, X., Chen, F.: A novel multimedia device ability matching technique for ubiquitous computing environments. EURASIP J. Wirel. Commun. Netw. (2013). doi:10.1186/1687-1499-2013-181
3. Schwotzer, T., Geihs, K.: Shark–a system for management, synchronization and exchange of knowledge in mobile user groups. J. Univ. Comput. Sci. **8**(6), 644–651 (2002)
4. WfMC, 2009, Binding, WfMC Standards, WFMC-TC-1023. http://www.wfmc.org (2000)
5. Debnath, N., Zorzan, F., Montejano, G., Riesco, D.: Management of software development projects based on SmallRUP methodology through a standard workflow engine. In: 2011 9th IEEE International Conference on Industrial Informatics (INDIN 2011), pp. 671–675 (2011)
6. Woheda, P., Russellb, N., ter Hofstedec, A.H.M., Anderssona, B., van der Aalst, W.M.P.: Patterns-based evaluation of open source BPM systems: the cases of jBPM, OpenWFE, and Enhydra Shark. Inf. Softw. Technol. **51**(8), 1187–1216 (2009)
7. Moser, O., Rosenberg, F., Dustdar, S.: Non-intrusive monitoring and service adaptation for WS-BPEL. In: Proceedings of the 17th International Conference on World Wide Web, pp. 815–824 (2008)

Oriented Research of Color Emotion in E-commerce Website Interface

Xiaoling Zhang[✉] and Fengmei Qin

Zhengda Software Polytechnic of Chongqing, Chongqing, China
410279513@qq.com, fmqin@zdsoft.cn

Abstract. This new round of cloud computing as the center of the IT industry revolution in the global emerging. Internet industry is full of "cloud computing" is the key word. Based on this premise that the sharing of resources, to the development of the Internet has brought opportunities as well as challenges. The E-commerce project in China is in the rapid development stage. The color of website has guiding function to influence consumer's purchase decision and to give consumption implication to consumer. This paper, by combing the website examples and practice, from the angle of E-commerce website interface, researches into color's guiding functions. It's a valuable try in the research of guiding function of color emotion in E-commerce website interface.

Keywords: Could computing · E-commerce · Website interface

1 Introduction

Donald A. Norman pointed out emotion's important position and function in design and in-depth analyzed how to integrate emotional effect into product design for the sake of solving the long bothering contradiction between usability and beauty in his book named ≪Emotional Design≫ [1]. The generation of certain desire in visitor is based on some reasons rather than groundless. This reason will guide visitor's mind and behavior. There is emotion in interface color of website and this emotion will guide visitor's mind and behavior. The expert of industrial design color, Anchor Hocking, pointed out that color was able to directly influence mankind's mind and psychology, which was the vital point for commodity production and sales [2]. He proved that color emotion has guiding function.

The orientation and direction-guidance can be considered as a kind of guiding to direction. The guiding function means the feature of letting things to develop towards a certain direction, such as the guidepost in public place or highway, which serves as direction guider. In the E-commerce website interface, there could be many elements of guiding functions. The guiding function of color emotion in the E-commerce website interface means the color design in E-commerce website interface carries certain emotion and this emotion can provide guiding function to the function, performance and all other aspects of the website [3].

In the design of E-commerce website interface, there are many elements of guiding function, such as shape, color and material. Besides, color has excellent sensory irritation to catch consumer's attention at the first glance and to leave

V.C.M. Leung and M. Chen (Eds.): CloudComp 2013, LNICST 133, pp. 222–228, 2014.
DOI: 10.1007/978-3-319-05506-0_21, © Institute for Computer Sciences, Social Informatics and Telecommunications Engineering 2014

impressive image to visitor. During this process, the emotion revealed by color can unconsciously arouse sympathy from visitor. Therefore, the designer is able to guide visitor by adopting the color emotion.

2 The Guiding Function of Color Emotion in E-commerce Website Interface

2.1 The Guidance for Aesthetics Appreciation

There are two kinds of color decoration and beautification: the integration between color and online content and the decoration of color to the interface of website. The latter means that color is only to decorate the interface and has no connection with content, as it only aims to provide visional appreciation. They aim to improve website image on the basis of visional art and to illustrate the beauty of interface. This kind of color gives the emotion of guiding visitors to appreciate the beauty of E-commerce website interface and helps website to build a colorfully beautiful interface.

2.2 The Fulfillment of Guiding Function

The practical function of color is able to help E-commerce website interface to realize its original functions. On one hand, some colors are special colors in the design of E-commerce website interface and they may indicate certain meaning or usage. Once these colors appear in the certain part in the interface, they will trigger the idea of associating them with certain function [4]. On the other hand, color has the identification function. Within the certain visional range, interfaces of different natures can be classified by different colors to help visitors in distinguishing different functions and to avoid the misunderstanding or time and energy loss caused by single color of confused colors.

2.3 The Motivation of Visitor's Inner Emotion

The color emotion is a kind of emotion to arouse visitor's psychological preference in-depth. It could interact with the psychology of visitors, guide visitor's psychological preference and guide visitor's behavior. Since there are countless colors in the world and they can carry different emotions, the application of different colors will result in remarkable difference in the demonstration of product function, shape and materials. The multi-functions of color provide unconscious function to color in arousing visitors' passion.

2.4 Establish Stable Visitor Group

With consumption improvement of netizen in E-commerce, the color in E-commerce website interface is no longer the color of aesthetic sense but an emotional extension of product. It aims to maintain a certain kind of tacit understating in the aspect of consumption psychology and consumption preference to maintain the stable consumer group. Galbraith, the famous modern American economist, once said "we have no reason to assume that the scientific and industrial achievement is the ultimate appreciation of mankind. When consumption develops to a certain degree, the preference beyond everything is the aesthetic appreciation" [5]. Therefore, we shall pay attention to visitor's psychological and spiritual demand. Once we manage to meet consumer's emotional need, the emotional satisfactory will be more powerful than pure material needs.

The successful website color choice and color collocation will attract visitor's attention from the aspect of vision and cause their imagination from the aspect of emotion. The reason why visitor will be impressed by the E-commerce website interface is that memory has three procedures during recognition, including marking, recalling and re-recognizing. During this process, the marking is the precondition for keeping it in memory and recalling is the review of memory while re-recognizing is result for verifying memory. Therefore, in order to let visitor to record E-commerce website interface color and cause recalling and re-recognizing, the color shall be of outstanding color character, so that color will indicate interface's culture feature and cause permanent memory to visitors.

2.5 Improve the Value of E-commerce Website Interface and Build Brand Image

Through color design in interface, excellent website image and brand recognition, it could arouse visitor's emotional sympathy and value orientation, which are the additional values of color to E-commerce website interface. Therefore, visitors will have different emotions in accordance with different colors. To improve website's appreciation value by increasing color's emotional value is one of the important strategies in modern market to improve guiding rate of color emotion from E-commerce website interface.

Color is one of the important languages to present website's external feature. The color will tend to cause initial impression to visitors when they watching a commodity. Visitors are not only able to sense the emotion and feeling carried by color, but also unconscious to present their pursuit of idea product to color by gaining emotional sympathy from psychological interaction with color. Color has the function of imagination and symbolization, as the application of certain color will bring imagination to its product or company, resulting in the recognition in company's reputation and brand quality. For example, the color of deep blue is not only the representative for website color but also leads the innovation and development of global business pattern, as blue provides the imagination of technology, presents the color emotion of vigor and builds the image of technology for enterprise. Red is another color with rich imaginations, such as blood, sun, red flag, vigor and passion, as well as stands for the bottle for Coca Cola, and red color of bottle with over a hundred years also serves effectively as the main color in its website. The certain color, as a kind of special language, can serve as the implication and mark for brand image. When visitors are browsing websites with this kind of marks, they could identify the brand and distinguish it from other websites even if there isn't any logo. It's the color emotion's guiding function that carries typical visional impact and impressive image [6].

3   The Method to Fulfill the Guiding Function of Color Emotion in E-commerce Website Interface

There are two kinds guiding functions for color emotion in E-commerce website interface, namely the behavior guiding and psychological guiding, while the behavior guiding function can be divided into cognitive behavior guiding and operational behavior guiding. Human is kind of senior social creatures with independent mind and emotion. Therefore, in most occasions in real life, emotion will influence people's mind and behavior. Color has no emotion but color could trigger visitor's emotions. When color is adopted to E-commerce website interface, the color emotion will either strengthen or weaken website's value. When colors are appropriately applied to the E-commerce website interface, they will cause effective effort and color emotion will provide more interface information to visitors by guiding them in operational behavior and emotional recognition. The method to fulfill the guiding function of color emotion in website interface is shown in Fig. 1.

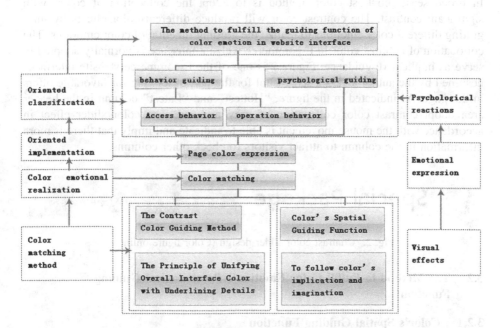

Fig. 1. The method to fulfill the guiding function of color emotion in website interface

3.1   Method to Fulfill Color Emotion's Behavior Guiding Function

3.1.1   The Principle of Unifying Overall Interface Color with Underlining Details

Generally speaking, E-commerce website interface normally has an overall color tone as the frequently used color. Different pages of a website shall have unified color tone and some specially designed pages to maintain systematic color emotion, so that it can bring a unified color sense to indicate the color emotion of the whole website. Meanwhile, the obvious visional effect will directly enhance a clear and unified color emotion. In case that this emotion triggers psychological sympathy with visitor, it can guide visitor's browsing behavior.

The unification of website color doesn't mean that there could only be colors of same system. The unified overall color and underlining local color will form a fierce contrast, which is the presentation of aesthetic principle of integrating unification in changes. When designing, we can adopt the collocation of different colors to underline details. The contrast between colorless and colorful parts as well as the application of contrast color and complementary color could underline details to attract visitor's attention, as, when visitors notice this kind of color, they will response to the color and color emotion. Therefore, color emotion will attract visitor's operational behavior and visiting behavior.

3.1.2   The Contrast Color Guiding Method

In broad sense, contrast color method is to adopt the collocation of colors with significant contrast. The contrast color will produce different color effects by integrating different color emotions to realize the guiding function of color emotions. The collocation of contrast color in E-commerce website interface is normally adopted to serve as implicative guidance. Figure 2 is one of the E-commerce website interfaces designed by the author and is a screenshot for the part of looking for favorable offers in the page. As indicated in the figure, "Hottest" and "Latest" column in the header area adopt contrast color collocation of grey and red. The color slider effect in accordance with the mouse movement is able to indicate and imply that there is more information in the column to attract visitors to check other columns.

Fig. 2.   Contrast color slider design (Color figure online).

3.2   The Method to Fulfill Color Emotion's Psychological Guiding Function

3.2.1   Color's Spatial Guiding Function

Spatial guiding method is to create multi-dimensional space feeling by adopting different colors in E-commerce website interface so as to guide visitor's emotion and behavior. The space created by different color collocation and contrast is a kind of virtual visional space. Judged from the aspect of visional sense, it's planar, psyche-delic and contradictory, in other words, the space created is a kind of illusion, since the 3D space is only an illusion based 2D plane, aiming to provide visitors more emotions created by colors and to enable these colors to influence visitor's psycho-logical changes for the sake of guiding their operational behavior and visiting behavior. Generally, we can adopt below color methods to build color space.

To create spatial feeling by overlapping [7]. The color contrast by overlapping a color onto another color will create the sense of front and back as well as up and down to produce the sense of spatial feeling.

To create spatial sense by the application of shadow. In the digital age, shadow can be changed to any color. The application of shadow will create the 3D feeling. In addition, the shadow can be adopted to present product's external shape.

To create contradictory space. The so-called contradictory space is the space cannot exist in real world but only in the imaginative world. The different collocation of colors will enable colors to present different shadows on the basis of plane.

To distinguish visional regions by the contrast of colors. The fast pace of modern life has unconsciously changed the design style for E-commerce website interface. People tend to prefer simple and direct reading effect. The shape guiding method based on color emotion is to adopt the contrast of colors to divide the E-commerce website interface into different clear areas and regions to guide visitor's mind, visiting and operation behavior.

3.2.2 To Follow Color's Implication and Imagination

After long term life experience accumulation, colors have been endowed with dif-ferent implications and imaginations. In the design of E-commerce website interface, only the connection of color imagination and implication with emotion of visitor can trigger visitor's psychological sympathy to improve website's click rate or even to bring business deals. The color imagination and implication are normally brought by basic colors. Such as green, which stands for peace, hope and life, as the olive branch in ancient Greek Mythology is green. Therefore, when people are visiting green pages, they will be implied by the symbol of this color. In the design, to follow color's imagination and implication will gain twice visional delivery effect.

4 Conclusion

The guiding function of color emotion is not only effective in improving interface's aesthetic appreciation but also effective in improving website's PV value as well as click rate. In the age of sensibility when color is widely adopted, we have to make good use of color's nature of carrying emotion and adopt this nature fully in the design of E-commerce websites.

Acknowledgement. The authors would like to thank the Chongqing Higher Education Reform Project 《Build the Curriculum System of "Integration of Knowledge and Quality" and Fulfill the Innovative Talent Training in Page Design Department》. Project Number: 1202112.

References

1. Norman, D.A.: Emotional Design. Basic Books, New York (2005)
2. Zhang, Z: Intuition and aesthetic freedom. Fudan University (2012)
3. Zhang, X.: User's experience in page design. Artist. Life **287** (2012)
4. Wan, J., Liu, Z., Zhou, K., Lu, R.: Mobile cloud computing: application scenarios and service models. In: Proceedings of the 9th IEEE International Wireless Communications and Mobile Computing Conference, Cagliari, Italy, July 2013
5. Li, G.: A research into color design on product on the basis of consuming behavior. Mall Mod. **17** (2007)
6. Bian, B.: The influence of user's experience on the conversion rate of business e-commerce website. In: The 4th China Management Annual Conference, Management Branch, Conference of China, 14 November 2009
7. Lai, C., Lai, Y., Chao, H., Wan, J.: Cloud-assisted real-time transrating for HTTP live streaming. IEEE Wirel. Commun. **20**(3), 62–70 (2013)

An Adaptive Variable Structure Control Approach Based on Neural Networks and Filter for Four-Wheel Omnidirectional Mobile Robots

Jianbin Wang[1], Jianping Chen[2($\boxtimes$)], and Yimin Yang[1]

[1] School of Automation, Guangdong University of Technology,
Guangzhou 510090, Guangdong, China
wangjianbin505@163.com
[2] School of Computer Science, Zhaoqing University,
Zhaoqing 526061, Guangdong, China
jpchen@zqu.edu.cn

Abstract. For dynamic model of a four-wheel omnidirectional mobile robot (FOMR) usually contains parameter uncertainties, in addition, with the influence of exogenous disturbances, the traditional method for motion control has not good performance. An adaptive variable structure control approach based on neural networks and filter (ANFVSC) is presented in this paper. According to the variable structure control theory and Radial Basis Function neural networks, combining the filter, the ANFVSC is applied to deal with the inherent buffeting with normal variable structure control method. The contribution of ANFVSC in improving the control system performance is shown via simulation. The results show that this method has good tracking robustness and a high control precision, simple achievement and effectively eliminated buffeting.

Keywords: Four-wheel · Omnidirectional mobile robot · Motion control · Dynamic model · Variable structure control · Adaptive · Neural networks · Filter

1 Introduction

Omnidirectional mobile robot has the function of omnidirectional mobility. It can move in any direction without changing any position and pose [1]. With its special motion advantage, the omnidirectional mobile robot is widely applied to the human production and life practice in recent years [2]. The traditional control problems of motion and regulation have been extensively studied in the field of mobile robotics. In particular, the differential and the omnidirectional mobile robots, also known, respectively, as the (2,0) and the (3,0) robots, have attracted the interest of many control researchers.

It is a common practice in mobile robotics to address control problems taking into account only a kinematic representation. From a kinematic perspective, the motion control problem of (2,0) type robot has been addressed and solved [3]. And the

V.C.M. Leung and M. Chen (Eds.): CloudComp 2013, LNICST 133, pp. 229–238, 2014.
DOI: 10.1007/978-3-319-05506-0_22, © Institute for Computer Sciences, Social Informatics and Telecommunications Engineering 2014

regulation and motion control problems for the omnidirectional mobile robot, have also received sustained attention. Considering, only its kinematic model, several control strategies have been proposed. It is designed a nonlinear controller based on a trajectory linearization strategy [4]. In [5] the trajectory-tracking problem is solved by means of an estimation strategy that predicts the future values of the system based on the exact nonlinear discrete-time model of the robot.

However, a good motion control for mobile robot with its kinematic model needs it to track the designed velocity perfectly, which is impossible in practical application. Then a few number of contributions have been focused on the dynamic representation of the omnidirectional mobile robot. It is described the mechanical design of a (3,0) robot and based on its dynamic model it is proposed a PID control for each robot wheel [6]. In the same spirit, in [7] the dynamic model of the mobile robot is considered in order to study the slipping effects between the wheels of the vehicle and the working surface. In literature [8] they solved the optimal velocity trajectory problem for a three-wheel omnidirectional mobile robot in translation motion with cost function of total energy drawn from the batteries. And the time-optimization problem of a desired trajectory is considered for a mobile robot subject to admissible input limits in order to obtain feedback laws that are based on the kinematic and aynamic models [9]. In [10] the trajectory tracking problem is addressed and solved by considering a modification of the well known computed-torque strategy. The achievements in these literatures are all usually supposed that their dynamic models and the parameters were always exactly known.

The analysis of dynamic model uncertainties and exogenous disturbances has produced some sliding mode strategies that have been developed in the area of robot motion control. In [11], based on the linearized system, an integral sliding mode control (ISMC) is designed for trajectory tracking control of an omnidirectional mobile robot. But it has inherent deficiency, which needs computing the upper boundedness of the system dynamics, and may cause high noise amplification. And furthermore, a robust neural network (NN)-based sliding mode controller (NNSMC), which uses an NN to identify the unstructured system dynamics directly, is further proposed to overcome the disadvantages of ISMC and reduce the online computing burden of conventional NN adaptive controllers [12]. However, it needs computing more parameter values and still causes high control cost.

We address and solve the motion control problem of a four-wheel omnidirectional mobile robot taking into account its dynamic model. An adaptive variable structure control approach based on Radial Basis Function neural networks (RBFNN) and filter is presented and this control strategy is robust to model uncertainties and exogenous disturbances. The stability of the closed-loop system, the convergence of the adapting process, and the boundedness of the RBFNN weight estimation errors are all strictly guaranteed. The effectiveness of the control scheme is demonstrated through simulation study, and is compared with the NNSMC. It is shown that the control system with the ANFVSC has better tracking performance of motion control.

2   Four-Wheel Omnidirectional Mobile Robot

Four-wheel robots are one of the models of robots, which are used in many domains. They are omnidirectional with four wheels that have the ability of moving to any direction at any time (they are holonomic mobile robots, in other words). Figure 1 shows the schematic of a four-wheel robot, the angles and directions of the four wheels.

2.1   Kinematic Model

According to the geometric relationship of Fig. 1, the robot pose (position and orientation) in the robot coordinate frame is expressed as $X_m = (x\ y\ \theta)^T$, and the robot pose can be presented in the world coordinate frame as $X_w = (X\ Y\ \theta)^T$, the relationship between X_m and X_w is as formula (1).

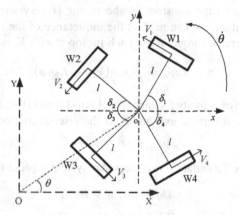

Fig. 1. Schematic model of a four-wheel robot. θ is the moving direction of robot, l is the distance from the wheel to the center of the robot and δ is the angle between the direction of the robot and direction of the wheel.

$$X_m = R(\theta) \cdot X_w = \begin{bmatrix} \cos\theta & -\sin\theta & 0 \\ \sin\theta & \cos\theta & 0 \\ 0 & 0 & 1 \end{bmatrix} \cdot X_w. \tag{1}$$

The kinetic model of mobile robot can be constructed as formula (2):

$$\begin{pmatrix} v_1 \\ v_2 \\ v_3 \\ v_4 \end{pmatrix} = r \cdot \begin{pmatrix} \omega_1 \\ \omega_2 \\ \omega_3 \\ \omega_4 \end{pmatrix} = \begin{pmatrix} -\sin(\delta_1 + \theta) & \cos(\delta_1 + \theta) & l \\ -\sin(\delta_2 - \theta) & -\cos(\delta_2 - \theta) & l \\ \sin(\delta_2 + \theta) & -\cos(\delta_2 + \theta) & l \\ \sin(\delta_1 - \theta) & \cos(\delta_1 - \theta) & l \end{pmatrix} \begin{pmatrix} \dot{X}_w \\ \dot{Y}_w \\ \dot{\theta} \end{pmatrix} = g(\theta)\dot{X}_w. \tag{2}$$

Where v_i denotes the linear velocity and ω_i is its angular velocity of each wheel, r is the radius of each wheel.

2.2   Dynamic Model

The force acting on the robot can be derived by applying the Newton's second law in the robot coordinate frame. Where $M = diag\{m, m, J\}$, m is the total mass of robot, J is the total inertia for robot rotation, and $f = (f_1 \ f_2 \ f_3 \ f_4)^T$ is the tangential force generated by DC motors at each wheel.

$$M\ddot{X}_w = g^T(\theta)f. \tag{3}$$

The dynamics of armature current of each DC motor can be described as formula (4). Where V_s is battery voltage, $u \in [-1, \ 1]$ is normalized control input, and L_a is reactance of the motor, R_a is armature resistance, K_b is back-emf constant, n is gear ratio and φ is angular of the each wheel.

$$L_a \frac{di_a}{dt} + R_a i_a = V_s u - K_b n \dot{\varphi}. \tag{4}$$

Since the electrical time constant of the motor is very small compared to the mechanical time constant, we can neglect the inductance of the motor electric circuit and describe the generated torque of the each motor τ, with K_t is the torque constant.

$$\tau = K_t n i_a = \frac{1}{R_a} K_t n (V_s u - K_b n \dot{\varphi}). \tag{5}$$

Dynamic equation of velocity for each wheel is as formula (6), where J_w is the inertia at center of wheel about vertical axis and F_v is the viscous friction factor in drive line.

$$J_w \ddot{\varphi}_i + F_v \dot{\varphi}_i = \tau_i - r f_i. \tag{6}$$

Then the dynamic formulation produces the system representation,

$$D\ddot{q} + C(\dot{q})\dot{q} = B\tau. \tag{7}$$

Where $q = X_w$, $\tau = (\tau_1 \ \tau_2 \ \tau_3 \ \tau_4)^T$, $B = R(\theta)g^T(0)$,

$$D = \begin{bmatrix} \frac{3J_w}{2r^2} + m & 0 & 0 \\ 0 & \frac{5J_w}{2r^2} + m & \frac{J_w}{r^2}(\sqrt{2} - \sqrt{3})l \\ 0 & \frac{J_w}{r^2}(\sqrt{2} - \sqrt{3})l & \frac{4J_w l^2}{r^2} + J \end{bmatrix},$$

$$C(\dot{q}) = \begin{bmatrix} \frac{3}{2} - \frac{J_w \dot{\theta}}{2r^2}\sin 2\theta & -\dot{\theta}(m + \frac{4J_w}{r^2}) & 0 \\ \dot{\theta}(m + \frac{4J_w}{r^2}) & \frac{5}{2} + \frac{J_w \dot{\theta}}{2r^2}\sin 2\theta & (\sqrt{2} - \sqrt{3})l \\ \frac{J_w \dot{\theta}}{r^2}(\sqrt{2} - \sqrt{3})l \cos\theta & (\sqrt{2} - \sqrt{3})l(\frac{J_w \dot{\theta}}{r^2}\sin\theta + 1) & 4l^2 \end{bmatrix}.$$

3   ANFVSC Design

3.1   Variable Structure Control Based on Filter

Considering the model uncertainties and exogenous disturbances, the dynamic formula (7) can be rewritten as,

$$D\ddot{q} + C(\dot{q})\dot{q} + E(t) = T. \tag{8}$$

With $T = B\tau$, $E(t)$ is bounded, which is the total parameter uncertainties and exogenous disturbances.

According to the theory of variable structure control and filter, the inherent buffeting may be eliminated with a low pass filter, where $\lambda_i > 0$, $i = 1, 2, \cdots, k$, k is the number of control input T.

$$Q(s) = \frac{\lambda_i}{s_i + \lambda_i}. \tag{9}$$

Given a feasible smooth bounded reference trajectory $q_d(t)$, the tracking error $e(t) = q(t) - q_d(t)$, such that for all trajectories starting at $q(t_0) = q_d(t_0)$, we have,

Theorem 1. Consider the system (8) in closed loop with the controller,

$$u = A^{-1}\dot{T} + T = -A^{-1}[H + \eta \, \text{sgn}(s)]. \tag{10}$$

Then the tracking error $e(t)$ is globally asymptotically stabilized to zero. Where $A = diag\{\lambda_1, \lambda_2, \cdots, \lambda_k\}$, $A_i = diag\{\lambda_{i1}, \lambda_{i2}, \cdots, \lambda_{ik}\}$, $\lambda_{ij} > 0$, $i = 1, 2, j = 1, 2, \cdots, k$, $H = D(A_1\ddot{e} + A_2\dot{e} - \dddot{q}_d) - (AD + C(\dot{q}))\dddot{q} - (AC(\dot{q}) + \dot{C}(\dot{q}))\dot{q} - AE(t) - \dot{E}(t)$.

Proof. The sliding mode switching function is designed as $s(t) = \ddot{e} + A_1\dot{e} + A_2 e$, and take now the following Lyapunov function candidate,

$$V = \frac{1}{2}s^T D s. \tag{11}$$

whose time derivative is given by, $\dot{V} = \frac{1}{2}(\dot{s}^T D \, s + s^T D \, \dot{s})$. From (8) and (10), we have,

$$D\dddot{q} + C(\dot{q})\ddot{q} + \dot{C}(\dot{q})\dot{q} + \dot{E} + AD\ddot{q} + AC(\dot{q})\dot{q} + AE = Au. \tag{12}$$

D is a constant symmetric, positive definite matrix, then $\dot{s}^T D s = s^T D \dot{s}$. Introducing (10) and (12) into the above equation, we have

$$
\begin{aligned}
\dot{V} &= s^T[D(\dddot{q} - \dddot{q}_d + A_1\ddot{e} + A_2\dot{e})] \\
&= s^T[Au + D(A_1\ddot{e} + A_2\dot{e} - \dddot{q}_d) - (AD + C(\dot{q}))\dddot{q} - (AC(\dot{q}) + \dot{C}(\dot{q}))\dot{q} - AE(t) - \dot{E}(t)] \\
&= s^T(Au + H) = -s^T\eta\text{sgn}(s) = -\eta|s| \leq 0.
\end{aligned}
\tag{13}
$$

By the variable structure control theory, the proof is completed.

3.2 Adaptive Variable Structure Control Based on Filter

The controller, whose representation is as (10), is applied by the expression of H has been known exactly. However, it is impossible in practical application. By using the estimated value $\hat{H}$ in stead of H, the estimated error $\tilde{H} = H - \hat{H}$, and assuming that parameters of H are slow time variable, we have,

Theorem 2. Consider the system (8) in closed loop with the new adaptive controller,

$$u == -A^{-1}[\hat{H} + \eta \mathrm{sgn}(s)]. \tag{14}$$

With adapting law of $\hat{H}$ is

$$\dot{\hat{H}} = \gamma s. \tag{15}$$

Then the tracking error $e(t)$ is globally asymptotically stabilized to zero.

Proof. Take the following Lyapunov function candidate,

$$V = \frac{1}{2}s^T D s + \frac{1}{2\sigma}\tilde{H}^T \tilde{H}, \sigma > 0. \tag{16}$$

Then introducing (14) and adapting law (15) into (16), we have,

$$\dot{V} = s^T(Au + H) - \frac{1}{\sigma}\tilde{H}^T\dot{\hat{H}} = s^T(Au + \hat{H}) + \tilde{H}^T s - \frac{1}{\sigma}\tilde{H}^T\dot{\hat{H}} \tag{17}$$
$$= -s^T\eta\mathrm{sgn}(s) = -\eta|s| \leq 0.$$

The proof is completed.

3.3 ANFVSC Design

The switching gain η is usually bigger than the boundedness of model uncertainties and exogenous disturbances, which needs computing the upper boundedness of the system dynamics, and may cause high noise amplification and high control cost, particularly for the complex dynamics of the omnidirectional mobile manipulator system. Therefore, a RBFNN is used to identify and approach the switching gain η. Using learning ability of RBFNN, ANFVSC can coordinately control the omnidirectional mobile robot with different dynamics effectively. By taking the sliding mode switching function s as input of RBFNN, and switching gain η is its output, then we have,

$$\eta = |WR(s)|. \tag{18}$$

With $R(s) = \exp(-\|s - c\|^2/b^2)$ is Gauss function, W is matrix of weights between hidden layer and output layer, where c is the center vector and b is the width vector of Radial Basis Function.

Take the adapting performance index is $J_p = s(t)\dot{s}(t)$, then the RBFNN weight-updating process is

$$W(t + 1) = W(t) + \Delta W + \alpha(W(t) - W(t - 1)). \tag{19}$$

Where $\Delta W = -\mu\frac{\partial J_p}{\partial W} = -\mu\frac{\partial s\dot{s}}{\partial u}\frac{\partial \eta\mathrm{sgn}(s)}{\partial \eta}\frac{\partial \eta}{\partial W}$, μ is learning ratio and α is inertial ratio. Then we have,

Theorem 3. Consider the system (8) in closed loop with the new controller (14) and (15), whose switching gain η is given by (18) and (19), the tracking error $e(t)$ is globally asymptotically stabilized to zero.

The similar proof process could be found in literature [12].

4 Numerical Simulation

We carried out numerical simulations to assess the performance of the controller given in Theorem 3. The values of the parameters correspond to a laboratory prototype built in our institution and they are found in Table 1.

Table 1. Parameter values of the robot.

Parameters	Value	Parameters	Value
F_v	1.86 [Nm/(rad/s)]	J_w	0.8 [gcm^2]
K_t	0.0259 [Nm/A]	V_s	24 [V]
K_b	0.0259 [V/(rad/s)]	m	23 [kg]
n	22	L	0.225 [m]
R_a	0.611 [Ω]	r	0.1 [m]
J	33.3 [gcm^2]		

It is desired to follow a circular trajectory, the total disturbances and uncertainties is $E(t) = [\ 2\sin(2\pi t)\ 1.5\cos(2\pi t)\ 3\sin(2\pi t)]^T$, and $q_d(t) = [\ \cos(\pi t)\ \sin(\pi t)\ \frac{\pi}{15}]^T$, $q_d(0) = [\ 0.5\ 0.5\ 0.5]^T$, adapting weight is $\gamma = 30$, learning ratio is $\mu = 0.05$ and inertial ratio is $\alpha = 0.05$. And the matrix $A_1 = diag\{15, 15, 15\}$, $A_2 = diag\{45, 45, 45\}$, $A = diag\{3.5, 3.5, 3.5\}$, $\eta = diag\{41, 94, 50\}$.

With the exact parameters of H in Table 1, Fig. 2 shows the evolution of the mobile robot when it is considered the control strategy proposed on this paper (ANFVSC). The control torque signals in X axis with ANFVSC and NNSMC [12] are shown on Fig. 3. While m in Table 1 is changed into 12 kg, the result of trajectory tracking and the torque signals in X axis are shown on Figs. 4 and 5.

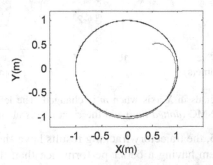

Fig. 2. Evolution of the mobile robot with exact parameters when it is considered ANFVSC. Reference trajectory (*dotted line*) and real tracking trajectory (*real line*) is shown on the figure.

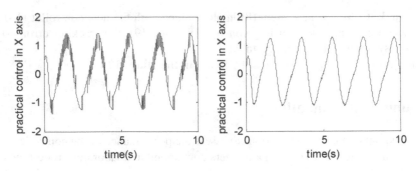

Fig. 3. Control torque signals in X axis with exact parameters. The left figure shows the signal when it is considered NNSMC (*dotted line*) and the right one is about ANFVSC (*real line*).

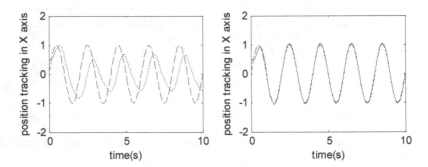

Fig. 4. Position tracking results in X axis when m is changed. The reference position trajectory (*dash line*) is as shown, the left figure shows the position tracking results when it is considered NNSMC (*dotted line*) and the right one is about ANFVSC (*real line*).

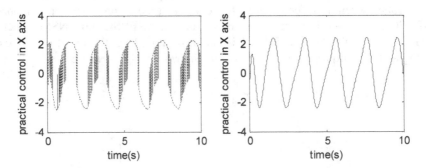

Fig. 5. Control torque signals in X axis when m is changed. The left figure shows the signal when it is considered NNSMC (*dotted line*) and the right one is about ANFVSC (*real line*).

From Figs. 2, 3, 4, 5, the trajectory tracking results have shown that the properties of the closed-loop system having a better performance than the control obtained by NNSMC, whether or not the parameter m is constant or changed. The inherent buffeting has been eliminated effectively when it is considered ANFVSC, however, NNSMC has caused high noise amplifications and high control costs.

5 Conclusions

The motion control with model for a four-wheel omnidirectional mobile robot considering its dynamic model uncertainties and exogenous disturbances has been addressed and solved by means of an adaptive variable structure control based on neural networks and filter. The asymptotic stability of the closed loop system is formally proved. Numerical simulations are proposed to illustrate the properties of the closed-loop system showing a better performance than the control obtained by NNSMC.

Acknowledgments. The work of this paper is supported by the Natural Science Fund Free Application Project of Guangdong Province (No. S2011010004006), the Industry-university-institute Cooperation Project of Guangdong Province and China's Ministry of Education (No. 2012B091100423), the Science and Technology Planning Project of Zhaoqing City (No. 2010F006, No. 2011F001), and the Research Initiation Fund of Zhaoqing University (No. 2012BS01). Associate professor Chen Jianping is corresponding author.

References

1. Jefri, E., Mohamed, R., Sazali, Y.: Designing omni-directional mobile robot with Mecanum wheel. Am. J. Appl. Sci. **3**(5), 1831–1835 (2006)
2. Kalmar-Nagy, T., Ganguly, P., D'Andrea, R.: Real-time trajectory generation for omnidirectional vehicles. In: American Control Conference, Anchorage, pp. 286–291 (2002)
3. Niño-Suárez, P.A., Aranda-Bricaire, E., Velasco-Villa, M.: Discrete-time sliding mode path-tracking control for a wheeled mobile robot. In: 45th IEEE Conference on Decision and Control, pp. 3052–3057. IEEE Press, San Diego (2006)
4. Liu, Y., Wu, X., Zhu, J., Lew, J.: Omni-directional mobile robot controller design by trajectory linearization. In: American Control Conference, Denver, pp. 3423–3428 (2003)
5. Velasco-Villa, M., del Muro-Cuellar, B., Alvarez-Aguirre, A.: Smith-predictor compensator for a delayed omnidirectional mobile robot. In: 15th Mediterranean Conference on Control and Automation, Athens, Greece, pp. T30–027 (2007)
6. Carter, B., Good, M., Dorohoff, M., Lew, J., Williams II, R.L., Gallina, P.: Mechanical design and modeling of an omni-directional RoboCup player. In: RoboCup International Symposium, Seattle (2001)
7. Williams, R.L., Carter, B.E., Gallina, P., Rosati, G.: Dynamic model with slip for wheeled omnidirectional robots. IEEE Trans. Robot. Autom. **18**, 285–293 (2006)
8. Hongjun, K., Byung, K.K.: Minimum-energy trajectory planning and control on a straight line with rotation for three-wheeled omni-directional mobile robots. In: IEEE/RSJ International Conference on Intelligent Robots and Systems (IROS), Vilamoura, pp. 3119–3124 (2012)
9. Kalmár-Nagy, T., D'Andrea, R., Ganguly, P.: Near-optimal dynamic trajectory and control of an omnidirectional vehicle. Rob. Auton. Syst. **46**, 47–64 (2004)
10. Velasco-Villa, M., Rodríguez-Cortés, H., Estrada-Sanchez, I., Sira-Ramírez, H., Vázquez, J.A.: Dynamic trajectory-tracking control of an omnidirectional mobile robot based on a passive approach. In: Hall, E. (ed.) Advances in Robot Manipulators, pp. 299–314. InTech Press, Rijeka (2010)

11. Sho-Tsung, K., Wan-Jung, C., Ming-Tzu, H.: Integral sliding mode control for trajectory tracking control of an omnidirectional mobile robot. In: 8th Asian Control Conference (ASCC), Kaohsiung, pp. 765–770 (2011)
12. Xu, D., Zhao, D.B., Yi, J.Y., Tan, X.M.: Trajectory tracking control of omnidirectional wheeled mobile manipulators: robust neural network-based sliding mode approach. IEEE Trans. Syst. Man Cybern. Part B Cybern. **39**, 788–799 (2009)

Radar Decision Criteria Based on Fuzzy Test of Hypotheses

Ahmed K. Elsherif[1(✉)], Chunming Tang[2], and Lei Zhang[1]

[1] College of information and communication engineering,
Harbin Engineering University, Harbin 15001, China
ahmedelsherif80@gmail.com
[2] College of Electronics and Information Engineering,
Tianjin Polytechnic University, Tianjin 300387, China

Abstract. In this paper we introduce one new step in the procedure of the solution given by S. Mahmoud Taheri and M. Arefi (2009), J. Buckley (2005) in which we can make a decision in more easier way without the need of numerical in calculating A_R and A_T. Second, we give three important tests of hypotheses for radar system to show how the crisp hypothesis decision is too rigid to be true for small changes. Finally, therefore we make the tests by fuzzy hypotheses which can deduce more scientific results with certain degree for accepting or rejecting null hypotheses.

Keywords: Fuzzy hypotheses · Radar detection · Membership function

1 Introduction

Radar Detection is a particular kind of binary decision problem. Initially, we shall make a simplifying assumption that the space consists of only two hypotheses and requires the receiver to determine in the presence of channel disturbance whether to accept or reject the null hypotheses.

Real observations of continuous quantities are not precise but more or less non-precise. Such observations are called non-precise number or fuzzy number. The fuzziness is different from measurement errors and stochastic uncertainty. Errors already are the difference between the exact and measured value and described by statistical model. But, fuzzy is a feature of single observations from continuous quantities. Traditionally, all statisticians assume that the hypotheses for which we provide a test are well defined. This limitation sometimes forces statistician to make decision procedure in unrealistic manner. To relax this rigidity we introduce a fuzzy test of hypotheses for radar detection. The objective of this paper is introducing new step in the procedure of the solution of the fuzzy test of hypotheses based on the procedure defined in [6]. Also show how fuzzy hypotheses are important in radar detection because it gives the advantage of accepting or rejecting the null hypotheses with certain degree. So far few researchers have studied fuzzy hypotheses, such as, Caslas and Gil (1989), Bernhard F. Arnold (1996) [13], Taheri and Behboodian (1999). Their approach has been extended by Torabi et al. (2006) in the cases when the data is fuzzy. Arnold (1996) has proposed the fuzzification of usual statistical hypotheses and considered the

V.C.M. Leung and M. Chen (Eds.): CloudComp 2013, LNICST 133, pp. 239–247, 2014.
DOI: 10.1007/978-3-319-05506-0_23, © Institute for Computer Sciences, Social Informatics
and Telecommunications Engineering 2014

hypotheses test under fuzzy constraints on type I and II error. Korner (2000) has presented an asymptotic test for expectation of random fuzzy variable. Montenegro et al. (2001) has assumed two sample hypotheses tests for mean by considering a fuzzy random variable in two populations. Taheri and Behboodian (2001) have applied Bayesian approach to fuzzy hypotheses testing [15]. Filzmoser, Viertl (2004) and Parchami et al. (2010–2011) [11] have considered p-value approach for problem of testing hypotheses in fuzzy environments. A. Parchami et al., study the fuzzy p-value in testing fuzzy hypotheses with crisp data [12]. Torabi and Behboodian (2007) have studied the likelihood ratio method for testing fuzzy hypotheses [9]. Many researchers have introduced their fuzzy work in pure mathematical algorithm and not applied it in specific application except a few researchers like A. Parchami et al., [8] have applied their p-value testing hypotheses on soil study. In this paper we will extend the fuzzy testing hypotheses in order to make more reasonable decision in radar detection. In Sect. 2 we give some preliminary concepts on fuzzy. In Sect. 3 we introduce three examples for radar detection by crisp test of hypotheses. And the same ones are considered by fuzzy test of hypotheses in Sect. 4. And it draws a conclusion in Sect. 5.

2   Preliminary Concepts

Some concepts on fuzzy hypothesis testing have been introduced.

(**Fuzzy hypotheses testing**): Any hypothesis of the form "$H : \theta$ is $H(\theta)$" is called fuzzy hypothesis, where "$H : \theta$ is $H(\theta)$" implies that θ is in fuzzy set of Θ (the parameter space) with membership function $H(\theta)$ i.e. a function from Θ to $[0,1]$.

Given that the ordinary hypothesis $H_i : \theta \in \Theta_i$ is a fuzzy hypothesis with membership function $H(\theta) = 1$ at $\theta \in \Theta_i$, and zero at $\theta \notin \Theta_i$.

(**One-sided fuzzy hypotheses**): Let the fuzzy hypothesis "$\tilde{H} : \theta$ is $H(\theta)$":

- H is a monotone function of θ.
- There exists $\theta_1 \in \Theta$ such that $H(\theta) = 1$ for $\theta \geq \theta_1$ (or for $\theta \leq \theta_1$).
- The range of H contains the interval $[0,1]$.

(**Two-sided fuzzy hypotheses**): Let the fuzzy hypothesis "$\tilde{H} : \theta$ is $H(\theta)$":

- There exists an interval $[\theta_1, \theta_2] \subset \Theta$ such that $H(\theta) = 1$ for $\theta \in [\theta_1, \theta_2]$ and $\inf\{\theta : \theta \in \Theta\} < \theta_1 < \theta_2 < \sup\{\theta : \theta \in \Theta\}$.
- H is increasing function of θ for $\theta \geq \theta_1$ and is decreasing for $\theta \geq \theta_2$).
- The range of H contains the interval $[0,1]$.

For the addition, subtraction, multiplication and division see [2]. Let R be a set of real numbers. For details see [12].

$$F_S(R) = \{S(a,b)/a, b \in R, a \leq b\}$$
$$F_B(R) = \{B(c,d)/c, d \in R, c \leq d\}$$
$$F_T(R) = \{T(a,b,c)/a, b, c \in R, a \leq b \leq c\}$$

(Boundary of fuzzy hypotheses): The boundary of fuzzy hypotheses $\tilde{H}$ is a fuzzy subset of Θ with a membership function H_b, defined as follows

- Left-sided test ($H \in F_B(R)$ and H is increasing) $H_{ob} = \begin{cases} H(\theta) \text{ for } \theta \leq \theta_1 \\ 0 \text{ for } \theta > \theta_1 \end{cases}$.

- Right-sided test ($H \in F_S(R)$ and H is decreasing) $H_{ob} = \begin{cases} H(\theta) \text{ for } \theta \geq \theta_1 \\ 0 \text{ for } \theta < \theta_1 \end{cases}$.

- Two sided test $H_{ob}(\theta) = H(\theta)$.

3 Crisp Hypotheses for Radar Detection System

Based on Neyman-Pearson criteria the decision is made by maximizing the probability of detection under a constraint, which is the probability of false alarm does not exceed a certain value. For detailed test of hypotheses see [3–5], the achievable combination of detection probability and false alarm probability are affected by the quality of the radar system and the design of a signal processor. However, as we all know, for fixed system, if we increase detection probability, probability of false alarm will increase as well (because of type II error being decreased). The radar system designer will confirm the probability value of false alarm depending on radar type, such as, for normal surveillance radar, the probability value of false alarm is in the range of 10^{-4} to 10^{-8}. The radar makes tens or hundreds of thousands, even millions of detection decision per second. To have a complete decision rule, each point in the space (each combination of N measured data values) must be assigned one decision, H_0 ("Target absent") or H_1 ("Target present"). Then when the radar measures a particular data set (observation of received power signal), the system chooses either "target absent" or "target present". In radar detection problem the prior probabilities density function are unknown, but for theoretical study we can consider it as a normal density function.

"Probability of false alarm" $= \alpha =$ Probability (reject H_0/H_0 true).
"Probability of miss" $= \beta =$ probability (accept H_0/H_1 true).
"Probability of detection" $= 1 - \beta$.
The hypothesis: $H_0 : \mu \leq \mu_0$ (Noise alone) $H_1 : \mu > \mu_0$ (Signal + Noise).

Example 1. Let $x_1, \ldots, x_{100}$ be a 100 random sample of a received power signals, having normal probability density function with unknown μ, and known σ^2, we test the hypothesis with $P_{fa} = \alpha = 0.05$ (theoretical value).

$H_0 : \mu \leq 0.5$ (Noise alone) $H_1 : \mu > 0.5$ (Signal + Noise)

Assume we make this experiment twice with sample means $\bar{x}_1 = 0.9$ microwatt (theoretical value) and $\bar{x}_2 = 1$ microwatt (theoretical value) and sample variance $\sigma^2 = 7.84$.

For $\bar{x}_1 = 0.9$ $Z_{C_1} = \frac{\bar{x}_1 - \mu_0}{\sigma/\sqrt{n}} = 1.428 < Z_\alpha = 1.65$

Then we accept H_0 (received signal due to noise).

For $\bar{x}_2 = 1$ $Z_{C_1} = \frac{\bar{x}_2 - \mu_0}{\sigma/\sqrt{n}} = 1.785 > Z_\alpha = 1.65$

Then we reject H_0 (received signal due to signal).

Example 2. Let $x_1, \ldots, x_{101}$ be a 101 random sample of a received power signals, having normal probability density function with unknown μ, σ^2, we test the hypothesis with $\alpha = 0.05$

$$H_0 : \sigma^2 \le 2.5 \,(\text{Same Target}) \qquad H_1 : \sigma^2 > 2.5 \,(\text{Different target})$$

This test measure if the echo signal is due to the same target or different target because different target returns different received power, so the value of the variance get larger when it returns from different target. And the value 2.5 depends on the radar's type and position. Assume we make this experiment twice with sample variances $s_1^2 = 3.1$ and $s_2^2 = 3.2$.

For $s_1^2 = 3.1$ $\chi_{c_1}^2 = \frac{(n-1)s_1^2}{\sigma^2} = 124 < \chi_{n-1,\alpha} = 1240342$

Accept H_0 (the received signal from the same target).

For $s_2^2 = 3.2$ $\chi_{c_2}^2 = \frac{(n-1)s_2^2}{\sigma^2} = 128 > \chi_{n-1,\alpha} = 1240342$

Reject H_0 (the received signal from the different target).

Example 3. Assume we have two auxiliary similar antennas with 180 degree in position and rotating together with 360 degree as shown in Fig. 1, the two ones having wide beam width and bandwidth. The radar transmitter must be powered off to avoid burning the two receivers. We make a test to determine which direction contains more noise (jamming), in order to make the radar receiver taking it in consideration while testing the hypothesis about the mean as in Example 1 in order to increase or decrease the threshold level. Assume $\alpha = $ type I $= 0.05$ we test:

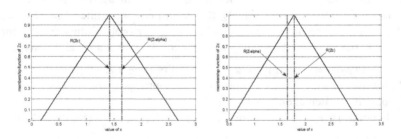

Fig. 1. Membership function of Z_C at mean of $\bar{x}_1$ and $\bar{x}_2$

$$H_0 : \mu_1 = \mu_2 \Rightarrow \mu_1 - \mu_2 = d = 0 \,(\text{Same amount of noise})$$

$$H_1 : \mu_1 \ne \mu_2 \Rightarrow \mu_1 - \mu_2 \ne d \ne 0 \,(\text{Different amount of noise})$$

Let $x_1, \ldots, x_{100}$ be a 100 random sample of a received power signals from the first antenna, having normal probability density function with unknown μ_1, and known σ_1^2 and $y_1, \ldots, y_{100}$ be a 100 random sample of a received power signals from the second antenna, with normal probability density function with unknown μ_2, and known σ_2^2.

Assume we make this experiment twice by changing the mean of the received signal power of the first antenna with sample means $\bar{x}_1 = 0.3$ microwatt $\bar{x}_2 = 0.31$ with the same variance $\sigma_1^2 = 0.5$ and $\bar{y}_1 = \bar{y}_2 = 0.1$ microwatt not changed with the same sample variance $\sigma_2^2 = 0.6$.

For $\bar{x}_1 = 0.3$, $\sigma_1^2 = 0.5$ and $\bar{y}_1 = 0.1$, $\sigma_2^2 = 0.6$

$$Z_{c_1} = \frac{\bar{x}_1 - \bar{y}_1}{\sqrt{\frac{\sigma_1^2}{n_1} + \frac{\sigma_2^2}{n_2}}} = 1.9164 < Z_{\frac{\alpha}{2}} = 1.96 \text{ accept } H_0 \text{(same amount of noise)}.$$

$$Z_{c_2} = \frac{\bar{x}_1 - \bar{y}_1}{\sqrt{\frac{\sigma_1^2}{n_1} + \frac{\sigma_2^2}{n_2}}} = 2.0122 > Z_{\frac{\alpha}{2}} = 1.96 \text{ reject } H_0 \text{ (different amount of noise)}.$$

These three given examples show that even a slightly change in signal value can make different decision based on crisp testing hypotheses. So we have to think of more realistic algorithm in testing hypotheses to solve this problem. Fuzzy mathematics has been introduced to address this challenge.

4   Fuzzy Hypotheses Test with Fuzzy Data in Radar Decision

Traditionally, all statisticians assume hypotheses are well defined. This limitation sometimes forces the statistician to make decision procedure in unrealistic manner. To relax this rigidity we introduce a fuzzy test of hypotheses for radar detection. The design of the threshold level must be a fuzzy threshold. As classical threshold give severe decision for slightly change in the sample received signal mean power. While fuzzy threshold give more scientific results because there is a degree of the acceptance or rejection and depending on your radar (surveillance or tracking) you adjust your fuzzy threshold. Suppose that, we are interested in testing the following fuzzy hypotheses:

$H_0 : \theta^* \leq \theta_0$ (θ^* is approximately less than θ_0)
$H_1 : \theta^* > \theta_0$ (θ^* is approximately larger than θ_0)

We introduce an approach for testing the above fuzzy hypotheses based on [6] with one new step:

- Calculate the $\delta - cut$ of H_{0b} (fuzziness due to hypotheses)

$$H_{0b} = \begin{cases} H(\theta) \, for \ \theta \geq \theta_1 \\ 0 \, for \ \theta < \theta_1 \end{cases}$$

With $H_{0b} = [\theta_1(0), \theta_2(0)] = [\theta_{0l}, \theta_{0h}]$
- Calculate the $\delta - cut$ of the fuzzy sample parameter (fuzziness due to data)
  $\Omega_{\delta=0} = [\Omega_l(0), \Omega_h(0)]$, where $\delta \in [0, 1)$
- Calculate the fuzzy test statistic Q_{0C} based on the first two steps.
- For (TFN): $Q_{0C} = T(a_1, b_1, c_1)$ and $Q_\alpha = T(a_2, b_2, c_2)$

$$R(Q_{0C}) = \frac{\gamma}{2}(a_1 + b_1) + \frac{1 - \gamma}{2}(b_1 + c_1)$$

$$R(Q_\alpha) = \frac{\gamma}{2}(a_2 + b_2) + \frac{1 - \gamma}{2}(b_2 + c_2).$$

Where γ is the measure of pessimistic and optimistic of your decision, with ($\gamma = 0$ pessimistic decision) and with ($\gamma = 1$ optimistic decision). In our case we consider $\gamma = 0.5$. This criterion considers the fuzziness in optimistic and pessimistic but it gives a rigid decision for detail see [17].

But here we give another formula to give a decision with a degree of acceptance.

In case right sided test of hypotheses:
If $R(Q_{0C}) > R(Q_\alpha)$
(i) $a_1 < R(Q_\alpha)$ reject $H_0 = \frac{R(Q_{0C})}{R(Q_{0C}) + R(Q_\alpha)}$, (ii) $a_1 > R(Q_\alpha)$ reject $H_0 = 1$
If $R(Q_{0C}) < R(Q_\alpha)$
(i) $c_1 > R(Q_\alpha)$ reject $H_0 = \frac{R(Q_{0C})}{R(Q_{0C}) + R(Q_\alpha)}$, (ii) $c_1 < R(Q_\alpha)$ accept $H_0 = 1$.

In case left sided test of hypotheses:
If $R(Q_{0C}) < R(Q_{1-\alpha})$
(i) $c_1 > R(Q_{1-\alpha})$ accept $H_0 = \frac{R(Q_{0C})}{R(Q_{0C}) + R(Q_{1-\alpha})}$, (ii) $c_1 < R(Q_{1-\alpha})$ reject $H_0 = 1$
If $R(Q_{0C}) > R(Q_{1-\alpha})$
(i) $a_1 < R(Q_{1-\alpha})$ accept $H_0 = \frac{R(Q_{0C})}{R(Q_{0C}) + R(Q_{1-\alpha})}$, (ii) $a_1 > (Q_{1-\alpha})$ accept $H_0 = 1$.

In case of two sided-tests of hypotheses:
If $R(Q_{0C}) > R\left(Q_{\alpha/2}\right)$:
(i) $a_1 < R(Q_{\frac{\alpha}{2}})$ reject $H_0 = \dfrac{R(Q_{0C})}{R(Q_{0C}) + R\left(Q_{\frac{\alpha}{2}}\right)}$, (ii) $a_1 > R\left(Q_{\frac{\alpha}{2}}\right)$ reject $H_0 = 1$

If $R(Q_{0C}) < R\left(Q_{\frac{\alpha}{2}}\right)$
(i) $c_1 > R\left(Q_{\frac{\alpha}{2}}\right)$ reject $H_0 = \dfrac{R(Q_{0C})}{R(Q_{0C}) + R\left(Q_{\frac{\alpha}{2}}\right)}$, (ii) $c_1 > R\left(Q_{\frac{\alpha}{2}}\right)$ accept $H_0 = 1$

If $R(Q_{0C}) < R\left(Q_{1-\frac{\alpha}{2}}\right)$
(i) $c_1 > R\left(Q_{1-\frac{\alpha}{2}}\right)$ accept $H_0 = \dfrac{R(Q_{0C})}{R(Q_{0C}) + R\left(Q_{1-\frac{\alpha}{2}}\right)}$, (ii) $c_1 < R\left(Q_{1-\frac{\alpha}{2}}\right)$ reject $H_0 = 1$

If $R(Q_{0C}) > R\left(Q_{1-\frac{\alpha}{2}}\right)$
(i) $a_1 > R\left(Q_{1-\frac{\alpha}{2}}\right)$ accept $H_0 = \dfrac{R(Q_{0C})}{R(Q_{0C}) + R\left(Q_{1-\frac{\alpha}{2}}\right)}$, (ii) $a_1 < \left(Q_{1-\frac{\alpha}{2}}\right)$ accept $H_0 = 1$.

Example 4. The same as Example 1 but with fuzzy test of hypotheses:
$H_0 : \theta^* = \mu \leq 0.5$(Noise alone) $H_1 : \theta^* = \mu < 0.5$(Signal + Noise)
With $H_0 : S(a,b) = \begin{cases} (1.5 - 2x) \text{ for } 0.25 < x \leq 0.75 \\ 0, \text{ elsewhere} \end{cases}$
In both cases: $\bar{x}_1 = TFN(0.8, 0.9, 1)$ and $\bar{x}_2 = TFN(0.9, 1, 1.9)$

For $\bar{x}_1 = TFN(0.8, 0.9, 1)$

- $H_{0b} = [0.25, 0.75 - 0.5\delta]_{\delta=0} = [0.25, 0.75]$, $\bar{x}(\delta = 0) = [0.8, 1]$

- $Z_C = \left[\dfrac{\bar{x}_l - \mu_{0h}}{\sigma/\sqrt{n}} - \dfrac{\bar{x}_h - \mu_{0l}}{\sigma/\sqrt{n}} \right] = [0.1785, 2.678]$

  $Z_C = TFN(0.1785, 1.42825, 2.678)$

- At $\gamma = 0.5$ $R(\tilde{Z}_C) = \dfrac{\gamma}{2}(a_1 + b_1) + \dfrac{1-\gamma}{2}(b_1 + c_1) = 1.42825$

  $R(Z_\alpha) = Z_\alpha = 1.65$(Because it is not fuzzy)

- The decision is to reject H_0 with 46.39 % or accept H_0 with 53.61 %.

For $\bar{x}_2 = TFN(0.9, 1, 1.1)$ $R(Z_C) = 1.7857$ and $R(Z_\alpha) = 1.65$
The decision is to reject H_0 with 51.97 % or accept H_0 with 48.03 %.

Example 5. The same as Example 2 but with fuzzy test of hypotheses:

    $H_0 : \theta^* = \sigma^2 \leq 2.5$(Same target) $H_1 : \theta^* = \sigma^2 > 2.5$ (Different target)

    With $H_0 : S(a, b) = \begin{cases} (3 - x) \ for \ 2 < x \leq 3 \\ 0, elsewhere \end{cases}$

At: $S_1^2 = TFN(3, 3.1, 3.2)$, $S_2^2 = TFN(3.1, 3.2, 3.3)$
For $S_1^2 = TFN(3, 3.1, 3.2)$

- $H_{0b} = [2, 3 - \delta]_{\delta=0} = [2, 3]$
- $S_1^2(\delta = 0) = [3, 3.2]$
- $\chi_C^2 = \left[\dfrac{(n-1)S_l^2}{\sigma_{0h}^2}, \dfrac{(n-1)S_h^2}{\sigma_{0l}^2} \right] = [100, 160]$, $\chi_C^2 = TFN(100, 130, 160)$
- At $\gamma = 0.5$ $R(\chi_C^2) = 130$ and $R(\chi_\alpha^2) = 140.169$
- The decision is to reject H_0 with 48.11 % or accept H_0 with 51.89 %.

For $S_2^2 = TFN(3.1, 3.2, 3.3)$ $R(\chi_C^2) = 134.1665$ and $R(\chi_\alpha^2) = 140.169$
Reject H_0 with 48.9 % or accept H_0 with 51.1 % (Fig. 2).

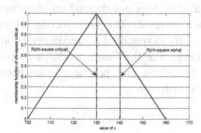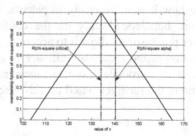

Fig. 2. Membership function of chi-square critical at s_1^2 and s_2^2

Example 6. The same as Example 3 but with fuzzy test of hypotheses:

$$H_0 : \theta^* \Rightarrow \mu_1 - \mu_2 \approx d = 0 \text{ (Same amount of noise)}$$

$$H_1 : \theta^* \Rightarrow \mu_1 - \mu_2 \neq d = 0 \text{ (Different amount of noise)}$$

With $H_0 : T(a, b, c) = T(0, 0.25, 0.5)$
For $\bar{x}_1 - \bar{y}_1 = TFN(0.1, 0.2, 0.3)$

- $H_{0b} = [0.05\delta - 0.05, 0.05 - 0.05\delta]_{\delta=0}$, $H_{0b} = [d_{0l}, d_{0h}] = [-0.05, 0.05]$
- $\bar{x}_1 - \bar{y}_1(\delta = 0) = [(\bar{x}_1 - \bar{y}_1)_l, (\bar{x}_1 - \bar{y}_1)_h]$, $\bar{x}_1 - \bar{y}_1 = [0.1.0.3]$

- $Z_C = \left[\dfrac{(\bar{x}_1 - \bar{y}_1)_l - d_{0h}}{\sqrt{\frac{\sigma_1^2}{n_1} + \frac{\sigma_2^2}{n_2}}}, \dfrac{(\bar{x}_1 - \bar{y}_1)_h - d_{0l}}{\sqrt{\frac{\sigma_1^2}{n_1} + \frac{\sigma_2^2}{n_2}}} \right] = [0.4767, 3.3371]$

  $Z_C = TFN(0.4767, 1.42985, 2.383)$

- $R(Z_C) = 1.42985$ $R\left(Z_{\frac{\alpha}{2}}\right) = Z_{\frac{\alpha}{2}} = 1.96$ and $R\left(Z_{1-\frac{\alpha}{2}}\right) = Z_{1-\frac{\alpha}{2}} = -1.96$

The decision is to reject H_0 with 49.31 % or accept H_0 with 50.69 %.

For $\bar{x}_2 - \bar{y}_2 = TFN(0.11, 0.21, 0.31)$
The decision is to reject H_0 with 50.53 % or accept H_0 with 49.47 % (Fig. 3).

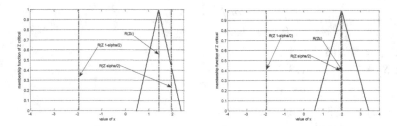

Fig. 3. Membership function of Z_C at $\bar{x}_1 - \bar{y}_1$ and $\bar{x}_2 - \bar{y}_2$

5   Conclusion

The statistical tests based on fuzzy test statistic are more flexible and give more scientific decision than the traditional ones. We showed in the new step of our procedure how it is more easily in calculation also it does not depend on membership function, but depend only on the confidence interval. The construction of radar receiver processor to allow it to accept or reject H_0 to specified degree depends on the application of the radar (surveillance or tracking). For the future work, theoretically we need to introduce more enhancement algorithms and practically we need to implement the receiver based on this detection criterion.

References

1. Skolnik, M.I.: Introduction to Radar System, 2nd edn. Mc Graw-Hill, New York (2008)
2. Kaufmann, A., Gupta, M.M.: Introduction to Fuzzy Arithmetic Theory and Application. Van Nostrand Reinhold Company, New York (1985)
3. Papoulis, A.: Probability Random Variable and Stochastic Processes, 3rd edn. Mc Graw-Hill, New York (1991)

4. Kreyszig, E.: Advanced Engineering Mathematics, 9th edn., pp. 991–1094. Willey, Hoboken (2006)
5. Lehmann, E.L., Romano, J.P.: Testing Statistical Hypotheses, 3rd edn. Springer, New York (2010)
6. Taheri, S.M., Arefi, M.: Testing fuzzy hypotheses based on fuzzy test statistic. Soft. Comput. 13, 617–625 (2009)
7. Arnold, B.F.: Testing fuzzy hypotheses with crisp data. Fuzzy Sets Syst. 94, 323–333 (1998)
8. Parchami, A., Ivani, R., Mashinchi, M.: An application of testing fuzzy hypotheses: soil study on bioavailability of cadmium. Scientia Iranica C 18(3), 470–478 (2011)
9. Torabi, H., Behboodian, J.: Likelihood ratio tests for fuzzy hypotheses testing. Stat. Pap. 48, 509–522 (2007)
10. Hryniewicz, O.: Possibilistic decisions and fuzzy statistical tests. Fuzzy Sets Syst. 157, 2665–2673 (2006)
11. Filzmoser, P., Viertl, R.: Testing hypotheses with fuzzy data: the fuzzy p-value. Metrika 59, 21–29 (2004)
12. Parchami, A., Taheri, S.M., Mashinchi, M.: Fuzzy p-value in testing fuzzy hypotheses with crisp data. Stat Paper 51, 209–226 (2010)
13. Arnold, B.F.: An approach to fuzzy hypothesis testing. Metrica 44, 119–126 (1996)
14. Grzegorzewski, P.: Testing statistical hypotheses with vague data. Fuzzy Sets Syst. 112, 501–510 (2000)
15. Taheri, S.M., Behboodian, J.: A Bayesian approach to fuzzy hypotheses testing. Fuzzy Sets Syst. 123, 39–48 (2001)
16. Falsafain, A., Taheri, S.M.: On Buckley's approach to fuzzy estimation. Soft. Comput. 15, 345–349 (2011)
17. Kumar, A., Singh, P., kaur, P., Kaur, A.: A new approach for ranking of L_R type generalized fuzzy numbers. Expert Syst. Appl. 38, 10906–10910 (2011)

Workshop Session 2

An Efficient Adaptive Neighbor Selection
Algorithm in Pear-to-Pear Networks

Xian Li$^{(\boxtimes)}$ and Aili Zhang

Guangdong Industrial Technical College, Guangzhou, Guangdong, China
qiangliu1977@gmail.com, 2002106018@gditc.edu.cn

Abstract. Based on analysis of fixed random neighbor selection algorithms, this paper presents an efficient adaptive and dynamic neighbor selection algorithm. The new algorithm adopts a comprehensive impact value to measure nodes. The different nodes have different impact values and have different transmission abilities. The nodes with bigger impact values can do more work in P2P system and thus are easier to be selected as neighbors. Simulations show that the new algorithm can reduce the transmission delay and improve the performance of P2P networks.

Keywords: Peer-to Peer network · Adaptive neighbor selection · Impact value

1 Introduction

With rapid development of cyber-physical systems [1, 2], mobile cloud computing [3, 4] and Internet of Things [5], there is an inevitable demand on applying P2P technologies to stream media transmission. But as we all know, the performance of P2P stream media system depends on the P2P network topology. The earlier P2P stream media models adopt multicast tree widely, which will cause the problems that algorithms can't balance between depth and width in constructing a multicast tree and also feel in dilemma in deciding whether leaf nodes attend data distribution or not [6]. For the above reasons, the later P2P systems are inclined to construct mesh topology. In the research field of P2P systems, several topologies are presented, such as centralized P2P structure, distributed P2P structure and hybrid P2P structure. These structures and topologies solved the problems brought by tree structure. But for the reason that all client nodes have different up-link bandwidth, the P2P system still can't utilize resources of the nodes that have high up-link bandwidth. Then the selection of these high quality nodes as P2P nodes has been a critical problem in constructing P2P topology [7]. For this question, an impact value for measuring ability of node is designed in this paper. The value can reflect one node's bandwidth, delay and computation ability comprehensively. The nodes in P2P networks can be evaluated and classified by this value. Based on this value and a fixed random neighbor selection algorithm (FRNS) [8], an efficient adaptive neighbor selection (EANS) algorithm is presented.

V.C.M. Leung and M. Chen (Eds.): CloudComp 2013, LNICST 133, pp. 251–257, 2014.
DOI: 10.1007/978-3-319-05506-0_24, © Institute for Computer Sciences, Social Informatics
and Telecommunications Engineering 2014

Most of the P2P live stream media systems select nodes based on bandwidth or delay. Two kinds of P2P topology construction and neighbor selection algorithms are used: method tree based [9] and method random selection based [10]. In the tree based method, the general way is to select parent node according bandwidth. In order to satisfy high bandwidth demand, some algorithms limit the out degree of nodes. The random selection based method is based on node's delay. Every node maintains only a small part of the state of neighbor nodes selected randomly. This can acquire a better extensive performance. When a node joins a P2P network, the search process begins to find other node's information, which can help the node to select its neighbors. Information of a node includes several aspects, such as online status, bandwidth, delay and computation ability et al. Compared with other parameters, delay is easier to measure. So many P2P systems select appropriate neighbors according node's delay. When a node joins a P2P network, it will select the nodes that have smallest delay to it as neighbors. Algorithms, such as Dagstream, ZIGZAG and AnySee, all adopt this method. Because the delay between two nodes can't reflect bandwidth, these nodes always have not enough bandwidth to satisfy stream media systems.

If the status of entire network and nodes has never changed, a better performance can be gotten by selecting nodes according to delay or bandwidth. But because of existence of many shared links or parent nodes in overlay network, the network performance will be greatly influenced in such dynamic network environment. Some P2P stream media networks, such as PRO [11], randomly select nodes in order to provide diverse paths and parent nodes. The node that sends out request in PRO will abide some rules to select appropriate node as its parent. PRIME [12] selects a node's neighbor by bandwidth bottleneck. The algorithm can get the minimal bandwidth bottleneck by analyzing all the nodes that have the ability to provide bandwidth. This algorithm only adapts to the overlay networks that exist directive parent-child relation between nodes. CoolStreaming [13] is a protocol based on Gossip. This algorithm is adaptable to mass P2P network. But some nodes randomly selected can't provide ideal high quality stream media. The resources of the nodes that have higher bandwidth can't be used.

Reference [8] presented a fixed random neighbor selection (FRNS) algorithm. In this algorithm, the neighbor number of request node is fixed whether in static or dynamic environment. At first step, the algorithm searches the online nodes that have the probability to become neighbors of the request node by message mechanism. Once such a node is found, the node's information will be stored in neighbor list and at the same time, a timer will start. Before this node in node list really becomes a neighbor of the request node and the timer is elapsed, the request node will delete this node from neighbor list. If the number of online node is greater than 0 and the neighbor number of the request node is less than the max neighbor number, the request node will select nodes from node list by a random number as it's neighbors.

When a node requests resources from server and FRNS algorithm is used, the low bandwidth nodes may become bottleneck in transmitting system resources. The nodes that have high bandwidth not used will reduce the transmitting performance. According to the faults of these algorithms and considering the character of stream media, this paper presents an efficient adaptive random neighbor selection algorithm.

The algorithm ranks node's ability by an impact value. The nodes with stronger ability are easier to be selected, which improved the performance of P2P stream media system and solved the problem of neighbor selection in a better way.

2 Problems and Solution

In the hybrid P2P systems, in order to satisfy request node's query request, the central server randomly records current position of every node. In FRNS algorithm, the nodes stored in neighbor list are randomly selected and their upload ability, such as bandwidth and delay, is not considered. For evaluating every node's ability, an impact value, which can be used to classify nodes, is introduced here. The request nodes with different impact values are assigned different max neighbor number. Nodes in neighbor list are no more in equal position and the ones that have bigger impact value is easier to be mapped to neighbor position.

According to above description, the critical part of new algorithm is to design an impact value. This parameter should reflect the influence of bandwidth, delay, loss ratio and computation ability. In this paper, we design this parameter as follows:

$$IV = \frac{B^\alpha C^\beta}{D^\gamma L^\lambda} \tag{1}$$

where:

IV—impact value of a node;
B—the bandwidth a node can provide;
C—the computation ability of a node (measured by idle ratio of CPU);
D—delay from source to a node;
L—loss ratio of a node;

α, β, γ, λ— influence exponent of every parameter, can be adapted according to detail application, but satisfy $\alpha + \beta + \gamma + \lambda = 1$;

From Eq. (1), we can see that the bigger the impact value, the stronger ability the node will have. Then the main part of the algorithm is described as follows.

As shown in line 4 in Fig. 1, the algorithm also finds online nodes by a message mechanism [8]. The nodes found are stored in neighbor list and become a candidate neighbor. In a real P2P network, because every node's detect and control ability is limited, once the number of node in P2P networks is greater than a threshold, the performance of the P2P system must decrease. Hence only part of candidate nodes can become neighbor nodes. Line 5 computes IV by Eq. (1). Stream media can endure a certain packet loss. The general loss ratio is 1 % to 3 %. The nodes whose loss ratio is less than 2 % are set to be the preferential candidate nodes. Operation in Line 15 is based on such a process that once a node is stored in the node list, a timer for it will be started. Before dead time arriving, if this node doesn't become neighbor, it will be deleted from neighbor list.

```
1    if (number of online nodes)>0 then
2        return
3    End if
4    create neighbor list by message query process
5    calculate nodes' IV in neighbor list
6    sort nodes in neighbor list by IV in descend
7    while (number of online nodes)>0 do
8        node_id=random(ids of all online nodes )
9        If node_id is not self then
10           If find(node_id, neighbor list)=true then
11               If (number of neighbor)< (max number of neighbor)
                 and (position of node_id in neighbor list)<=
                 (max number of neighbor) then
12                   Label node_id in neighbor list as a neighbor
13               Else
14                   If dead time of node_id in neighbor list arrives then
15                       Delete node_id from neighbor list
16                   End if
17               End if
18           End if
19        End if
20   End while
```

Fig. 1. The efficient adaptive neighbor selection (EANS) algorithm

3   Simulation and Performance Evaluation

In this part, we will evaluate performance of our algorithm by simulation and compare it with FRNS algorithm in sever load, play delay, and network throughput.

3.1   Simulation Environment

The network topology, which includes 1000 routers and 2000 nodes, is generated by GT-IMT [14] tool. The output bandwidth of each node is randomly distributed in [0, 8000] Kbps. The access bandwidth is randomly distributed in [500, 2000] Kbps. The stream session lasts 60 min and media file is divided into 60 blocks. The parameters in Eq. (1) are set as follows: $\alpha = 0.3$, $\beta = 0.2$, $\gamma = 0.3$, $\lambda = 0.2$. This can increase the influence of bandwidth and delay.

All simulations are completed under NS2 simulation environment. In simulation process, ten nodes join the P2P network per second until there are 1500 nodes in P2P system.

3.2   Server Load

This parameter is measured by increasing network scale gradually. Simulation result is shown in Fig. 2. From the figure, we can see that with node increasing, server flow becomes to decrease. This is because that more nodes can be found to share their cache content. At the same time, compared with our algorithm, FRNS demands more server flow. This is because the neighbor nodes found by FRNS may not have enough

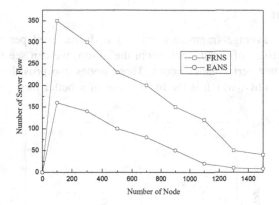

Fig. 2. Server load comparison between two algorithms

resource to provide data flow. Especially when the P2P system has a mass scale, EANS is easier to find appropriate neighbor nodes than FRNS and can relieve server load effectively.

3.3 Average Play Delay

Average play delay means the average time a packet from source to every on-demand destination. Every packet a node received includes a time field, which is used to record the time from source to it. The average play delay can be calculated by the sum of all time fields. The average play delay is influenced by frequency of node loss, the time a new node spends in joining network and packet loss ratio. Figure 3 illustrates the average delay comparison between two algorithms. We can find that our algorithm has a lower delay. This is because the nodes in our algorithms have stronger computation and transmission ability.

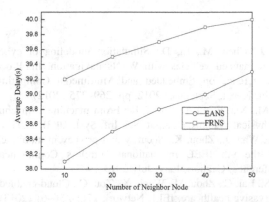

Fig. 3. Comparison of average delay between two algorithms

3.4 Throughput

Throughput is the average fragment number a node received per second. Figure 4 illustrates the statistics of throughput. From the graph, we can see that EANS algorithm can find better performance nodes. These nodes can provide more bandwidth and computation ability, which is the main cause of a better throughput.

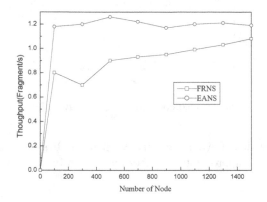

Fig. 4. Comparison of throughput between two algorithms

4 Conclusions

Algorithms of neighbor selection in P2P stream media networks are studied in this paper. Base on the problems in these algorithms, an efficient adaptive and dynamic neighbor selection algorithm is presented. The new algorithm can evaluate node's ability by an impact value. Simulations show that the new algorithm has better performance. In future work, the parameters and their influences in impact value need to be studied further.

References

1. Zou, C., Wan, J., Chen, M., Li, D.: Simulation modeling of cyber-physical systems exemplified by unmanned vehicles with WSNs navigation. In: Proceedings of the 7th International Conference on Embedded and Multimedia Computing Technology and Service, Gwangju, Korea, September 2012, pp. 269–275 (2012)
2. Wan, J., Chen, M., Xia, F., Li, D., Zhou, K.: From machine-to-machine communications towards cyber-physical systems. Comput. Sci. Inf. Syst. **10**(3), 1105–1128 (2013)
3. Suo, H., Liu, Z., Wan, J., Zhou, K.: Security and privacy in mobile cloud computing. In Proceedings of the 9th IEEE International Wireless Communications and Mobile Computing Conference, Cagliari, Italy, July 2013
4. Wan, J., Ullah, S., Lai, C., Zhou, M., Wang, X., Zou, C.: Cloud-enabled wireless body area networks for pervasive healthcare. IEEE Network **27**(5), 56–61 (2013)
5. Suo, H., Wan, J., Zou, C., Liu, J.: Security in the internet of things: a review. In: Proceedings of 2012 International Conference on Computer Science and Electronic Engineering, Hangzhou, China, March 2012, pp. 648–651 (2012)

6. Lai, C.F., Huang, Y.M., Chao, H.C.: DLNA-based multimedia sharing system for OSGI framework with extension to P2P network. IEEE Syst. J. **4**(2), 262–270 (2010)
7. Rowstron, A., Druschel, P.: Pastry: scalable, decentralized object location and routing for large scale peer-to-peer systems. In: ACM International Conference on Distributed Systems Platforms, pp. 329–350. Springer, London (2001)
8. Chang, J.H., Lai, C.F., Huang, Y.M.: 3PRS: a personalized and popular programs recommend system of digital TV for P2P social network. Multimed. Tools Appl. **47**(1), 31–48 (2010)
9. Chen, M., Leung, V., Mao, S.: Cross-layer and path priority scheduling based real-time video communications over wireless sensor networks. In: IEEE 67th Vehicular Technology Conference (VTC'08), pp. 213–216. IEEE Press, Singapore (2008)
10. Stoica, I., Morris, R., Liben, D.: Chord: a scalable peer-to-peer lookup protocol for internet applications. IEEE/ACM Trans. Network. **11**, 17–32 (2003)
11. Shah, N., Qian, D.: Cross-layer design to merge structured P2P networks over MANET. In: Parallel and Distributed Systems, pp. 851–856. IEEE Press, Shanghai (2010)
12. Magharei N., Rejaie R.: Prime: peer-to-peer receiver-driven mesh based streaming. In: The 26th IEEE International Conference on Computer and Communications Societies (INFOCOM 2007), pp. 1415–1423. IEEE Press, New York (2006)
13. Zhang, Z.: Approach to construct cluster in unstructured P2P networks based on small-world theory. In: The 3rd International Symposium on Information Processing, pp. 117–120. IEEE Press, Qingdao (2010)
14. Wumnava, S.V., Crosby G.V., Kapasi A.: Adaptive network modeling scheme. In: IEEE SoutheastCon 2001, pp. 109–113. IEEE Press, Clemson (2001)

Design Support Tools of Cyber-Physical Systems

Keliang Zhou, Binbin Liu$^{(\boxtimes)}$, Cen Ye, and Ling Liang

College of Electrical Engineering and Automation,
Jiangxi University of Science and Technology, Ganzhou, China
nyzkl@sina.com, liu554802016@163.com

Abstract. With the development of technology on cloud computing, wired/wireless communications, sensor networks and automatic control methods, these technologies make the foundation for a new system, i.e., Cyber-Physical Systems (CPS). The proposal of CPS points out the research direction of the large-scale complex information systems in the future. The design of CPS is a complex task because CPS contains many subsystems, such as computing system, networking system, and physical process. The support design tools are essential in the design process. As a new complicated system, CPS is also based on all kinds of subsystems. The tools for these subsystems have gradually matured. In this article, we classify the tools, including embedded development tools, network analysis and simulation tools, co-design tools, and domain-specific tools. Some specific tools for each aspect are enumerated, and some comparisons for these tools are also proposed. The future challenges for the design support tools are described in brief.

Keywords: Cyber-Physical Systems · Design support tools · Embedded systems · Co-design

1   Introduction

With the development of cloud computing, wired/wireless communications, sensor networks, and advanced control technologies, these theories and techniques make the foundation for a new system, i.e., Cyber-Physical Systems (CPS) [1–3]. A CPS integrates the virtual world (e.g., cyber world) with the real world (e.g., physical world). The sensor network is the communication medium between the cyber world and the physical world. CPS is a system that has a feedback control loop, embedded computers, networks monitor and physical processes in the loop. With the feedback control loop, computations in the cyber world and physical processes in the physical world can affect each other (see Fig. 1). Cyber-Physical Energy Systems (CPES) and Medical Cyber-Physical Systems (MCPS) are the typical applications of CPS. These systems all have below characteristics, such as dependable, secure, safe, efficient, real-time, scalable, cost-efficient and adaptive. Some related research results have been achieved, such as robust and resilient control for CPS and autonomic computing technologies in CPS. Researches regarding the application of CPS have a huge potential value for the economy and society.

V.C.M. Leung and M. Chen (Eds.): CloudComp 2013, LNICST 133, pp. 258–267, 2014.
DOI: 10.1007/978-3-319-05506-0_25, © Institute for Computer Sciences, Social Informatics and Telecommunications Engineering 2014

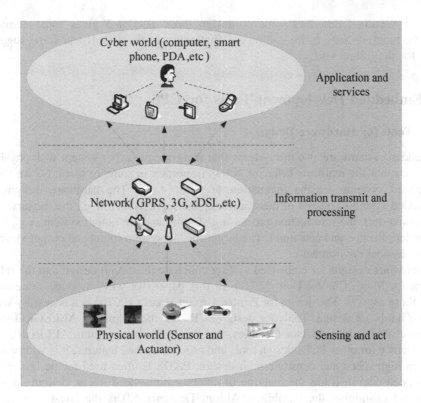

Fig. 1. A CPS framework model

Since CPS consists of many subsystems, we think that the design of CPS includes subsystem implementation and integrations of these subsystems. In the design processing, we will use some design support tools to help us with the complex design. We classify the tools, including embedded development tools, network analysis and simulate tools, co-design tools and domain-specific tools. In the design of embedded system, the tools for hardware design and software design will be used. The network analysis and simulation tools will help the designer to analyze the data transmission and the performance of the network. Co-design is an important issue in the real-time system. The co-design tools can provide the integration of scheduling and control. In some specific applications, some domain-specific tools will be used. The researchers in Berkeley and Vanderbilt have began the researches in CPS long before. And they developed some relate tools for CPS design. COSMIC and CIAO are the modeling tools, they are developed by the researches in Vanderbilt. They also developed some system execution modeling tools (e.g., CoSmic, and CUTS) and some tools for networked systems (e.g., NCSWT). The researchers in Berkeley developed a system named Ptolemy II as a co-design tool for CPS design, and we have compared it with other co-design tools in this survey.

The rest of this survey is outlined as follows. Section 2 introduces the tools for embedded systems. The network analysis and simulation tools are illustrated in

Sect. 3. Section 4 describes some co-design tools. Section 5 gives some domain-specific tools. In Sect. 6, we outline the challenges of these tools and some suggestions for the future work.

2 Embedded Development Tools for CPS

2.1 Tools for Hardware Design

Embedded systems are also the systems that integrate the cyber system with physical processes, but the real-time behavior is less important in some of them. So we think embedded systems are the foundation of CPS [4, 5]. The hardware design for embedded systems consists of these aspects: the input system (e.g., the sensors, and A/D converter), the information-processing system, and the output system (e.g., D/A converter, display, and actuators). The target for I/O system (input and output system) is the physical environment.

Hardware designs for embedded system conclude the circuit design and the relate design for Micro Control Unit (MCU). In this paper, we will introduce some tools from these aspects. The design for Printed Circuit Boards (PCBs) is a necessary work for the hardware design. Tools for design PCBs are the following: ALLEGRO from Cadence, PADS from Mentor Graphics, and PROTEL from Altium. ALLEGRO has the interface for other PCBs design tools and other enhanced features. It is widespread used in high speed and density circuit design. PADS is often used for designing the high-speed circuit. It has the function of creating high-speed traces, defining design rules and examining the feasibility. Altium Designer 6.0 is the latest edition for PROTEL. It has the function of design FPGA and SOPC, so that the designer can combine the designing for FPGA and PCBs with the design for embedded system. A comparison of these tools is shown in Table 1.

Table 1. PCBs design tools

Software name	Company	Operability	Characteristic
ALLEGRO	Cadence	Complex	High speed and density circuit design
PROTEL	Altium	Easy	Integrate the design for FPGA and PCBs
PADS	Mentor Graphics	General	Interactive layout function

Compared with the traditional artificially design, these automatic design tools make the PCB design become more efficient, and the quality of drawing possesses the high resolution [6]. Particularly, the complexity and real-time of control system change quickly, the problems, such as signal integrity and resource utilization, become the important aspects in PCBs design, then these tools provide a good way to solve these problems. They have specific arrangement on the hardware configuration, matched data input process, and management requirement. The development of these tools gives the assistance for designing the high speed PCBs.

The design support tools for MCU play an important role in the systems design. The mainstream MCU in the world are single-chip microcomputer, ARM, DSP, and FPGA. Proteus is a tool for co-simulation with single-chip microcomputer and its peripheral circuit. Keil is a develop system for single-chip microcomputer, and it also can support for ARM in Keil uVision4. It has the compiler and the debug tools. ARM ADS, RealView MDK and Multi 2000 are the integrated development environment for ARM. Multi 2000 also supports the development of DSP. CCS is the tool developed by TI, it is used for design DSP project. The main suppliers for FPGA are Altera and Xilinx. They have each development platform for their products. Quartus II is the platform for Altera and ISE is the platform for Xilinx. The design support tools for MCU turn the abstract algorithm into hardware implementation, and the related support work also have been started. Some tools can help designers make the algorithm into code directly, thus the code design becomes more convenient. These tools often are developed by the chip makers, so these tools only support for each of their products. So they have the poor generality for other products. The general tools should be designed for these MCUs.

The software based on the hardware platform is also the indispensable part in hardware design. Labview is developed by NI (National Instruments). The user can build virtual instrument in the develop environment. It was often used with Multisim (a simulate tool for design analog/digital circuit). They can help the designers to simulate and test the design. These tools provide the virtual instruments to replace the real instrument. They fully reflect the computer effect with instrument, and they have been widely been used in the measurement, control area, and simulation.

2.2   Tools for Software Design

The software of an embedded system consists of these components: embedded operating system (OS), device driver, and middleware and application software. Embedded Linux, Windows CE, QNX and other general-purpose systems are the mainstream embedded OS. The design for other software like application software can not leave the support from OS. The design support tools for OS mainly are divided into these categories: embedded programming language and tools (e.g., embedded-C, C++, embedded-Java, hardware support layer (BSP) software- development kit (SDK)), other GUI/Windowing toolkits (e.g., QT, Microsoft Embedded Visual C++, and Microsoft Visual Studio), GNUPro tools (e.g., GNUPro C compiler, GNUPro C++ compiler, and a range of additional tools and utilities), vendor specific and standard OS toolset.

These OS above are often used in high level MCU: ARM, MIPS, Intel X86, but in some application environment, we need smaller OS [7], such as μC/OS-II, OSEK Works, Ariel and TinyOS. They are general lightweight and static. VEST is a toolkit for these systems to perform extensive static analysis. They also need the supports from the programming language, such as NesC, AspectC, AspectJ, C and C++ are also widely used in these systems, and they have the simulation tools like TOSSIM for TinyOS. In some MCU, such as single-chip microcomputer, they don't have the resources to execute an operating system, so they often work without an OS and the programming languages for them are assembly language and C. To develop an embedded system is system engineering, the design support tools for hardware and software should provide, and with the speed development of the internet, the embedded OS unites network system has become inevitable. The embedded systems nowadays have the characteristic of networked and cyber ability.

Sometimes, we need a simulate tool for language programming. Modelsim is a simulate software for HDL. It can support the simulation for VHDL and Verilog. Another software support for the MCU (e.g., single-chip, and DSP) can also simulate for the codes. We can use Keil and CCS for code simulation. CCSLink is a toolkit developed by TI and Mathworks. It can be used for simulating algorithm in DSP software design.

Software design for embedded system has been speedily developing in the last decades. Hardware and software designs often take into account at the same time. The hardware and software components influence each other. So the design for the embedded system is hardware and software co-design [8–11]. These design support tools have a trend, i.e., hardware-software co-design. They have the function of both hardware custom and software design, then the design efficiency is improved and the development time is also shortened.

3 Network Analysis and Simulation Tools

Network plays a critical role in the communication system. The works on analysis and simulation network are very important for the communication system of CPS. There is a mount of tools for network analysis and simulation. The tools for network analysis and simulation are given as follows: Ns-2, OMNeT++, OPNET, SPW, J-sim, GloMosim, and SSFnet [12–14]. These tools for network simulation can help the designer know the reliability of network, and they also can be used for the optimal design and the future expansion. It helps the design for new network at the same time. These tools have each characteristic. The comparisons of these tools are given in the Table 2.

These tools are frequently used in the network design. Next we will introduce some tools that may not usually be used. TOSSIM is a tool for Tiny OS sensor

Table 2. Comparisons of network analysis and simulation tools

Software name	Interface configuration	Support language	Component library supporting	Cost
Ns-2	TCL script code	C++, Otcl	Rich organizational modularity	Free
OMNeT++	GUI\Code	C++	Rich	Free
OPNET	GUI\Code	Proto-c	Rich	Commercial
SPW	GUI\Code	C/HDL	Rich component library	Commercial
J-sim	GUI\Code	Java, Tcl	Rich component library	Free
GloMosim	GUI\Code	C/C++/PARSEC	Rich component library	Free
SSFnet	DML	JAVA/C++	Rich component library	Free

networks. It focuses on the simulation of TinyOS and its execution, and it can simulate the network at a bit-level. Network in A Box (NAB) is a tool for simulating the large-scale senor networks, it is written by OCAML and based on event-driven programming. The recent researches for Ns-3 are also on the way. Ns-3 is designed to replace the current popular Ns-2 and it uses the C++ programs and Python scripting. The more integration of software and support for virtualization are also the improvement based on Ns-2. Truetime is also a tool for network simulation. But compared with the tools above, it is oversimplified. Its function of co-simulation makes it become an important position in these tools. It is often used with other additional co-simulation facilities (e.g., Simulink) to simulate the latency-related aspects of the network communication and the dynamics of the physical environment.

As the development of the new technology of network and the increasing complexness of data network, it is impossible to have performance testing and network planning in the real network environment. Network analysis and simulation become a more and more desperately need in the network design. The network analysis and simulation tools become the essential elements in this work. These tools can be used for analyzing the physical components of network and the data transmission performance, such as packet loss rate and data latency. With the widely use of the tools, the reliability and the accuracy of network can be assured, and they can reduce the cost on the network. It seems that with the open sourced and well designed embedded object-orient programming feature used in the academia and industry, the tools which are easy to learn and use and more organizations and more specialized in the documentation can be well developed and more popular.

4 Co-Design Tools

The real-time behavior is essential for some CPS applications. Task scheduling is a typical issue in real-time control algorithm implementation. The performances of a real-time control systems are not only based on the control polices but also based on the scheduling performance. Limited resources, hardware without optimized and software components introduce the uncertain factors in the real-time system [15–20]. So, we need the tools to consider the problems, such as the optimal use of computing resources, the control algorithm and the control software design. The tools presented are the following: Jitterbug, Truetime, AIDA, XILO, Ptolemy II, RTSIM, Syndex and Orccad. A comparison for these tools has been given in Table 3.

Co-design is the most difficult problem for the real-time control system design. Task scheduling in the real-time design will affect the control and vice versa. Tools support gives a good solution to simplify the design process. This paper attempts to introduce some important tools. However the tools nowadays have the disadvantages to focus on the actual part of co-design, and they aim at the analysis in the design. The methods and the theories on design and synthesis should be developed to enhance the function of co-design tools.

Table 3. Comparisons of real-times system co-design tools

Software name	Inputs	Outputs	Support language	Extensibility
Jitterbug	Signal model, timing model	Performance index	C++, Matlab-code	Bad
TrueTime	Script for each kernel block	Different output graphs	C++, Matlab-code	General
AIDA	Execution times, system model	Response times bounds, timing information	DOME, C++	Well
XILO	Drag-and-drop approach	Timing analysis parameters ordinary Simulink outputs	C++, Matlab-code	Well
Ptolemy II	Timed multitasking model	Different outputs on different simulation hierarchy	Java	Well
RTSIM	Functional and architectural model, parameters for simulation	Execution traces and statistical timing, quantities for control performance	C++	Well
Syndex	The algorithm, data-transfers, target hardware	Mapping of operations and data-transfers, executable code	SIGNAL, SyncCharts	Well
Orccad	System descriptions	C code of the system analyze results	Esterel, C	Not supported

5   Domain-Specific Tools

CPS has gradually been used in the industrial processes, medical system, and traffic system. Airbus, vehicle and building are just a few parts of them [21]. When designing a domain-specific CPS, we must consider the characteristics of the control objects, such as the security for a vehicle control system. So we need the design support tools for these specific systems. The research of Complex Vehicles System (CVS) is a novel issue in traffic area. Some design support tools in this area are presented. AMESim developed by Imagine is a tool of modeling, simulation and the dynamic analysis of hydraulic and mechanical system. Dymola is a modeling language for large dynamical systems like CVS. The programming tool Parallel Virtual Machine (PVM) and CORBA are used for the simulation of the CVS.

Cyber-Physical Energy Systems (CPES) is the application of CPS in energy management. It contains smart grid, electric vehicles and home automation. In a design for smart grid, the control system for an electric power grid is a complex system with cyber and physical system. Some tools are used in the design process. For example, RT-SPIN is used to analyze and verify the model and RT-PROMELA program is the input for the RT-SPIN. As the smart gird is also large-scale dynamic systems, then some tools for this style of the system are also used, like Monte-Carlo is used for estimating contingency statistics. The security of the electric power grid is very important. So the security tools are used. Computerized Oracle and Password System (COPS) is a tool for check security, it can detect security problems as an aid to system administrators. Some specific tools are used in some special application of CPES, such as a charging system for electric vehicles. Programmable Logic Controller (PLC) is used in this design, some support tools for PLC (e.g., Simatic, and MCGS) are necessary.

The research of applications on medical becomes a potential issue of CPS. Medical Cyber-Physical Systems (MCPS) are the systems combine CPS with the medical system [22–25]. MCDF is an open-source toolset for messaging system in the complex MCPS. A series of verification tools are also used in the system (e.g., TIMES, Z nation, and Circus).

With more and more applications of CPS, a series of new design support tools should be developed. In these specific areas, the control object and the control environment are very complex, the modeling tools should be researched, and they need the specific validation and verification tools to ensure the system requirement.

6   Conclusions

In this survey, we have a brief introduction to the tools for CPS design. According to CPS related to the computer filed, communication area and control world, we introduce them from each aspect, including embedded system tools, network analysis and simulation tools, co-design tools, and domain-specific tools. However, the assisted tools cannot meet requirements of CPS design because of the heterogeneity of these subsystems. So the new support design tools for CPS need to develop. The new tools should consider the characteristics of each subsystem, but this behavior brings bad effects. The specialty and the productivity of the tools may lose, and then the costs for the design lead to increase. The tools for CPS design should remove or reduce the heterogeneity between the subsystems, and they must balance the other characteristics of CPS (e.g., security). The special tools for CPS should be developed. The researches on this aspect should be considered.

Acknowledgments. This project was supported in part by grants from the National Natural Science Foundation of China (No. 61262013, 61363011) and the Science and Technology Research Project of education department of Jiangxi province (No. GJJ13429).

References

1. Yan, H., Liu, Z., Wan, J., Zhou, K.: Improving spectator sports safety by cyber-physical systems: challenges and solutions. In: Proceedings of the 8th International Conference on Embedded and Multimedia Computing, Taipei, Taiwan (2013)
2. Chun, I., Park, J., Kim, W., Kang, W., Lee, H., Park, S.: Autonomic computing technologies for cyber-physical systems. In: The 12th International Conference on Advanced Communication Technology (ICACT), pp. 1009–1014 (2010)

3. Yan, H., Wan, J., Li, D., Tu, Y., Zhang, P.: Codesign of networked control systems: a review from different perspectives. In: Proceedings of the IEEE International Conference on Cyber Technology in Automation, Control, and Intelligent Systems, pp. 84–90 (2011)
4. Camposano, R., Wilberg, J.: Embedded system design. Des. Autom. Embed. Syst. 1(1–2), 5–50 (1996)
5. Marwedel, P.: Embedded System Design. Springer, New York (2005)
6. Schmitz, A., Wanger, S., Hahn, R., Uzun, H., Hebling, C.: Stability of planar PEMFC in printed circuit board technology. J. Power Sources 127(1–2), 197–205 (2004)
7. Henriksson, D.: Resource-constrained embedded control and computing systems. Ph.D. thesis, Department of Automatic Control, Lund University (2006)
8. Ernst, R.: Codesign of embedded systems: status and trends. IEEE Des. Test Comput. 15(2), 45–54 (1998)
9. Hsiung, P.-A.: Embedded software verification in hardware–software codesign. J. Syst. Archit. 46(15), 1435–1450 (2000)
10. Vidal, J., de Lamotte, F., Gogniat, G., Soulard, P., Diguet, J.P.: A co-design approach for embedded system modeling and code generation with UML and MARTE. In: Design, Automation & Test in Europe Conference & Exhibition, 2009. DATE '09, pp. 226–231 (2009)
11. Chen, M., Wan, J., Li, F.: Machine-to-machine communications: architectures, standards, and applications. KSII Trans. Internet Inf. Syst. 6(2), 547–565 (2012)
12. Zou, C., Wan, J., Chen, M., Li, D.: Simulation modeling of cyber-physical systems exemplified by unmanned vehicles with WSNs navigation. In: Proceedings of the 7th International Conference on Embedded and Multimedia Computing Technology and Service. pp. 269–275. Springer, Netherlands, Gwangju, Korea (2012)
13. Shu, Z., Li, D., Hu, Y., Ye, F., Wan, J.: From models to code: automatic development process for embedded control system. In: Proceedings of the IEEE International Conference on Network, Sensor and Control, pp. 660–665. IEEE Press, Shanya, China (2008)
14. Wan, J., Chen, M., Xia, F., Li, D., Zhou, K.: From machine-to-machine communications towards cyber-physical systems. Comput. Sci. Inf. Syst. 10(3), 1105–1128 (2013)
15. Yan, H., Wan, J., Suo, H.: Adaptive resource management for cyber-physical systems. In: Proceedings of the 2011 International Conference on Mechatronics and Applied Mechanics, pp. 747–751, HongKong (2011)
16. Yan, H., Wan, J., Li, D., Tu, Y., Zhang, P.: Codesign of networked control systems: a review from different perspectives. In: Proceedings of the IEEE International Conference on Cyber Technology in Automation, Control, and Intelligent Systems, pp. 84–90. IEEE Press (2011)
17. Feng, X., Youxian, S.: Control-scheduling codesign: a perspective on integrating control and computing. Dyn. Contin. Discrete Impuls. Syst. Ser. B 13(S1), 1352–1358 (2008)
18. Arzen, K.E., Cervin, A., Eker, J., Sha, L.: An introduction to control and scheduling co-design. In: Proceedings of the 39th IEEE Conference on Decision and Control, pp. 4865–4870. IEEE Press (2000)
19. Cervin, A.: Integrated control and real-time scheduling. Ph.D. thesis, Department of Automatic Control, Lund Institute of Technology, Sweden (2003)
20. Marti, P., Yepez, J., Velasco, M., Villa, R., Fuertes, J.M.: Managing quality-of-control in network-based control systems by controller and message scheduling co-design. IEEE Trans. Ind. Electron. 51(6), 1159–1167 (2004)

21. Leonardi, F., Pinto, A., Carloni, L.P.: Synthesis of distributed execution platforms for cyber-physical systems with applications to high-performance buildings. In: 2011 IEEE/ACM International Conference on Cyber-Physical Systems (ICCPS), pp. 215–224. IEEE Press (2011)
22. Cheng, A.M.K.: Cyber-physical medical and medication systems. In: The 28th International Conference on Distributed Computing Systems Workshops, pp. 529–532 (2008)
23. Insup, L., Sokolsky, O.: Medical cyber physical systems. In: Design Automation Conference (DAC), 2010 47th ACM/IEEE, pp. 743–748. IEEE Press (2010)
24. Sokolsky, O.: Medical cyber-physical systems. In: 18th IEEE International Conference and Workshops on Engineering of Computer Based Systems (ECBS), pp. 2–2. IEEE Press (2011)
25. Li, Y.: The building of medical image communication system based on web and MySQL. IJACT: Int. J. Adv. Comput. Technol. 4(20), 131–140 (2012)

Study on Collaborative Awareness Model Based on Working Tree

Zuomin Luo$^{(\boxtimes)}$, Yinzhao Lin, and Haolu Hou

School of Computer Science and Engineering,
Xi'an University of Technology, Xi'an, China
lzm@xaut.edu.cn, lyz6869467@gmail.com

Abstract. With difficulties for complex collaborative network in acquiring better effects and real-time collaborative awareness, collaborative awareness model based on a working tree is proposed. The working tree, priority queue of node information distribution and preferential information multicast tree are established in this model on the respective basis of node functions, node weight and node need degree, which not only ensures the preferential distribution of major node information and preferential reception of information badly needed, but performs an incremental transmission of information in accordance with transmission modes selected by clustering attract value. This model was applied to the collaborative work platform of a certain municipal government, which verified its better effect of awareness.

Keywords: Collaborative network · Node weight · Node need degree · Collaborative awareness · Working tree

1 Introduction

Computer supported collaborative work (CSCW) has achieved rapid development and realized the wide application in the field of military affairs, industry, medical treatment, scientific research and so on since it was proposed by Iren Grief from MIT and Paul from DEC in a seminar in 1984. How to solve the naturalness and convenience in the interactive process not only between people and collaborative work environments but between man and man? The first is to solve the problem of awareness in collaborative work environments which is the key technology and also one of important and difficult points to study CSCW.

With the wide application of cloud computing, computing resources and information resources can be collected anytime and anywhere by different portable equipment, which makes people participate in or constitute collaborative work. The technology convergence of pervasive computing and CSCW will be performed on a deeper level to promote the derivation and development of more collaborative applications. The collaborative application supported by multiple types of network and multiple computing platforms will be the prevailing application in pervasive computing environment. The complexity of the network environment and the diversity of the Client make it difficult for users in different locations to acquire better effects and real-time collaborative awareness of cooperation in shared virtual geographic

V.C.M. Leung and M. Chen (Eds.): CloudComp 2013, LNICST 133, pp. 268–277, 2014.
DOI: 10.1007/978-3-319-05506-0_26, © Institute for Computer Sciences, Social Informatics and Telecommunications Engineering 2014

environment (VGE), which surely is a major restraining factor for practical demand of increasingly close collaborative relationship between current users, high cooperation efficiency and complex cooperation tasks and environments. Therefore, the study on collaborative awareness in complex network environment has a practical significance of great importance.

To meet the requirements of efficient and safe hybrid transmission of collaborative network, Luo Zuomin et al. provided a strategy to select transmission modes based on transmission clustering attract value [1]; Correa et al. made a research on heterogeneous collaborative system [2]; Prasanna Ganesan and Vagner Sacramento et al. made a research on collaborative awareness of mobile environment [3–5]; Benitez-Guerrero and Belkadi et al. made a research on context awareness [6, 7]; Salvadores et al. made a research on collaborative awareness model by semantic context [8]; however, it is relatively rare to study collaborative awareness in complex network environment through constructing working tree.

From the perspective of node functions in collaborative work, this paper makes a full consideration of node need degree for cooperators' work information and the node weight in the overall collaborative work so as to construct the working tree in accordance with the relation between nodes and study on the awareness information which shall be transmitted by nodes and transmission modes; moreover, the collaborative awareness model based on working tree is proposed to make each collaborative node obtain required information timely in the complex network environment and be aware of the current working conditions of its related cooperator, so that the further decisions and actions can be performed safely and timely.

2 The Collaborative Awareness Model Based on the Working Tree

2.1 The Working Tree

In real life, it is necessary to divide the work if one piece of work shall be completed by many people, thus hierarchical relation emerges between man and man because of different duties the gradual subdivision of which will give rise to the formation of tree structure for interpersonal relationship. The tree structure, one of the most common data structure models, can display the inclusion relation and hierarchical relation generalizing many relations in real life. Therefore, the tree structure can be applied to show a group doing collaborative work with its nodes on behalf of roles with various subdivisions. A series of divisions of labor are implemented on the basis of roles' hierarchical relation, which finally construct a working tree. Figure 1 is a simplified working tree.

To realize collaborative work, each node must know what other nodes can do and want to do and tell other nodes what it can do. To finish the work task of cooperation, the mutual transmission of information between nodes is always performed to realize the awareness of collaborative environment and information state of other nodes, or to inform its nodes of the changes of its information. For nodes, information interaction is divided into two parts of information transmission and reception. The path to

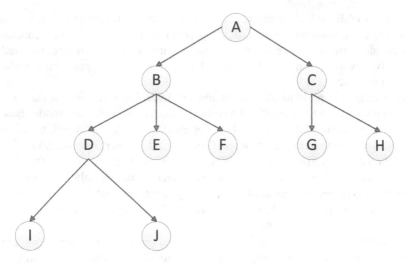

Fig. 1. A simplified working tree

transmit and receive information is not necessarily symmetrical for the same node. The concept of node weight and node need degree is introduced herein to ensure the safe, flexible and controllable transmission of awareness information.

2.2 Node Weight and Need Degree

(1) Node weight
Each member plays a different role in the collaborative work and its hierarchical relationship in group working reflects its status in the group. In other words, with higher status, it has a wider and stronger influence. Weight is a set of data used to quantize range of influence and influence power of nodes within the scope in the work of collaborative awareness. Node weight depends on its level in the working tree, which means that the node weight is greater if it is closer to the root node. In addition, node weight only has an influence on itself and its child nodes because weight only has a downward impact.

In Fig. 1, depth means the depth of the working tree; level (A) means the level of node A; degree (A) means the degree of node A. As for node B, its computational formula of the weight in the overall collaborative work is: $W = \text{depth-level (B)}$; moreover, its range of influence is: $N = \{D, E, F, I, J\}$.

To make it convenient for discussion, every node is numbered and see Table 1 for the node number in Fig. 1.

Table 1. Corresponding table for nodes and serial number

Node	A	B	C	D	E	F	G	H	I	J
No.	0	1	2	3	4	5	6	7	8	9

Table 2 is a weight matrix used to store the value of node weight, for example, W [0] [3] = 4 refers to the weight ratio between node A and node D is 4.

Table 2. Weight matrix

No. Node	0	1	2	3	4	5	6	7	8	9
0	4	4	4	4	4	4	4	4	4	4
1	0	3	0	3	3	3	0	0	3	3
2	0	0	3	0	0	0	3	3	0	0
3	0	0	0	2	0	0	0	0	2	2
4	0	0	0	0	2	0	0	0	0	0
5	0	0	0	0	0	2	0	0	0	0
6	0	0	0	0	0	0	2	0	0	0
7	0	0	0	0	0	0	0	2	0	0
8	0	0	0	0	0	0	0	0	1	0
9	0	0	0	0	0	0	0	0	0	1

(2) Node need degree

In the collaborative work, the node needs work information from nodes in relation to its work task. To be specific, if other nodes are closer related to the node's work task, it is in the increasing need of their work information. Therefore, each node has different need degree for other nodes' work information. Node need degree reflects the awareness range of the node and its need degree for the awareness information. Define the max need degree as 1 in collaborative awareness system and node need degree for itself as 1. The node need degree for its ancestor node which is upward need decreases with the increasing number of nodes. Child nodes are directly connected with father nodes, and the max node need degree for its father node is 1. In brief, the node need degree for its ancestor node is inversely proportional to the product of the degree of interval nodes between nodes. Take the Fig. 1 as an example, need [I] [A] = 1/ (degree (D)*degree (B)), need [I] [A] means the need degree of node I for node D with degree (D) and degree (B) respectively representing the degree of node D and node B.

Downward need means the need degree of the node for its child nodes. There is an independent collaborative work system which is constructed between father nodes and child nodes. The need degree of father nodes for their child nodes is 1 without exception because father nodes are only interested in their child nodes.

Relative need degree means the need degree between brother nodes which need awareness information of each other so that they can successfully carry out collaborative work. The need degree between brother nodes is 1/degree (father).

The need degree matrix stores the value of need degree as shown in Table 3. For instance, need [0] [3] = 0 means the need degree of Node A for node D is 0.

Table 3. Need degree matrix

No. Node	0	1	2	3	4	5	6	7	8	9
0	1	1	1	0	0	0	0	0	0	0
1	1	1	1/2	1	1	1	0	0	0	0
2	1	1/2	1	0	0	0	1	1	0	0
3	1/3	1	0	1	1/3	1/3	0	0	1	1
4	1/3	1	0	1/3	1	1/3	0	0	0	0
5	1/3	1	0	1/3	1/3	1	0	0	0	0
6	1/2	0	1	0	0	0	1	1/2	0	0
7	1/2	0	1	0	0	0	1/2	1	0	0
8	1/6	1/2	0	1	0	0	0	0	1	1/2
9	1/6	1/2	0	1	0	0	0	0	1/2	1

2.3   Collaborative Awareness Model Based on a Working Tree

After the quantization of node need degree and node weight in accordance with the working tree, the awareness information processing model is provided as shown in Fig. 2 for the major purpose of ensuring the preferential distribution of major node information and preferential reception of information badly needed, in the perspective of how to collect and describe work information and what information transmission mode will be applied.

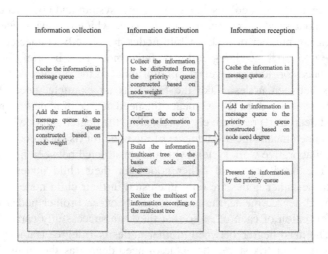

Fig. 2. The awareness model based on the working tree

Figure 2 consists of information collection, information distribution and information reception. In information collection, if multiple nodes correspond to only one server, the information shall be firstly cached in message queue to ensure the preferential distribution of major node information, and then the information in message queue shall be added to the priority queue constructed based on node weight; in information distribution, to ensure preferential reception of information badly needed and information security, first collect the information to be distributed from the priority queue constructed based on node weight, confirm its receiving node in accordance with the need degree for information generated by other nodes and finally realize the multicast of information according to the information multicast tree which shall be preferentially built on the basis of node need degree; in information reception, the information shall be firstly cached in message queue, and then the information in message queue shall be added to the priority queue constructed based on the need degree of receiving node for information generated by other nodes and present the information complying with the priority queue.

3 The Management of Weight and Need Degree

3.1 The Management of Weight and Need Degree

Weight and need degree, the basis of collaborative awareness model based on the working tree, decide the rapid, safe and efficient collection and analysis of mutual information by their appropriateness. The working tree carries out descriptions by applying WorkingTree.xml, so as to overcome the dynamic update problems existed in the distribution of the need degree. Once the working tree changes or adds new nodes, the relevant contents corresponding to WorkingTree.xml will be updated timely; moreover, the node needs degree and node weight matrix will be recalculated.

3.2 Information Collection

It is inevitable that there exists simultaneous operation of multiple nodes in collaborative work which is a distributed multi-node application. When multiple nodes are in simultaneous operation, the transmission of multi-node work information by the server depends on the value of node weight, which means the server first transmits the work information from nodes with greater weight to other relevant nodes and later transmits the work information from nodes with smaller weight to other relevant nodes. If multiple nodes correspond to only one server, the information which is firstly cached in message queue shall be added to the priority queue constructed based on node weight to ensure the preferential distribution of the node information with greater weight. The priority queue constructed on the basis of heapsort, in nature, is a sequential storage binary tree with better time and spatial performance.

3.3 Information Distribution

Information distribution includes distribution order, objects to distribute and communication mode. To ensure the preferential distribution of major node information, node information shall be distributed in accordance with the priority of node weight, i.e. the information to distribute shall be collected successively from the priority queue constructed based on the node weight. The nodes in collaborative work have different needs for the information because of their different duties and jobs. The need degree of a certain node for the work information from a node decides whether its work information will be transmitted to the certain node or not. Presume that there are n collaborative nodes and the need degree of node i for node j is r (need [i] [j] = 1). If r = 0, node i does not need any work information from node j and there is no need for node j to transmit its work information to node i; otherwise, it is necessary for node j to transmit its work information to node i. The need degree for the information generated by other nodes decides whether this information will be received or not, i.e. objects to distribute are decided by node need degree. Communication mode in the network includes unicast, broadcast and multicast. The multicast is a one-to-many (group) communication mode and presents advantages of unicast and broadcast, which makes it especially suitable for the cooperation between nodes. The information multicast is performed on the basis of the multicast tree which is constructed in accordance with node delay and bandwidth. With the same node delay and bandwidth, the node with greater need degree shall be preferentially added to the optimal father nodes with the min delay and max bandwidth of the multicast tree. The information shall be encrypted to guarantee information security for the multicast; moreover, to prevent the congestion of the multicast, the degree of each node of the multicast tree is limited to 3 and it is necessary to add nodes with smaller delay and larger available degree to the multicast tree to the greatest extent in accordance with the bandwidth and overall consideration of the delay and available degree of nodes.

3.4 Information Transmission

The terminal nodes involved in collaborative network are PC, Personal Digital Assistant (PDA) and Smartphone (SP) and main transmission modes are HTTP, TCP and named pipe (IPC). Under the circumstances, nodes shall take all attributes and transmission modes suitable for their application programs into consideration, recognize attributes quite important to their application programs and transmission modes beneficial to each attribute, and then select transmission modes best for their attribute set. Main attributes are composed of diagnosis (automatic detection of connectivity problems of the transmission), load bearing, inspection, lag time, distance join, security, throughput and tools etc. Thus the complicated relationship among the collaborative terminal, the transmission mode and the attribute is formed. Every kind of transmission mode has different attribute sets, so the transmission mode shall be selected by the collaborative terminal based on attribute sets. The strategy to select transmission modes based on transmission clustering attract value analyzes the betweenness of the relation net of node attributes though the relation between intensity and attribute, deduces the ratio of attribute betweenness and clustering coefficient and evaluates the transmission clustering attract value; finally, the transmission mode is defined by the range of the transmission clustering attract value worked out with the application of kernel clustering and hierarchical cluster analysis [1]. As for the transmission of the node information, the incremental transmission shall be performed by adopting the transmission mode confirmed by the strategy to select transmission modes based on transmission clustering attract value.

3.5   Information Presentation

In the collaborative work, it is possible for a node to cooperate with one other node or multiple other nodes. If a node cooperates with multiple other nodes, this node will receive the work information from multiple other nodes, which results in the simultaneous arrival of the work information from multiple other nodes to this node. Generally, the higher the node need degree is, the stronger the node's need for information is. The work information from multiple other nodes simultaneously arrived shall be presented by the receiving node according to its need degree for other nodes and their information, which can be ensured by constructing the heapsort-based priority queue in accordance with the need degree of the receiving node for other nodes.

4   Application Effects Sing the Template

There are various jobs in government sector, including information entry, receipt and dispatch of official documents, file edition, records & letter filing and searching, report production, mailing and meeting arrangement etc. One piece of work is generally finished by multiple office staff in cooperation in accordance with some office procedure, which is the characteristic of jobs in government sector. All of shared jobs consist of a task set and a set of process relations between tasks. The former is an independent set of work items which is handled respectively by specific personnel or agent. See Fig. 3 for the collaborative office system model of a certain municipal government.

OA workflow management environment, the core of system model, is responsible for solving cooperation problems of official documents between various roles in office environment. The daily office work has quite complex content from which a principle line shall be arranged with a good design and then the relation between various contents shall be developed based on the principle line. Traditional collaborative office system solidifies the workflow generated by the abstraction of some fixed process and other various businesses are developed upon workflow. With the combination of the collaborative awareness model based on the working tree and traditional OA workflow management, various permissions for different roles shall be set in accordance with office duties and of task requirements; moreover, relevant weight

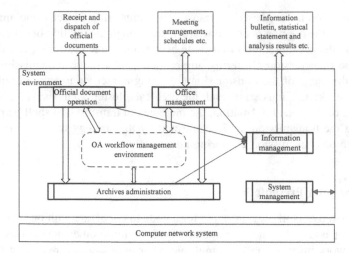

Fig. 3. The collaborative office system model of a certain municipal government

and need degree for other nodes will be distributed to roles on the basis of their working tree; furthermore, priority queue of node information distribution and preferential information multicast tree are established on the respective basis of node weight and node need degree, and the incremental transmission of information is performed in accordance with transmission modes selected by clustering attract value. Compared with the original system, the faster transmission of official documents, more rational and efficient meeting arrangements, more thorough implementation of leadership decision, more compact cooperation between nodes and obvious improvement of collaborative work efficiency have explained the better awareness effect of this model.

5   Conclusion

With the analysis of the research status of current collaborative awareness model in this paper, it is found that the current collaborative awareness model pays less attention to the node weight in collaborative work and node need degree for work information from other nodes, which might make the major nodes and nodes badly in need of work information from other nodes in complex collaborative network unable to get information needed in time, and have an effect on the smooth implementation of collaborative work. The collaborative awareness model based on the working tree is proposed herein to preferentially ensure nodes with greater weight and nodes badly in need of work information from other nodes can collect information needed timely and improve the existing model.

Acknowledgment. The thesis supported by Dr. Start-up Fund of Xi'an University of Technology (116-211105), the Technology Plan Projects of Shaanxi Province (2012JM8047), the Technology Plan Projects of Xi'an (CXY1341(2)).

References

1. Luo, Z.M., Fu, Y.L., Hou, H.L.: Selection and application of transmission modes of collaborative network. CIMS **17**(10), 2309–2315 (2011)
2. Correa, C.D., Marsic, I.: An optimization approach to group coupling in heterogeneous collaborative systems. In: The 2005 International ACM SIGGROUP Conference on Supporting Group Work, pp. 274–283. ACM Press, New York (2005)
3. Ganesan, P., Karmouch, A.: Context awareness in ad-hoc communication. In: Proceedings of IEEE Pacific Rim Conference on Communications, Computers and Signal Processing, pp. 28–30. IEEE Press, New York (2003)
4. Sacramento, V., Endler, M., Rubinsztejn, H.K.: MoCA: a middle ware for developing collaborative applications for mobile users. IEEE Distrib. Syst. Online **5**(10), 1–14 (2004). (IEEE, New York)
5. Campolo, C., Antonio, L., Militano, L.: Scenario-adaptive and gain-aware content sharing policies for collaborative wireless environments. Comput. Commun. **35**(10), 1259–1271 (2012). (Elsevier, Amsterdam)
6. Edgard, B.G., Carmen, M.G., Luis, G.M.J.: Context-aware mobile collaborative systems: conceptual modeling and case study. Sensors **12**(10), 13491–13507 (2012)
7. Belkadi, F., Bonjour, E., Camargo, M.: A situation model to support awareness in collaborative design. Int. J. Hum. Comput. Stud. **71**(1), 110–129 (2013). (Elsevier, Amsterdam)
8. Salvadores, M., Herrero, P., Luis, J.L.: A semantic collaborative awareness model to deal with resource sharing in grids. Future Gener. Comput. Syst. **26**(2), 276–280 (2010). (Elsevier, Amsterdam)

Study on the Transformation Method
of AADL-Based Reliability Model
in the Embedded System

Liu Jianjun[1], Meng Haining[2]([☒]), Huang Yinglan[1], and Zhong Shan[1]

[1] Aeronautics Computing Technique Research Institute, Xi'an 710068, China
jjliu_imu@163.com
[2] Xi'an Technology University, Xi'an 710048, China
mengning2001ji@gmail.com

Abstract. Architecture analysis and design language (AADL) is an important method for architecture modeling, performance analysis and verification in embedded field. And the system reliability is an important attribute of software quality metrics in embedded system. In this paper, we first established an AADL-based reliability model to describe the system functional requirements and the reliability information of the runtime embedded system. Then, by analyzing the differences of syntax, semantics and mathematical presentation between the AADL-based reliability model and the SPN model, we present the rules and methods to automatically transform the AADL-based reliability model to the stochastic Petri net (SPN) model, which is convenient for system designers to assess and measure system reliability in the design phase of system development. Finally, an example of model transformation process for an automaton in aviation systems is shown to verify the effectiveness of model transformation rules and methods.

Keywords: Embedded system · Architecture analysis and design language · Stochastic Petri net · Model transformation

1 Introduction

With the development of microelectronics, communications and software technology, the increasing complexity of software systems improves major concerns in the embedded domain, in particular with respect to the verification and analysis of performance and reliability requirements. And the development method has changed from the traditional code level to the model level, which is convenient for the system feasibility analysis in the early system integration process.

Model-driven architecture (MDA) which was launched by the object management group (OMG) is a software design approach for the development of software systems through model transformations [1]. It provides a set of guidelines for the structuring of specifications, which are expressed as models based on UML and relevant industry standards. In order to adapt to the development of embedded systems, it requires not only establishing the mapping relationship between system model and hardware structure to satisfy the functional, non-functional requirements, but also providing the

V.C.M. Leung and M. Chen (Eds.): CloudComp 2013, LNICST 133, pp. 278–286, 2014.
DOI: 10.1007/978-3-319-05506-0_27, © Institute for Computer Sciences, Social Informatics and Telecommunications Engineering 2014

diverse model analysis method of the system design solution in system design phase. Therefore, extended on the UML and emphasis on the embedded domain, AADL is released to model the software and hardware architecture of an embedded, real-time system by SEI, Honeywell, Boeing, Lockheed Martin, the U.S. Army/Navy and other organizations together [2].

AADL can be used to establish the architectural model of system platform, and describe the key characteristics of system timing requirements and task states. The AADL working group expands the core language and creates the error model annex (EMA) [3], to describe the reliability information of runtime system. In the previous literatures, the mathematical models of system reliability analysis, such as Petri Net model [4] and Markov chains (MA) model [5], were based on system characteristics. At present, many mature software tools have integrated the analysis and calculation function for FTA, MA and SPN, such as Isograph, SPNP and etc. However, these mathematical models are quite different with AADL models in the aspects of syntax and semantics expression, and it requires the system designer to be familiar with the relevant mathematical knowledge. Therefore, in order to enable designers to focus on the system design process and reduce their burdens on mathematical model establishment, it urgent to study on the automatic model transformation method from the AADL model to the mathematical analysis model.

In this paper, aiming at the embedded system, we set up an AADL-based reliability model and present a method for transforming the AADL-based reliability model to the SPN analysis model based on C-based stochastic Petri net language (CSPL) [6]. Then the transformation rules and methods were described in detail to analyze and evaluate the system reliability. Finally, an example of model transformation process for an automaton in aviation systems is shown to validate the effectiveness of transformation rules and methods.

2   The AADL-Based Model Transformation Method

When a fault causes the system to deviate from the correct runtime states, the error will appear [7]. The EMA describes an information model in which the components are in different error states due to variable faults occurrence. Thus, the model described by the EMA is usually called the error model. The AADL-based reliability analysis process consists of three steps [8, 9]. First, the EMA error model is added to the architecture model of each component, and the AADL-based reliability analysis model is established. Secondly, the AADL-based reliability analysis model is transformed into the mathematical measurement model. Finally, by applying the numerical calculation software to analyze and obtain the reliability parameters through the mathematical measurement model.

2.1   The AADL-Based Reliability Analysis Model

The AADL-based reliability analysis model consists of the AADL-based architecture model and the EMA error model. The AADL-based architecture model illustrates system task design, reliability strategy (such as fault tolerance, N version design) and the relationships between components. The EMA error model describes not only the reliability information of a single component, but also the information between components affected by error propagation. The reliability information of a single component includes component faults, error states, error state transition paths and the random parameters of faults. And the information between components consists of input and output guards of error propagations for interactive components, error state mapping rules for subordinate components, and guards of component mode changes under different fault-tolerant mechanisms.

The AADL Meta model defines the semantics and rules of the AADL core language. And the EMA integrated with AADL compiler through Meta model reuse. The EMA Meta model is divided into two parts: the error annex library and the error annex subclause. Correspondingly, the information of the EMA error model can be divided into the reusable information and the specific information of a component to describe a semantic determined, information consistent and complete error model.

The error annex library is expressed as the subclass of core language annex library. It contains a number of named error model identifiers which can be error model types or error model implementations. An error model type mainly includes error states, error propagations and error events. An error model implementation describes the error state transition path, in which the trigger conditions of state transition is consistent with the error event and the error propagation, and the transferred state is consistent with the error state in the error model types.

Similarly, the error annex subclause is expressed as the subclass of core language annex subclause. It contains six error model properties that are associated with a component to specify its reliability information as follows:

(1) *ComponentErrorModelProperty* shows the error model for a component by specifying the error model identifier.
(2) *ModelHierarchyProperty* declares the error model for a subcomponent that the developer considers to be significant in the modeling process.
(3) *ReportErrorProperty* declares the error state or error propagation that the developer considers to be significant in the modeling process.
(4) *DerivedErrorStateMappingGuard* describes the state mapping rules between base component and subcomponent using Boolean expression.
(5) *ErrorGuard* describes the guards of port event occurrence, input and output of error propagation and mode change by Boolean expression which is composed of error source name (*ErrorSourceName*) and logic operation. And the error source name consists of an error state name and an error propagation event name for a component.
(6) *OccurrenceProperty* is a specific property that can be included in the error annex library or the error annex subclause.

2.2 Model Transformation Rules

Model transformation rules closely correlate with the representation of destination model. The AADL-based reliability model is transformed to the SPN model which is described using CSPL language. SPNP is adopted to receive the SPN model as the input. Then the SPN model is transformed to MA matrix to calculate the steady and transient solution.

The error annex library contains Meta model specifications of error events, error propagations, error states and error transformations. They describe the fault, operation states and state transition paths of each component, reflects the state transition relationship. Therefore, the part of error annex library is transformed to the net function of CSPL.

Table 1 lists the CSPL code templates transformed from some elements in error annex library.

Table 1. The CSPL code templates of the error annex library

Elements in error annex library	CSPL code templates
ErrorState	place (" f(ErrorState.getName()) ");
ErrorEvent	trans (" f(ErrorEvent.getName()) ");
OccurrenceProperty	rateval("f(ErrorEventOrPropagation.getName())", ErrorEvent property value);
ErrorPropagation	imm("f(ErrorPropagation.getName())"); guard("f(ErrorPropagation.getName())", "f1(ErrorPropagation.getName())");
ErrorTransition	iarc("f(ErrorEventOrPropagation.getName())", "f(ErrorState.getName())"); oarc("f(ErrorEventOrPropagation.getName())", "f(ErrorState.getName())");

The error annex subclause contains the error propagation guards, event generation guards, mode change guards, state mapping guards and the Meta model specification of all properties such as *report* property. The templates of these guards are similar, and it will generate a function that returns value 1 or 0. In order to ensure the generated code to be successfully checked by CSPL compiler, the function declaration and definition are put after the include statement in CSPL file and before the function such as options which CSPL should define. The function name is generated by mapping rules. The function body is composed of the CSPL if statements. When the condition of if statement holds, the return value is 1. On the contrary, when the condition does not hold, the return value is 0.

Table 2 lists the CSPL code templates of error propagation guards and state mapping guards. f1 (ErrorPropagationRule object.getName ()) is the string of function name, and the function declaration is put before all function definitions. The error propagation rule *ErrorpropagationRule* and the error state mapping rule *ErrorStateMappingRule* involve the transformation of the Boolean expression which is composed of a Boolean expression type and an error source name.

Table 3 gives the CSPL code templates of the Boolean expression type and the error source name. A Boolean expression type is transformed into a CSPL operator. The error source name represents the error state or the error propagation of a component. When the component is in the error state, the error source name is transformed

Table 2. The CSPL code templates of error propagation guard and state mapping guard

Guard name	Rule	CSPL code template

Error propagation guard	ErrorPropagationRule	int
		f1([1]Object.getName())()
		{
		  Bool expression CSPL template
		  return 1;
		}

State mapping guard	ErrorStateMappingRule	int
		f1([2]Object.getName())()
		{
		  Bool expression CSPL template
		  return 1;
		}

Table 3. The CSPL code templates of the Boolean expression type and the error source name

Element in Meta model	CSPL code template
BooleanExpressionType	not: ! and: && or: ‖ ormore: >= orless: <=
ErrorSourceName	ErrorState: mark("f(ErrorState.getName())") ! = 0 PropagationName: f1(ErrorPropagation.getName())()

to the conditional expression which judges whether tokens exist in the current state through calling the *mark* function. If the error source name represents the error propagation, then it transforms into the function named f1 (ErrorPropagation.get-Name) ()).

The *report* element describes the error state or the error propagation in the analysis method. While in the SPN-based analysis method, the error state described by *report* element is taken as UP state of MC that is isomorphic to SPN. When the component is in the error state described by *report* element, it means that the component is available or does not fail. Thus, the report property is transformed into double type CSPL function that returns value 1 or 0.

The CSPL function can judge whether a component is in the error state described by *report* element. The transformed error states have the "OR" relationship with each other. f2 is a string mapping rule to ensure the automatically generated function names will not conflict with each other. f2(s) represents the string generated from string *s* by using f2 mapping rule. f2(component.GetName()) is the function name. The function calls template of *ReportErrorProperty* associates the generated function with the component through the *pr_expected* function, and it is taken as the statement of *ac_final* function. This makes the output file derived the probability when the return value of function f2(component.GetName()) is 1. Thus the reliability parameters of the component are obtained.

Table 4 lists the CSPL code templates for *ReportErrorProperty* to transform into declarations, definitions and calls of component reliability calculation function.

Table 4. The CSPL code templates of *ReportErrorProperty*

CSPL code template of	ReportErrorProperty in EMA model
function statement	double f2(component.getName())();
function definition	double f2(component.getName())(){
	if(mark("f(ErrorState1.getName())") ! =0
	|| mark("f(ErrorState2.getName())") ! =0)
	...
	return 1;
	return 0;
	}
function call	pr_expected("component.getName()",
	"f2(component.getName()");

2.3   Model Transformation Methods

Model transformation methods can be divided into the method of manual transformation, template-based code generation technology, model transformation based on relationship algebra, mapping rule between the Meta models and design pattern, and etc. [10]. We adopted the template-based code generation technology to transform the AADL-based reliability analysis model to the SPN with CSPL (CSPL_SPN) measurement model.

The process of model transformation is composed of four parts: the AADL-based reliability analysis model, the CSPL_SPN measurement model, the transformation rule library, and the model transformation controller. The AADL-based reliability analysis model, namely the source model, is the input of the transformation process. The CSPL_SPN measurement model, namely the destination model after transformation, is the output of the transformation process. The transformation rule library is composed of error annex library rules and error annex subclause rules. The model transformation controller is used to control the whole transformation process. In the transformation process, firstly the model transformation controller reads and analyzes the information of the source model, and acquires the interactive information or inherited relationship information between the components according to the AADL architecture model. Secondly, the EMA error model of component is analyzed to obtain the corresponding elements in the EMA Meta model. Thirdly, in the basis of obtained elements in the EMA model, the appropriate CSPL code templates are selected from the transformation rule library. Finally, to generate the CSPL code file that stores the SPN destination model. The generated CSPL code file is used to be the input of SPNP for system reliability analysis.

3 An Example

Based on the above transformation rules and methods, an example of an automaton in aviation systems is given to show how to transform the reliability analysis model that is descried by AADL and EMA to the CSPL_SPN model.

The reliability analysis model is taken as the source model, and the CSPL_SPN model is considered as the destination model. The source model of the automaton is shown in Fig. 1, which describes two error states, one error event and one error propagation event. It can be seen that when the error event occurs or the corrupted data is input to the automaton, system fails and stops working.

```
annex Error_Model {**
    error model BinState
    features
      ErrorFree: initial error state;
      Failed: error state;
      Fault: error event;
      CorruptedData: in error propagation{Occurrence => fixed 0.8};
    end BinState;

    error model implementation BinState.basic
    transitions
      ErrorFree -[ Fail]-> Failed;
      ErrorFree -[ in CorruptedData]-> Failed;
    properties
      occurrence => poisson 1.0E-4 applies to Fault;
    end BinState.basic;
**};
```

Fig. 1. The source model of reliability analysis model

Figure 2 shows the SPN model with CSPL after the transformation of the source model. By calling *place* the *net* function defines two location of SPN named p_1 and p_2 separately, to represent the states of ErrorFree and Failed. Where, the *init* function p_1 initially has a token. In the *trans* function, the timed transition is named as t_12 representing the error event, and the firing rate of transition t_12 is designated 10^{-4} by *rateval*. Due to the immediate transition is associated with the logic conditions, the *imm_12_func* function representing logic conditions is connected with the immediate transition *imm_12* together to be the input of *CorruptedData*. And it can be seen from *probval* that when the logic conditions hold, the probability that transition *imm_12* fired is 0.8.

In the process of model transformation, the precision of calculation and the time of reliability analysis are configurable parameters, they are assumed to be 10^{-9} in the *option* function and 3600 s in the *ac_final* function.

In summary, the net function defines all elements in SPN such as positions, transitions and arcs, and sets the value of the transition with parameter attributes. In the analysis process, the newly discovered mark does not require verifications, so

```
#include <stdio.h>
#include "user.h"
int imm_12_func(){
    if( mark("p_1") == 2)
        return (1);
        return (0);
}
void net() {
    place("p_1");   place("p_2");
    trans("t_12");  rateval("t_12",1E-4);
    init("p_1",1);  imm("imm_12");
    probval("imm_12", 1.0);  guard("imm_12", imm_12_func);
    iarc("t_12","p_1");  oarc("t_12","p_2");
    iarc("imm_12","p_1");    oarc("imm_12","p_2");
}
void options(){
    iopt(IOP_TSMETHOD,VAL_TSUNIF);
    fopt(FOP_PRECISION,1E-09);
}
int assert() { return(RES_NOERR); }
void ac_init() {}
Void ac_reach() {}
void ac_final() {solve(3600);}
```

Fig. 2. The destination model of CSPL_SPN

there is only return statement in the *assert* function. Although there is not any statement in the *ac_reach* and *ac_init* functions, they are still an essential part of the CSPL file.

4   Conclusions and Future Work

In this paper, the rules and methods to automatically transform the AADL-based reliability analysis model to the SPN model are presented. This method combines system design method with reliability analysis method in embedded system, and provides effective support to realize automatic transformation process.

Future research mainly includes establishing a reusable SPN Meta model, and the study on transformation rules from the EMA model to the SPN model.

Acknowledgements. The author would like to thank the sponsors of the Scientific Research Plan Project of Shaanxi Education Department of China under Grant No. 09JK642, Doctoral Fund No. 116-210912 and Scientific Research Plan Project of Xi'an Technology University under Grant No. 116-210907.

References

1. Object Management Group, MDA guide version 1.0.1. OMG/03-06-01 (2003)
2. SAE-AS5506, Architecture Analysis and Design Language. Society of Automotive Engineers. www.aadl.info (2004)
3. SAE-AS5506_1, SAE Architecture Analysis and Design Language Annex Volume 1. Society of Automotive Engineers. www.aadl.info (2006)
4. Mura, I., Bondavalli, A.: Markov regenerative stochastic Petri nets to model and evaluate phased mission systems dependability. IEEE Trans. Comput. **50**(12), 1337–1351 (2001). (IEEE Press, New York)
5. Dugan, J.B., Bavuso, S.J., Boyd, M.A.: Fault trees and Markov models for reliability analysis of fault-tolerant digital systems. Reliab. Eng. Syst. Saf. **39**(3), 291–307 (1993). (Elsevier LTD, England)
6. Center for Advanced Computing and Communication (CACC), Department of Electrical and Computer Engineering, Duke University. SPNP User's Manual (1999)
7. Clark, J.A., Pradhan, D.K.: Fault injection: a method for validating computer-system dependability. IEEE Comput. **28**(6), 47–56 (1995). (IEEE Press, New York)
8. Shu, Z., Li, D., Hu, Y., Ye, F., Wan, J.: From models to code: automatic development process for embedded control system. In: IEEE International Conference on Network, Sensor and Control, pp. 660–665. IEEE Press, New York (2008)
9. Liu, J.J., Zhong, S., Ye, H.: Reliability modeling for airborne equipment system using AADL. Aeronaut. Comput. Tech. **39**(2), 90–94 (2009). (Aeronautics Computing Technique Research Institute, Xi'an)
10. Wang, X.B., Wu, Q.Y., Shi, D.X.: Model transformation approaches in MDA. Comput. Eng. Sci. **28**(11), 133–135 (2006). (National University of Defense Technology, Changsha)

Distributed IPv6 Sensor Network Networking Method Based on Dynamic Regional Agents

Jiye Wang[1], Zhihua Cheng[1], and Jinghong Guo[2(✉)]

[1] State Grid Corporation of China, No. 86 West Changan St., Beijing, China
{Jiye-wang,Zhihua-cheng}@sgcc.com.cn
[2] China Electric Power Research Institute, No. 15 Xiaoying East Rd.,
Beijing, China
Guojinghong@epri.sgcc.com.cn

Abstract. In order to network a distributed IPv6 sensor network with the idea of decentralization, we propose a networking method based on the dynamic regional agent. The method is based on the two-layer architecture and dynamically elects the regional agent node when the network running. We then propose two algorithms to elect the regional agent node, which are common election algorithm and general election algorithm, and they will be used in the different environment. We give detailed introduces to the trigger condition and the algorithm itself. The experimental results show that the proposed networking method has good performance in the consuming time needed in networking, simplify the complexity of network maintenance.

Keywords: Distributed IPv6 sensor network · Regional agent node · Dynamic region agent

1 Introduction

Distributed sensor network is a hot, multi-interdisciplinary subject, which is widely used in many important areas, such as military, industry, agriculture, medical treatment, city management and environmental monitoring, and is regarded as one of the enormous influence technology in the 21st century [1].

The outstanding characteristics of the distributed sensor network are the number of sensors within it is very large and at the same time, adopt the one-layer, full connective network mechanism with a static management node. This manner of mechanism on the one hand will make the data increase sharply when an event happens, and lots of nodes will have to deal with lots of irrelevant information; on the other hand will make the management node overload, and the scale of the whole network will be limited by the performance of the management node. Further more, the rapid growth of the Internet has led to the anticipated consumption of address in the current version of the Internet protocol (IP), i.e., IPv4. This consumption has given rise to s newer version of the IP, i.e., IP version6 (Ipv6). IPv6 provides sufficient address space to meet the increase of the Internet. So, how to form the distributed IPv6 sensor network with the idea of decentralization is the first problem needed to be resolved in the collaborative observation system.

V.C.M. Leung and M. Chen (Eds.): CloudComp 2013, LNICST 133, pp. 287–296, 2014.
DOI: 10.1007/978-3-319-05506-0_28, © Institute for Computer Sciences, Social Informatics and Telecommunications Engineering 2014

In order to solve the above problem, we research into the networking method of the distributed IPv6 sensor network, propose a networking method based on dynamic regional agent. The method is based on the two-layer architecture, firstly classifies the sensors into different regions based on their geographical positions, and then elects the regional agents for each of these regions. The two-layer architecture can avoid information explosion and overload of the centered node. We then propose two kinds of agent node election algorithm, which include common election algorithm and general election algorithm. We give detailed introduces to the trigger condition and the algorithm itself. The experimental results show that the proposed networking method has good performance in the consuming time needed in networking.

2 Related Work

At present, the commonly used distributed sensor network networking mechanisms are SWE (Sensor Web Enablement) proposed by OGC (Open Geospatial Consortium), NICTA Open Sensor Web Architecture (NOSA), The German Indonesian Tsunami Early Warning System (GITEWS) and Fire Emergency Response System (RFERS). These networking mechanisms are similar, but they have different style when involving the specific business content.

SWE commits itself to provide the real-time sensor access function [2], with the aim to develop a standard to make the sensor to detect event, exchange information and monitor environment possible. NOSA is a basic platform of software based on SWE, and provides a reuse, retractable, extendible and interoperable services [3]. GITEWS is a Germany research project of geography, and is mainly used in the early warning of tsunamis and sharing related information [4]. It makes the best of the basic service provided by SWE. RFERS concentrates on the early warning of the fire, provides the geography-based subscription service for the resource planning in distributed sensor network [5], but there are not any comparison between RFERS and other systems. All these networking mechanisms did not discuss the address configuration algorithm and the routing algorithm using IPv6.

Researchers proposed many solutions to the large number of the sensors in the distributed sensor network. Gnutella architecture used point-to-point transmission method in order to decentralize the overload of the management node, but it can not avoid the broadcast storm because it used the broadcast transmission manner. A.M. Jovanovic's research work resolve the broadcast storm, but decrease the accessibility of information, which isn't be acceptable in the emergency response system. Other researchers resolve the problem based on the classification of the sensors [7–9]. They mainly concentrate on how to classify these sensors. But due to the limitation of the sensing distance of the sensors, we must take the hop count of each sensor into account, and we need to connect the sensor network to the IPv6 network. So networking methods must support IPv6 address configuration.

3 Sensor Network Architecture Based on Dynamic Regional Agent

3.1 Traditional Network Architecture

The hierarchical structure is a common architecture used in the traditional network, which is shown in Fig. 1.

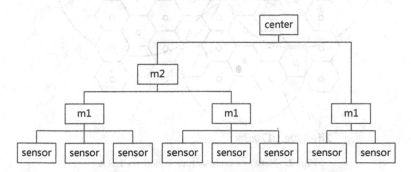

Fig. 1. Traditional network architecture

The advantage of the above architecture is obvious, and it can easily be expended to embrace more sensors. But the shortcomings of thus architecture is also clear: firstly, the management node will have to deal with lots of data; secondly, with the increment of the layer, all the data from the lower layer will to be dealt with or transferred by the management node, which will make the management node always under the high load condition. Once the management fails, all the nodes subjected to management node will also fail.

3.2 Dynamic Regional Agent Method Based on a Two-Layer Architecture

In order to avoid the shortcomings of the above traditional architecture, we propose a distributed sensor networking method based on dynamic regional agents (DRA). The idea of this architecture is shown in Fig. 2.

DRA-based networking method first classify the sensors into different regions based on their geographical positions, and then elect the regional agent node for each regions to manage the other nodes in this region. Different region are in different network segment. Figure 2 include three different regions, which is represented using the first three segment of IP in the IPv6, i.e. 2ffe:320e:1:170::1:x, 2ffe:320e:1:170::1:x and 2ffe:320e:1:170::1:x. All the IP of the node in a certain region will within the range of the segment. If using IPv6, the last part of the IP of any node will range from 0 to 255, and 0 represents the broadcast address. The biggest number of the sensors of a certain region will be 255. The *id* of any node is represented based on its IP address.

From the figure, we can see that the DRA-based architecture is a two-layer structure. Due to the limitation of the scale of a certain region, the sensors of any

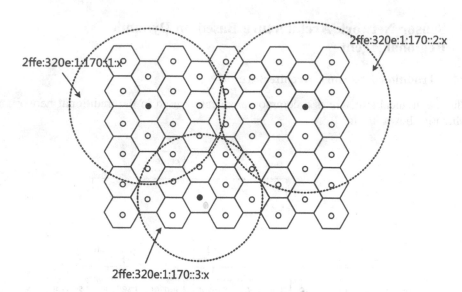

Fig. 2. Network architecture based on DRA

region will not too much, so the DRA-based architecture can avoid the overload of the management node in the traditional hierarchical architecture. Besides the above advantage, the regional agent in the DRA-based architecture is elected dynamically, so any node will get the same chance to act as the agent node. All in all, the DRA-based architecture has the following two advantages: on the one hand, this architecture can avoid the losses of the management node too fast; on the other hand, this architecture can reduce the over-reliance on certain key nodes. Once the current regional agent node failed, the DRA-based architecture can elect the new regional agent node dynamically, which can ensure that the whole network works steadily.

4 Dynamic Election Mechanism of Regional Agents

There are two kinds of election: common election and general election.

Common election is usually used when the network is initialized or when the network recovers from the breakdown. There is not management node during the election, and all the nodes will part in the election, until the new regional agent is elected. The common election algorithm will be triggered when a new sensor node join the network and cannot receive any response after it sending three WIA (who is agent) messages.

General election is a periodical election when the network runs normally, and has an active regional agent. In order to prevent the unexpected invalidation of the nodes, it is necessary to elect periodically new regional agent, which is critical to repair the disconnected region and average the sensor losses among all the sensors. When the term of office of the current agent is over, it will trigger the general election by sending a WIN (who is next) message. The other nodes will part in the election after they receive this message.

Figure 3 compare the information exchange process of these two elections. From the figure, we can see that any two nodes will exchange information in the common election, whereas the ordinary nodes only exchange information with the current regional agent in the general election.

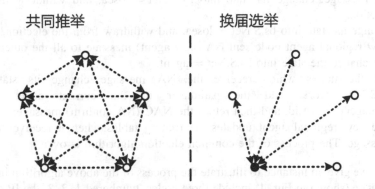

共同推举   换届选举

Fig. 3. The information exchange in election

4.1　Common Election Algorithm

Before introducing the algorithm, we firstly give the definition of agent rate, which is an important judgment standard of the common election algorithm.

Definition 1 Agent Rate: agent rate (recorded as ar) is defined to be the ratio between atime and ltime, that is ar = atime/ltime, where atime is the duration during which a node acts as agent, and ltime is the duration during which a node is in working state.

During the common election, the nodes with the smaller agent rate have priority to become the next agents. The common election algorithm always tries its best to let each node has the same chance to be elected as agent, so as time go on, agent rate of every node will be 1/N, that is $\lim_{t \to +\infty} ar = 1/N$, where N is the number of sensors in the network.

Now, we give the common election algorithm which as follows:

(1) All the nodes are in initialization state, so for a nodes set BS = {bs1, bs2... bsm}, we will have ∀bs (bs ∈ BS → bs.S.Net = init);

(2) Every node sends a broadcast message CL = <ltime, atime> to recommend itself to act as an agent and at the same time set its state bs.S.Net = prea, where atime is the duration during which a node acts as agent, and ltime is the duration during which a node is in working state, prea represent the current state, the meaning of the state is the node parts in the election and has not been selected.

(3) Suppose the number of all the nodes in this region is N, and then all the nodes will receive N–1 recommendation messages.

(4) Suppose the agent rate of each node is computed using ar = atime/ltime, the agent rate of the current node is arself, and the agent rate of other nodes are another. If arself < arother or arself = arother ∧ bsself.id < bsother.id, then the

current node send a denial message CLD to other nodes, the current continue to send CL message and go to the (5) step; or else the algorithm go to (6) step.

(5)   If the current node does not receive the CLD message from other nodes after it send three CL messages, which shows that no nodes object to the current node to be elected as agent, and then go to step (7); or else the current stop sending the CL message, change its state into bs.S.Net = losea, and withdraw from the election.

(6)   Change its state into bs.S.Net = losea, and withdraw from the election.

(7)   New regional agent node sent NA (new agent) message to all the other nodes, and change the state into bs.S.Net = agent.

(8)   All the nodes which receive the NA message change its state into bs.S.Net = work, add the parameter of the current node: bs.bParam.agent = NA.id, and then return the NAC (NA confirm) message.

(9)   The new regional agent updates the routing tables when it receives a NAC message. The process of the common election algorithm is over.

Now, we give an instance to illustrate the process of the above algorithm in detail. The instance (shown in Fig. 4) include three nodes, numbered 1, 2, 3, the IP of these three nodes are 2ffe:320e:1:170::1:1, 2ffe:320e:1:170::1:2, 2ffe:320e:1:170::1:3, respectively. The current agent rates of these three nodes are 0.3, 0.3, and 0.5, respectively.

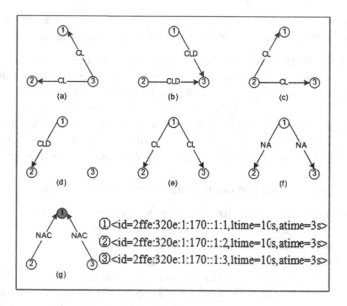

Fig. 4. Instance of common election

From Fig. 4, we can see that the whole election process consists of the following seven steps:

(1)   Node 3 sends CL message to node 1 and node 2 to recommend itself to act the next regional agent.

(2)   Through comparing, node 1 and node 2 will find that their own agent rates are smaller than that of node 3, then node 1 and node 2 will send CLD message to node 3 to turn down the application of node 3.

(3)   Then, node 2 sends CL message to node 1 and node 3 to recommend itself to act the next regional agent.

(4)   The agent rate of node 1 is equal to that of node 2, but the id of node 1 is smaller than that of node 2, so node 1 will send CLD message to node 2 to turn down the application of node 2. Now, node 3 is already withdrawing from the election, so it will not send any message.

(5)   Then, node 1 sends CL message to node 2 and node 3 to recommend itself to act the next regional agent.

(6)   Node 1 does not receive any denial message after it send three CL messages, then send NA message to declare itself to be the new agent, and change its state.

(7)   Node 2 and node 3 return NAC message, the election is over.

4.2   General Election Algorithm

The general election algorithm is triggered by the current regional agent node, and the new regional agent node will be elected under the management of the current agent. The general election algorithm is as follows:

(1)   The states of all the nodes except the regional agent node are work, that is to say, for the node set BS = {bs1, bs2… bsm}, ∀bs (bs ∈ BS → bs.S.Net = work).

(2)   Current regional agent node sends the NE (new election) message to all the other nodes in this region.

(3)   Each node will send NEC (NE confirm) message after they receive the NE message, NEC = <ltlme, atlme>

(4)   Once receiving all the NEC messages, the current regional agent selects the node with the smallest agent rate, i.e. min ({atime/ltime | NECi = <ltimei, atimei> ∧ i ∈ N}), sends AA (appointment agent) to the selected node, and change its state into work, i.e. bs.S.Net = work.

(5)   After it receives the AA message, the new regional agent sends NA (new agent) to all the other nodes, change its state to agent, i.e. bs.S.Net = agent. The general election is over.

Now, we also give an instance to illustrate the process of the above general election algorithm in detail. The instance (shown in Fig. 5) include five nodes, numbered 1, 2, 3, 4, 5, the IP of these three nodes are 2ffe:320e:1:170::1:1, 2ffe:320e:1:170::1:2, 2ffe:320e:1:170::1:3, 2ffe:320e:1:170::1:4, 2ffe:320e:1:170::1:5, respectively. The current agent rates of these three nodes are 0.3, 0.2, 0.1, 0.2 and 0.1, respectively.

From Fig. 5, we can see that the whole election process consists of the following four steps, where node 1 is the current regional agent node:

(1)   Node 1 sends NE message to node 2, node 3, node 4 and node 5 to trigger the general election.

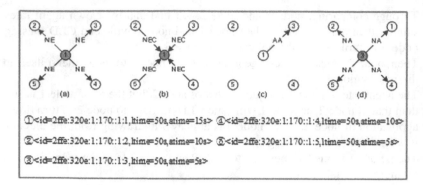

Fig. 5. Instance of general election

(2)   These four nodes return NEC message to node 1.

(3)   Node 1 will analyze the agent rates of these four nodes, and will find out that node 3 and node 5 have the smallest agent rate. And the id of node 3 is smaller than node 5, so node 1 will finally select node 3 as the new regional agent, and send AA message to it.

(4)   Node 3 broadcast NA message to declare that it is the new regional agent, and change its state to agent, the process is over.

5   Experimental Results and Analysis

During the networking, the election of the regional agent node is the most time-consuming work. Once the regional agent node is elected, the networking is over. Speeding up the election of the regional agent can provide basic guarantee of network for the collaborative observation system. Once the network tends towards stability, the election of regional agent is mostly based on the general election, so we will only give the performance of the general election algorithm in the following experiments. The performance of the common election algorithm is similar with that of the general election algorithm and will not be described here.

The factors influencing the networking time are usually include the number of the sensors in the region and the network delay. Figure 6 gives the change of the time needed to elect the regional agent based on general election algorithm along with the change of the number of sensors, where the network delay is set to 500 ms.

From the figure, we can see that the time consuming of the networking does not change apparently with the number of sensors increasing from 100 to 1000, and is always around 600 ms to 800 ms. When the number of the sensors is equal to 600 and 800, the consuming time falls in a small scale. The reason maybe that all the NEC messages happen to reach the regional agent node at the same time, the node can carry out the election immediately, which can reduce the time consuming. If the NEC messages cannot reach the node at the same time, the regional agent will have to wait for their coming before it carry out the election, which lead to the increase of the

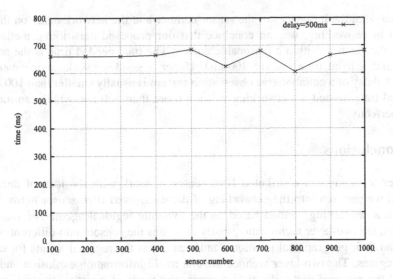

Fig. 6. Relations between network time and number of sensors

consuming time. All in all, the influence of the number of the sensor on the time needed in networking is small.

Figure 7 is the change graph of the time needed in networking with the change of network delay (the number of sensors is set to 1000). We can find out that the time rises sharply with the network delay range from 100 ms to 1000 ms. The relations between them appear to be a kind of linear relation.

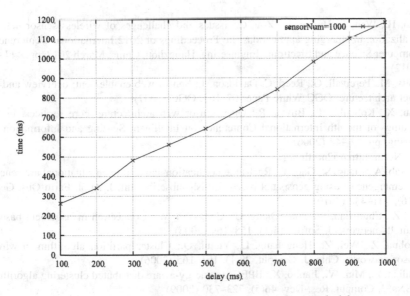

Fig. 7. Relations between networking time and network delay

Analyzing the influences of the sensor number and the network delay on the time needed in networking, we can conclude that our proposed networking method can realize the election within a reasonable during. The final needed time is the network delay and a fixed time (nearly 200 ms). Under a good network environment, the network delay of a collaborative observation system is usually smaller than 100 ms, so the final time needed in networking will not more than 300 ms, which can meet the need perfectly.

6 Conclusions

In order to organize a distributed IPv6 sensor network with the idea of decentralization, we research into the networking of the distributed IPv6 sensor network, and propose a networking method based on the dynamic regional agent. The method is based on the two-layer architecture, firstly classifies the sensors into different regions based on their geographical positions, and then elects the regional agents for each of these regions. The two-layer architecture can avoid information explosion and overload of the centered node. We then propose two kinds of agent node election algorithm, which include common election algorithm and general election algorithm. We give detailed introduces to the trigger condition and the algorithm itself. The experimental results show that the proposed networking method has good performance in the consuming time needed in networking. Our proposed networking method has taken IPv6 address configuration into account and could support IPv6 network well.

References

1. Suo, H., Wan, J., Huang, L., Zou, C.: Issues and challenges of wireless sensor networks localization in emerging applications. In: Proceedings of 2012 International Conference on Computer Science and Electronic Engineering, Hangzhou, China, March 2012, pp. 447–451 (2012)
2. Botts, M., Percivall, G., Reed, C. Davidson, J.: Sensor web enablement: overview and high level architecture. OGC White Paper 07–165. OGC (2007)
3. Chu, X., Kobialka, T., Buyya, R.: Open sensor web architecture: core services. In: Proceedings of the 4th International Conference on Intelligent Sensing and Information Processing, pp. 42–44 (2006)
4. 52° North. http://52north.org
5. Kassab, A., Liang, S., Gao, Y.: Real-time notification and improved situational awareness in fire emergencies using geospatial-based publish/subscribe. Int. J. Appl. Earth Obs. Geoinf. 12(6), 431–438 (2010)
6. Lei, Z., Chun-Jian, P., Yong-Qiang, G., Cong-Yin, W.: Connection management based on Gnutella network. J. Softw. 16(1), 158–164 (2005)
7. Baohua, Z., Wei, Z., Hengchang, L., Yugui, Q.: Cluster partition algorithm in wireless sensor networks. Chin. J. Comput. 29(1), 161–165 (2006)
8. Xinlian, Z., Min, W., Jianbo, X.: BPEC: an energy-aware distributed clustering algorithm in WSNs. J. Comput. Res. Dev. 46(5), 723–730 (2009)
9. Xiong, J., Wang, Q., Wan, J., Ye, B., Xu, W., Liu, J.: Detection of outliers in sensor data based on adaptive moving average fitting. Sens. Lett. 11(5), 877–882 (2013)

Author Index